VAMPIRES:

FIRST BLOOD

VOLUME II

THE VAMPIRE LADIES

Edited by James Grant Goldin

A Basilisk Book

Vampires: First Blood Volume II: The Vampire Ladies

A Basilisk Book

https://jamesgrantgoldinbooks.com

ISBN-13: 978-1-7335690-2-6 (paperback)
ISBN-13: 978-1-7335690-5-7 (Kindle)
ISBN-13-978-1-7335690-3-3 (ebook)

To Lisa

who can recite immense summaries of Anne Rice from memory

NOTES ON THE TEXTS:

Since the stories and poems in this anthology were first published, there have been some changes in the conventions of punctuation and spelling. This edition makes a few—but only a few—concessions to 21st century tastes.

Nineteenth-century versions of words like "some one," "every one," "to-day," "to-morrow," etc., have been mostly modernized to "someone," "everyone," "today," "tomorrow," and so forth.

The original British spellings of words like "ardour," "glamour," etc. have usually been kept, but less familiar British versions have been Americanized; so "shew" is "show," "surprize" is "surprise," etc. The use of long dashes to conceal profanity, a date or a name ("D—", "the year 17—", "the little village of C——") has been happily retained.

A glossary is provided at the end of each story or poem to explain various now-obscure terms.

THE VAMPIRE LADIES:

INTRODUCTION:

DEADLIER THAN THE MALE

Why split the history of the vampire's literary development, up to the publication of Bram Stoker's *Dracula* in 1897, into two books, and divide them by gender?

Because the vampire lord and the vampire lady developed along different paths and represented different fantasies.

Volume I: The Vampire Lords argued that almost all male vampires in fiction are aristocrats, whether or not they have actual titles of nobility; partly because the real-life Lord Byron (1788-1824) was the model for the first mass-media vampire star, Lord Ruthven (who made his debut in *The Vampyre,* 1819), and partly because a veneer of manners and class softened the edges of what became, increasingly, a fantasy of rape, with the victim, usually a woman, as a passive or willing figure.

So what about "the female of the species" (to quote Kipling)?

It's true that fictional female vampires became just as aristocratic as their male counterparts; you'll find no 19th century tales of vampire barmaids. And, just as with the male vampire of the 1800's, the development of the female vampire's accepted powers and limitations changed from story to story.

But, beyond that, there are significant differences.

A male aristocrat already has power; as a vampire, he just has more power. Alive or undead, he seduces and rapes, using the force of his personality to manipulate others. He might feel guilty, but he soothes his feelings of remorse by declaring, "This is my nature." In other words, the vampire lord is not essentially different than he was as a human being, but now he has superior strength and magical abilities.

But women had little power in the real world. Yes, countesses and queens could be ruthless and cruel; but to the men who made up the majority of writers, such rulers were exceptions. Was a woman who used power really a woman at all? If there was any sort of power a woman could rightfully claim, men decreed, it was the power of a mother's love. If a woman also exercised "masculine" power, such as killing someone or choosing her own sexual partner, she was no woman, but a monster. It was even worse if she didn't want children; some of the female vampires in these pages menace children, in a way that male vampires rarely if ever do. (This trope reaches a climax in *Dracula* itself, where the Count's three wives actually eat a baby; and when the heroine's friend Lucy is vampirized, she stalks young children.)

Still, pre-20th century lady vampires did more than attack boys and girls. Writers were faced with the fact that a woman who became a vampire was suddenly stronger than the men who could have mastered her in life. So, if a woman is more powerful than a man, what does she *do?* Does she become a super-seductress? Does she become a mindless destroyer, like the women in Euripides's *The Bacchae*? A version of Shakespeare's Lady Macbeth? Does she embrace her undead-ness, or fight it? Does she seek love—or revenge—or just another meal?

There has never been one single type of lady vampire. Some are overtly threatening; others, extremely enticing. While some vampire women see humans simply as prey, others, against all odds, yearn for a committed relationship, even if it means fighting their own bloodlust.

One thing's clear, though: the power of the vampire woman is, to use a current critical term, *transgressive.* If she attacks children, she transgresses the core role of woman-as-mother, as mandated by the patriarchy; if she seduces other women, it's a transgression of the patriarchy's established rules of sexuality; if she attacks men, then it's not just a transgression, but an overturning of the way things are supposed to be: woman as aggressor, man as passive victim.

And yet, the lady *nosferatu* is sometimes presented as being completely, passionately, devoted to the human male protagonist. So the super-woman is partially tamed by emphasizing the female desire for the tenderest of emotions. The dominatrix is partially dominated by her love for the passive man.

This, however, is just one of many possibilities. The female vampire is constantly being reinterpreted, and has been for centuries, with the essential challenge to the patriarchy always there under the surface, even in the most patriarchal prose.

Which brings us to the character who's been called the first vampire of them all. She's been reinterpreted again and again over thousands of years, undergoing transformations from demon to superstition to feminist icon…

LILITH

**And Lilith said, "We two are equal,
for we both come from earth."**

Several thousand years ago in the Middle East, children who died young were said to be the victims of night-demons. The Sumerians called the demon Dimme; the Akkadians called it Lamashtu.

During the Babylonian Captivity, in the 6th century BC, Lamashtu evolved or morphed into Lilitu, the demon "Lilith" of Jewish legend.

Lilith was a proto-vampire; she drained the life-force from children, sometimes by strangling them, sometimes by drinking their blood, sometimes by vaguer, more mystical means. She also tormented men who slept alone, causing them to have wet dreams—so she could gather up the spilled sperm for herself and have massive amounts of demon babies. (Although later stories had her marry a fallen angel named Samael, who was the father of her many, many children.)

Lilith made it into the Bible, briefly, in Isaiah 34:14, where the prophet imagines a post-catastrophe wilderness:

> The wild beasts of the desert shall also meet the wild beasts of the island and the satyr[1] shall cry to his fellow; Lilith[2] also shall rest here, and find for herself a place of rest.

What did Lilith look like? Early on, she may have been a kind of owl-demon; but she was also a beautiful woman with wings and long, sometimes red, hair (of which she was very proud). But Lilith's springboard to lasting fame came during the Dark Ages, when rabbis noticed some textual problems in The Book of Genesis.

The problem was this: Genesis 1:27 says:

---

[1]What's a satyr doing in the Bible? A mystery for another day…

[2] There are different translations; the King James Version translates the Hebrew "lilit" as "screech owl,"; other versions have "night creature" or "night hag."

> God created man in His own image, in the image of God created He him; male and female created He them.

But in the second *chapter of* Genesis, *the story of creation is told* again, *with several crucial differences, especially in* Genesis 2:7, *where it says,*

> ...God formed man of the dust of the ground....

So humanity consisted of just one man—Adam, whose name means "earth." Then God put Adam in the Garden of Eden and...

> ...God said, It is not good that the man should be alone...and he took one of his ribs...and...made he a woman, and brought her unto the man. And Adam said, This is now bone of my bones, and flesh of my flesh: she shall be called Woman, because she was taken out of Man. Therefore shall a man leave his father and his mother, and shall cleave unto his wife: and they shall be one flesh. (Genesis 2:18-24)

Because the Bible is, as some scholars put it, "a composite work," two versions of the same story got tossed into the mix. The first story implied an equality between men and women, while the second established woman's inferior status—a status which was of course confirmed in the real patriarchal world for thousands of years. So if Genesis 2 *was right, was* Genesis 1 *wrong? For the rabbis, who considered* Genesis *to be a unified work written by Moses under the direct inspiration of God, inconsistency was not an option.*

So the two creation myths had to be reconciled.

The biggest sticking point was the line, "male and female created He them." Were the first humans hermaphrodites (an idea that might have been taken from Plato's Symposium*)? Or—and this idea was the one that, for some reason, caught on—did Adam have a wife before Eve, a woman who was not taken from him but created with him?*

Finally, in the anonymous The Alphabet of Ben Sira, *a collection of stories and advice probably written between 900 and 1000 AD, the notion of Adam's first wife was permanently connected with Lilith. The framing story of the* Alphabet *tells of a wise Jewish scholar, Ben Sira, at the court of the ancient Babylonian king Nebuchednezzar II. At one point, Ben Sira prepares a magic amulet to heal the king's son. The king asks why the names of three angels are inscribed on the charm, and Ben Sira explains with the following story...*

LILITH

From "The Alphabet of Ben Sira"

When God created Adam, the first man, God said, "It is not good for man to be alone." And God created a woman for Adam, from the earth like Adam, and God called her Lilith.

But from the beginning, Adam and Lilith did not get along.

Lilith said, "I will not lie below you!"

And Adam said, "*I* will not lie below *you*, but *above*, for you are fit for being below and I am fit for being above!"

And Lilith said, "We two are equal, for we both come from earth."

And they would never agree.

Seeing this, Lilith spoke the holy name of God and flew off into the air.

Adam prayed to his Maker, "Master of the Universe, the woman you gave me fled from me!"

At once, the Holy One sent three angels, Sanoy, Sansenoy, and Samangelof, to bring Lilith back. God told them, "If she wishes to return, good. If not, let her know that every day, one hundred of her children shall die."

So the three angels pursued Lilith and overtook her in the raging waters of the same sea where the Egyptians would one day drown. They told her what God had said.

Nevertheless, she said she would not go back to Adam.

The angels threatened to drown her in the sea, but she told them, "Let me be! I was created only to make babies sick! If they are boys, I will have power over them until they are eight days old; if they are girls, I will have power over them until their twentieth day!"

When the angels heard this, they begged Lilith to come back to Adam, but she swore an oath in the name of the living God that whenever she would see a baby with an amulet that bore the angels' names or images, she would not harm that baby. And she accepted God's order that one hundred of her own children would die every day.

And so a hundred of Lilith's demons die every day, which is why we write the names of the three angels on amulets for young children. Because when Lilith sees the amulets, she recalls her oath and the child is kept safe from harm.

GLOSSARY

Holy name of God: According to Biblical scholars, the true name of God was never fully spelled out—the Hebrew letters, without vowels, correspond to YHVH; adding vowels gives us names like Yahweh or the Anglicized Jehovah. Since nobody knows what vowels are really supposed to go between the consonants, the true name of God is unknown—but if a magician knew it, it would be a spell of great power. Lilith, apparently, knows God's name; when she speaks it, she either uses it as a magic spell to give herself wings so she can fly away—or she uses it as a curse, and is cursed with wings. When Adam calls God to whine about his wife leaving him, he doesn't call God by name—he uses a safe epithet. When Lilith swears her oath with the angels, she likewise swears, not by God's actual name, but "in the name of" God; in the same way that a witness at trial who says "so help me God" swears a binding oath without using the actual name of the Deity.

One hundred of her own children: As noted earlier, Lilith had children with stolen human sperm and/or by her second husband, a fallen angel. There was another tradition that, after Cain's murder of Abel, a distraught Adam had a 130-year trial separation from Eve, and during that time Lilith came back to him and they had tens of thousands of demon children.

AFTERWORD

After Ben Sira's explanation, the amulet protects the king's son from Lilith, and all is well in Babylon. (Anti-Lilith charms have been found dating back to at least the 7th century BC, and were being made well into the 1800's.)

The story became familiar to Christian theologians, who, by the 13th century, associated Lilith with the serpent that tempted Adam and Eve—which is why, in the Renaissance, Michelangelo portrayed the serpent as a half-human red-haired woman on the ceiling of the Sistine Chapel.

Things started changing in the mid-20th century. In early 1971, an illustrated version of the Lilith story appeared in the Warren comic magazine Vampirella, *with the "vain and arrogant" Lilith branded as "the first vampire." A 1974 Marvel comic magazine,* Vampire Tales, *featured another retelling,* Lilith: The First Vampire, *and in this version, the first woman specifically "refused to submissively agree that she was less than Adam's equal"—a reflection of the increasingly mainstream feminist movement of the early 1970's. Later in 1974, Marvel introduced* Lilith, Daughter of Dracula*—a beautiful vampire who hated her father and possessed the bodies of young women who were being mistreated by their own fathers, giving them the power to destroy their patriarchal abusers. Jewish feminists had started claiming Lilith as a symbol of power and resistance starting in 1972.* Lilith, *a magazine of Jewish feminism, debuted in 1976, and the (non-religious, non-vampiric) female-centric music festival* Lilith Fair *began in 1997.*

If Lilith treads the line between good and evil, our next vampire could be said to be firmly on the side of the angels...except that she is very much against everything having to do with Christianity...

THE BRIDE OF CORINTH

**Each is with the other's thought possess'd.
His hot ardour's flood
Warms her chilly blood,
But no heart is beating in her breast.**

With the Central European "vampire plagues" of the early 18th century (see the story of Arnold Paul and others in Volume I: The Vampire Lords*), the concept of blood-drinking corpses became familiar in the West, and writers began to use the vampire as a metaphor for various other things.*

In 1748, as noted in Volume I, the German poet Heinrich Ossenfelder saw vampirism as a form of anti-Christian protest, and as a male fantasy of heterosexual rape; but in 1797, during the Romantic Era—when the idea of the emancipated woman was just gaining ground for the first time—another German poet created a new female vampire…

Like Ossenfelder before him, Johann Wolfgang von Goethe sets his vampire in opposition to a stifling mother and a sexless, joyless Christianity. But, unlike Ossenfelder's metaphorical male seducer, Goethe's heroine is an actual vampire—and she isn't part of a rape fantasy; the undead Bride is an avatar of an older and purer religion, and she's filled with honest feeling, true passion and genuine love.

THE BRIDE OF CORINTH

Johann Wolfgang von Goethe

Once a stranger youth to Corinth came,
Who in Athens lived, but hoped that he
From a certain townsman there might claim,
As his father's friend, kind courtesy.
Son and daughter, they
Had been wont to say
Should thereafter bride and bridegroom be.
But can he that boon so highly prized,
Save 'tis dearly bought, now hope to get?
They are Christians and have been baptized,
He and all of his are heathens yet.
For a newborn creed,
Like some loathsome weed,
Love and truth to root out oft will threat.
Father, daughter, all had gone to rest,
And the mother only watches late;
She receives with courtesy the guest,
And conducts him to the room of state.
Wine and food are brought,
Ere by him besought
Bidding him good night, she leaves him straight.
But he feels no relish now, in truth,
For the dainties so profusely spread;
Meat and drink forgets the wearied youth,
And, still dress'd, he lays him on the bed.

Scarce are closed his eyes,
When a form in-hies

Through the open door with silent tread.
By his glimmering lamp discerns he now
How, in veil and garment white array'd,
With a black and gold band round her brow,
Glides into the room a bashful maid.
But she, at his sight,
Lifts her hand so white,
And appears as though full sore afraid.
"Am I," cries she, "such a stranger here,
That the guest's approach they could not name?
Ah, they keep me in my cloister drear,
Well nigh feel I vanquish'd by my shame.
On thy soft couch now
Slumber calmly thou!
I'll return as swiftly as I came."

"Stay, thou fairest maiden!" cries the boy,
Starting from his couch with eager haste:
"Here are Ceres', Bacchus' gifts of joy;
Amor bringest thou, with beauty grac'd!
Thou art pale with fear!
Loved one, let us here
Prove the raptures the Immortals taste."

"Draw not nigh, O Youth! afar remain!
Rapture now can never smile on me;
For the fatal step, alas! is ta'en,
Through my mother's sick-bed fantasy.
Cured, she made this oath:
'Youth and nature both
Shall henceforth to Heav'n devoted be.'
"From the house, so silent now, are driven
All the gods who reign'd supreme of yore;

One Invisible now rules in heaven,
On the cross a Saviour they adore.
Victims slay they here,
Neither lamb nor steer,
But the altars reek with human gore."
And he lists, and ev'ry word he weighs,
While his eager soul drinks in each sound:
"Can it be that now before my gaze
Stands my loved one on this silent ground?
Pledge to me thy troth!
Through our father's oath:
With Heav'ns blessing will our love be crown'd."
"Kindly youth, I never can be thine!
'Tis my sister they intend for thee.
When I in the silent cloister pine,
Ah, within her arms remember me!
Thee alone I love,
While love's pangs I prove
Soon the earth will veil my misery."
"No! for by this glowing flame I swear,
Hymen hath himself propitious shown:
Let us to my father's house repair,
And thou'lt find that joy is not yet flown,
Sweetest, here then stay,
And without delay
Hold we now our wedding feast alone!"
Then exchange they tokens of their truth;
She gives him a golden chain to wear,
And a silver chalice would the youth
Give her in return of beauty rare.
"That is not for me;
Yet I beg of thee,
One lock only give me of thy hair."

Now the ghostly hour of midnight knell'd,
And she seem'd right joyous at the sign;
To her pallid lips the cup she held,
But she drank of nought but blood-red wine.
For to taste the bread
There before them spread,
Nought he spoke could make the maid incline.
To the youth the goblet then she brought,–
He too quaff'd with eager joy the bowl.
Love to crown the silent feast he sought,
Ah! full love-sick was the stripling's soul.
From his prayer she shrinks,
Till at length he sinks
On the bed and weeps without control.
And she comes, and lays her near the boy:
"How I grieve to see thee sorrowing so!
If thou think'st to clasp my form with joy,
Thou must learn this secret sad to know;
Yes! the maid, whom thou
Call'st thy loved one now,
Is as cold as ice, though white as snow."
Then he clasps her madly in his arm,
While love's youthful might pervades his frame:
"Thou might'st hope, when with me, to grow warm.
E'en if from the grave thy spirit came!
Breath for breath, and kiss!
Overflow of bliss!
Dost not thou, like me, feel passion's flame?"
Love still closer rivets now their lips,
Tears they mingle with their rapture blest,
From his mouth the flame she wildly sips,
Each is with the other's thought possess'd.
His hot ardour's flood

Warms her chilly blood,
But no heart is beating in her breast.
In her care to see that nought went wrong,
Now the mother happen'd to draw near;
At the door long hearkens she, full long,
Wond'ring at the sounds that greet her ear.
Tones of joy and sadness,
And love's blissful madness,
As of bride and bridegroom they appear.
From the door she will not now remove
'Till she gains full certainty of this;
And with anger hears she vows of love,
Soft caressing words of mutual bliss.
"Hush! the cock's loud strain!
But thou'lt come again,
When the night returns!"–then kiss on kiss.
Then her wrath the mother cannot hold,
But unfastens straight the lock with ease
"In this house are girls become so bold,
As to seek e'en strangers' lusts to please?"
By her lamp's clear glow
Looks she in,–and oh!
Sight of horror!–'tis her child she sees.
Fain the youth would, in his first alarm,
With the veil that o'er her had been spread,
With the carpet, shield his love from harm;
But she casts them from her, void of dread,
And with spirit's strength,
In its spectre length,
Lifts her figure slowly from the bed.
"Mother! mother!"–Thus her wan lips say:
"May not I one night of rapture share?
From the warm couch am I chased away?
Do I waken only to despair?

It contents not thee
To have driven me
An untimely shroud of death to wear?
But from out my coffin's prison-bounds
By a wond'rous fate I'm forced to rove,
While the blessings and the chaunting sounds
That your priests delight in, useless prove.
Water, salt, are vain
Fervent youth to chain,
Ah, e'en Earth can never cool down love!
"When that infant vow of love was spoken,
Venus' radiant temple smiled on both.
Mother! thou that promise since hast broken,
Fetter'd by a strange, deceitful oath.
Gods, though, hearken ne'er,
Should a mother swear
To deny her daughter's plighted troth.
From my grave to wander I am forc'd,
Still to seek The Good's long-sever'd link,
Still to love the bridegroom I have lost,
And the life-blood of his heart to drink;
When his race is run,
I must hasten on,
And the young must 'neath my vengeance sink.
Beauteous youth! no longer may'st thou live;
Here must shrivel up thy form so fair;
Did not I to thee a token give,
Taking in return this lock of hair?
View it to thy sorrow!
Grey thou'lt be to-morrow,
Only to grow brown again when there.
Mother, to this final prayer give ear!
Let a funeral pile be straightway dress'd;
Open then my cell so sad and drear,

That the flames may give the lovers rest!
When ascends the fire
From the glowing pyre,
To the gods of old we'll hasten, blest."

GLOSSARY

Amor: Latin for "love."
Bacchus: Roman god of wine, counterpart to the Greek Dionysius.
Ceres: Roman goddess of grain and harvest; counterpart to the Greek Demeter.
Corinth: A city in South-Central Greece. An ancient city-state, and the site of the early Christian church to which St. Paul wrote his "Letters to the Corinthians."
Hymen: Greek god of marriage.
In-hies: Comes inside.
Quaff'd: Drank.
Venus: Roman goddess of love, counterpart to the Greek Aphrodite.

AFTERWORD

Goethe's Bride is a powerful, active heroine who is sure of final victory and acceptance by the true heavenly powers. It's a cry of defiance from the Romantic Age. Ironically, the English had laughed at vampires in the 18th century, dismissing them as a silly superstition from Central or Eastern Europe. But as the 19th century dawned, British writers reconsidered the literary vampire as a figure of horror…

ONEIZA

"A Fiend; a manifest Fiend!"

Robert Southey was England's Poet Laureate from 1813 until his death thirty years later. Before that, he was one of the Romantic "Lake Poets" along with Wordsworth and Coleridge. His 1801 epic poem Thalaba the Destroyer *is set in an Arabian Nights-like Middle East—"Oriental" fantasy mixed with "Gothic."*

Thalaba is a young man who defeats a series of evil sorcerers and other creatures. His tutor, Moath, has a beautiful daughter, Oneiza; she and Thalaba plan to marry, but she dies before their wedding. Thalaba and Moath discover that evil sorcery has been at work in her tomb…

Excerpt from

THALABA THE DESTROYER

Robert Southey

...The Old Man looked at him incredulous.
"Nightly," the youth pursued,
"Thy daughter comes to drive me to despair.
Moath thou thinkest me mad,
But when the Cryer from the Minaret
Proclaims the midnight hour,
Hast thou a heart to see her?"
In the Meidan now
The clang of clarions and of drums
Accompanied the Sun's descent.
"Dost thou not pray? my son!"
Said Moath, as he saw
The white flag waving on the neighbouring Mosque;
Then Thalaba's eye grew wild,
"Pray!" echoed he, "I must not pray!"
And the hollow groan he gave
Went to the Old Man's heart,
And bowing down his face to earth,
In fervent agony he called on God.

A night of darkness and of storms!
Into the Chamber of the Tomb
Thalaba led the Old Man,
To roof him from the rain.

A night of storms! the wind
Swept through the moonless sky,
And moan'd among the pillar'd sepulcheres;
And in the pauses of its sweep
They heard the heavy rain
Beat on the monument above.
In silence on Oneiza's grave
Her father and her husband sate.
The Cryer from the Minaret
Proclaim'd the midnight hour.
"Now, now!" cried Thalaba;
And o'er the chamber of the tomb
There spread a lurid gleam,
Like the reflections of a sulphur fire;
And in that hideous light
Oneiza stood before them. It was She. . .
Her very lineaments. . .and such as death
Had changed them, livid cheeks and lips of blue;
But in her eye there dwelt
Brightness more terrible
Than all the loathsomeness of death.
"Still art thou living, wretch?"
In hollow tones she cried to Thalaba;
"And must I nightly leave my grave
To tell thee, still in vain,
God hath abandoned thee?"
"This is not she!" the Old Man exclaim'd;
"A Fiend; a manifest Fiend!"
And to the youth he held his lance;
"Strike and deliver thyself!"
"Strike HER!" cried Thalaba,
And palsied of all power,
Gazed fixedly upon the dreadful form.
"Yea, strike her!" cried a voice, whose tones

Flow'd with such a sudden healing through his soul,
As when the desert shower
From death deliver'd him;
But unobedient to that well-known voice,
His eye was seeking it,
When Moath, firm of heart,
Perform'd the bidding: through the vampire corpse
He thrust his lance; it fell,
And howling with the wound,
Its fiendish tenant fled,
A sapphire light fell on them,
And garmented with glory, in their sight
Oneiza's Spirit stood.

GLOSSARY

Lineaments: Distinctive characteristics, especially facial features.
Meidan: An open space in a city.
Palsied: Paralyzed.
Sepulcheres: Sepulchres; tombs.

AFTERWORD

The vampire Thalaba battles is not **actually** ***Oneiza, but a kind of demonic doppelganger—and when her true spirit is freed, Oneiza guides Thalaba through his further adventures. In most vampire***

stories, of course, the vampire is an actual body, transformed, of a dead person—although without a soul, which is why Stoker's vampires cast no reflection or shadow. Early 18th century records of "actual" vampire cases made it clear that staking or impalement was the basic way to kill an undead corpse. The reason behind the impaling was, however, not always clear. It may have been to secure the vampire to the earth, to prevent it rising from the grave. In Stoker's Dracula, *though, impalement through the vampire's heart frees the vampire's soul and opens the door to salvation and eternal rest. We may see the beginning of this end-of-the-19th-century idea at the beginning of the 19th century, in Southey's Oneiza.*

But, in the poem, Thalaba doesn't know this as he enters "the chambers of the tomb," and he is, at first, put off by the image of his beloved. Southey has another "first," here, because in the "real-life" vampire cases, there's no record of any hesitation on the part of the villagers staking the vampires who used to be their friends and neighbors. Stoker, and, through Stoker, dozens of vampire films of the mid-20th century, would make the hesitation before staking a key moment of drama.

Oneiza's fate, though, can also be seen as an early example of another trope: the necessary destruction by a man of a woman who's out of control—or out of male control. She can't be reasoned with or prayed or magicked back to normal. She can only be destroyed—and saved--through an act of violent murder. Thalaba doesn't want to do it, but his father tells the hero to, in essence, "be a man" and stab. Thalaba doesn't know what's going to happen—but he trusts his patriarchal tutor, and what seems like an act of murder actually frees his beloved from having her spirit trapped by an evil demon…which is literally a fate worse than death.

The act of impalement is a kind of mirror image of the deflowering of a virgin. Instead of "deflowering" or "soiling" the woman—to use some 19th century terms—penetration restores virgin innocence. What seems like killing—and a very phallic killing—is actually liberation and salvation.

In the 20th century, staking the female vampire would become a kind of fetish in movies, a parallel to the earlier scene where the lovely woman lies in her bed and the male vampire comes in to penetrate and possess her.

But in the staking scene, the vampire woman lies, not in her bed, but her coffin. Usually asleep and always motionless—until the stake goes in and she screams—the female victim can't resist the thrust of the stake. On the hero's part, the penetration is performed with a combination of terror and altruism, because, even if the woman yells and screams, "it's for her own good."

Male vampires are also sometimes staked while they sleep in their coffins, but the star vampire, the vampire lord, is usually more active—perhaps the staker's timing is off and the vampire lord is awake or has left the coffin, to present a dynamic threat that can only be overcome by an unexpected shaft of sunlight or the pointy end of a broken fence or wheel.

Female vampires don't have to exert themselves. A beautiful sleeping woman is dangerous enough, just lying there…

BRUNHILDA

...the flame of that youthful blood, of which she drained the veins of others, rioted in her own...

Ernst Benjamin Salomo Raupach, who was primarily a dramatist, wrote Laßt die Todten ruhen (Let the Dead Rest) *for a collection of German stories called* Minerva *in 1823. It was subtitled "Ein Märchen" or "A Fairy Tale."*

The story, apparently originally aimed at female readers, was almost immediately translated into English as Wake Not the Dead, *and was included in the 1823 English anthology,* Popular Tales and Romances of the Northern Nations. *In 1830, the English dramatist George Blink turned it into a stage melodrama:* The Vampire Bride, or Wake Not the Dead.

Raupach sets his story in late Medieval, or perhaps early Renaissance, times. True to its sub-title, the story has the form of a fairy tale—one of those grown-up, grim ones, where someone is granted a wish he should never have asked for in the first place. It deals with issues of class, sexuality and the role of women in society, but in a "once upon a time" context, full of Romantic images of storms and violence.

And the ending will *surprise you.*

WAKE NOT THE DEAD

Ernst Benjamin Salomo Raupach

"Wilt thou forever sleep? Wilt thou never more awake, my beloved, but henceforth repose forever from thy short pilgrimage on earth? O yet once again return! and bring back with thee the vivifying dawn of hope to one whose existence hath, since thy departure, been obscured by the dunnest shades. What! dumb? forever dumb? Thy friend lamenteth, and thou heedest him not? He sheds bitter, scalding tears, and thou reposest unregarding his affliction? He is in despair, and thou no longer openest thy arms to him as an asylum from his grief? Say then, doth the pale shroud become thee better than the bridal veil? Is the chamber of the grave a warmer bed than the couch of love? Is the spectre death more welcome to thy arms than thy enamoured consort? Oh! return, my beloved, return once again to this anxious disconsolate bosom."

Such were the lamentations which Walter poured forth for his Brunhilda, the partner of his youthful passionate love; thus did he bewail over her grave at the midnight hour, what time the spirit that presides in the troublous atmosphere, sends his legions of monsters through mid-air; so that their shadows, as they flit beneath the moon and across the earth, dart as wild, agitating thoughts that chase each other o'er the sinner's bosom:--thus did he lament under the tall linden trees by her grave, while his head reclined on the cold stone.

Walter was a powerful lord in Burgundy, who, in his earliest youth, had been smitten with the charms of the fair Brunhilda, a beauty far surpassing in loveliness all her rivals; for her tresses, dark as the raven face of night, streaming over her shoulders, set off to the utmost advantage the beaming lustre of her slender form, and the rich dye of a cheek whose tint was deep and brilliant as that of the western heaven; her eyes did not resemble those burning orbs whose pale glow gems the vault of night, and whose immeasurable distance fills the soul with deep thoughts of eternity, but rather as the sober beams which cheer this nether world, and which, while they enlighten, kindle the sons of earth to joy and love.

Brunhilda became the wife of Walter, and both being equally enamoured and devoted, they abandoned themselves to the enjoyment of a passion that rendered them reckless of aught besides, while it lulled them in a fascinating dream. Their sole apprehension was lest aught should awaken them from a delirium which they prayed might continue forever. Yet how vain is the wish that would arrest the decrees of destiny! as well might it seek to divert the circling planets from their eternal course. Short was the duration of this frenzied passion; not that it gradually decayed and subsided into apathy, but death snatched away his blooming victim, and left Walter to a widowed couch.

Impetuous, however, as was his first burst of grief, he was not inconsolable, for ere long another bride became the partner of the youthful nobleman.

Swanhilda also was beautiful; although nature had formed her charms on a very different model from those of Brunhilda. Her golden locks waved bright as the beams of morn: only when excited by some emotion of her soul did a rosy hue tinge the lily paleness of her cheek: her limbs were proportioned in the nicest symmetry, but also possessed that luxuriant fullness of animal life. Her eye beamed eloquently, but it was with the milder radiance of a star, tranquillizing to tenderness rather than exciting to warmth. Thus formed, it was not possible that she should steep him in his former delirium, although she rendered happy his waking hours—tranquil and serious, yet cheerful, studying in all things her husband's pleasure, she restored order and comfort in his family, where her presence shed a general influence all around. Her mild benevolence tended to restrain the fiery, impetuous disposition of Walter, while at the same time her prudence recalled him in some degree from his vain, turbulent wishes, and his aspirings after unattainable enjoyments, to the duties and pleasures of actual life.

Swanhilda bore her husband two children, a son and a daughter; the latter was mild and patient as her mother, well contented with her solitary sports, and even in these recreations displayed the serious turn of her character. The boy possessed his father's fiery, restless disposition, tempered, however, with the solidity of his mother. Attached by his offspring even more tenderly towards their mother, Walter now lived for several years very happily: his thoughts would frequently, indeed, recur to Brunhilda, but without their former violence, merely as we dwell upon the memory of a friend of our earlier days, borne from us on the rapid current of time to a region where we know that he is happy.

But clouds dissolve into air, flowers fade, the sands of the hourglass run imperceptibly away, and even so do human feelings dissolve, fade, and pass away; and with them too, human happiness. Walter's inconstant breast again sighed for the ecstatic dreams of those days which he had spent with his equally romantic, enamoured Brunhilda—again did she present herself to his ardent fancy in all the glow of her bridal charms, and he began to draw a parallel between the past and the present; nor did imagination, as it is wont, fail to array the former in her brightest hues, while it proportionably obscured the latter; so that he pictured to himself, the one much more rich in enjoyment, and the other, much less so than they really were.

This change in her husband did not escape Swanhilda; whereupon, redoubling her attentions towards him, and her cares towards their children, she expected, by this means, to reunite the knot that was slackened; yet the more she endeavoured to regain his affections, the colder did he grow, the more intolerable did her caresses seem, and the more continually did the image of Brunhilda haunt his thoughts. The children, whose endearments were now become indispensable to him, alone stood between the parents as genii eager to affect a reconciliation; and, beloved by them both, formed a uniting link between them.

Yet, as evil can be plucked from the heart of man, only ere its root has yet struck deep, its fangs being afterwards too firm to be eradicated; so was Walter's diseased fancy too far affected to have its disorder stopped, for, in a short time, it completely tyrannized over him. Frequently of a night, instead of retiring to his consort's chamber, he repaired to Brunhilda's grave, where he murmured forth his discontent, saying: "Wilt thou sleep forever?"

One night as he was reclining on the turf, indulging in his wonted sorrow, a sorcerer from the neighbouring mountains, entered into this field of death for the purpose of gathering, for his mystic spells, such herbs as grow only from the earth wherein the dead repose, and which, as if the last production of mortality, are gifted with a powerful and supernatural influence. The sorcerer perceived the mourner, and approached the spot where he was lying.

"Wherefore, fond wretch, dost thou grieve thus, for what is now a hideous mass of mortality—mere bones, and nerves, and veins? Nations have fallen unlamented; even worlds themselves, long ere this globe of ours was created, have mouldered into nothing; nor hath any one wept over them; why then shouldst thou indulge this vain affliction for a child of the dust—a being as frail as thyself, and like thee the creature but of a moment?"

Walter raised himself up:—"Let yon worlds that shine in the firmament," replied he, "lament for each other as they perish. It is true, that I who am myself clay, lament for my fellow-clay: yet is this clay impregnated with a fire,—with an essence, that none of the elements of creation possess—with love: and this divine passion I felt for her who now sleepeth beneath this sod."

"Will thy complaints awaken her: or could they do so, would she not soon upbraid thee for having disturbed that repose in which she is now hushed?"

"Avaunt, cold-hearted being: thou knowest not what is love. Oh! that my tears could wash away the earthy covering that conceals her from these eyes;—that my groan of anguish could rouse her from her slumber of death!—No, she would not again seek her earthy couch."

"Insensate that thou art, and couldst thou endure to gaze without shuddering on one disgorged from the jaws of the grave? Art thou too thyself the same from whom she parted; or hath time passed o'er thy brow and left no traces there? Would not thy love rather be converted into hate and disgust?"

"Say rather that the stars would leave yon firmament, that the sun will henceforth refuse to shed his beams through the heavens. Oh! that she stood once more before me;—-that once again she reposed on this bosom!—-how quickly should we then forget that death or time had ever stepped between us."

"Delusion! mere delusion of the brain, from heated blood, like to that which arises from the fumes of wine. It is not my wish to tempt thee;—to restore to thee thy dead; else wouldst thou soon feel that I have spoken truth."

"How! restore her to me," exclaimed Walter casting himself at the sorcerer's feet. "Oh! if thou art indeed able to effect that, grant it to my earnest supplication; if one throb of human feeling vibrates in thy bosom, let my tears prevail with thee; restore to me my beloved; so shalt thou hereafter bless the deed, and see that it was a good work."

"A good work! a blessed deed!"—-returned the sorcerer with a smile of scorn; "for me there exists nor good nor evil; since my will is always the same. Ye alone know evil, who will that which ye would not. It is indeed in my power to restore her to thee: yet, bethink thee well, whether it will prove thy weal. Consider too, how deep the abyss between life and death; across this, my power can build a bridge, but it can never fill up the frightful chasm."

Walter would have spoken, and sought to prevail on this powerful being with fresh entreaties, but the latter prevented him, saying: "Peace! bethink thee well! and return hither to me tomorrow at midnight. Yet once more do I warn thee, 'Wake not the dead.' "

Having uttered these words, the mysterious being disappeared. Intoxicated with fresh hope, Walter found no sleep on his couch; for fancy, prodigal of her richest stores, expanded before him the glittering web of futurity; and his eye, moistened with the dew of rapture, glanced from one vision of happiness to another. During the next day he wandered through the woods, lest wonted objects by recalling the memory of later and less happier times, might disturb the blissful idea that he should again behold her—again fold her in his arms, gaze on her beaming brow by day, repose on her bosom at night: and, as this sole idea filled his imagination, how was it possible that the least doubt should arise; or that the warning of the mysterious old man should recur to his thoughts?

No sooner did the midnight hour approach, than he hastened before the grave-field where the sorcerer was already standing by that of Brunhilda. "Hast thou maturely considered?" inquired he.

"Oh! restore to me the object of my ardent passion," exclaimed Walter with impetuous eagerness. "Delay not thy generous action, lest I die even this night, consumed with disappointed desire; and behold her face no more."

"Well then," answered the old man, "return hither again tomorrow at the same hour. But once more do I give thee this friendly warning, 'Wake not the dead.' "

All in the despair of impatience, Walter would have prostrated himself at his feet, and supplicated him to fulfil at once a desire now increased to agony; but the sorcerer had already disappeared. Pouring forth his lamentations more wildly and impetuously than ever, he lay upon the grave of his adored one, until the grey dawn streaked the east.

During the day, which seemed to him longer than any he had ever experienced, he wandered to and fro, restless and impatient, seemingly without any object, and deeply buried in his own reflections, inquest as the murderer who meditates his first deed of blood: and the stars of evening found him once more at the appointed spot.

At midnight the sorcerer was there also. "Hast thou yet maturely deliberated?" inquired he, "as on the preceding night?"

"Oh what should I deliberate?" returned Walter impatiently. "I need not to deliberate; what I demand of thee, is that which thou hast promised me--that which will prove my bliss. Or dost thou but mock me? If so, hence from my sight, lest I be tempted to lay my hand on thee."

"Once more do I warn thee," answered the old man with

undisturbed composure, " 'Wake not the dead'—let her rest."

"Aye, but not in the cold grave: she shall rather rest on this bosom which burns with eagerness to clasp her."

"Reflect, thou mayst not quit her until death, even though aversion and horror should seize thy heart. There would then remain only one horrible means."

"Dotard!" cried Walter, interrupting him, "how may I hate that which I love with such intensity of passion? how should I abhor that for which my every drop of blood is boiling?"

"Then be it even as thou wishest," answered the sorcerer; "step back."

The old man now drew a circle round the grave, all the while muttering words of enchantment. Immediately the storm began to howl among the tops of the trees; owls flapped their wings, and uttered their low voice of omen; the stars hid their mild, beaming aspect, that they might not behold so unholy and impious a spectacle; the stone then rolled from the grave with a hollow sound, leaving a free passage for the inhabitant of that dreadful tenement. The sorcerer scattered into the yawning earth roots and herbs of most magic power, and of most penetrating odour, so that the worms crawling forth from the earth congregated together, and raised themselves in a fiery column over the grave: while rushing wind burst from the earth, scattering the mould before it, until at length the coffin lay uncovered. The moonbeams fell on it, and the lid burst open with a tremendous sound. Upon this the sorcerer poured upon it some blood from out of a human skull, exclaiming at the same time, "Drink, sleeper, of this warm stream, that thy heart may again beat within thy bosom." And, after a short pause, shedding on her some other mystic liquid, he cried aloud with the voice of one inspired: "Yes, thy heart beats once more with the flood of life: thine eye is again opened to sight. Arise, therefore, from the tomb."

As an island suddenly springs forth from the dark waves of the ocean, raised upwards from the deep by the force of subterraneous fires, so did Brunhilda start from her earthy couch, borne forward by some invisible power.

Taking her by the hand, the sorcerer led her towards Walter, who stood at some little distance, rooted to the ground with amazement.

"Receive again," said he, "the object of thy passionate sighs: mayest thou never more require my aid; should that, however, happen, so wilt thou find me, during the full of the moon, upon the mountains in that spot and where the three roads meet."

Instantly did Walter recognize in the form that stood before him, her whom he so ardently loved; and a sudden glow shot through his frame at finding her thus restored to him: yet the night-frost had chilled his limbs and palsied his tongue. For a while he gazed upon her without either motion or speech, and during this pause, all was again become hushed and serene; and the stars shone brightly in the clear heavens.

"Walter!" exclaimed the figure; and at once the well-known sound, thrilling to his heart, broke the spell by which he was bound.

"Is it reality? Is it truth?" cried he, "or a cheating delusion?"

"No, it is no imposture; I am really living:—conduct me quickly to thy castle in the mountains."

Walter looked around: the old man had disappeared, but he perceived close by his side, a coal-black steed of fiery eye, ready equipped to conduct him thence; and on his back lay all proper attire for Brunhilda, who lost no time in arraying herself.

This being done, she cried; "Haste, let us away ere the dawn breaks, for my eye is yet too weak to endure the light of day."

Fully recovered from his stupor, Walter leaped into his saddle, and catching up, with a mingled feeling of delight and awe, the beloved being thus mysteriously restored from the power of the grave, he spurred on across the wild, towards the mountains, as furiously as if pursued by the shadows of the dead, hastening to recover from him their sister.

The castle to which Walter conducted his Brunhilda was situated on a rock between other rocks rising up above it. Here they arrived, unseen by any save one aged domestic, on whom Walter imposed secrecy by the severest threats.

"Here will we tarry," said Brunhilda, "until I can endure the light, and until thou canst look upon me without trembling as if struck with a cold chill."

They accordingly continued to make that place their abode: yet no one knew that Brunhilda existed, save only that aged attendant, who provided their meals. During seven entire days they had no light except that of tapers: during the next seven, the light was admitted through the lofty casements only while the rising or setting-sun faintly illumined the mountain-tops, the valley being still enveloped in shade.

Seldom did Walter quit Brunhilda's side: a nameless spell seemed to attach him to her; even the shudder which he felt in her presence, and which would not permit him to touch her, was not unmixed with pleasure, like that thrilling awful emotion felt when strains of sacred music float under the vault of some temple; he rather sought, therefore, than avoided this feeling. Often too as he had indulged in calling to mind the beauties of Brunhilda, she had never appeared so fair, so fascinating, so admirable when depicted by his imagination, as when now beheld in reality. Never till now had her voice sounded with such tones of sweetness; never before did her language possess such eloquence as it now did, when she conversed with him on the subject of the past. And this was the magic fairy-land towards which her words constantly conducted him. Ever did she dwell upon the days of their first love, those hours of delight which they had participated together when the one derived all enjoyment from the other: and so rapturous, so enchanting, so full of life did she recall to his imagination that blissful season, that he even doubted whether he had ever experienced with her so much felicity, or had been so truly happy. And, while she thus vividly portrayed their hours of past delight, she delineated in still more glowing, more enchanting colours, those hours of approaching bliss which now awaited them, richer in enjoyment than any preceding ones.

In this manner did she charm her attentive auditor with enrapturing hopes for the future, and lull him into dreams of more than mortal ecstasy; so that while he listened to her siren strain, he entirely forgot how little blissful was the latter period of their union, when he had often sighed at her imperiousness, and at her harshness both to himself and all his household.

Yet even had he recalled this to mind would it have disturbed him in his present delirious trance? Had she not now left behind in the grave all the frailty of mortality? Was not her whole being refined and purified by that long sleep in which neither passion nor sin had approached her even in dreams? How different now was the subject of her discourse! Only when speaking of her affection for him, did she betray anything of earthly feeling: at other times, she uniformly dwelt upon themes relating to the invisible and future world; when in descanting and declaring the mysteries of eternity, a stream of prophetic eloquence would burst from her lips.

In this manner had twice seven days elapsed, and, for the first time, Walter beheld the being now dearer to him than ever, in the full light of day. Every trace of the grave had disappeared from her countenance; a roseate tinge like the ruddy streaks of dawn again beamed on her pallid cheek; the faint, mouldering taint of the grave was changed into a delightful violet scent; the only sign of earth that never disappeared. He no longer felt either apprehension or awe, as he gazed upon her in the sunny light of day: it was not until now, that he seemed to have recovered her completely; and, glowing with all his former passion towards her, he would have pressed her to his bosom, but she gently repulsed him, saying:—"Not yet—spare your caresses until the moon has again filled her horn."

Spite of his impatience, Walter was obliged to await the lapse of another period of seven days: but, on the night when the moon was arrived at the full, he hastened to Brunhilda, whom he found more lovely than she had ever appeared before. Fearing no obstacles to his transports, he embraced with all the fervour of a deeply enamoured and successful lover. Brunhilda, however, still refused to yield to his passion.

"What!" exclaimed she, "is it fitting that I who have been purified by death from the frailty of mortality, should become thy concubine, while a mere daughter of the earth bears the title of thy wife: never shall it be. No, it must be within the walls of thy palace, within that chamber where I once reigned as queen, that thou obtainest the end of thy wishes,—and of mine also," added she, imprinting a glowing kiss on his lips, and immediately disappeared.

Heated with passion, and determined to sacrifice everything to the accomplishment of his desires, Walter hastily quitted the apartment, and shortly after the castle itself. He travelled over mountain and across heath, with the rapidity of a storm, so that the turf was flung up by his horse's hoofs; nor once stopped until he arrived home.

Here, however, neither the affectionate caresses of Swanhilda, or those of his children could touch his heart, or induce him to restrain his furious desires. Alas! is the impetuous torrent to be checked in its devastating course by the beauteous flowers over which it rushes, when they exclaim:—"Destroyer, commiserate with our helpless innocence and beauty, do not lay us waste"?—the stream sweeps over them unregarding, and a single moment annihilates the pride of a whole summer.

Shortly afterwards did Walter begin to hint to Swanhilda that they were ill-suited to each other; that he was anxious to taste that wild, tumultuous life, so well according with the spirit of his sex, while she, on the contrary, was satisfied with the monotonous circle of household enjoyments:—that he was eager for whatever promised novelty, while she felt most attached to what was familiarized to her by habit: and lastly, that her cold disposition, bordering upon indifference, but ill assorted with his ardent temperament: it was therefore more prudent that they should seek apart from each other that happiness which they could not find together.

A sigh, and a brief acquiescence in his wishes was all the reply that Swanhilda made: and, on the following morning, upon his presenting her with a paper of separation, informing her that she was at liberty to return home to her father, she received it most submissively: yet, ere she departed, she gave him the following warning: "Too well do I conjecture to whom I am indebted for this our separation. Often have

I seen thee at Brunhilda's grave, and beheld thee there even on that night when the face of the heavens was suddenly enveloped in a veil of clouds. Hast thou rashly dared to tear aside the awful veil that separates the mortality that dreams, from that which dreameth not? Oh! then woe to thee, thou wretched man, for thou hast attached to thyself that which will prove thy destruction."

She ceased: nor did Walter attempt any reply, for the similar admonition uttered by the sorcerer flashed upon his mind, all obscured as it was by passion, just as the lightning glares momentarily through the gloom of night without dispersing the obscurity.

Swanhilda then departed, in order to pronounce to her children a bitter farewell, for they, according to national custom, belonged to the father; and, having bathed them in her tears, and consecrated them with the holy water of maternal love, she quitted her husband's residence, and departed to the home of her father's.

Thus was the kind and benevolent Swanhilda driven an exile from those halls where she had presided with grace;—from halls which were now newly decorated to receive another mistress.

The day at length arrived on which Walter, for the second time, conducted Brunhilda home as a newly made bride. And he caused it to be reported among his domestics that his new consort had gained his affections by her extraordinary likeness to Brunhilda, their former mistress. How ineffably happy did he deem himself as he conducted his beloved once more into the chamber which had often witnessed their former joys, and which was now newly gilded and adorned in a most costly style: among the other decorations were figures of angels scattering roses, which served to support the purple draperies whose ample folds o'ershadowed the nuptial couch. With what impatience did he await the hour that was to put him in possession of those beauties for which he had already paid so high a price, but, whose enjoyment was to cost him most dearly yet! Unfortunate Walter! revelling in bliss, thou beholdest not the abyss that yawns beneath thy feet, intoxicated with the luscious perfume of the flower thou hast plucked, thou little deemest how deadly is the venom with which it is fraught, although, for a short season, its potent fragrance bestows new energy on all thy feelings.

Happy, however, as Walter was now, his household were far from being equally so. The strange resemblance between their new lady and the deceased Brunhilda filled them with a secret dismay,—an undefinable horror; for there was not a single difference of feature, of tone of voice, or of gesture. To add too to these mysterious circumstances, her female attendants discovered a particular mark on her back, exactly like one which Brunhilda had. A report was now soon circulated, that their lady was no other than Brunhilda herself, who had been recalled to life by the power of necromancy. How truly horrible was the idea of living under the same roof with one who had been an inhabitant of the tomb, and of being obliged to attend upon her, and acknowledge her as mistress! There was also in Brunhilda much to increase this aversion, and favour their superstition: no ornaments of gold ever decked her person; all that others were wont to wear of this metal, she had formed of silver: no richly coloured and sparkling jewels glittered upon her; pearls alone, lent their pale lustre to adorn her bosom. Most carefully did she always avoid the cheerful light of the sun, and was wont to spend the brightest days in the most retired and gloomy apartments: only during the twilight of the commencing or declining day did she ever walk abroad, but her favourite hour was when the phantom light of the moon bestowed on all objects a shadowy appearance and a sombre hue; always too at the crowing of the cock an involuntary shudder was observed to seize her limbs.

Imperious as before her death, she quickly imposed her iron yoke on everyone around her, while she seemed even far more terrible than ever, since a dread of some supernatural power attached to her, appalled all who approached her. A malignant withering glance seemed to shoot from her eye on the unhappy object of her wrath, as if it would annihilate its victim. In short, those halls which, in the time of Swanhilda were the residence of cheerfulness and mirth, now resembled an extensive desert tomb.

With fear imprinted on their pale countenances, the domestics glided through the apartments of the castle; and in this abode of terror, the crowing of the cock caused the living to tremble, as if they were the spirits of the departed; for the sound always reminded them of their mysterious mistress. There was no one but who shuddered at meeting her in a lonely place, in the dusk of evening, or by the light of the moon, a circumstance that was deemed to be ominous of some evil: so great was the apprehension of her female attendants, they pined in continual disquietude, and, by degrees, all quitted her. In the course of time even others of the domestics fled, for an insupportable horror had seized them.

The art of the sorcerer had indeed bestowed upon Brunhilda an artificial life, and due nourishment had continued to support the restored body: yet this body was not able of itself to keep up the genial glow of vitality, and to nourish the flame whence springs all the affections and passions, whether of love or hate; for death had forever destroyed and withered it: all that Brunhilda now possessed was a chilled existence, colder than that of the snake. It was nevertheless necessary that she should love, and return with equal ardour the warm caresses of her spell-enthralled husband, to whose passion alone she was indebted for her renewed existence. It was necessary that a magic draught should animate the dull current in her veins and awaken her to the glow of life and the flame of love—a potion of abomination—one not even to be named without a curse—human blood, imbibed whilst yet warm, from the veins of youth. This was the hellish drink for which she thirsted: possessing no sympathy with the purer feelings of humanity; deriving no enjoyment from aught that interests in life and occupies its varied hours; her existence was a mere blank, unless when in the arms of her paramour husband, and therefore was it that she craved incessantly after the horrible draught. It was even with the utmost effort that she could forbear sucking even the blood of Walter himself, reclined beside her. Whenever she beheld some innocent child whose lovely face denoted the exuberance of infantine health and vigour, she would entice it by soothing words and fond caresses into her most secret apartment, where, lulling it to sleep in her arms, she would suck from its bosom the warm, purple tide of life. Nor were youths of either sex safe from her horrid attack: having first breathed upon her unhappy victim, who never failed immediately to sink into a lengthened sleep, she would then in a similar manner drain his veins of the vital juice. Thus children, youths, and maidens quickly faded away, as flowers gnawn by the cankering worm: the fullness of their limbs disappeared; a sallow line succeeded to the rosy freshness of their cheeks, the liquid lustre of the eye was deadened, even as the sparkling stream when arrested by the touch of frost; and their locks became thin and grey, as if already ravaged by the storm of life.

Parents beheld with horror this desolating pestilence devouring their offspring; nor could simple or charm, potion or amulet avail aught against it. The grave swallowed up one after the other; or did the miserable victim survive, he became cadaverous and wrinkled even in the very morn of existence. Parents observed with horror this devastating pestilence snatch away their offspring--a pestilence which, nor herb however potent, nor charm, nor holy taper, nor exorcism could avert. They either beheld their children sink one after the other into the grave, or their youthful forms, withered by the unholy, vampire embrace of Brunhilda, assume the decrepitude of sudden age.

At length strange surmises and reports began to prevail; it was whispered that Brunhilda herself was the cause of all these horrors; although no one could pretend to tell in what manner she destroyed her victims, since no marks of violence were discernible. Yet when young children confessed that she had frequently lulled them asleep in her arms, and elder ones said that a sudden slumber had come upon them whenever she began to converse with them, suspicion became converted into certainty, and those whose offspring had hitherto escaped unharmed, quitted their hearths and home—all their little possessions—the dwellings of their fathers and the inheritance of their children, in order to rescue from so horrible a fate those who were dearer to their simple affections than aught else the world could give.

Thus daily did the castle assume a more desolate appearance; daily did its environs become more deserted; none but a few aged, decrepit old women and grey-headed menials were to be seen remaining of the once numerous retinue. Such will in the latter days of the earth be the last generation of mortals, when childbearing shall have ceased, when youth shall no more be seen, nor any arise to replace those who shall await their fate in silence.

Walter alone noticed not, or heeded not, the desolation around him; he apprehended not death, lapped as he was in a glowing Elysium of love. Far more happy than formerly did he now seem in the possession of Brunhilda. All those caprices and frowns which had been wont to overcloud their former union had now entirely disappeared. She even seemed to dote on him with a warmth of passion that she had never exhibited even during the happy season of bridal love; for the flame of that youthful blood, of which she drained the veins of others, rioted in her own. At night, as soon as he closed his eyes, she would breathe on him till he sank into delicious dreams, from which he awoke only to experience more rapturous enjoyments. By day she would continually discourse with him on the bliss experienced by happy spirits beyond the grave, assuring him that, as his affection had recalled her from the tomb, they were now irrevocably united. Thus fascinated by a continual spell, it was not possible that he should perceive what was taking place around him. Brunhilda, however, foresaw with savage grief that the source of her youthful ardour was daily decreasing, for, in a short time, there remained nothing gifted with youth, save Walter and his children, and these latter she resolved should be her next victims.

On her first return to the castle, she had felt an aversion towards the offspring of another, and therefore abandoned them entirely to the attendants appointed by Swanhilda. Now, however, she began to pay considerable attention to them, and caused them to be frequently admitted into her presence. The aged nurses were filled with dread at perceiving these marks of regard from her towards their young charges, yet they dared not oppose the will of their terrible and imperious mistress.

Soon did Brunhilda gain the affection of the children, who were too unsuspecting of guile to apprehend any danger from her; on the contrary, her caresses won them completely to her. Instead of ever checking their mirthful gambols, she would rather instruct them in new sports: often too did she recite to them tales of such strange and wild interest as to exceed all the stories of their nurses. Were they wearied either with play or with listening to her narratives, she would take them on her knees and lull them to slumber.

Then did visions of the most surpassing magnificence attend their dreams: they would fancy themselves in some garden where flowers of every hue rose in rows one above the other, from the humble violet to the tall sunflower, forming a parti-coloured broidery of every hue, sloping upwards towards the golden clouds where little angels whose wings sparkled with azure and gold descended to bring them delicious cakes or splendid jewels; or sung to them soothing melodious hymns. So delightful did these dream in short time become to the children that they longed for nothing so eagerly as to slumber on Brunhilda's lap, for never did they else enjoy such visions of heavenly forms. They were they most anxious for that which was to prove their destruction:—yet do we not all aspire after that which conducts us to the grave—after the enjoyment of life? These innocents stretched out their arms to approaching death because it assumed the mask of pleasure; for, which they were lapped in these ecstatic slumbers, Brunhilda sucked the life-stream from their bosoms.

On waking, indeed, they felt themselves faint and exhausted, yet did no pain nor any mark betray the cause. Shortly, however, did their strength entirely fail, even as the summer brook is gradually dried up: their sports became less and less noisy; their loud, frolicsome laughter was converted into a faint smile; the full tones of their voices died away into a mere whisper.

Their attendants were filled with horror and despair; too well did they conjecture the horrible truth, yet dared not to impart their suspicions to Walter, who was so devotedly attached to his horrible partner. Death had already smote his prey: the children were but the mere shadows of their former selves, and even this shadow quickly disappeared.

The anguished father deeply bemoaned their loss, for,

notwithstanding his apparent neglect, he was strongly attached to them, nor until he had experienced their loss was he aware that his love was so great.

His affliction could not fail to excite the displeasure of Brunhilda: "Why dost thou lament so fondly," said she, "for these little ones? What satisfaction could such unformed beings yield to thee unless thou wert still attached to their mother? Thy heart then is still hers? Or dost thou now regret her and them because thou art satiated with my fondness and weary of my endearments? Had these young ones grown up, would they not have attached thee, thy spirit and thy affections more closely to this earth of clay—to this dust and have alienated thee from that sphere to which I, who have already passed the grave, endeavour to raise thee? Say is thy spirit so heavy, or thy love so weak, or thy faith so hollow, that the hope of being mine forever is unable to touch thee?"

Thus did Brunhilda express her indignation at her consort's grief, and forbade him her presence. The fear of offending her beyond forgiveness and his anxiety to appease her soon dried up his tears; and he again abandoned himself to his fatal passion, until approaching destruction at length awakened him from his delusion.

Neither maiden, nor youth, was any longer to be seen, either within the dreary walls of the castle, or the adjoining territory:—all had disappeared; for those whom the grave had not swallowed up had fled from the region of death. Who, therefore, now remained to quench the horrible thirst of the female vampire save Walter himself? and his death she dared to contemplate unmoved; for that divine sentiment that unites two beings in one joy and one sorrow was unknown to her bosom. Was he in his tomb, so was she free to search out other victims and glut herself with destruction, until she herself should, at the last day, be consumed with the earth itself, such is the fatal law to which the dead are subject when awoke by the arts of necromancy from the sleep of the grave.

She now began to fix her blood-thirsty lips on Walter's breast, when cast into a profound sleep by the odour of her violet breath he reclined beside her quite unconscious of his impending fate: yet soon did his vital powers begin to decay; and many a grey hair peeped through his raven locks. With his strength, his passion also declined; and he now frequently left her in order to pass the whole day in the sports of the chase, hoping thereby to regain his wonted vigour.

As he was reposing one day in a wood beneath the shade of an oak, he perceived, on the summit of a tree, a bird of strange appearance, and quite unknown to him; but, before he could take aim at it with his bow, it flew away into the clouds; at the same time letting fall a rose-coloured root which dropped at Walter's feet, who immediately took it up and, although he was well acquainted with almost every plant, he could not remember to have seen any at all resembling this. Its delightfully odoriferous scent induced him to try its flavour, but ten times more bitter than wormwood it was even as gall in his mouth; upon which, impatient of the disappointment, he flung it away with violence. Had he, however, been aware of its miraculous quality and that it acted as a counter charm against the opiate perfume of Brunhilda's breath, he would have blessed it in spite of its bitterness: thus do mortals often blindly cast away in displeasure the unsavoury remedy that would otherwise work their weal.

When Walter returned home in the evening and laid him down to repose as usual by Brunhilda's side, the magic power of her breath produced no effect upon him; and for the first time during many months did he close his eyes in a natural slumber. Yet hardly had he fallen asleep, ere a pungent smarting pain disturbed him from his dreams; and, opening his eyes, he discerned, by the gloomy rays of a lamp, that glimmered in the apartment what for some moments transfixed him quite aghast, for it was Brunhilda, drawing with her lips, the warm blood from his bosom. The wild cry of horror which at length escaped him, terrified Brunhilda, whose mouth was besmeared with the warm blood.

"Monster!" exclaimed he, springing from the couch. "Is it thus that you love me?"

"Aye, even as the dead love," replied she, with a malignant coldness.

"Creature of blood!" continued Walter, "the delusion which has so long blinded me is at an end: thou are the fiend who hast destroyed my children—who hast murdered the offspring of my vassels." Raising herself upwards and, at the same time, casting on him a glance that froze him to the spot with dread, she replied. "It is not I who have murdered them;—I was obliged to pamper myself with warm youthful blood, in order that I might satisfy thy furious desires—-thou art the murderer!"—These dreadful words summoned, before Walter's terrified conscience, the threatening shades of all those who had thus perished; while despair choked his voice.

"Why," continued she, in a tone that increased his horror, "why dost thou make mouths at me like a puppet? Thou who hadst the courage to love the dead—to take into thy bed one who had been sleeping in the grave, the bed-fellow of the worm—who hast clasped in thy lustful arms, the corruption of the tomb—dost thou, unhallowed as thou art, now raise this hideous cry for the sacrifice of a few lives?—They are but leaves swept from their branches by a storm.—Come, chase these idiot fancies, and taste the bliss thou hast so dearly purchased." So saying, she extended her arms towards him; but this motion served only to increase his terror, and exclaiming: "Accursed Being,"—he rushed out of the apartment.

All the horrors of a guilty, upbraiding conscience became his companions, now that he was awakened from the delirium of his unholy pleasures. Frequently did he curse his own obstinate blindness, for having given no heed to the hints and admonitions of his children's nurses, but treating them as vile calumnies. But his sorrow was now too late, for, although repentance may gain pardon for the sinner, it cannot alter the immutable decrees of fate—it cannot recall the murdered from the tomb.

No sooner did the first break of dawn appear, than he set out for his lonely castle in the mountains, determined no longer to abide under the same roof with so terrific a being; yet vain was his flight, for, on waking the following morning, he perceived himself in Brunhilda's arms, and quite entangled in her long raven tresses, which seemed to involve him, and bind him in the fetters of his fate; the powerful fascination of her breath held him still more captivated, so that, forgetting all that had passed, he returned her caresses, until awakening as if from a dream he recoiled in unmixed horror from her embrace.

During the day he wandered through the solitary wilds of the mountains, as a culprit seeking an asylum from his pursuers; and, at night, retired to the shelter of a cave; fearing less to couch himself within such a dreary place, than to expose himself to the horror of again meeting Brunhilda; but alas! it was in vain that he endeavoured to flee her. Again, when he awoke, he found her the partner of his miserable bed. Nay, had he sought the centre of the earth as his hiding place; had he even imbedded himself beneath rocks, or formed his chamber in the recesses of the ocean, still had he found her his constant companion; for, by calling her again into existence, he had rendered himself inseparably hers; so fatal were the links that united them.

Struggling with the madness that was beginning to seize him, and brooding incessantly on the ghastly visions that presented themselves to his horror-stricken mind, he lay motionless in the gloomiest recesses of the woods, even from the rise of sun till the shades of eve. But, no sooner was the light of day extinguished in the west, and the woods buried in impenetrable darkness, than the apprehension of resigning himself to sleep drove him forth among the mountains. The storm played wildly with the fantastic clouds, and with the rattling leaves, as they were caught up into the air, as if some dread spirit was sporting with these images of transitoriness and decay: it roared among the summits of the oaks as if uttering a voice of fury, while its hollow sound rebounding among the distant hills, seemed as the moans of a departing sinner, or as the faint cry of some wretch expiring under the murderer's hand: the owl too, uttered its ghastly cry as if foreboding the wreck of nature. Walter's hair flew disorderly in the wind, like black snakes wreathing around his temples and shoulders; while each sense was awake to catch fresh horror. In the clouds he seemed to behold the forms of the murdered; in the howling wind to hear their laments and groans; in the chilling blast itself he felt the dire kiss of Brunhilda; in the cry of the screeching bird he heard her voice; in the mouldering leaves he scented the charnel-bed out of which he had awakened her.

"Murderer of thy own offspring," exclaimed he in a voice making night and the conflict of the element still more hideous, "paramour of a blood-thirsty vampire, reveller with the corruption of the tomb!"—while in his despair he rent the wild locks from his head.

Just then the full moon darted from beneath the bursting clouds; and the sight recalled to his remembrance the advice of the sorcerer, when he trembled at the first apparition of Brunhilda rising from her sleep of death;—namely, to seek him at the season of the full moon in the mountains, where three roads met. Scarcely had this gleam of hope broke in on his bewildered mind than he flew to the appointed spot.

On his arrival, Walter found the old man seated there upon a stone as calmly as though it had been a bright sunny day and completely regardless of the uproar around.

"Art thou come then?" exclaimed he to the breathless wretch, who, flinging himself at his feet, cried in a tone of anguish:—

"Oh save me—succour me—rescue me from the monster that scattereth death and desolation around her. Wherefore a mysterious warning? why didst thou not rather disclose to me at once all the horrors that awaited my sacrilegious profanation of the grave?"

"And wherefore a mysterious warning? why didst thou not perceive how wholesome was the advice—'Wake not the dead.' Wert thou able to listen to another voice than that of thy impetuous passions? Did not thy eager impatience shut my mouth at the very moment I would have cautioned thee?"

"True, true:—thy reproof is just: but what does it avail now;—I need the promptest aid."

"Well," replied the old man, "there remains even yet a means of rescuing thyself, but it is fraught with horror and demands all thy resolution."

"Utter it then, utter it; for what can be more appalling, more hideous than the misery I now endure?"

"Know then," continued the sorcerer, "that only on the night of the new moon does she sleep the sleep of mortals; and then all the supernatural power which she inherits from the grave totally fails her. 'Tis then that thou must murder her."

"How! murder her!" echoed Walter.

"Aye," returned the old man calmly, "pierce her bosom with a sharpened dagger, which I will furnish thee with; at the same time renounce her memory forever, swearing never to think of her intentionally, and that, if thou dost involuntarily, thou wilt repeat the curse."

"Most horrible! yet what can be more horrible than she herself is?— I'll do it."

"Keep then this resolution until the next new moon."

"What, must I wait until then?" cried Walter. "Alas, ere then, either her savage thirst for blood will have forced me into the night of the tomb, or horror will have driven me into the night of madness."

"Nay," replied the sorcerer, "that I can prevent;" and, so saying, he conducted him to a cavern further among the mountains. "Abide here twice seven days," said he; "so long can I protect thee against her deadly caresses. Here wilt thou find all due provision for thy wants; but take heed that nothing tempt thee to quit this place. Farewell, when the moon renews itself, then do I repair hither again." So saying, the sorcerer drew a magic circle around the cave, and then immediately disappeared.

Twice seven days did Walter continue in this solitude, where his companions were his own terrifying thoughts, and his bitter repentance. The present was all desolation and dread; the future presented the image of a horrible deed which he must perforce commit; while the past was empoisoned by the memory of his guilt. Did he think on his former happy union with Brunhilda, her horrible image presented itself to his imagination with her lips defiled with dropping blood: or, did he call to mind the peaceful days he had passed with Swanhilda, he beheld her sorrowful spirit with the shadows of her murdered children. Such were the horrors that attended him by day:

those of night were still more dreadful, for then he beheld Brunhilda herself, who, wandering round the magic circle which she could not pass, called upon his name till the cavern reechoed the horrible sound.

"Walter, my beloved," cried she, "wherefore dost thou avoid me? art thou not mine? for ever mine—mine here, and mine hereafter? And dost thou seek to murder me?—ah! commit not a deed which hurls us both to perdition—thyself as well as me."

In this manner did the horrible visitant torment him each night, and, even when she departed, robbed him of all repose.

The night of the new moon at length arrived, dark as the deed it was doomed to bring forth. The sorcerer entered the cavern. "Come," said he to Walter, "let us depart hence, the hour is now arrived:" and he forthwith conducted him in silence from the cave to a coal-black steed, the sight of which recalled to Walter's remembrance the fatal night. He then related to the old man Brunhilda's nocturnal visits and anxiously inquired whether her apprehensions of eternal perdition would be fulfilled or not.

"Mortal eye," exclaimed the sorcerer, "may not pierce the dark secrets of another world, or penetrate the deep abyss that separates earth from heaven." Walter hesitated to mount the steed. "Be resolute," exclaimed his companion, "but this once is it granted to thee to make the trial, and, should thou fail now, nought can rescue thee from her power."

"What can be more horrible than she herself?—I am determined:" and he leaped on the horse, the sorcerer mounting also behind him.

Carried with a rapidity equal to that of the storm that sweeps across the plain they in brief space arrived at Walter's castle. All the doors flew open at the bidding of his companion, and they speedily reached Brunhilda's chamber, and stood beside her couch. Reclining in a tranquil slumber; she reposed in all her native loveliness, every trace of horror had disappeared from her countenance; she looked so pure, meek and innocent that all the sweet hours of their endearments rushed to Walter's memory, like interceding angels pleading in her behalf. His unnerved hand could not take the dagger which the sorcerer presented to him.

"The blow must be struck even now:" said the latter, "shouldst thou delay but an hour, she will lie at daybreak on thy bosom, sucking the warm life drops from thy heart."

"Horrible! most horrible!" faltered the trembling Walter, and turning away his face, he thrust the dagger into her bosom, exclaiming—"I curse thee forever!"—and the cold blood gushed upon his hand.

Opening her eyes once more, she cast a look of ghastly horror on her husband, and, in a hollow dying accent said—"Thou too art doomed to perdition."

"Lay now thy hand upon her corpse," said the sorcerer, "and swear the oath."

Walter did as commanded, saying, "Never will I think of her with love, never recall her to mind intentionally, and, should her image recur to my mind involuntarily, so will I exclaim to it: *be thou accursed*."

"Thou hast now done everything," returned the sorcerer;—"restore her therefore to the earth, from which thou didst so foolishly recall her; and be sure to recollect thy oath: for, shouldst thou forget it but once, she would return, and thou wouldst be inevitably lost. Adieu—we see each other no more." Having uttered these words he quitted the apartment, and Walter also fled from this abode of horror, having first given direction that the corpse should be speedily interred.

Again did the terrific Brunhilda repose within her grave; but her image continually haunted Walter's imagination, so that his existence was one continued martyrdom, in which he continually struggled to dismiss from his recollection the hideous phantoms of the past; yet, the stronger his effort to banish them, so much the more frequently and the more vividly did they return; as the night-wanderer, who is enticed by a fire-wisp into quagmire or bog, sinks the deeper into his damp grave the more he struggles to escape. His imagination seemed incapable of admitting any other image than that of Brunhilda: now he fancied he beheld her expiring, the blood streaming from her beautiful bosom: at others he saw the lovely bride of his youth, who reproached him with having disturbed the slumbers of the tomb; and to both he was compelled to utter the dreadful words, *"I curse thee forever."* The terrible imprecation was constantly passing his lips; yet was he in incessant terror lest he should forget it, or dream of her without being able to repeat it, and then, on awaking, find himself in her arms. Else would he recall her expiring words, and, appalled at their terrific import, imagine that the doom of his perdition was irrecoverably passed. Whence should he fly from himself? or how erase from his brain these images and forms of horror? In the din of combat, in the tumult of war and its incessant pour of victory to defeat; from the cry of anguish to the exultation of victory--in these he hoped to find at least the relief of distraction: but here too he was disappointed. The giant fang of apprehension now seized him who had never before known fear; each drop of blood that sprayed upon him seemed the cold blood that had gushed from Brunhilda's wound; each dying wretch that fell beside him looked like her, when expiring, she exclaimed,—"Thou too art doomed to perdition"; so that the aspect of death seemed more full of dread to him than aught beside, and this unconquerable terror compelled him to abandon the battle-field.

At length, after many a weary and fruitless wandering, he returned to his castle. Here all was deserted and silent, as if the sword, or a still more deadly pestilence had laid everything waste: for the few inhabitants that still remained, and even those servants who had once shown themselves the most attached, now fled from him, as though he had been branded with the mark of Cain. With horror he perceived that, by uniting himself as he had done with the dead, he had cut himself off from the living, who refused to hold any intercourse with him.

Often, when he stood on the battlements of his castle, and looked down upon desolate fields, he compared their present solitude with the lively activity they were wont to exhibit, under the strict but benevolent discipline of Swanhilda. He now felt that she alone could reconcile him to life, but durst he hope that one, whom he so deeply aggrieved, could pardon him, and receive him again? Impatience at length got the better of fear; he sought Swanhilda, and, with the deepest contrition, acknowledged his complicated guilt; embracing her knees as he beseeched her to pardon him, and to return to his desolate castle, in order that it might again become the abode of contentment and peace.

The pale form which she beheld at her feet, the shadow of the lately blooming youth, touched Swanhilda. "The folly," said she gently, "though it has caused me much sorrow, has never excited my resentment or my anger. But say, where are my children?"

To this dreadful interrogation the agonized father could for a while frame no reply: at length he was obliged to confess the dreadful truth. "Then we are sundered forever," returned Swanhilda; nor could all his tears or supplications prevail upon her to revoke the sentence she had given.

Stripped of his last earthly hope, bereft of his last consolation, and thereby rendered as poor as mortal can possibly be on this side of the grave, Walter returned homewards; when, as he was riding through the forest in the neighbourhood of his castle, absorbed in his gloomy meditations, the sudden sound of a horn roused him from his reverie. Shortly after he saw appear a female figure clad in black, and mounted on a steed of the same colour: her attire was like that of a huntress, but, instead of a falcon, she bore a raven in her hand; and she was attended by a gay troop of cavaliers and dames. The first salutations bring passed, he found that she was proceeding the same road as himself; and, when she found that Walter's castle was close at hand, she requested that he would lodge her for that night, the evening being far advanced. Most willingly did he comply with this request, since the appearance of the beautiful stranger had struck him greatly; so wonderfully did she resemble Swanhilda, except that her locks were brown, and her eye dark and full of fire.

With a sumptuous banquet did he entertain his guests, whose mirth and songs enlivened the lately silent halls. Three days did this revelry continue, and so exhilarating did it prove to Walter that he seemed to have forgotten his sorrows and his fears; nor could he prevail upon himself to dismiss his visitors, dreading lest, on their departure, the castle would seem a hundred times more desolate than beforehand his grief be proportionally increased. At his earnest request, the stranger consented to stay seven, and again another seven days. Without being requested, she took upon herself the superintendence of the household, which she regulated as discreetly and cheerfully as Swanhilda had been wont to do, so that the castle, which had so lately been the abode of melancholy and horror, became the residence of pleasure and festivity, and Walter's grief disappeared altogether in the midst of so much gaiety.

Daily did his attachment to the fair unknown increase; he even made her his confidant; and, one evening as they were walking together apart from any of her train, he related to her his melancholy and frightful history.

"My dear friend," returned she, as soon as he had finished his tale, "it ill beseems a man of thy discretion to afflict thyself on account of all this. Thou hast awakened the dead from the sleep of the grave and afterwards found what might have been anticipated, that the dead possess no sympathy with life. What then? thou wilt not commit this error a second time. Thou hast however murdered the being whom thou hadst thus recalled again to existence—but it was only in appearance, for thou couldst not deprive that of life which properly had none. Thou hast, too, lost a wife and two children: but at thy years such a loss is most easily repaired. There are beauties who will gladly share thy couch, and make thee again a father. But thou dreadst the reckoning of hereafter:—go, open the graves and ask the sleepers there whether that hereafter disturbs them."

In such manner would she frequently exhort and cheer him, so that, in a short time, his melancholy entirely disappeared.

He now ventured to declare to the unknown the passion with which she had inspired him, nor did she refuse him her hand.

Within seven days afterwards the nuptials were celebrated, and the very foundations of the castle seemed to rock from the wild tumultuous uproar of unrestrained riot. The wine streamed in abundance; the goblets circled incessantly; intemperance reached its utmost bounds, while shouts of laughter almost resembling madness burst from the numerous train belonging to the unknown.

At length Walter, heated with wine and love, conducted his bride into the nuptial chamber: but, oh! horror! scarcely had he clasped her in his arms ere she transformed herself into a monstrous serpent, which entwining him in its horrid folds, crushed him to death.

Flames crackled on every side of the apartment; in a few minutes after, the whole castle was enveloped in a blaze that consumed it entirely: while, as the walls fell in with a tremendous crash, a voice exclaimed aloud—*"Wake not the dead!"*

GLOSSARY

Burgundy: A region of France, named for the Burgundians, an East German tribe.
Elysium: The Greek paradise.
Simple: An herb with medicinal properties; a folk remedy.

AFTERWORD

Who is the snake woman? Maybe the primeval Leviathan, a variation of the Babylonian Tiamat, the chaotic female principle who was tamed or destroyed or sublimated so that an ordered universe could flourish. But the cosmic serpent is never destroyed, just waiting to strike when unregulated male desire really needs some punishing. Because, even though Brunhilda is obviously a monster, her vampiric state is just a side-effect of Walter's obsession. Regarding the evolution of the literary vampire: Brunhilda doesn't need to sleep in her grave, and avoids gold, rather than silver—because gold is associated with the sun, and silver is the metal of the moon. Silver being fatal to vampires and werewolves is a later idea.

ALINSKA

...a portion of her garment ripped, and Raoul could perceive, beneath the left breast of the Hungarian, a wound from which a few drops of blood escaped.

So far, the vampires in this book have prowled in long-ago times, from the early Renaissance all the way back to the creation of the world. But the vampire craze in European literature was set in motion by the April 1819 publication of Dr. John Polidori's The Vampyre, *with the Byronic Lord Ruthven in contemporary London. Well, near-contemporary; the tale technically takes place in "17—" but the locale is a recognizable world of gambling dens, European tours, English country houses, horse-drawn carriages, etc. Polidori's tale prompted other writers to take up the challenge of bringing vampires into contact with the modern Western world—where such things weren't supposed to exist.*

In 1820, the German master of fantastic fiction, E.T.A. Hoffmann, wrote a story that had no title but which others called Vampirismus; *it dealt with Aurelie, a young woman in a contemporary German city who, her husband learns to his utter shock and horror, eats corpses with others of her kind. Aurelie almost made it into this collection; but, in spite of the title, the heroine of Hoffmann's tale is not really vampire, draining life from the living, but a ghoul, a devourer of the dead.*

So you won't find Aurelie here—and we look instead to a lady named Alinska to represent the first female vampire in a modern setting.

Alinska is the heroine of La Vampire, ou la Vierge de Hongrie (The Vampire, or the Virgin of Hungary) *written in late 1824 (some sources say 1825) by the Frenchman Léon de Lamothe-Langon.*

The story takes place in Toulouse (where Lamothe-Langon was born) in 1816-17. A mysterious young woman has moved into town. The people are intrigued by her beauty and puzzled that she never goes to church. We eventually learn that the woman, Alinska, is a Hungarian who fell in love with, and was deserted by, a French soldier during the Napoleonic wars. The heartbroken Hungarian killed herself with a knife to her heart. Suicide, a mortal sin in Catholic doctrine, was, according to superstition, one of the most likely ways to become a vampire. But Alinska's undead state isn't only a punishment for herself—it seems to have turned her into an instrument of divine wrath, an undead weapon forged to avenge the wrong done to her. Her former beloved, now a retired colonel, has moved on, married a Frenchwoman, and has two small children. Alinska plots against them.

In the preface to his novel, Lamothe-Langon makes much of the fact that his vampire is a woman. He points to his unprecedented use of the female article "La" with the word "vampire," which is traditionally masculine in French. Nevertheless, Alinska's avenging persona owes much to the Bride of Corinth, if not to Lilith herself. Often implacable and terrifying in her single-mindedness, Alinska is also a deeply sympathetic heroine who comes to an unfortunate end. Although supernatural, she ends up as the pawn of even greater forces.

What follows is a translated, and slightly edited, excerpt from Chapter VII of Lamothe-Langon's novel. (Brian Stableford has made his own translation of the entire work, published by Black Coat Press in 2011 as The Virgin Vampire.*)*

Raoul, attached to the colonel's household as a kind of aide, is a career military man, a former sergeant-major who introduced Colonel Edouard Delmont to Alinska back in Hungary. The Colonel saved Raoul's life on the battlefield, and when Raoul learns that the mysterious stranger is the girl his master abandoned, he writes a letter, asking the Colonel what he would like to do. But the letters disappear before being sent—apparently intercepted by Alinska, who can come and go like a ghost.

When Raoul first meets Alinska, she warns him, vaguely, that she has special powers and a supernatural mission, and that he should stay out of her way. But she doesn't come right out and tell him that she killed herself and is now a vampire. Raoul just thinks she's crazy, but knows she could still be dangerous. After all, Alinska feels betrayed and Raoul suspects she's up to something…

Excerpt from

THE VAMPIRE OR THE VIRGIN OF HUNGARY

Étienne-Léon de Lamothe-Langon

How was it possible to steal the letters? Who could have possessed the triple keys of the room, the wardrobe, and the drawer? Was there a traitor inside the house? Among the workmen? Or among the two serving-women?

Raoul lost himself in the chaos of reflections; he only saw insoluble difficulties; and yet there was, through all this, an incontestable reality, which disturbed all the calculations of human prudence. More than ever, he, who scarcely believed in another life (such was the misfortune of his education), was almost forced to admit the existence of these intermediary beings between the creature and the Creator.

In his moments of weakness, he returned to cursing and dreading the fears of the magicians of Hungary, whom he had heard so much from during his stay in that kingdom. Were there such terrible things as vampires? Those larvae of Christians, who, according to the accounts of an entire nation, abandon the tomb that should keep the dead inside forever, to wander on the land of which they are the stain and horror, which, in the shadow of nights, seek in the veins of an unfortunate, whose blood they suck, the foundation of a frightful existence which is not entirely life, and which nevertheless is not death?

But, more often, Raoul rejected these superstitions, these gross errors; he returned to more natural, more plausible suspicions. It was the possibility of intrigue and betrayal that he dreaded; and he promised himself to find the person who was assisting the Hungarian Alinska.

However, before beginning this kind of war, which was little in harmony with his open character, he formed the desire to see the principal enemy, who commanded the light troops. He promised himself the next morning to go down to the house in the woods; and this idea let him rest for a hours that night.

He rose, more convinced than ever of the necessity of his interview with the stranger; and when he thought he might even speak on friendly terms with her, he took the road to the manor where she lived.

When he arrived, the door was shut. He knocked, but none answered; he knocked a second time with more force, but the silence of the interior was not broken. The longer he waited, the more his impatience grew; and he began to shake the door-knocker a third time, without obtaining more success. What should he do? Was the house abandoned? Or did she not want to open it? Should he abandon the siege, or continue it with more vigor the next day?

While hesitating as to what to do, he heard not far from him a rather slight noise; he turned quickly, and found himself face to face with Alinska's old servant. He was of a colossal size; his head, stripped of hair, was exposed to the changing weather; a frightful paleness reigned over his thin face. His eyes, half-lit, were motionless; they did not move beneath their lids. The sound of his voice was drawn and hoarse, and a foul smell escaped from her mouth, in which only a few teeth were visible. A frock coat of coarse cloth covered this gigantic personage. It proclaimed the lassitude of a too-prolonged existence, and contempt for all that could please the common man.

"Hello, friend," Raoul said when he saw him, refusing to be frightened by the man's unpleasant exterior, "has your mistress already taken flight? Does she run in the fields to find the young birds in their nests?"

"Friend," replied the servant, who gives you the right to put such a question to me? Do we know one another well enough to speak with so much familiarity?" The tone of this reply was not friendly.

Raoul, despite his confidence in himself, was somewhat dumbfounded. Nevertheless, not wishing to appear vanquished at the very start of hostilities, he replied in his turn: "Come, grandfather, do not be angry; I come to speak to your mistress; I knock like a deaf man, but I receive a sign of life; you come up behind me with no sound—well, this all seems to me nothing but natural, and you must not take offense. You're not by chance one of those characters who finds it easier to be angry than to answer correctly? Your unnecessary wish to quarrel would make me suspect it."

"If you knew me, my *friend*," replied the old man, pressing on that last word, "you would easily see that there may be nothing in common between you and me. You follow your path, and mine has been over for a long time. It is not that I will suffer any injury or threat for that; but I hope we will not come to that, for you would soon be finished with me. What do you want from my mistress, since mistress she is? I can tell her, even though you would do it yourself."

"No, please, *friend*," replied Raoul, stung by with the manner in which he was being treated by an individual whom he did not believe was of a condition superior to his own; "my business with Alinska cannot have an intermediary. It is likely, however, that you know some of it, that perhaps you have taken your part in the sleight-of-hand that brings me here; but I do not like to take you into my confidence. I only want to talk to the Hungarian woman, do you hear?"

"I hear; but that did not lead me to serve you more, as you wish. The Hungarian woman, as you please call her, has nothing to do with you. So, take your leave; and as you seem to me to have been a soldier, do what you call an about-face to the right, and go your way."

"Do you know, old man, that to make me retire would require more artillery?"

"Well! We will find it," said the servant, as calmly as ever; and at the same time, before Raoul was able to suspect his project, he threw himself on him, seized him with one hand with such extraordinary strength that he lifted him from the ground, despite the efforts of the ex-Sergeant, and carried him from the door to some distance down the path.

Ah! How much at that moment Raoul regretted not wearing his sword, which had served him to extract a quick revenge for an action which dishonored him in his own eyes! But that steel, the weapon of his courage, was not there to defend him, and his rude adversary had at the same time wrested from him the walking-stick which he could have used. No auxiliary means showed itself to his attentive gaze. The soil of that country, generally throughout Lauraguais, is of such a nature that it can be traversed frequently for a league without encountering a single pebble; everywhere it is composed only of a clayey and compact fertile soil.

However, how can one allow such an offense to go unpunished? Rage did not blind the Sergeant-Major; he felt that it would be impossible for him to fight hand-to-hand with a man who only looked old, for his muscular strength was superior to that of the most vigorous men that Raoul had ever met. To challenge him to a duel was all he could do; so, in a voice half-hoarse by an impetuous transport, he made a sudden appeal to his bravery.

The stranger, who during this time had not lost the imperturbable tranquility which reigned on his face, looked at him without becoming more excited. "What do you want from me?" He said. "Is it to get me to use other weapons than those employed hitherto to humble your pride? Do not flatter yourself. I do not duel. I defend myself, and I immediately get rid of anyone who would not fear to insult me. You have learned to know me; go on your way, weak child of daring and vanity, and do not come back again."

The ferocious tone with which these words were pronounced, the gesture of death which accompanied them, the homicidal flame which shone suddenly in the eyes of the old man, had a meaning so easy to guess, that Raoul, despite his proven courage, could not say or do anything in reply. He was still wondering whether to utter his challenge again, when the door of the house opened, and Alinska, in a black dress which lent a strange expression to her face, suddenly showed herself.

"Well! Ladislas," said she to her servant, "will you always forget that I have forbidden you to give yourself up to the violence of your character? Is it that you still preserve a portion of human madness? And should you insult those who want to converse with me?"

The old man, at the words of his mistress, shuddered suddenly; but he did not show on his impassive face either respect or confusion: only an atrocious smile touched his lips; he did not reply, but he moved away, and returned to the mansion slowly, as if he had not been the main actor in the rather extraordinary scene that had just happened.

The presence of Alinska was at this moment what Raoul most desired. It was to talk to her that he had come down from the chateau, and the brutal manners of the porter did not allow him to hope to fulfill his wish. It was therefore happy to see the Hungarian woman ready to listen to him, and so he did not hesitate to get up and take the path back to the house; but as he drew near, he could not restrain his expressions of unhappiness as to the insulting manner in which he had been treated.

"Certainly, Alinska," he said, "your jailer, for that is the name he deserves, must give thanks to Providence for the deed of grace that made the King of France judge it wise to rid me of a piece of iron that did not leave my side in Hungary. If at that time he had acted with the insolence which he has lately shown, I would have gently insinuated through his ugly chest a few inches of steel, of which you would have received news. But, patience, he will not always find me unprepared, and I will take care, one of these mornings, to pay him the account he has just established with me."

"Come, come, Raoul," replied the Hungarian, "do not worry about this unpleasant incident. Ladislas no doubt has done some wrongs, but yours are not less; you have provoked him by your insistence; judging only on the appearance of his age, you thought it would be easy to make him submit to your wishes; the mistake was soon dispelled. Believe me, forget what happened; you cannot do better for your peace of mind. Whatever you try will fall back on your head, and your revenge will overwhelm you."

"It is well and good to say, but a soldier does not let himself be led like a recruit; I have passed the age of conscription, and I will never suffer an outrage. Besides, am I to be more satisfied with the mistress than with the valet? Do not we also have a business to discuss between us? Do not you play the role of trickster? Is that right or good? And will I bear it that you come to my country to deceive me, by yourself and those who work for you, and then to disturb the repose of my colonel's family?"

"Raoul," Alinksa replied coldly, "I do not know which higher power pushes you toward your destruction. How do you dare to complain to me? Which of us has done greater wrongs towards the other? Is it not you, miserable one, who, in my father's house, was the chief agent of my loss? Do not you remember that disastrous time, when, to serve the Colonel's evil projects, you never ceased to speak of his perfidious tenderness? Were you not relentlessly near me, seeking to trap me, to deceive my virtue? Unhappy tempter! First cause of my misfortune! It ill behooves you to raise an arrogant voice, and to pretend that I have done wrong to you! Remove yourself from my presence, if you hold to life, worm in the mud, for I should have already crushed you!"

"Devil! Alinska, how you talk! You do not spare your words; and if I had the desire to think myself a gentleman, you would make me remember, in spite of myself, that I am born of a good peasant of Bourbonnais. But your birth was not more illustrious; your father cultivated good vineyards, but I never said that he came down from the magnate houses of Esterhazyy or Palffy."

"You are wrong, Raoul, or you want to trick me. It is not to dispute with you about the dangers of destiny, that I show you a just contempt. You have a complaint about me, you dare to say; I want to remind you of the past, to let you judge yourself who is the first, the real criminal."

"It does not matter to me, I do not remember what happened so many years ago. If you were credulous, only blame yourself. But what matters to me, what I will not allow, is that one discovers my secrets, it is that one puts their hands on my correspondence, and that finally one spies in the house of my benefactors."

Alinska did not answer; she glanced at Raoul, a look in which a remarkable malignity was contained, like the triumph of vengeance assured.

"I repeat to you," he went on, "that I am tired of your intrigues and juggling. There are two letters that you've prevent from leaving; for who other than you could have acted in this circumstance? I do not know the means you use to achieve your goal, but keep in mind that if I meet one of your accomplices in some way that I can catch them in the act, his job will not continue; I will pay him on the back the arrears of our debt."

"What! You would do this, even with respect to old Ladislas!" said Alinska, accompanying this malicious remark with a smile that doubled its bitterness.

"Ah! A thousand thunderclaps! Let him come before anyone else! I still have a loaded rifle, with which I will make him thoroughly acquainted, and against whom the strength of his wrist will be insufficient."

"Raoul, for the last time I repeat to you, you are walking the road to your imminent destruction."

"And you, Alinska, towards the end of your criminal designs. I will not bear them any longer; if a third letter does not reach the Colonel, we will see if the magistrates will not render us justice."

"Foolish! What will be your complaint? On what plausible basis will you be able to establish your accusation? Will you make me responsible for your madness? Who will believe that I can put obstacles between you and your master? You will become, by complaining, a joke, and I will be satisfied in parts. Poor toy of the one who speaks to you, you will not carry far the insolent audacity of your speeches."

"Alinska, you can tell me anything you like. I know that I have wronged your good faith—if it is wrong to bring a young and elegant soldier to a good girl. But in the name of God! Forget the past, and leave me alone."

"I promised to let you be, and even to reward you if you promised not to let Edouard know that I am here. Why do you want to persist in refusing me something so simple? Let him come back; suffer that for the last time I speak to him; his happiness, his tranquility, his very existence, all depend on our interview. You will fight in vain against me. I will use, to defeat you, means that you cannot prevent. Tremble especially, if from you escapes a single word that makes me known to the happy rival who holds my place with Edouard; your indiscretion would cost you your life. Yes, Raoul, I will immolate you on the spot."

Alinska, in pronouncing these last words, made so impetuous a movement, that a portion of her garment ripped, and Raoul could perceive, beneath the left breast of the Hungarian, a wound from which a few drops of blood escaped. The involuntary shudder which agitated his body with this sinister sight, did not escape his interlocutor; she easily saw the cause, and tried to repair with her hand the disorder of her dress.

Raoul, for his part, was confounded, and felt a sudden pity in his soul: "Oh! unhappy girl," he exclaimed, "what have you done? Can you, in the state you are in, indulge such a dangerous passion? Return, return quickly to your home; you have a wound that has reopened, you do not know the danger you are running."

"What danger are you talking about? I do not know any more on earth."

"But your blood is flowing, the bandage must have come loose; do not waste time putting it back. If my care is needed, do not hesitate to accept it."

"Do not worry about what you see; my blood cannot flow, for I have no more blood; it has long since exhausted itself to the last drop; I know where to get that which replaces it. So let it flow, without care."

Listening to these strange words, Raoul did not doubt that the misfortunes of the Hungarian had weakened her reason; all the anger he felt about her disappeared. Instantly, he tried to bring her, by mildness, to calmer thoughts, he advanced to take her under the arm and support her, while he noticed that a frightening paleness covered her face."

"Do not come near me," she cried in a hoarse and weak voice, "do not touch me; rather, flee at once! It is not right that what is about to happen should strike your sight. Ladislas!" She cried again, "Ladislas! Come to me, or I cannot fulfill the mission I was entrusted with."

Ladislas heard this call; he left the house in time to catch Alinska, who, half fainting, dropped into his arms. The old man, having examined her for a moment, looked around him without speaking, and made a gesture, as if to urge Raoul to retire.

He did not seem disposed to obey him; but a sudden reflection changed his mind. He feared that being obstinate might cause the death of the foreign woman, and, directed by this motive, he returned to the path and went up the hill. At a turn in the road which brought him back to face the place where Alinska lay on the grass, he thought he could examine what was going on there.

He saw, or thought he saw, the old servant bending over her, pouring in her mouth a red liquid; but at the same time Raoul received a violent blow on the head which knocked him down. He rose quickly, to face the enemy who had struck him.

No one was near.

GLOSSARY

Bourbonnais: A region in central France.
"...these larvae of the Christian": An obscure phrase. The larva is the intermediate stage between egg and, say, a butterfly; and a vampire is in an intermediate stage between Christian life and death. Also, a larva such as a caterpillar has only one goal: to feed.
Esterhazy: The Esterhazys were the largest landowners in Hungary from the 18th century until the Communist takeover in 1945..
Palffy: A noble Hungarian family, prominent since the 16th century.

AFTERWORD

Alinska's story bears some similarity to Alexandre Dumas' and Auguste Maquet's The Count of Monte Cristo, *written twenty years later: a wronged person acquires wealth and power and exacts a long and sometimes messy revenge, acting as an instrument of God's vengeance. But there are differences; one, the Count only* considers *himself an instrument of God; Alinska, the novel reveals, actually* is. *The Count is superhuman, but Alinska is supernatural.*

Another difference is what *is being avenged; Young Edmond Dantes was imprisoned after being falsely accused of treason by men who are jealous of him. This is, in most civilized societies, a possible but relatively uncommon event, which makes it romantic. Yes, false imprisonment became much more common after the early 20th century; but the point is that, even when corrupt regimes go on for decades, it's seen to be an exception to what should be the normal rule of law. Alinska, on the other hand, was a girl wooed and deserted by a foreign soldier. It had and has happened countless times, in the finest armies of the most civilized societies. To the colonel, Alinska was nothing; a soldier's indiscretion never to be mentioned to the decent girlfriend back home. Alinska was one of millions over the millennia. But she didn't stay put. Her vengeance is not for a devious conspiracy, but for an everyday occurrence, and she embodies more than her own individual pain.*

THE VAMPIRE BRIDE

"I am come—I am come! once again from the tomb,
In return for the ring which you gave,
That I am thine, and that thou art mine,
This nuptial pledge receive."

Horror movies of the 20th century confirmed the idea that the best defense against vampires was a cross. But, although the notion of the vampire as a creature opposed to God goes back to Lilith, the cross was not used in the pre-Victorian vampire fiction written in the primarily Protestant countries of Germany and England. The paraphernalia of the Church were more often called upon to fight vampires in Catholic France. (Alinska avoids the local church—as it turns out, for a very good reason. Her aversion to holy places may have been inspired by the Medieval legend of Melusine, a beautiful woman who, when forced to attend Mass, turned into a demon and flew away.)

The following excerpt from the poem The Vampire Bride *may feature the first use of a crucifix against a vampire; and, although set in an unnamed Catholic country, it was written by a Protestant Englishman.*

Henry Thomas Liddell spent most of his public life as a Tory member of Parliament. He was favorably inclined toward Catholicism, and supported bills to remove social and political restrictions against English Catholics. A part-time poet, Liddell wrote The Vampire Bride *in 1833. (Not to be confused with George Blink's 1830 melodrama,* The Vampire Bride, or Wake Not the Dead.*) The full text is available online, but only the last two-thirds of the poem are included here.*

It begins with Count Albert (the only character the poem names) marrying a lovely young woman. The ceremony, in a church called St. Peter's, features an exchange of rings. But as Albert hands his bride a sapphire ring, he drops it—partly because he isn't serious about getting married, partly because of mysterious vibrations from underneath the church...

The ceremony goes forward anyway, and bride and groom celebrate separately. Albert still has the sapphire ring that belongs to his bride. After a game of tennis, he drops the ring again *near a marble statue of a nude woman with a "girdle" or "zone" wrapped around her waist...*

And words unknown on the circling zone
  Mysteriously were trac'd.

If these are magical incantations, Albert doesn't notice. As a kind of drunken joke, he puts his bride's sapphire ring on the statue's marble finger. Hours go by, and it's finally time to meet his lovely bride in their bedchamber...

Excerpt from

THE VAMPIRE BRIDE

Henry Thomas Liddell

...A page stood near Count Albert's chair,
  To wait his lord's behest,
With laughing cheek and rosy neck
  Beneath his 'broider'd vest.

"Come hither, come hither, my little foot-page,
  For eye yon sand be run,
By the torch's light, or the moonbeam bright,
  An errand must be done.

"To the courts below thou must quickly go,
  To the court where we toss the ball;
There with outstretched hand doth a statue stand.
  On its marble pedestal.

"With incautious haste, on that hand I placed
  This noon a sapphire stone,
No more may it linger on the marble finger—
  So haste thee, my page, and begone;

"And mark me, take a hammer, to break
  The finger that's doubled down;
For *there* is the ring that I bid thee bring;
  Now speed me my errand—and run."

The sand is run, the errand is done—
  But the boy came trembling back;
And the rosy red from his cheek hath fled,
  And his limbs they quiver and quake.

"Oh! master dear, no ring is there!
  No finger bent at all!
But the statue doth stand, with extended hand,
  On its lofty pedestal!

"It gleam'd wan and white, in the pale moonlight,
  And the courts look'd chill and drear;
Methought it did smile as I gazed the while—!
 I wellnigh swoon'd for fear.

"Unmoved by a breeze, the tall cypress-trees
  Moan'd and waved in the silent air;
And a meteor-star shot swift and far
  Through the sparkling hemisphere.

"And the bats unclean, with leathern skin,
  Flapp'd heavily around;
And a strange dog did howl, while shriek'd the owl,
  And like a grave smell'd the ground."

Back shrunk the page, for an ashen hue
  Spread wide over Albert's cheek;
And there stood on his brow clammy drops of dew,
  And in vain he essay'd to speak.

But the red wine he quaff'd, and he fearfully laugh'd,
  But he drew a long sigh between;
His hand he pass'd o'er his brow in haste,
  Then rose and changed the scene.

The bridesmaids are gone, and the bride left alone,
  And the sounds of mirth are fled;
And Albert, released from the dance and the feast,
  Hath sought the nuptial bed.

But his heart beat quick, and his breath came thick,
  And a nameless dread crept o'er him;
Yet he turned with delight to his lady bright,
  Reclin'd in her beauty before him.

He turned unto his lady true,
  And he felt her flutt'ring breath;
When an icy chill thro' his veins did thrill,
  And he shrunk from the grasp of death.

And a bitter, bitter cry broke forth in agony,—
  "Save me! for mercy! save!"
For in his arms he did hold a figure damp and cold,
  And the couch smell'd like a grave.

"Thou this day didst me wed, and I come to thy bed,
  Thy nuptial joys to share;
And in token true, the sapphire blue
  On my finger still I wear."

Another bitter cry, and he senseless did lie—
  For the phantom marble prest
Its loathsome form 'gainst his bosom warm,
  And weigh'd down his lab'ring breast.

And ever and anon murmur'd the lips of stone,—
  "This bridal couch is thine;
To this bed I come, but ere three days are gone,
  Albert, thou com'st to mine."

The morning light hath dispell'd the night
  Unhappy Albert lay
With throbbing head on his nuptial bed,
  Cold as the coffin'd clay.

But the Demon guest from his struggling breast
  Hath its icy grip withdrawn;
Away it flew, as the first cock crew
  In sign of the blushing dawn.

And his faithful bride, who lay by his side,
  Awoke in the self-same hour;
For a slumber deep did her sense steep
  While the spectre Bride had power.

Devoutly she pray'd to the Virgin for aid,
  For her heart beat with nameless fears;
She laid her warm cheek on her Albert's neck,
  And fast fell the trickling tears.

And she folded his face in her tender embrace,
  And her soft and balmy breath
Thaw'd the icy chains which froze his veins,
  And dispell'd the shades of death.

"Now send for the priest, let my sins be confest,
  Short space to me is given;
Though the Demon claim my mortal frame,
  Yet my soul may find rest in Heaven."

The holy priest hath his sins confest,
  And now, with shuddering cold,
Of his summons dread to the Phantom's bed
  Hath Albert darkly told:—

And how by some spell of the powers of Hell
  She had gain'd his sapphire stone;
And in right of that ring, how the foul damp thing
  Did claim him for her own.

The priest turn'd pale at the ghostly tale,
  And he shook his tonsured head;
And the livelong day he did fast and pray
  Beside the suff'rer's bed.

Cold horror sate in those halls of state,
  Which had echoed with nuptial song;
And the bridal wreath seem'd the emblem of death,
  And fear froze every tongue.

The second night came, but the taper's flame
  Dispell'd the thickening gloom;
For they trusted with prayer the fiend to scare,
  If again she sought the room.

And a cross of gold the priest did hold,
  And at intervals they raise,
In chorus meet, the vespers sweet,
  To the Blessed Virgin's praise.

And his faithful bride lay awake by his side,
  Till St Peter's clock toll'd one;
When a slumber deep o'er her senses did creep,
  For the Demon's power had begun.

The taper's light was extinguished quite,
  And the choristers all dropp'd to rest;
And the priest dropp'd down, like a monument stone,
  With the cross on his bosom prest.

And again a bitter cry broke forth in agony,—
  "Save me! for mercy! save!"
For Albert did hold the Spectre damp and cold,
  And the couch smell'd like a grave!

"I am come—I am come! once again from the tomb,
  In return for the ring which you gave,
That I am thine, and that thou art mine,
  This nuptial pledge receive."

He lay like a corse 'neath the Demon's force,
  And she wrapp'd him in a shroud;
And she fix'd her teeth his heart beneath,
  And she drank of the warm life-blood!

And ever and anon murmur'd the lips of stone,
  "Soft and warm is this couch of thine,
Thou'lt to-morrow be laid on a colder bed—
  Albert! that bed will be mine!"

Another bitter cry, and he senseless did lie,
  For the fiend sucked his stifled breath;
And the blood flowed fast from his wounded breast,
  And he suffered the pangs of death.

The morning light hath chased the night,
  And the fiend hath its grasp withdrawn;
Away it flew, as the first cock crew
  In sign of the blushing dawn.

And the startled priest, and the watchers, in haste,
  From unearthly slumbers broke:
For the nightmare's weight on their lungs had sate,
  And the breath in their throats did choke.

With stiffened limb and eyeballs dim,
  Cold as the coffin'd clay,
Where his blood ran red o'er the nuptial bed,
  Expiring Albert lay.

But his faithful bride, who lay by his side,
  Was still wrapp'd in slumber deep;
And her soft lips smiled, like a dreaming child,
  'Twas a pure and an holy sleep.

At length like the rose in the morning that blows,
  Her eyelids from slumber awake;
And like dewdrops hear tears, mingle soft with her prayers
  For her suffering Albert's sake.

But she folded his face in her tender embrace,
  And her warm and virgin breath
Thaw'd the icy chains that froze his veins,
  And dispell'd the shades of death.

And words of good cheer she breathed in his ear,
  And with steady hand and calm,
And with cheek unblench'd, his wound she staunch'd,
  With juice of the healing balm.

"Oh Albert! be cheered, my prayers have been heard,
  For lo! in her mercy mild,
The mother of God before me stood,
  And kiss'd her sleeping child:

"She bade me dig dawn, 'neath the altar stone,
  In St Peter's holy dome,
And thence shall I bring the sapphire ring
  In triumph from the tomb!"

She is gone to the fane, with a priestly train,
  With vestment, and banner, and cross;
The church bells they ring, and the choristers sing,
  And the censers they zealously toss:

Then with pick-axe and spade, ten lab'rers essay'd
  The ponderous stone to move,
And though the priests sung, and the censers swung,
  In vain the labourers strove.

But with purpose stout, and with heart devout,
  Is the virtuous maiden gone:
When the virtuous maid lent her feeble aid,
  Up sprung the lighten'd stone.

Five yards under ground a coffin they found,
  Of strange unwonted shape;
And the cold wet clay was red where it lay,
  And the coffin-lid did gape!

They lifted the lid, and the shroud they undid,
  But what they saw underneath—
The horrible sight that congeal'd them quite—
  I almost fear to breathe.

Beneath a shroud, stain'd and spotted with blood,
  A female naked lay!
On her clenched hand shone a sapphire stone,
  In her corpse there was no decay!

Her eyes did stare with a demon glare,
  A girdle bound her waist;
And words unknown on the charmed zone
  Mysteriously were traced.

Her veins accurs'd seemed ready to burst,
  She was gorged with infernal food;
And the vampire mouth foam'd with crimson froth;
  Her very pores oozed blood.

The lab'rers shrunk—and, fainting, sunk
  Back from the hideous sight;
And the priests fled the church, and rush'd out at the porch—
  They almost went mad with affright.

But the Virgin Bride in her maiden pride,
  In her love and virtue brave,
A crucifix press'd to her noble breast,
  And sprung into the grave.

"That which was given in the sight of Heaven,
  I bid thee, Fiend, restore;
That ring I claim in His awful name,
  Whom the Powers of Hell adore:

"By His holy sign, I bid thee resign,
  Demon, thy right for ever;—
Whom God doth join at His sacred shrine,
  Presume not thou to sever."

The Vampire shook at the words she spoke,
  In an instant the palm open'd wide;
From its finger she drew the sapphire blue,
  As drops from the icicle glide.

When the zone they unlaced from around its waist,
  Its bright eyes with fury gleam'd;
When they thrust a dart through its swollen heart,
  It convulsively shivered and screamed;

And the red blood thereout did gush and did spout,
  Till it sprinkled the chancel roof;
So vehement it sprung, that no fountain e'er flung
  With like force its waters aloof.

But the carcass foul of the carrion Goule
  Grew flaccid, and meagre, and thin—
As a huge bladder blown, when the air is gone,
  Shrivels up into wrinkled skin.

They lifted the bier from its sepulchre,
  Holy water they sprinkled around,
And lo! where it lay on the blood-stained clay,
  A passage went under ground.

It led to the tombs and the long catacombs
  Beneath the churchyard wall;
Where the Goules and Sprites keep on Sabbath nights
  Their unholy Carnival.

And spiders unclean, and huge earth-grubs, were seen
  Beneath the coffin to twine;
But the spider and worm own'd the pow'r of the charm,
  For never a one crawl'd within.

From the loathing shrine of Saint Peter divine
  They cast the Vampire forth,
But none could declare how it ever came there,
  In consecrated earth.

To the ramparts they hurried the carcass unburied,
  Where the murder's limbs are thrown,
Where the foxes howl, and the gaunt wolves prowl,
  As they gnash the mangled bone.

’Twas noon, but a lurid and sulphurous glare
  Eclipsed the meridian sun;
A sickly heat taints the murky air,
  A whirlwind comes rushing on!

“It came rushing and roaring, like a cataract pouring
  Over a mountain rock;”
And the crashing thunder rent the vapours asunder—
  It was felt like an earthquake’s shock!

The flashing levin, from the blood-red Heaven,
  Blazed o’er the Vampire dead;
When the hurricane roar was heard no more,
  Corpse, coffin, and girdle were fled!

And the self-same flash to the pavement did dash
  In fragments the cinctured stone:—
So the wrath Divine, in Philistia’s shrine,
  Hurl’d Dagon from his throne.

’Twere long to relate what joys await
  Albert recalled to life;
But this believe, that none e’er did receive
  A more faithful and virtuous wife.

When he saw the well-known ring of sapphire stone,
  Tears of joy stream’d down his cheek;
When his bride he press’d to his grateful breast
  His heart swell’d, but he could not speak.

But once in each year the live-long night
  Is spent in devotion and prayer;
On the fatal night of the Vampire’s bite
  Blood runs from his bosom’s scar.

And till morning light doth his lady bright
  Hymns to the Virgin sing—
As the fiendish wail sounds along the gale,
  Bemoaning the sapphire ring.

GLOSSARY

Chancel roof: The area of a church, east of the nave, where the sanctuary and choir are.
Cinctured: Encircled; although it isn't clear how this would apply to the large stone.
Corse: Corpse.
Dart: Presumably, a stake or spear.
Fane: Temple; the meaning here is the church.
Goule: Ghoul; used here as a general term for a frightening, bloodthirsty phantom.
"It came rushing and roaring, like a cataract pouring / Over a mountain rock": Liddell provided the following note as part of the original poem: 'These two lines are borrowed from Southey's ballad, "The Old Woman of Berkeley," and throughout the whole of these stanzas the author pleads guilty to the appropriation of many thoughts and phrases which may be found *passim* in former tales of horror and wonder. I have, indeed, been informed that [the Irish poet Thomas] Moore has written a ballad upon this very subject; but I have never seen it, or heard of it in any edition of his works.'
Levin: Lightning.
Meridian: Midday; noon.
Own'd: Admitted, acknowledged; the spiders and worms acknowledge the supernatural power that keeps them from going into the vampire's coffin.
Sabbath: The Witches' Sabbath. (Original poet's note.)
So the wrath Divine, in Philistia's shrine, / Hurl'd Dagon from his throne: A reference to the Old Testament story of Samson bringing down the Philistine temple of the sea-god Dagon.
Sprites: Spirits, as in ghostly spirits.
Tonsured: The priest has had the crown of his head shaved as a sign of his admission into the priesthood. The practice in Roman Catholicism began to decline after the Middle Ages, and was abandoned in 1972.

Unwonted: Unusual
Vespers: Evening prayers.
Zone: Something that binds in a circle; here, the skirt or girdle around the vampire's waist.

AFTERWORD

The discovery of the Vampire Bride in her coffin directly recalls the account of the "actual" 18th century vampire Arnold Paul, which is included in Volume I. The geyser of blood is Liddell's invention; as is the notion that a vampire, when not entombed, could be a statue (or could inhabit a statue?), although stories of statues coming to life go back to Greek mythology.

In the Arnold Paul account, Church and State come together as a united community to destroy a vampire plague. In The Vampire Bride, ***though, the monster lurks under the very foundation of the Church, and the individual efforts of the priests and other attendants are almost useless against the Bride's power. Only the true bride can defeat her—and her mission gives Albert's wife miraculous strength. Notice that, while she wields the power of the crucifix, her plan and power are given to her by the Virgin Mary; the poem presents three sacred and profane personifications of female energy—Mary, Albert's wife, and the Vampire Bride. Two sacred, one profane.***

One can only hope that Albert sobers up and proves himself worth the effort. As it is, the poem's greatest mystery is what the Vampire Bride sees in him. But this is a recurring theme in female vampire literature.

It might be noted that, in addition to the heavy emphasis on the crucifix and other Catholic aspects, the poem is one of the very first, and possibly the ***first, to associate bats with vampires, when the page boy recounts that***

…the bats unclean, with leathern skin,
Flapp'd heavily around…

Two more interesting items about Henry Thomas Liddell. He was the first cousin once removed of Alice Liddell, the inspiration for Lewis Carroll's Alice. And, when his father died, he assumed the family title of Lord Ravensworth. Which is about as good a name as an author of vampire fiction could have.

CLARIMONDE

*That exquisite perfection of bodily form,
although purified and made sacred
by the shadow of death, affected me
more voluptuously than it should
have done...*

The idea of the supernatural woman offering herself to a mortal goes back to ancient mythology (think, for example, of the nymph Calypso keeping Odysseus with her on her island). In the Middle Ages, there were many stories of men falling in love with women who were really demons of some kind. Aside from Melusine, there was the Queen of Elfland entrancing Tam Lin or Thomas the Rhymer. All this inspired John Keats' poem La Belle Dame Sans Merci ("The Beautiful Lady Without Mercy")*—which was published in 1819, the same year as Polidori's* The Vampyre, *and had a huge impact on the image of the dangerous supernatural temptress, with such lines as:*

> I saw pale kings and princes too,
>   Pale warriors, death-pale were they all;
> They cried—"La Belle Dame sans Merci
>   Thee hath in thrall!"

Clarimonde, however, the vampire of the next story, seems quite sincere in her affection. Unfortunately, the Church doesn't approve of liaisons between the living and the undead...especially when the living is a priest.

The author, Théophile Gautier, never achieved the fame of his French contemporaries Victor Hugo or Alexandre Dumas, but his work as a poet, novelist, and critic had a substantial influence. He co-wrote the libretto of the supernatural ballet Giselle, *and Oscar Wilde included two of his poems in* The Picture of Dorian Gray.

His 1836 story, La Morte Amoureuse, *was translated into English in 1910 as* Clarimonde, or The Dead in Love, *and is remarkable for its treatment of vampire sex. The relationship between priest and vampire which is judged harshly within the story, but the opinions of the male protagonist, and especially that of his strict Abbé, are not necessarily those of Gautier himself...*

CLARIMONDE, OR, THE DEAD IN LOVE

Théophile Gautier

Translated by Lafcadio Hearn

Brother, you ask me if I have ever loved. Yes. My story is a strange and terrible one; and though I am sixty-six years of age, I scarcely dare even now to disturb the ashes of that memory. To you I can refuse nothing; but I should not relate such a tale to any less experienced mind. So strange were the circumstances of my story, that I can scarcely believe myself to have ever actually been a party to them. For more than three years I remained the victim of a most singular and diabolical illusion. Poor country priest though I was, I led every night in a dream—would to God it had been all a dream!—a most worldly life, a damning life, a life of Sardanapalus. One single look too freely cast upon a woman well-nigh caused me to lose my soul; but finally by the grace of God and the assistance of my patron saint, I succeeded in casting out the evil spirit that possessed me. My daily life was long interwoven with a nocturnal life of a totally different character. By day I was a priest of the Lord, occupied with prayer and sacred things; by night, from the instant that I closed my eyes I became a young nobleman, a fine connoisseur in women, dogs, and horses; gambling, drinking, and blaspheming; and when I awoke at early daybreak, it seemed to me, on the other hand, that I had been sleeping, and had only dreamed that I was a priest. Of this somnambulistic life there now remains to me only the recollection of certain scenes and words which I cannot banish from my memory; but although I never actually left the walls of my presbytery, one would think to hear me speak that I were a man who, weary of all worldly pleasures, had become a religious, seeking to end a tempestuous life in the service of God, rather than a humble seminarist who has grown old in this obscure curacy, situated in the depths of the woods and even isolated from the life of the century. Yes, I have loved as none in the world ever loved—with an insensate and furious passion—so violent that I am astonished it did not cause my heart to burst asunder. Ah, what nights—what nights!

From my earliest childhood I had felt a vocation to the priesthood, so that all my studies were directed with that idea in view. Up to the age of twenty-four my life had been only a prolonged novitiate. Having completed my course of theology I successively received all the minor orders, and my superiors judged me worthy, despite my youth, to pass the last awful degree. My ordination was fixed for Easter week.

I had never gone into the world. My world was confined by the walls of the college and the seminary. I knew in a vague sort of a way that there was something called Woman, but I never permitted my thoughts to dwell on such a subject, and I lived in a state of perfect innocence. Twice a year only I saw my infirm and aged mother, and in those visits were comprised my sole relations with the outer world.

I regretted nothing; I felt not the least hesitation at taking the last irrevocable step; I was filled with joy and impatience. Never did a betrothed lover count the slow hours with more feverish ardour; I slept only to dream that I was saying mass; I believed there could be nothing in the world more delightful than to be a priest; I would have refused to be a king or a poet in preference. My ambition could conceive of no loftier aim.

I tell you this in order to show you that what happened to me could not have happened in the natural order of things, and to enable you to understand that I was the victim of an inexplicable fascination.

At last the great day came. I walked to the church with a step so light that I fancied myself sustained in air, or that I had wings upon my shoulders. I believed myself an angel, and wondered at the sombre and thoughtful faces of my companions, for there were several of us. I had passed all the night in prayer, and was in a condition well-nigh bordering on ecstasy. The bishop, a venerable old man, seemed to me God the Father leaning over His Eternity, and I beheld Heaven through the vault of the temple.

You well know the details of that ceremony—the benediction, the communion under both forms, the anointing of the palms of the hands with the Oil of Catechumens, and then the holy sacrifice offered in concert with the bishop.

Ah, truly spake Job when he declared that the imprudent man is one who hath not made a covenant with his eyes! I accidentally lifted my head, which until then I had kept down, and beheld before me, so close that it seemed that I could have touched her—although she was actually a considerable distance from me and on the further side of the sanctuary railing—a young woman of extraordinary beauty, and attired with royal magnificence. It seemed as though scales had suddenly fallen from my eyes. I felt like a blind man who unexpectedly recovers his sight. The bishop, so radiantly glorious but an instant before, suddenly vanished away! the tapers paled upon their golden candlesticks like stars in the dawn, and a vast darkness seemed to fill the whole church. The charming creature appeared in bright relief against the background of that darkness, like some angelic revelation. She seemed herself radiant, and radiating light rather than receiving it.

I lowered my eyelids, firmly resolved not to again open them, that I might not be influenced by external objects, for distraction had gradually taken possession of me until I hardly knew what I was doing.

In another minute, nevertheless, I reopened my eyes, for through my eyelashes I still beheld her, all sparkling with prismatic colours, and surrounded with such a penumbra as one beholds in gazing at the sun.

Oh, how beautiful she was! The greatest painters, who followed ideal beauty into heaven itself, and thence brought back to earth the true portrait of the Madonna, never in their delineations even approached that wildly beautiful reality which I saw before me. Neither the verses of the poet nor the palette of the artist could convey any conception of her. She was rather tall, with a form and bearing of a goddess. Her hair, of a soft blonde hue, was parted in the midst and flowed back over her temples in two rivers of rippling gold; she seemed a diademed queen. Her forehead, bluish-white in its transparency, extended its calm breadth above the arches of her eyebrows, which by a strange singularity were almost black, and admirably relieved the effect of sea-green eyes of unsustainable vivacity and brilliancy. What eyes! With a single flash they could have decided a man's destiny. They had a life, a limpidity, an ardour, a humid light which I have never seen in human eyes; they shot forth rays like arrows, which I could distinctly *see* enter my heart. I know not if the fire which illumined them came from Heaven or from Hell, but assuredly it came from one or the other. That woman was either an angel or a demon, perhaps both. Assuredly she never sprang from the flank of Eve, our common mother. Teeth of the most lustrous pearl gleamed in her ruddy smile, and at every inflection of her lips little dimples appeared in the satiny rose of her adorable cheeks. There was a delicacy and pride in the regal outline of her nostrils bespeaking noble blood. Agate gleams played over the smooth lustrous skin of her half-bare shoulders, and strings of great blonde pearls—almost equal to her neck in beauty of colour—descended upon her bosom. From time to time she elevated her head with the undulating grace of a startled serpent or peacock, thereby imparting a quivering motion to the high lace ruff which surrounded it like a silver trellis-work.

She wore a robe of orange-red velvet, and from her wide ermine-lined sleeves there peeped forth patrician hands of infinite delicacy, and so ideally transparent that, like the fingers of Aurora, they permitted the light to shine through them.

All these details I can recollect at this moment as plainly as though they were of yesterday, for notwithstanding I was greatly troubled at the time, nothing escaped me; the faintest touch of shading, the little dark speck at the point of the chin, the imperceptible down at the corners of the lips, the velvety floss upon the brow, the quivering shadows of the eyelashes upon the cheeks—I could notice everything with astonishing lucidity of perception.

And gazing I felt opening within me gates that had until then remained closed; vents long obstructed became all clear, permitting glimpses of unfamiliar perspectives within; life suddenly made itself visible to me under a totally novel aspect. I felt as though I had just been born into a new world and a new order of things. A frightful anguish commenced to torture my heart as with red-hot pincers. Every successive minute seemed to me at once but a second and yet a century. Meanwhile the ceremony was proceeding, and I shortly found myself transported far from that world of which my newly born desires were furiously besieging the entrance. Nevertheless I answered "Yes" when I wished to say "No," though all within me protested against the violence done to my soul by my tongue. Some occult power seemed to force the words from my throat against my will. Thus it is, perhaps, that so many young girls walk to the altar firmly resolved to refuse in a startling manner the husband imposed upon them, and that yet not one ever fulfils her intention. Thus it is, doubtless, that so many poor novices take the veil, though they have resolved to tear it into shreds at the moment when called upon to utter the vows. One dares not thus cause so great a scandal to all present, nor deceive the expectation of so many people. All those eyes, all those wills seem to weigh down upon you like a cope of lead, and, moreover, measures have been so well taken, everything has been so thoroughly arranged beforehand and after a fashion so evidently irrevocable, that the will yields to the weight of circumstances and utterly breaks down.

As the ceremony proceeded the features of the fair unknown changed their expression. Her look had at first been one of caressing tenderness; it changed to an air of disdain and of mortification, as though at not having been able to make itself understood.

With an effort of will sufficient to have uprooted a mountain, I strove to cry out that I would not be a priest, but I could not speak; my tongue seemed nailed to my palate, and I found it impossible to express my will by the least syllable of negation. Though fully awake, I felt like one under the influence of a nightmare, who vainly strives to shriek out the one word upon which life depends.

She seemed conscious of the martyrdom I was undergoing, and, as though to encourage me, she gave me a look replete with divinest promise. Her eyes were a poem; their every glance was a song.

She said to me:

"If thou wilt be mine, I shall make thee happier than God Himself in His paradise. The angels themselves will be jealous of thee. Tear off that funeral shroud in which thou art about to wrap thyself. I am Beauty, I am Youth, I am Life. Come to me! Together we shall be Love. Can Jehovah offer thee aught in exchange? Our lives will flow on like a dream, in one eternal kiss.

"Fling forth the wine of that chalice, and thou art free. I will conduct thee to the Unknown Isles. Thou shalt sleep in my bosom upon a bed of massy gold under a silver pavilion, for I love thee and would take thee away from thy God, before whom so many noble hearts pour forth floods of love which never reach even the steps of His throne!"

These words seemed to float to my ears in a rhythm of infinite sweetness, for her look was actually sonorous, and the utterances of her eyes were reechoed in the depths of my heart as though living lips had breathed them into my life. I felt myself willing to renounce God, and yet my tongue mechanically fulfilled all the formalities of the ceremony. The fair one gave me another look, so beseeching, so despairing that keen blades seemed to pierce my heart, and I felt my bosom transfixed by more swords than those of Our Lady of Sorrows.

All was consummated; I had become a priest.

Never was deeper anguish painted on human face than upon hers. The maiden who beholds her affianced lover suddenly fall dead at her side, the mother bending over the empty cradle of her child, Eve seated at the threshold of the gate of Paradise, the miser who finds a stone substituted for his stolen treasure, the poet who accidentally permits the only manuscript of his finest work to fall into the fire, could not wear a look so despairing, so inconsolable. All the blood had abandoned her charming face, leaving it whiter than marble; her beautiful arms hung lifelessly on either side of her body as though their muscles had suddenly relaxed, and she sought the support of a pillar, for her yielding limbs almost betrayed her. As for myself, I staggered toward the door of the church, livid as death, my forehead bathed with a sweat bloodier than that of Calvary; I felt as though I were being strangled; the vault seemed to have flattened down upon my shoulders, and it seemed to me that my head alone sustained the whole weight of the dome.

As I was about to cross the threshold a hand suddenly caught mine—a woman's hand! I had never till then touched the hand of any woman. It was cold as a serpent's skin, and yet its impress remained upon my wrist, burnt there as though branded by a glowing iron. It was she. "Unhappy man! Unhappy man! What hast thou done?" she exclaimed in a low voice, and immediately disappeared in the crowd.

The aged bishop passed by. He cast a severe and scrutinising look upon me. My face presented the wildest aspect imaginable: I blushed and turned pale alternately; dazzling lights flashed before my eyes. A companion took pity on me. He seized my arm and led me out. I could not possibly have found my way back to the seminary unassisted. At the corner of a street, while the young priest's attention was momentarily turned in another direction, a Negro page, fantastically garbed, approached me, and without pausing on his way slipped into my hand a little pocket-book with gold-embroidered corners, at the same time giving me a sign to hide it. I concealed it in my sleeve, and there kept it until I found myself alone in my cell. Then I opened the clasp. There were only two leaves within, bearing the words, *Clarimonde. At the Concini Palace.* So little acquainted was I at that time with the things of this world that I had never heard of Clarimonde, celebrated as she was, and I had no idea as to where the Concini Palace was situated. I hazarded a thousand conjectures, each more extravagant than the last; but, in truth, I cared little whether she were a great lady or a courtesan, so that I could but see her once more.

My love, although the growth of a single hour, had taken imperishable root. I did not even dream of attempting to tear it up, so fully was I convinced such a thing would be impossible. That woman had completely taken possession of me. One look from her had sufficed to change my very nature. She had breathed her will into my life, and I no longer lived in myself, but in her and for her. I gave myself up to a thousand extravagancies. I kissed the place upon my hand which she had touched, and I repeated her name over and over again for hours in succession. I only needed to close my eyes in order to see her distinctly as though she were actually present; and I reiterated to myself the words she had uttered in my ear at the church porch: "Unhappy man! Unhappy man! What hast thou done?" I comprehended at last the full horror of my situation, and the funereal and awful restraints of the state into which I had just entered became clearly revealed to me. To be a priest!—that is, to be chaste, to never love, to observe no distinction of sex or age, to turn from the sight of all beauty, to put out one's own eyes, to hide forever crouching in the chill shadows of some church or cloister, to visit none but the dying, to watch by unknown corpses, and ever bear about with one the black soutane as a garb of mourning for oneself, so that your very dress might serve as a pall for your coffin.

And I felt life rising within me like a subterranean lake, expanding and overflowing; my blood leaped fiercely through my arteries; my long-restrained youth suddenly burst into active being, like the aloe which blooms but once in a hundred years, and then bursts into blossom with a clap of thunder.

What could I do in order to see Clarimonde once more? I had no pretext to offer for desiring to leave the seminary, not knowing any person in the city. I would not even be able to remain there but a short time, and was only waiting my assignment to the curacy which I must thereafter occupy. I tried to remove the bars of the window; but it was at a fearful height from the ground, and I found that as I had no ladder it would be useless to think of escaping thus. And, furthermore, I could descend thence only by night in any event, and afterward how should I be able to find my way through the inextricable labyrinth of streets? All these difficulties, which to many would have appeared altogether insignificant, were gigantic to me, a poor seminarist who had fallen in love only the day before for the first time, without experience, without money, without attire.

"Ah!" cried I to myself in my blindness, "were I not a priest I could have seen her every day; I might have been her lover, her spouse. Instead of being wrapped in this dismal shroud of mine I would have had garments of silk and velvet, golden chains, a sword, and fair plumes like other handsome young cavaliers. My hair, instead of being dishonoured by the tonsure, would flow down upon my neck in waving curls; I would have a fine waxed moustache; I would be a gallant." But one hour passed before an altar, a few hastily articulated words, had forever cut me off from the number of the living, and I had myself sealed down the stone of my own tomb; I had with my own hand bolted the gate of my prison! I went to the window. The sky was beautifully blue; the trees had donned their spring robes; nature seemed to be making parade of an ironical joy. The *Place* was filled with people, some going, others coming; young beaux and young beauties were sauntering in couples toward the groves and gardens; merry youths passed by, cheerily trolling refrains of drinking-songs—it was all a picture of vivacity, life, animation, gaiety, which formed a bitter contrast with my mourning and my solitude. On the steps of the gate sat a young mother playing with her child. She kissed its little rosy mouth still impearled with drops of milk, and performed, in order to amuse it, a thousand divine little puerilities such as only mothers know how to invent. The father standing at a little distance smiled gently upon the charming group, and with folded arms seemed to hug his joy to his heart. I could not endure that spectacle. I closed the window with violence, and flung myself on my bed, my heart filled with frightful hate and jealousy, and gnawed my fingers and my bedcovers like a tiger that has passed ten days without food.

I know not how long I remained in this condition, but at last, while writhing on the bed in a fit of spasmodic fury, I suddenly perceived the Abbé Sérapion, who was standing erect in the center of the room, watching me attentively. Filled with shame of myself, I let my head fall upon my breast and covered my face with my hands.

"Romuald, my friend, something very extraordinary is transpiring within you," observed Sérapion, after a few moments" silence; "your conduct is altogether inexplicable. You—always so quiet, so pious, so gentle—you to rage in your cell like a wild beast! Take heed, brother—do not listen to the suggestions of the Devil. The Evil Spirit, furious that you have consecrated yourself for ever to the Lord, is prowling around you like a ravening wolf and making a last effort to obtain possession of you. Instead of allowing yourself to be conquered, my dear Romuald, make to yourself a cuirass of prayers, a buckler of mortifications, and combat the enemy like a valiant man; you will then assuredly overcome him. Virtue must be proved by temptation, and gold comes forth purer from the hands of the assayer. Fear not. Never allow yourself to become discouraged. The most watchful and steadfast souls are at moments liable to such temptation. Pray, fast, meditate, and the Evil Spirit will depart from you."

The words of the Abbé Sérapion restored me to myself, and I became a little more calm. "I came," he continued, "to tell you that you have been appointed to the curacy of C———. The priest who had charge of it has just died, and Monseigneur the Bishop has ordered me to have you installed there at once. Be ready, therefore, to start to-morrow." I responded with an inclination of the head, and the Abbé retired. I opened my missal and commenced reading some prayers, but the letters became confused and blurred under my eyes, the thread of the ideas entangled itself hopelessly in my brain, and the volume at last fell from my hands without my being aware of it.

To leave to-morrow without having been able to see her again, to add yet another barrier to the many already interposed between us, to lose forever all hope of being able to meet her, except, indeed, through a miracle! Even to write to her, alas! would be impossible, for by whom could I dispatch my letter? With my sacred character of priest, to whom could I dare unbosom myself, in whom could I confide? I became a prey to the bitterest anxiety.

Then suddenly recurred to me the words of the Abbé Sérapion regarding the artifices of the Devil; and the strange character of the adventure, the supernatural beauty of Clarimonde, the phosphoric light of her eyes, the burning imprint of her hand, the agony into which she had thrown me, the sudden change wrought within me when all my piety vanished in a single instant—these and other things clearly testified to the work of the Evil One, and perhaps that satiny hand was but the glove which concealed his claws. Filled with terror at these fancies, I again picked up the missal which had slipped from my knees and fallen upon the floor, and once more gave myself up to prayer.

Next morning Sérapion came to take me away. Two mules freighted with our miserable valises awaited us at the gate. He mounted one, and I the other as well as I knew how.

As we passed along the streets of the city, I gazed attentively at all the windows and balconies in the hope of seeing Clarimonde, but it was yet early in the morning, and the city had hardly opened its eyes. Mine sought to penetrate the blinds and window-curtains of all the palaces before which we were passing. Sérapion doubtless attributed this curiosity to my admiration of the architecture, for he slackened the pace of his animal in order to give me time to look around me. At last we passed the city gates and commenced to mount the hill beyond. When we arrived at its summit I turned to take a last look at the place where Clarimonde dwelt. The shadow of a great cloud hung over all the city; the contrasting colours of its blue and red roofs were lost in the uniform half-tint, through which here and there floated upward, like white flakes of foam, the smoke of freshly kindled fires. By a singular optical effect one edifice, which surpassed in height all the neighbouring buildings that were still dimly veiled by the vapours, towered up, fair and lustrous with the gilding of a solitary beam of sunlight—although actually more than a league away it seemed quite near. The smallest details of its architecture were plainly distinguishable—the turrets, the platforms, the window-casements, and even the swallow-tailed weather-vanes.

"What is that palace I see over there, all lighted up by the sun?" I asked Sérapion. He shaded his eyes with his hand, and having looked in the direction indicated, replied: "It is the ancient palace which the Prince Concini has given to the courtesan Clarimonde. Awful things are done there!"

At that instant, I know not yet whether it was a reality or an illusion, I fancied I saw gliding along the terrace a shapely white figure, which gleamed for a moment in passing and as quickly vanished. It was Clarimonde.

Oh, did she know that at that very hour, all feverish and restless—from the height of the rugged road which separated me from her, and which, alas! I could never more descend—I was directing my eyes upon the palace where she dwelt, and which a mocking beam of sunlight seemed to bring nigh to me, as though inviting me to enter therein as its lord? Undoubtedly she must have known it, for her soul was too sympathetically united with mine not to have felt its least emotional thrill, and that subtle sympathy it must have been which prompted her to climb—although clad only in her nightdress—to the summit of the terrace, amid the icy dews of the morning.

The shadow gained the palace, and the scene became to the eye only a motionless ocean of roofs and gables, amid which one mountainous undulation was distinctly visible. Sérapion urged his mule forward, my own at once followed at the same gait, and a sharp angle in the road at last hid the city of S——— forever from my eyes, as I was destined never to return thither. At the close of a weary three-days' journey through dismal country fields, we caught sight of the cock upon the steeple of the church which I was to take charge of, peeping above the trees, and after having followed some winding roads fringed with thatched cottages and little gardens, we found ourselves in front of the façade, which certainly possessed few features of magnificence. A porch ornamented with some mouldings, and two or three pillars rudely hewn from sandstone; a tiled roof with counterforts of the same sandstone as the pillars—that was all. To the left lay the cemetery, overgrown with high weeds, and having a great iron cross rising up in its center; to the right stood the presbytery under the shadow of the church. It was a house of the most extreme simplicity and frigid cleanliness. We entered the enclosure. A few chickens were picking up some oats scattered upon the ground; accustomed, seemingly, to the black habit of ecclesiastics, they showed no fear of our presence and scarcely troubled themselves to get out of our way. A hoarse, wheezy barking fell upon our ears, and we saw an aged dog running toward us. It was my predecessor's dog. He had dull bleared eyes, grizzled hair, and every mark of the greatest age to which a dog can possibly attain. I patted him gently, and he proceeded at once to march along beside me with an air of satisfaction unspeakable. A very old woman, who had been the housekeeper of the former curé, also came to meet us, and after having invited me into a little back parlour, asked whether I intended to retain her. I replied that I would take care of her, and the dog, and the chickens, and all the furniture her master had bequeathed her at his death. At this she became fairly transported with joy, and the Abbé Sérapion at once paid her the price which she asked for her little property.

As soon as my installation was over, the Abbé Sérapion returned to the seminary. I was, therefore, left alone, with no one but myself to look to for aid or counsel. The thought of Clarimonde again began to haunt me, and in spite of all my endeavours to banish it, I always found it present in my meditations. One evening, while promenading in my little garden along the walks bordered with box-plants, I fancied that I saw through the elm trees the figure of a woman, who followed my every movement, and that I beheld two sea-green eyes gleaming through the foliage; but it was only an illusion, and on going round to the other side of the garden, I could find nothing except a footprint on the sanded walk—a footprint so small that it seemed to have been made by the foot of a child. The garden was enclosed by very high walls. I searched every nook and corner of it, but could discover no one there. I have never succeeded in fully accounting for this circumstance, which, after all, was nothing compared with the strange things which happened to me afterward.

For a whole year I lived thus, filling all the duties of my calling with the most scrupulous exactitude, praying and fasting, exhorting and lending ghostly aid to the sick, and bestowing alms even to the extent of frequently depriving myself of the very necessaries of life. But I felt a great aridness within me, and the sources of grace seemed closed against me. I never found that happiness which should spring from the fulfilment of a holy mission; my thoughts were far away, and the words of Clarimonde were ever upon my lips like an involuntary refrain. Oh, brother, meditate well on this! Through having but once lifted my eyes to look upon a woman, through one fault apparently so venial, I have for years remained a victim to the most miserable agonies, and the happiness of my life has been destroyed forever.

I will not longer dwell upon those defeats, or on those inward victories invariably followed by yet more terrible falls, but will at once proceed to the facts of my story. One night my door-bell was long and violently rung. The aged housekeeper arose and opened to the stranger, and the figure of a man, whose complexion was deeply bronzed, and who was richly clad in a foreign costume, with a poniard at his girdle, appeared under the rays of Barbara's lantern. Her first impulse was one of terror, but the stranger reassured her, and stated that he desired to see me at once on matters relating to my holy calling. Barbara invited him upstairs, where I was on the point of retiring. The stranger told me that his mistress, a very noble lady, was lying at the point of death, and desired to see a priest. I replied that I was prepared to follow him, took with me the sacred articles necessary for extreme unction, and descended in all haste. Two horses black as the night itself stood without the gate, pawing the ground with impatience, and veiling their chests with long streams of smoky vapour exhaled from their nostrils. He held the stirrup and aided me to mount upon one; then, merely laying his hand upon the pommel of the saddle, he vaulted on the other, pressed the animal's sides with his knees, and loosened rein. The horse bounded forward with the velocity of an arrow. Mine, of which the stranger held the bridle, also started off at a swift gallop, keeping up with his companion. We devoured the road. The ground flowed backward beneath us in a long streaked line of pale gray, and the black silhouettes of the trees seemed fleeing by us on either side like an army in rout. We passed through a forest so profoundly gloomy that I felt my flesh creep in the chill darkness with superstitious fear. The showers of bright sparks which flew from the stony road under the ironshod feet of our horses remained glowing in our wake like a fiery trail; and had any one at that hour of the night beheld us both—my guide and myself—he must have taken us for two spectres riding upon nightmares. Witch-fires ever and anon flitted across the road before us, and the night-birds shrieked fearsomely in the depth of the woods beyond, where we beheld at intervals the glow of the phosphorescent eyes of wild cats. The manes of the horses became more and more dishevelled, the sweat streamed over their flanks, and their breath came through their nostrils hard and fast. But when he found them slacking pace, the guide reanimated them by uttering a strange, gutteral, unearthly cry, and the gallop recommenced with fury. At last the whirlwind race ceased; a huge black mass pierced through with many bright points of light suddenly rose before us, the hoofs of our horses echoed louder upon a strong wooden drawbridge, and we rode under a great vaulted archway which darkly yawned between two enormous towers. Some great excitement evidently reigned in the castle. Servants with torches were crossing the courtyard in every direction, and above lights were ascending and descending from landing to landing. I obtained a confused glimpse of vast masses of architecture—columns, arcades, flights of steps, stairways—a royal voluptuousness and elfin magnificence of construction worthy of fairyland. A Negro page—the same who had before brought me the tablet from Clarimonde, and whom I instantly recognised—approached to aid me in dismounting, and the major-domo, attired in black velvet with a gold chain about his neck, advanced to meet me, supporting himself upon an ivory cane. Large tears were falling from his eyes and streaming over his cheeks and white beard. "Too late!" he cried, sorrowfully shaking his venerable head. "Too late, sir priest! But if you have not been able to save the soul, come at least to watch by the poor body."

He took my arm and conducted me to the death-chamber. I wept not less bitterly than he, for I had learned that the dead one was none other than that Clarimonde whom I had so deeply and so wildly loved. A *prie-dieu* stood at the foot of the bed; a bluish flame flickering in a bronze paten filled all the room with a wan, deceptive light, here and there bringing out in the darkness at intervals some projection of furniture or cornice. In a chiselled urn upon the table there was a faded white rose, whose leaves—excepting one that still held—had all fallen, like odorous tears, to the foot of the vase. A broken black mask, a fan, and disguises of every variety, which were lying on the armchairs, bore witness that death had entered suddenly and unannounced into that sumptuous dwelling. Without daring to cast my eyes upon the bed, I knelt down and commenced to repeat the Psalms for the Dead, with exceeding fervour, thanking God that He had placed the tomb between me and the memory of this woman, so that I might thereafter be able to utter her name in my prayers as a name forever sanctified by death. But my fervour gradually weakened, and I fell insensibly into a reverie. That chamber bore no semblance to a chamber of death. In lieu of the fetid and cadaverous odours which I had been accustomed to breathe during such funereal vigils, a languorous vapour of Oriental perfume—I know not what amorous odour of woman—softly floated through the tepid air. That pale light seemed rather a twilight gloom contrived for voluptuous pleasure, than a substitute for the yellow-flickering watch-tapers which shine by the side of corpses. I thought upon the strange destiny which enabled me to meet Clarimonde again at the very moment when she was lost to me forever, and a sigh of regretful anguish escaped from my breast. Then it seemed to me that someone behind me had also sighed, and I turned round to look. It was only an echo. But in that moment my eyes fell upon the bed of death which they had till then avoided. The red damask curtains, decorated with large flowers worked in embroidery and looped up with gold bullion, permitted me to behold the fair dead, lying at full length, with hands joined upon her bosom. She was covered with a linen wrapping of dazzling whiteness, which formed a strong contrast with the gloomy purple of the hangings, and was of so fine a texture that it concealed nothing of her body's charming form, and allowed the eye to follow those beautiful outlines—undulating like the neck of a swan—which even death had not robbed of their supple grace . She seemed an alabaster statue executed by some skillful sculptor to place upon the tomb of a queen, or rather, perhaps, like a slumbering maiden over whom the silent snow had woven a spotless veil.

I could no longer maintain my constrained attitude of prayer. The air of the alcove intoxicated me, that febrile perfume of half-faded roses penetrated my very brain, and I commenced to pace restlessly up and down the chamber, pausing at each turn before the bier to contemplate the graceful corpse lying beneath the transparency of its shroud. Wild fancies came thronging to my brain. I thought to myself that she might not, perhaps, be really dead; that she might only have feigned death for the purpose of bringing me to her castle, and then declaring her love. At one time I even thought I saw her foot move under the whiteness of the coverings, and slightly disarrange the long straight folds of the winding-sheet.

And then I asked myself: "Is this indeed Clarimonde? What proof have I that it is she? Might not that black page have passed into the service of some other lady? Surely, I must be going mad to torture and afflict myself thus!" But my heart answered with a fierce throbbing: "It is she; it is she indeed!" I approached the bed again, and fixed my eyes with redoubled attention upon the object of my incertitude. Ah, must I confess it? That exquisite perfection of bodily form, although purified and made sacred by the shadow of death, affected me more voluptuously than it should have done; and that repose so closely resembled slumber that one might well have mistaken it for such. I forgot that I had come there to perform a funeral ceremony; I fancied myself a young bridegroom entering the chamber of the bride, who all modestly hides her fair face, and through coyness seeks to keep herself wholly veiled. Heartbroken with grief, yet wild with hope, shuddering at once with fear and pleasure, I bent over her and grasped the corner of the sheet. I lifted it back, holding my breath all the while through fear of waking her. My arteries throbbed with such violence that I felt them hiss through my temples, and the sweat poured from my forehead in streams, as though I had lifted a mighty slab of marble. There, indeed, lay Clarimonde, even as I had seen her at the church on the day of my ordination. She was not less charming than then. With her, death seemed but a last coquetry. The pallor of her cheeks, the less brilliant carnation of her lips, her long eyelashes lowered and relieving their dark fringe against that white skin, lent her an unspeakably seductive aspect of melancholy chastity and mental suffering; her long loose hair, still intertwined with some little blue flowers, made a shining pillow for her head, and veiled the nudity of her shoulders with its thick ringlets; her beautiful hands, purer, more diaphanous, than the Host, were crossed on her bosom in an attitude of pious rest and silent prayer, which served to counteract all that might have proven otherwise too alluring—even after death—in the exquisite roundness and ivory polish of her bare arms from which the pearl bracelets had not yet been removed. I remained long in mute contemplation, and the more I gazed, the less could I persuade myself that life had really abandoned that beautiful body forever. I do not know whether it was an illusion or a reflection of the lamplight, but it seemed to me that the blood was again commencing to circulate under that lifeless pallor, although she remained all motionless. I laid my hand lightly on her arm; it was cold, but not colder than her hand on the day when it touched mine at the portals of the church. I resumed my position, bending my face above her, and bathing her cheek with the warm dew of my tears. Ah, what bitter feelings of despair and helplessness, what agonies unutterable did I endure in that long watch! Vainly did I wish that I could have gathered all my life into one mass that I might give it all to her, and breathe into her chill remains the flame which devoured me. The night advanced, and feeling the moment of eternal separation approach, I could not deny myself the last sad sweet pleasure of imprinting a kiss upon the dead lips of her who had been my only love.... Oh, miracle! A faint breath mingled itself with my breath, and the mouth of Clarimonde responded to the passionate pressure of mine. Her eyes unclosed, and lighted up with something of their former brilliancy; she uttered a long sigh, and uncrossing her arms, passed them around my neck with a look of ineffable delight. "Ah, it is thou, Romuald!" she murmured in a voice languishingly sweet as the last vibrations of a harp. "What ailed thee, dearest? I waited so long for thee that I am dead; but we are now betrothed: I can see thee and visit thee. Adieu, Romuald, adieu! I love thee. That is all I wished to tell thee, and I give thee back the life which thy kiss for a moment recalled. We shall soon meet again." Her head fell back, but her arms yet encircled me, as though to retain me still. A furious whirlwind suddenly burst in the window, and entered the chamber. The last remaining leaf of the white rose for a moment palpitated at the extremity of the stalk like a butterfly's wing, then it detached itself and flew forth through the open casement, bearing with it the soul of Clarimonde. The lamp was extinguished, and I fell insensible upon the bosom of the beautiful dead.

When I came to myself again I was lying on the bed in my little room at the presbytery, and the old dog of the former curé was licking my hand, which had been hanging down outside of the covers. Barbara, all trembling with age and anxiety, was busying herself about the room, opening and shutting drawers, and emptying powders into glasses. On seeing me open my eyes, the old woman uttered a cry of joy, the dog yelped and wagged his tail, but I was still so weak that I could not speak a single word or make the slightest motion. Afterward I learned that I had lain thus for three days, giving no evidence of life beyond the faintest respiration. Those three days do not reckon in my life, nor could I ever imagine whither my spirit had departed during those three days; I have no recollection of aught relating to them. Barbara told me that the same coppery-complexioned man who came to seek me on the night of my departure from the presbytery had brought me back the next morning in a close litter, and departed immediately afterward. When I became able to collect my scattered thoughts, I reviewed within my mind all the circumstances of that fateful night. At first I thought I had been the victim of some magical illusion, but ere long the recollection of other circumstances, real and palpable in themselves, came to forbid that supposition. I could not believe that I had been dreaming, since Barbara as well as myself had seen the strange man with his two black horses, and described with exactness every detail of his figure and apparel. Nevertheless it appeared that none knew of any castle in the neighbourhood answering to the description of that in which I had again found Clarimonde.

One morning I found the Abbé Sérapion in my room. Barbara had advised him that I was ill, and he had come with all speed to see me. Although this haste on his part testified to an affectionate interest in me, yet his visit did not cause me the pleasure which it should have done. The Abbé Sérapion had something penetrating and inquisitorial in his gaze which made me feel very ill at ease. His presence filled me with embarrassment and a sense of guilt. At the first glance he divined my interior trouble, and I hated him for his clairvoyance.

While he inquired after my health in hypocritically honeyed accents, he constantly kept his two great yellow lion-eyes fixed upon me, and plunged his look into my soul like a sounding-lead. Then he asked me how I directed my parish, if I was happy in it, how I passed the leisure hours allowed me in the intervals of pastoral duty, whether I had become acquainted with many of the inhabitants of the place, what was my favourite reading, and a thousand other such questions. I answered these inquiries as briefly as possible, and he, without ever waiting for my answers, passed rapidly from one subject of query to another. That conversation had evidently no connection with what he actually wished to say. At last, without any premonition, but as though repeating a piece of news which he had recalled on the instant, and feared might otherwise be forgotten subsequently, he suddenly said, in a clear vibrant voice, which rang in my ears like the trumpets of the Last Judgment:

"The great courtesan Clarimonde died a few days ago, at the close of an orgy which lasted eight days and eight nights. It was something infernally splendid. The abominations of the banquets of Belshazzar and Cleopatra were re-enacted there. Good God, what age are we living in? The guests were served by swarthy slaves who spoke an unknown tongue, and who seemed to me to be veritable demons. The livery of the very least among them would have served for the gala-dress of an emperor. There have always been very strange stories told of this Clarimonde, and all her lovers came to a violent or miserable end. They used to say that she was a ghoul, a female vampire; but I believe she was none other than Beelzebub himself."

He ceased to speak, and commenced to regard me more attentively than ever, as though to observe the effect of his words on me. I could not refrain from starting when I heard him utter the name of Clarimonde, and this news of her death, in addition to the pain it caused me by reason of its coincidence with the nocturnal scenes I had witnessed, filled me with an agony and terror which my face betrayed, despite my utmost endeavours to appear composed. Sérapion fixed an anxious and severe look upon me, and then observed: "My son, I must warn you that you are standing with foot raised upon the brink of an abyss; take heed lest you fall therein. Satan's claws are long, and tombs are not always true to their trust. The tombstone of Clarimonde should be sealed down with a triple seal, for, if report be true, it is not the first time she has died. May God watch over you, Romuald!"

And with these words the Abbé walked slowly to the door. I did not see him again at that time, for he left for S——— almost immediately.

I became completely restored to health and resumed my accustomed duties. The memory of Clarimonde and the words of the old Abbé were constantly in my mind; nevertheless no extraordinary event had occurred to verify the funereal predictions of Sérapion, and I had commenced to believe that his fears and my own terrors were over-exaggerated, when one night I had a strange dream. I had hardly fallen asleep when I heard my bed-curtains drawn apart, as their rings slid back upon the curtain rod with a sharp sound. I rose up quickly upon my elbow, and beheld the shadow of a woman standing erect before me. I recognised Clarimonde immediately. She bore in her hand a little lamp, shaped like those which are placed in tombs, and its light lent her fingers a rosy transparency, which extended itself by lessening degrees even to the opaque and milky whiteness of her bare arm. Her only garment was the linen winding-sheet which had shrouded her when lying upon the bed of death. She sought to gather its folds over her bosom as though ashamed of being so scantily clad, but her little hand was not equal to the task. She was so white that the colour of the drapery blended with that of her flesh under the pallid rays of the lamp. Enveloped with this subtle tissue which betrayed all the contour of her body, she seemed rather the marble statue of some fair antique bather than a woman endowed with life. But dead or living, statue or woman, shadow or body, her beauty was still the same, only that the green light of her eyes was less brilliant, and her mouth, once so warmly crimson, was only tinted with a faint tender rosiness, like that of her cheeks. The little blue flowers which I had noticed entwined in her hair were withered and dry, and had lost nearly all their leaves, but this did not prevent her from being charming—so charming that, notwithstanding the strange character of the adventure, and the unexplainable manner in which she had entered my room, I felt not even for a moment the least fear.

She placed the lamp on the table and seated herself at the foot of my bed; then bending toward me, she said, in that voice at once silvery clear and yet velvety in its sweet softness, such as I never heard from any lips save hers:

"I have kept thee long in waiting, dear Romuald, and it must have seemed to thee that I had forgotten thee. But I come from afar off, very far off, and from a land whence no other has ever yet returned. There is neither sun nor moon in that land whence I come: all is but space and shadow; there is neither road nor pathway: no earth for the foot, no air for the wing; and nevertheless behold me here, for Love is stronger than Death and must conquer him in the end. Oh what sad faces and fearful things I have seen on my way hither! What difficulty my soul, returned to earth through the power of will alone, has had in finding its body and reinstating itself therein! What terrible efforts I had to make ere I could lift the ponderous slab with which they had covered me! See, the palms of my poor hands are all bruised! Kiss them, sweet love, that they may be healed!" She laid the cold palms of her hands upon my mouth, one after the other. I kissed them, indeed, many times, and she the while watched me with a smile of ineffable affection.

I confess to my shame that I had entirely forgotten the advice of the Abbé Sérapion and the sacred office wherewith I had been invested. I had fallen without resistance, and at the first assault. I had not even made the least effort to repel the tempter. The fresh coolness of Clarimonde's skin penetrated my own, and I felt voluptuous tremors pass over my whole body. Poor child! in spite of all I saw afterward, I can hardly yet believe she was a demon; at least she had no appearance of being such, and never did Satan so skillfully conceal his claws and horns. She had drawn her feet up beneath her, and squatted down on the edge of the couch in an attitude full of negligent coquetry. From time to time she passed her little hand through my hair and twisted it into curls, as though trying how a new style of wearing it would become my face. I abandoned myself to her hands with the most guilty pleasure, while she accompanied her gentle play with the prettiest prattle. The most remarkable fact was that I felt no astonishment whatever at so extraordinary an adventure, and as in dreams one finds no difficulty in accepting the most fantastic events as simple facts, so all these circumstances seemed to me perfectly natural in themselves.

"I loved thee long ere I saw thee, dear Romuald, and sought thee everywhere. Thou wast my dream, and I first saw thee in the church at the fatal moment. I said at once, 'It is he!' I gave thee a look into which I threw all the love I ever had, all the love I now have, all the love I shall ever have for thee—a look that would have damned a cardinal or brought a king to his knees at my feet in view of all his court. Thou remainedst unmoved, preferring thy God to me!

"Ah, how jealous I am of that God whom thou didst love and still lovest more than me!

"Woe is me, unhappy one that I am! I can never have thy heart all to myself, I whom thou didst recall to life with a kiss—dead Clarimonde, who for thy sake bursts asunder the gates of the tomb, and comes to consecrate to thee a life which she has resumed only to make thee happy!"

All her words were accompanied with the most impassioned caresses, which bewildered my sense and my reason to such an extent, that I did not fear to utter a frightful blasphemy for the sake of consoling her, and to declare that I loved her as much as God.

Her eyes rekindled and shone like chrysoprases. "In truth?—in very truth?—as much as God!" she cried, flinging her beautiful arms around me. "Since it is so, thou wilt come with me; thou wilt follow me whithersoever I desire. Thou wilt cast away thy ugly black habit. Thou shalt be the proudest and most envied of cavaliers; thou shalt be my lover! To be the acknowledged lover of Clarimonde, who has refused even a Pope! That will be something to feel proud of. Ah, the fair, unspeakably happy existence, the beautiful golden life we shall live together! And when shall we depart, my fair sir?"

"Tomorrow! Tomorrow!" I cried in my delirium.

"Tomorrow, then, so let it be!" she answered. "In the meanwhile I shall have opportunity to change my toilet, for this is a little too light and in nowise suited for a voyage. I must also forthwith notify all my friends who believe me dead, and mourn for me as deeply as they are capable of doing. The money, the dresses, the carriages—all will be ready. I shall call for thee at this same hour. Adieu, dear heart!" And she lightly touched my forehead with her lips. The lamp went out, the curtains closed again, and all became dark; a leaden, dreamless sleep fell on me and held me unconscious until the morning following.

I awoke later than usual, and the recollection of this singular adventure troubled me during the whole day. I finally persuaded myself that it was a mere vapour of my heated imagination. Nevertheless its sensations had been so vivid that it was difficult to persuade myself that they were not real, and it was not without some presentiment of what was going to happen that I got into bed at last, after having prayed God to drive far from me all thoughts of evil, and to protect the chastity of my slumber.

I soon fell into a deep sleep, and my dream was continued. The curtains again parted, and I beheld Clarimonde, not as on the former occasion, pale in her pale winding-sheet, with the violets of death upon her cheeks, but gay, sprightly, jaunty, in a superb travelling-dress of green velvet, trimmed with gold lace, and looped up on either side to allow a glimpse of satin petticoat. Her blond hair escaped in thick ringlets from beneath a broad black felt hat, decorated with white feathers whimsically twisted into various shapes. In one hand she held a little riding-whip terminated by a golden whistle. She tapped me lightly with it, and exclaimed: "Well, my fine sleeper, is this the way you make your preparations? I thought I would find you up and dressed. Arise quickly, we have no time to lose."

I leaped out of bed at once.

"Come, dress yourself, and let us go," she continued, pointing to a little package she had brought with her. "The horses are becoming impatient of delay and champing their bits at the door. We ought to have been by this time at least ten leagues distant from here."

I dressed myself hurriedly, and she handed me the articles of apparel herself one by one, bursting into laughter from time to time at my awkwardness, as she explained to me the use of a garment when I had made a mistake. She hurriedly arranged my hair, and this done, held up before me a little pocket-mirror of Venetian crystal, rimmed with silver filigree-work, and playfully asked: "How dost find thyself now? Wilt engage me for thy *valet de chambre*?"

I was no longer the same person, and I could not even recognise myself. I resembled my former self no more than a finished statue resembles a block of stone. My old face seemed but a coarse daub of the one reflected in the mirror. I was handsome, and my vanity was sensibly tickled by the metamorphosis.

That elegant apparel, that richly embroidered vest had made of me a totally different personage, and I marvelled at the power of transformation owned by a few yards of cloth cut after a certain pattern. The spirit of my costume penetrated my very skin and within ten minutes more I had become something of a coxcomb.

In order to feel more at ease in my new attire, I took several turns up and down the room. Clarimonde watched me with an air of maternal pleasure, and appeared well satisfied with her work. "Come, enough of this child's play! Let us start, Romuald, dear. We have far to go, and we may not get there in time." She took my hand and led me forth. All the doors opened before her at a touch, and we passed by the dog without awaking him.

At the gate we found Margheritone waiting, the same swarthy groom who had once before been my escort. He held the bridles of three horses, all black like those which bore us to the castle—one for me, one for him, one for Clarimonde. Those horses must have been Spanish genets born of mares fecundated by a zephyr, for they were fleet as the wind itself, and the moon, which had just risen at our departure to light us on the way, rolled over the sky like a wheel detached from her own chariot. We beheld her on the right leaping from tree to tree, and putting herself out of breath in the effort to keep up with us. Soon we came upon a level plain where, hard by a clump of trees, a carriage with four vigorous horses awaited us. We entered it, and the postillions urged their animals into a mad gallop. I had one arm around Clarimonde's waist, and one of her hands clasped in mine; her head leaned upon my shoulder, and I felt her bosom, half bare, lightly pressing against my arm. I had never known such intense happiness. In that hour I had forgotten everything, and I no more remembered having ever been a priest than I remembered what I had been doing in my mother's womb, so great was the fascination which the evil spirit exerted upon me. From that night my nature seemed in some sort to have become halved, and there were two men within me, neither of whom knew the other. At one moment I believed myself a priest who dreamed nightly that he was a gentleman, at another that I was a gentleman who dreamed he was a priest. I could no longer distinguish the dream from the reality, nor could I discover where the reality began or where ended the dream. The exquisite young lord and libertine railed at the priest, the priest loathed the dissolute habits of the young lord. Two spirals entangled and confounded the one with the other, yet never touching, would afford a fair representation of this bicephalic life which I lived. Despite the strange character of my condition, I do not believe that I ever inclined, even for a moment, to madness. I always retained with extreme vividness all the perceptions of my two lives. Only there was one absurd fact which I could not explain to myself—

namely, that the consciousness of the same individuality existed in two men so opposite in character. It was an anomaly for which I could not account—whether I believed myself to be the curé of the little village of C———, or *Il Signor Romualdo*, the titled lover of Clarimonde.

Be that as it may, I lived, at least I believed that I lived, in Venice. I have never been able to discover rightly how much of illusion and how much of reality there was in this fantastic adventure. We dwelt in a great palace on the Canaleio, filled with frescoes and statues, and containing two Titians in the noblest style of the great master, which were hung in Clarimonde's chamber. It was a palace well worthy of a king. We had each our gondola, our *barcarolli* in family livery, our music hall, and our special poet. Clarimonde always lived upon a magnificent scale; there was something of Cleopatra in her nature. As for me, I had the retinue of a prince's son, and I was regarded with as much reverential respect as though I had been of the family of one of the twelve Apostles or the four Evangelists of the Most Serene Republic. I would not have turned aside to allow even the Doge to pass, and I do not believe that since Satan fell from Heaven, any creature was ever prouder or more insolent than I. I went to the Ridotto, and played with a luck which seemed absolutely infernal. I received the best of all society—the sons of ruined families, women of the theatre, shrewd knaves, parasites, hectoring swashbucklers. But notwithstanding the dissipation of such a life, I always remained faithful to Clarimonde. I loved her wildly. She would have excited satiety itself, and chained inconstancy. To have Clarimonde was to have twenty mistresses; aye, to possess all women: so mobile, so varied of aspect, so fresh in new charms was she all in herself—a very chameleon of a woman, in sooth. She made you commit with her the infidelity you would have committed with another, by donning to perfection the character, the attraction, the style of beauty of the woman who appeared to please you. She returned my love a hundred-fold, and it was in vain that the young patricians and even the Ancients of the Council of Ten made her the most magnificent proposals. A Foscari even went so far as to offer to espouse her. She rejected all his overtures. Of gold she had enough. She wished no longer for anything but love—a love youthful, pure, evoked by herself, and which should be a first and last passion. I would have been perfectly happy but for a cursed nightmare which recurred every night, and in which I believed myself to be a poor village curé, practising mortification and penance for my excesses during the day. Reassured by my constant association with her, I never thought further of the strange manner in which I had become acquainted with Clarimonde. But the words of the Abbé Sérapion concerning her recurred often to my memory, and never ceased to cause me uneasiness.

For some time the health of Clarimonde had not been so good as usual; her complexion grew paler day by day. The physicians who were summoned could not comprehend the nature of her malady and knew not how to treat it. They all prescribed some insignificant remedies, and never called a second time. Her paleness, nevertheless, visibly increased, and she became colder and colder, until she seemed almost as white and dead as upon that memorable night in the unknown castle. I grieved with anguish unspeakable to behold her thus slowly perishing; and she, touched by my agony, smiled upon me sweetly and sadly with the fateful smile of those who feel that they must die.

One morning I was seated at her bedside, and breakfasting from a little table placed close at hand, so that I might not be obliged to leave her for a single instant. In the act of cutting some fruit I accidentally inflicted rather a deep gash on my finger. The blood immediately gushed forth in a little purple jet, and a few drops spurted upon Clarimonde. Her eyes flashed, her face suddenly assumed an expression of savage and ferocious joy such as I had never before observed in her. She leaped out of her bed with animal agility—the agility, as it were, of an ape or a cat—and sprang upon my wound, which she commenced to suck with an air of unutterable pleasure. She swallowed the blood in little mouthfuls, slowly and carefully, like a connoisseur tasting a wine from Xeres or Syracuse. Gradually her eyelids half closed, and the pupils of her green eyes became oblong instead of round. From time to time she paused in order to kiss my hand, then she would recommence to press her lips to the lips of the wound in order to coax forth a few more ruddy drops. When she found that the blood would no longer come, she arose with eyes liquid and brilliant, rosier than a May dawn; her face full and fresh, her hand warm and moist—in fine, more beautiful than ever, and in the most perfect health.

"I shall not die! I shall not die!" she cried, clinging to my neck, half mad with joy. "I can love thee yet for a long time. My life is thine, and all that is of me comes from thee. A few drops of thy rich and noble blood, more precious and more potent than all the elixirs of the earth, have given me back life."

This scene long haunted my memory, and inspired me with strange doubts in regard to Clarimonde; and the same evening, when slumber had transported me to my presbytery, I beheld the Abbé Sérapion, graver and more anxious of aspect than ever. He gazed attentively at me, and sorrowfully exclaimed: "Not content with losing your soul, you now desire also to lose your body. Wretched young man, into how terrible a plight have you fallen!" The tone in which he uttered these words powerfully affected me, but in spite of its vividness even that impression was soon dissipated, and a thousand other cares erased it from my mind. At last one evening, while looking into a mirror whose traitorous position she had not taken into account, I saw Clarimonde in the act of emptying a powder into the cup of spiced wine which she had long been in the habit of preparing after our repasts. I took the cup, feigned to carry it to my lips, and then placed it on the nearest article of furniture as though intending to finish it at my leisure. Taking advantage of a moment when the fair one's back was turned, I threw the contents under the table, after which I retired to my chamber and went to bed, fully resolved not to sleep, but to watch and discover what should come of all this mystery. I did not have to wait long, Clarimonde entered in her nightdress, and having removed her apparel, crept into bed and lay down beside me. When she felt assured that I was asleep, she bared my arm, and drawing a gold pin from her hair, commenced to murmur in a low voice:

"One drop, only one drop! One ruby at the end of my needle... Since thou lovest me yet, I must not die!. Ah, poor love! His beautiful blood, so brightly purple, I must drink it. Sleep, my only treasure! Sleep, my god, my child! I will do thee no harm; I will only take of thy life what I must to keep my own from being forever extinguished. But that I love thee so much, I could well resolve to have other lovers whose veins I could drain; but since I have known thee all other men have become hateful to me.... Ah, the beautiful arm! How round it is! How white it is! How shall I ever dare to prick this pretty blue vein!" And while thus murmuring to herself she wept, and I felt her tears raining on my arm as she clasped it with her hands. At last she took the resolve, slightly punctured me with her pin, and commenced to suck up the blood which oozed from the place. Although she swallowed only a few drops, the fear of weakening me soon seized her, and she carefully tied a little band around my arm, afterward rubbing the wound with an unguent which immediately cicatrised it. Further doubts were impossible. The Abbé Sérapion was right. Notwithstanding this positive knowledge, however, I could not cease to love Clarimonde, and I would gladly of my own accord have given her all the blood she required to sustain her factitious life. Moreover, I felt but little fear of her. The woman seemed to plead with me for the vampire, and what I had already heard and seen sufficed to reassure me completely. In those days I had plenteous veins, which would not have been so easily exhausted as at present; and I would not have thought of bargaining for my blood, drop by drop. I would rather have opened myself the veins of my arm and said to her, "Drink, and may my love infiltrate itself throughout thy body together with my blood!" I carefully avoided ever making the least reference to the narcotic drink she had prepared for me, or to the incident of the pin, and we lived in the most perfect harmony.

Yet my priestly scruples commenced to torment me more than ever, and I was at a loss to imagine what new penance I could invent in order to mortify and subdue my flesh. Although these visions were involuntary, and though I did not actually participate in anything relating to them, I could not dare to touch the body of Christ with hands so impure and a mind defiled by such debauches whether real or imaginary. In the effort to avoid falling under the influence of these wearisome hallucinations, I strove to prevent myself from being overcome by sleep. I held my eyelids open with my fingers, and stood for hours together leaning upright against the wall, fighting sleep with all my might; but the dust of drowsiness invariably gathered upon my eyes at last, and finding all resistance useless, I would have to let my arms fall in the extremity of despairing weariness, and the current of slumber would again bear me away to the perfidious shores. Sérapion addressed me with the most vehement exhortations, severely reproaching me for my softness and want of fervour. Finally, one day when I was more wretched than usual, he said to me: "There is but one way by which you can obtain relief from this continual torment, and though it is an extreme measure it must be made use of; violent diseases require violent remedies. I know where Clarimonde is buried. It is necessary that we shall disinter her remains, and that you shall behold in how pitiable a state the object of your love is. Then you will no longer be tempted to lose your soul for the sake of an unclean corpse devoured by worms, and ready to crumble into dust. That will assuredly restore you to yourself." For my part, I was so tired of this double life that I at once consented, desiring to ascertain beyond a doubt whether a priest or a gentleman had been the victim of delusion. I had become fully resolved either to kill one of the two men within me for the benefit of the other, or else to kill both, for so terrible an existence could not last long and be endured. The Abbé Sérapion provided himself with a mattock, a lever, and a lantern, and at midnight we wended our way to the cemetery of ———, the location and place of which were perfectly familiar to him. After having directed the rays of the dark lantern upon the inscriptions of several tombs, we came at last upon a great slab, half concealed by huge weeds and devoured by mosses and parasitic plants, whereupon we deciphered the opening lines of the epitaph:

Here lies Clarimonde
Who was famed in her life-time
As the fairest of women

"It is here without a doubt," muttered Sérapion, and placing his lantern on the ground, he forced the point of the lever under the edge of the stone and commenced to raise it. The stone yielded, and he proceeded to work with the mattock. Darker and more silent than the night itself, I stood by and watched him do it, while he, bending over his dismal toil, streamed with sweat, panted, and his hard-coming breath seemed to have the harsh tone of a death rattle. It was a weird scene, and had any persons from without beheld us, they would assuredly have taken us rather for profane wretches and shroud-stealers than for priests of God. There was something grim and fierce in Sérapion's zeal which lent him the air of a demon rather than of an apostle or an angel, and his great aquiline face, with all its stern features, brought out in strong relief by the lantern-light, had something fearsome in it which enhanced the unpleasant fancy. I felt an icy sweat come out upon my forehead in huge beads, and my hair stood up with a hideous fear. Within the depths of my own heart I felt that the act of the austere Sérapion was an abominable sacrilege; and I could have prayed that a triangle of fire would issue from the entrails of the dark clouds, heavily rolling above us, to reduce him to cinders. The owls which had been nestling in the cypress-trees, startled by the gleam of the lantern, flew against it from time to time, striking their dusty wings against its panes, and uttering plaintive cries of lamentation; wild foxes yelped in the far darkness, and a thousand sinister noises detached themselves from the silence. At last Sérapion's mattock struck the coffin itself, making its planks re-echo with a deep sonorous sound, with that terrible sound nothingness utters when stricken. He wrenched apart and tore up the lid, and I beheld Clarimonde, pallid as a figure of marble, with hands joined; her white winding-sheet made but one fold from her head to her feet. A little crimson drop sparkled like a speck of dew at one corner of her colourless mouth. Sérapion, at this spectacle, burst into fury: "Ah, thou art here, demon! Impure courtesan! Drinker of blood and gold!" And he flung holy water upon the corpse and the coffin, over which he traced the sign of the cross with his sprinkler. Poor Clarimonde had no sooner been touched by the blessed spray than her beautiful body crumbled into dust, and became only a shapeless and frightful mass of cinders and half-calcined bones.

"Behold your mistress, my Lord Romuald!" cried the inexorable priest, as he pointed to these sad remains. "Will you be easily tempted after this to promenade on the Lido or at Fusina with your beauty?" I covered my face with my hands, a vast ruin had taken place within me. I returned to my presbytery, and the noble Lord Romuald, the lover of Clarimonde, separated himself from the poor priest with whom he had kept such strange company so long. But once only, the following night, I saw Clarimonde. She said to me, as she had said the first time at the portals of the church: "Unhappy man! Unhappy man! What hast thou done? Wherefore have hearkened to that imbecile priest? Wert thou not happy? And what harm had I ever done thee that thou shouldst violate my poor tomb, and lay bare the miseries of my nothingness? All communication between our souls and our bodies is henceforth forever broken. Adieu! Thou wilt yet regret me!" She vanished in air as smoke, and I never saw her more.

Alas! she spoke truly indeed. I have regretted her more than once, and I regret her still. My soul's peace has been very dearly bought. The love of God was not too much to replace such a love as hers. And this, brother, is the story of my youth. Never gaze upon a woman, and walk abroad only with eyes ever fixed upon the ground; for however chaste and watchful one may be, the error of a single moment is enough to make one lose Eternity.

GLOSSARY

Barcarolli: Gondoliers who sing folk songs called barcarolles.

Belshazzar: A prince of Babylon; featured in the Old Testament Book of Daniel.

Chrysoprases: Chrysoprase is a green-colored gemstone, a variety of chalcedony.

Concini Palace: Named for Concino Concini, an Italian politician who was the first minister of France; he must have given the palace to Clarimonde in or before 1617, since that was the year he was murdered, as part of a plot by Louis XIII. It's unclear if Clarimonde was alive or undead at the time. (Interestingly, in real life, Concini's wife was accused of sorcery, beheaded, and burned.)

Council of Ten: Venice's governing body from 1310 to 1797.

Doge: The most senior elected official in Venice; an office that existed from around 700 to 1797.

Foscari: An illustrious Venetian family.

"…I am sixty-six…": Romuald was ordained at the age of twenty-four; the story was published in 1836. If Romuald is speaking contemporaneously, then he met Clarimonde in 1794.

Oil of Catechumens: An oil blessed by a bishop to anoint a new Christian or a new priest.

Our Lady of Sorrows: Another name for the Virgin Mary.

Paten: A metal plate for holding a candle or the Host.

Prie-Dieu: A piece of furniture for use in prayer, usually having a surface for kneeling (sometimes cushioned), a narrow upright front, and a flat surface for resting books or elbows.

Ridotto: A famous casino in Venice, 1638-1774.

Sardanapalus: Legendary king of Assyria, famed for his decadence.

Syracuse: An Italian city.

Xeres: A wine named for Jerez de la Frontera, a region in Spain; also the source of the word "sherry."

AFTERWORD

Romuald says Clarimonde "never sprang from the flank of Eve..." which may tie her in with Lilith. She is certainly one more female vampire whose chief enemy is Christianity and the patriarchy. When Sérapion sprinkles the holy water on Clarimonde, he's just trying to eradicate her, not save her soul. Nevertheless, Clarimonde is clearly the heroine and the Abbé the villain of the piece.

Gautier presents vampirism as a sexual act—Clarimonde climaxes while sucking on Romuald—but it's very different from the rape fantasy at the center of the male vampire trope. Romuald is a very ordinary person, but he's the world to Clarimonde. All he has to do is lie back while she goes to work on him with her mouth—and she's as satisfied as he is, if not more so. A dream of oral sex.

THE LADY BRIGHT

And then the knichte – "Oh ladye brichte,
What chance hes broucht you here…"

James Clerk Maxwell (1831-1879) was a Scottish physicist who formulated the theory electromagnetic radiation and the theory of kinetic gases. He laid the groundwork for both special relativity and quantum mechanics. In a poll taken in 1999, Maxwell was voted the third greatest physicist of all time, after Einstein and Newton.

And he wrote a poem about a lady vampire.

Composed in 1845 when Maxwell was a teenager (and when the penny dreadful Varney the Vampyre *began), the poem is deliberately "medieval" in tone, and clearly inspired by the work of Robert Burns, as well as ballads like* The Demon Lover *and* Thomas the Rhymer. *It's written in the Scots dialect, so* "knichte" *is* "knight," "ladye brichte" *is* "lady bright," *etc. The glossary provides a full translation into standard English. But try the original first. The year before he wrote* The Lady Bright, *Maxwell, then 13, won both the Edinburgh Academy's medal in mathematics and took first prize in English and poetry. So he knew what he was doing...*

THE VAMPIRE

James Clerk Maxwell

Thair is a knichte rydis through the wood,
  And a douchty knichte is hee,
And sure hee is on a message sent,
  He rydis sae hastilie.
Hee passit the aik, and hee passit the birk,
  And hee passit monie a tre,
Bot plesant to him was the saugh sae slim,
  For beneath it hee did see

The boniest ladye that ever he saw,
  Scho was sae schyn and fair.
And there scho sat, beneath the saugh,
  Kaiming hir gowden hair.
And then the knichte – "Oh ladye brichte,
  What chance hes broucht you here,
But say the word, and ye schall gang
  Back to your kindred dear."
Then up and spok the Ladye fair -
  "I have nae friends or kin,
Bot in a littel boat I live,
  Amidst the waves' loud din."
Then answered thus the douchty knichte -
  "I'll follow you through all,
For gin ye bee in a littel boat,
  The world to it seemis small."
They gaed through the wood, and through the wood
  To the end of the wood they came:

And when they came to the end of the wood
  They saw the salt sea faem.
And then they saw the wee, wee boat,
  That daunced on the top of the wave,
And first got in the ladye fair,
  And then the knichte sae brave;

They got into the wee, wee boat,
  And rowed wi' a' their micht;
When the knichte sae brave, he turnit about,
  And lookit at the ladye bricht;
He lookit at her bonie cheik,
  And hee lookit at hir twa bricht eyne,
Bot hir rosie cheik growe ghaistly pale,
  And scho seymit as scho deid had been.
The fause knichte growe pale wi frichte,
  And his hair rose up on end,
For gane-by days cam to his mynde,
  And his former luve he kenned.
Then spake the ladye, - "Thou, fause knichte,
  Hast done to mee much ill,
Thou didst forsake me long ago,
  Bot I am constant still;
For though I ligg in the woods sae cald,
  At rest I canna bee
Until I sucke the gude lyfe blude
  Of the man that gart me dee."
Hee saw hir lipps were wet wi' blude,
  And hee saw hir lyfelesse eyne,
And loud hee cry'd, "Get frae my syde,
  Thou vampyr corps uncleane!"
Bot no, hee is in hir magic boat,
  And on the wyde sea;
And the vampyr suckis his gude lyfe blude,

Sho suckis hym till hee dee.
So now beware, whoe're you are,
That walkis in this lone wood;
Beware of that deceitfull spright,
The ghaist that suckis the blude.

GLOSSARY

There is a knight that rides through the wood,
And a fearless knight is he.
And sure he is on a message sent,
He rides so hastily.
He passed the oak, and he passed the birch,
And he passed by many a tree;
But pleasant to him was the willow so slim,
For beneath it he did see

The bonniest lady that ever he saw,
She was so shining and fair.
And there she sat, beneath the willow
Combing her golden hair,
And then the knight– "Oh lady bright,
What chance has brought you here?
But say the word, and you shall go
Back to your kindred dear."
Then up and spoke the Lady fair -
"I have no friends or kin,
But in a little boat I live,
Amidst the waves' loud din."
Then answered thus the fearless knight -
"I'll follow you through all,
For though you be in a little boat,
The world to it seems small."
They went through the wood, and through the wood
To the end of the wood they came;
And when they came to the end of the wood
They saw the salt sea foam.

And then they saw the small, small boat,
That danced on the top of the wave,
And first got in the lady fair,
And then the knight so brave;

They got into the small, small boat,
And rowed with all their might;
When the knight so brave, he turned about
And looked at the lady bright;
He looked at her lovely cheek,
And he looked at her two bright eyes,
But her rosy cheek grew ghostly pale,
And she seemed as though she were dead.
The false, false knight grew pale with fright,
And his hair rose up on end,
For long-gone days came to his mind,
And his former love he knew.
Then spoke the lady - "You, false knight,
Have done to me much ill,
You did forsake me long ago,
But I am constant still;
For though I live in the woods so cold,
At rest I cannot be
Until I suck the good life-blood
Of the man that caused me to die."
He saw her lips were wet with blood,
And he saw her lifeless eyes.
And loud he cried, "Get from my sight,
You vampire corpse unclean!"

But no, he is in her magic boat,
And on the wide, wide sea;
And the vampire sucks his good life-blood
She sucks till dead is he;
So now beware, whoever you are,
That walk in this lone wood;
Beware of that deceitful sprite,
The ghost that sucks the blood.

AFTERWORD

The Lady Bright *is perhaps the clearest example in this book of vampirism empowering a woman's vengeance, even more so than Alinska. An interesting artistic choice for a 14-year-old boy in early Victorian Scotland.*

CLARA CROFTON

The lid moved, and a strange sound was heard from within…

The first twenty chapters of Varney the Vampyre, an English "penny dreadful" serialized from 1845 to 1847, have been excerpted in Volume I: The Vampire Lords. *The vampiric Sir Francis Varney threatens the Bannerworth family, especially the brave and lovely Flora. She is repeatedly bitten, but finally escapes becoming a "vampire."*

The turning of a victim into one of the undead has always been more of an art than a science. In the official reports of "real" vampires, Petar Blagojevic seems to have killed his victims without vampirizing them; Arnold Paul, however, was turned by a Turkish vampire, and at least some of his alleged victims were infected. In William Stagg's 1812 poem The Vampyre, *the victim is being gradually drained to death and fears he will rise again after his burial. In John Polidori's 1819 story,* The Vampyre: A Tale, *Lord Ruthven's victims are just dead. In this volume, several vampires can take just enough blood to satisfy their needs without endangering the lives of their beloved victims.*

Clara Crofton, however, is not so fortunate. Her saga comes towards the end of Varney's 667,000 word epic, and is excerpted in the following pages.

In the original penny dreadfuls, the Clara Crofton chapters were numbered as 185 through 208; however, due to various editorial and printing errors, they should really be numbered 202 through 225. In the following pages, the chapters are not numbered, but they retain their original evocative sub-headings...which really should become standard practice in literature again!

The vampirized young woman, Clara Crofton, is given only a few words of dialogue while she's alive, none after she's undead, and almost no characterization—but she is the hub around which everything revolves.

To set the scene: Sir Francis Varney, disgusted by his centuries of undead wickedness, attempts suicide by drowning himself so deep in the sea that the rays of the moon, which always revive him, can't reach him. Ironically, two brothers, Charles and Edwin Crofton, rescue him, thinking they've done a good deed. Varney, his plans thwarted, decides to do something terrible to them.

He journeys to the Grange, the large country house where Charles and Edwin live with their widowed father, Sir George Crofton, and their sisters Emma and Clara. On his way there, Varney sees a young man fall off his horse. Varney does not bite the unconscious man; instead, he robs him, and takes a woman's portrait hanging around the man's neck. "She is fair, very fair," Varney says to himself, adding, "she would make a fit victim for me." The woman in the portrait is Clara, and the young man is her fiancé, Mr. Ringwood.

At the Grange, Varney pretends to be "Mr. Smith," grateful to have been rescued from drowning, and is welcomed by the Croftons. He accepts an offer to spend the night. Then the injured Ringwood is brought to the Grange, where the local physician, Dr. North, tends him.

Ringwood, recovering from his concussion, dreams about Clara being attacked by a "vampyre," but nobody takes it seriously—and "Mr. Smith" especially pooh-poohs the matter. Everyone retires for the night...until screams echo through the house...and Sir George rushes to Clara's bedroom...

Excerpt from

VARNEY, THE VAMPYRE; OR, THE FEAST OF BLOOD.

James Malcom Rymer

THE SIGHT OF TERROR.—THE DOCTOR'S SUSPICIONS.—THE NIGHT WATCH.

The sight that met the eyes of the father in his daughter's chamber, was, indeed, one calculated in every respect to strike him with horror and misery. Emma was lying insensible at the side of the bed, and Clara seemed to be dead, for she was ghastly pale, and there was blood upon her neck.

The father staggered to a seat, but Dr. North at once rushed forward, and held the light to the eyes of Clara, at the same time, that he placed his finger on her wrist to note if there was any pulsation.

"Only a fainting fit," he said.

"But the blood—the—the blood," cried Sir George.

"That I know nothing about, just at present, but let us see what's the matter here."

He raised Emma from the floor, and found that she too had fainted, but she appeared to be perfectly uninjured. She slightly recovered as he lifted her up, and he resigned her at once to the care of some of the female servants, who now made their appearance in the chamber, all terribly alarmed at the shriek that had awakened them.

"This is strange," said Dr. North, "here is a small puncture upon the throat of your daughter Clara, that almost looks like the mark of a tooth."

"A tooth!"

"Yes, but of course that cannot be."

"Hear me, oh, hear me," cried Emma, at this moment. "Horror—horror!"

"What would you say—speak at once, and clear up this mystery if you can. What has happened?"

"I heard a noise, and came from my own chamber to this. There was some one bending over the bed. 'Twas I who shrieked."

"You?"

"Yes, oh yes! 'Twas I. I know not what then happened, for I either fell or was struck down, and I felt that my senses left me. What has happened? I too ask; oh, Clara! What was it? what was it?"

"Imagination, most likely," said the doctor. "You had better go to your room again, Miss Emma, for you are trembling with cold and apprehension. Perhaps in the morning, all this affair will assume a different shape. At present we are all too much flurried to take proper cognisance of it. There your sister is rapidly recovering. How do you feel now, Miss Clara?"

"I—I—am mad!"

"Oh, pho! pho! nonsense!"

"Oh, God help me! How horrifying ! How more than dreadful! That awful face! Those hideous teeth!—I am mad!—I am mad!"

"Why, my dear child, you will drive me mad," cried Sir George, "if you talk in such a strain. Oh, let me beg of you not."

"Don't heed her," said Dr. North. "This will soon pass away. Come, Miss Clara, you must tell me freely, as your medical man, what has happened. Let us hear the full particulars, and then you know well, that if any human means can aid you, you shall be aided."

This calm mode of discourse had evidently a great effect upon her, and after the silence of a few moments, she spoke much more collectedly than before, saying,—

"Oh, no—no! I cannot think it a dream."

"What, a dream?"

"You—you shall hear. But do not drag me from my home, and from all I love, if I am mad; I pray you do not—I implore you!"

"You are quite safe. Why, what a ridiculous girl you are, to be sure. Nobody wants to drag you from your home, and nobody will attempt such a thing, I assure you. You have only to tell us all unreservedly, and you will then be quite safe. If you refuse us you confidence how can we act for you in any way?"

This argument seemed to be effective, and to reach her understanding quite, so that after a shudder, and a glance around her of great dread and dismay, she spoke, saying in a low, faltering voice,—

"Something came; something not quite human, yet having the aspect of a man. Something that flew at me, and fastened its teeth upon my neck."

"Teeth! everybody says 'teeth!' " exclaimed the father.

"Hush!" said the doctor, with an admonitory wave of his hand; "keep that a secret from her, whatever you do. I implore you, keep quiet on that head. Well, is that all, Clara?"

"Yes—yes."

"Then it was a dream, and nothing else, I can assure you. Nothing but a dream; make yourself comfortable, and think no more of it. I dare say you will have a quiet sleep now, after this. But you had better let your sister Emma lay with you, as your nerves are a little shattered."

"Oh, yes, yes."

Emma, who truth to tell, was very little better than her sister, professed her readiness to stay, and the doctor giving Sir George a nod, as much as to say, "Let no more be said about it just now," led the way from the room at once.

When he reached the corridor, where Varney and the two sons were waiting, he said,—

"We shall none of us after this, I am certain, feel inclined to sleep; suppose we go downstairs at once and think and talk this matter over together; there is more in it, perhaps, than meets the eye; I will follow you in a moment, when I have just seen that my patient is all right."

They all proceeded down stairs to the dining-room, and in a few minutes, the doctor followed; lights were procured, and they sat down, all looking at the doctor who had taken the lead in the affair, and who evidently had some very disagreeable, if not very true, ideas upon the subject matter of the evening's disturbance.

"Well, doctor," said Sir George, "we rely upon you to give us your opinion upon this business, and some insight into its meaning."

"In the first place then," said the doctor, "I don't understand it."

"Well, that's coming to the point."

"Stop a bit; it was no dream."

"You think not."

"Certainly not a dream, two people don't dream of the same thing at the same time; I don't of course deny the possibility of such a thing, but it is too remarkable a coincidence to believe all at once; but Emma avows that she saw a somebody in her sister's room."

"Ah," said Sir George; "she did, I had in my confusion forgotten that horrible confirmation of Clara's story. She did so, and before Clara was well recovered too, so she could not have put the idea into her head. Good God! what am I to think? For the love of Heaven some of you tell me what are your opinions upon this horrible affair, which looks so romantically unreal, and yet so horribly real."

All except the doctor looked at each other in surprise.

"Well," he said, "I will tell you what the thing suggests; not what it is, mind you, for the affair to me is too out of the way of natural causes to induce me to come to a positive conclusion. Before I speak, however, I should like to have your opinion, Mr. Smith; I am convinced it will be valuable."

"Really I have formed none," replied Varney; "I am only exceedingly surprised that somebody should have fastened me in my bedroom. I know that that circumstance gave me a terrible fright, for when I heard all the outcry and confusion, I thought the house was on fire."

"Ah! the locking of us in our rooms, too," said the doctor, "there's another bit of reality. Who did that?"

"It puzzles me beyond all comprehension," said Sir George; "how the doors could be locked I cannot imagine; for as I told you the keys are in a drawer in my library."

"At all events, the doors could not lock themselves, with or without keys," said Charles; "and that circumstance shows sufficiently evidently that someone has been at work in the business whom we have still to discover."

"True," said Mr. Smith.

"Well, gentlemen," added the doctor, "I will tell you what I suggest; and that is contained in a letter, written a long while ago by a distant relation of mine, likewise a surgeon. Mind, I do not of course pledge myself at the present time, for the truth and accuracy of a man who was dead long before I was born; he might too have been a very superstitious man."

"But what did he suggest?"

"He did more than suggest; he wrote for a medical publication of that day an account, only of course suppressing names, of the appearance of a vampyre."

"A what?"

"A vampyre!"

"I have heard of such horrors," said Mr. Smith, "but really at the present day, no one can think of believing such things. Vampyres indeed! No—that is too great a claim upon one's credulity. These existences, or supposed existences, have gone the same way as the ghosts, and so on."

"One would think so, but you shall hear."

Sir George Crofton and his sons looked curious, and thought that the doctor was going to draw upon his memory in the matter to which he alluded, but he took from his pocket a memorandum book, and from it extracted some printed papers.

"The communication was so curious," he said, "that I cut it out of the old volume in which it appeared, and kept it ever since."

"Pray," said Mr. Smith, "what was the name of your distant relation, the medical man?"

"Chillingworth."

"Oh, indeed; an odd name rather, I don't recollect ever hearing of it."

"No, sir, it is not likely you should. Dr. Chillingworth has been dead many years, and no one else of his name is at present in the medical profession to my knowledge. But you shall hear, at all events, what he says about it."

The doctor then opened the folded paper, and read as follows:—

"Notwithstanding the incredulity that has been shown regarding vampyres, I am in a condition from my own knowledge to own the existence of one, I think he is dead now. His name was Varney, at least that was the name he went by, and he came strangely enough under my observation, in connection with some dear friends of mine named B———."

"Is that all?" said Mr. Smith.

"Not quite," replied Dr. North, "He goes on to say that but for touching the feeling of living persons, he could and would unfold some curious particulars respecting vampyres, and that if he lived long enough he will perhaps do so, by which I suppose he meant if he outlived the parties whose feelings he was afraid of hurting by any premature disclosures."

"And—and," faltered Sir George, "do you draw a conclusion from all that, that my daughter has been visited by one of these persons—surely not."

"Maybe, Sir George; I draw no conclusions at all, I merely throw out the matter for your consideration. It is always worthwhile considering these matters in any possible aspect. That is all."

"A most horrible aspect," said Sir George.

"Truly dreadful," said Mr. Smith.

"This shall be settled," said Charles, "Edwin and I will take upon ourselves tomorrow night to set this question completely at rest."

At this moment there was a loud cry of "Help, help, help," in the voice of Emma, and they all rushed up stairs with great speed.

"Oh, this way, this way," she cried, meeting them at the head of the stairs. "Come to Clara."

They followed her, and when they reached the room, they found to their horror and surprise that Clara was dead!

FAMILY TROUBLES.—THE HOUSE OF MOURNING.

It was too true. It was not the mere appearance of death, but the reality of the fell destroyer that the Crofton family had to mourn. She who, but a few short hours since, was in all the bloom of apparent health, and youth, and beauty was now no more.

The poor father, the sisterless sister, the astonished, indignant, and agonised brothers formed a group that was too sad to contemplate. As they gazed upon the wreck of her whom they had all loved so fondly, they could scarcely believe that death had indeed claimed her as her own; they "Thought her more beautiful than death," and could not, as they gazed tremblingly upon her still form, bring themselves to believe that she had indeed gone from them forever.

Dr. North, however, soon put all doubt upon the subject to rest by an announcement that her spirit had really fled. In vain he tried all the means that his art suggested. That mysterious and mighty something which we call life, which we miss and yet see no loss, which is so great, yet so evanescent and impalpable, was gone.

"Come away," he said, "we can do no good here now. Come away, all of you!"

"Oh, no, no," cried Sir George. "Why should we leave my child?"

"That," said the doctor, as he pointed to the corpse, "that is not your child."

The old man shuddered, and with an aspect upon his face, as if ten years of added age had at least passed over him in those few moments, he suffered them to lead him from the room. They all passed down stairs again, leaving Emma in her own chamber along with the female servants, so hastily again called up to remain with her.

When the dining-room was reached once more, Mr. Smith, who bore all the appearance of being quite thunder-struck by what had passed, spoke in the most feeling manner, saying,—

"This is truly one of the most affecting circumstances I ever remember. It is dreadful; a young girl to be at once snatched from a circle of admiring and loving friends in this manner, is too sad a picture for anyone with a heart to feel for the distresses of others to contemplate. What, sir, is your opinion," to Dr. North, "of the actual cause of death?"

"The shock to the nervous system I suspect has induced some sudden action of the heart that has been too much for vitality."

"Dreadful!"

"Alas, alas!" sobbed Sir George. "What have I done, that Heaven should thus launch against me the bolts of its bitterest vengeance? Why should I be robbed of my child? Surely there were angels enough in Heaven without taking mine from me."

"Hush, hush," said Dr. North; "you are in grief, sir, and know not what you say. These were not else the words that would fall from the lips of such a man as you are."

The bereaved father was silent, and the sons looked at him with countenances in which dismay was most strongly pictured. They seemed as if as yet they had not become fully alive to the loss they had sustained, or of what had really happened within the once happy domestic circle, of which the fairest portion was now so ruthlessly dragged from them.

"It is like a dream," said Edwin, addressing his brother Charles in a whisper. "It is much more like a dream than aught else in the world."

"It is, it is. Oh, tell me that this is not real."

"It is too real," said the doctor, "you must bow with what amount of resignation you can call to your aid to that stroke of destiny which you cannot control; you should consider that as regards her who has gone from you, that she is now no object of pity. Death is an evil to you in your loss, but it is the end of all evil and pain to her; and then again, she has but gone a few years, after all, earlier than usual, for how long shall we—ay, the best and strongest of us—be behind her?"

This was consolation of the right sort, and was sure to have its effect upon persons in the habit of conversing coolly and calmly upon general subjects, so that in a short time, the father even felt much better, and although the sons were quite convinced of their loss they no longer looked at each other with such bewildered aspects, but exhibited the rational grief of men.

Charles spoke after a time with great energy, saying,—

"It is true that we may call our reason to our aid, and contrive to rid ourselves of our grief in a great measure; but there is another duty we have to perform, and that is, to diligently inquire why and how it was, that our sister got this horrible fright, that has had the effect of hurrying her into eternity."

"Yes, brother," said Edwin, "you are right! our sister's memory shall be vindicated, and woe be to him who has brought this desolation and grief upon us."

Sir George looked from one of his sons to the other, but said nothing; he appeared to be prostrated too much by his feelings, and the doctor strongly urging him to retire to rest, he shortly did so, where we will leave him for a time, hoping that he will find the oblivion of sleep creep over him, and "Knit up the ravelled sleeve of care."

"Now," said Dr. North, "here we are four men with cool heads, and active enough judgments. For God's sake, let us try to come to some sort of conclusion about this dreadful affair. What do you say, Charles?"

"In the first place, I should recommend that the house be searched diligently, in order that we may see if any stranger is in it, or discover any means by which an entrance to the premises has been effected. We don't know but that after all some robbery may be the aim, and that the fright of our sister which has had so fatal an effect, may be the consequence merely of the appearance of a thief in her room."

"Agreed," said Edwin, "let the search of the house be our first step."

Two of the new servants were summoned with lights, and the party of four proceeded to an examination of the house, which on account of its size was not a very short process, for there were so many staircases and rooms opening the one into the other, that the hiding places were numerous enough.

At length, however, they were not only satisfied that no one was concealed on the premises, but likewise that all the fastenings were quite secure, and had been made so before the servants retired to rest. The mystery therefore was rather increased.

Had there not been the collateral evidence of Emma and the singular fact of the fastening up of the doors of the doctor's and Mr. Smith's bedchambers, no doubt the whole affair would have rested where it was, and have been put down as a remarkable death arising from the influence of a dream.

But that was out of the question—somebody had been seen, and whether that somebody was really not an inhabitant of this world was the question.

In the midst of all this, the day began to dawn.

Sir George had had no sleep, but he had done himself some good in the solitude of his own chamber. He had prayed long and earnestly, and his prayers had had the effect which they almost invariably have upon all imaginative persons, namely, of bringing him an amount of mental calmness, peace, and resignation, highly desirable in his circumstances.

The breakfast table was laid in silence by the servants, and when Sir George met his sons and his guests, he spoke calmly enough, saying to them,—

"You will no more hear from me the accents of grief or of despair. I accept what consolation I can find, but as a man, and a father I will have justice; my child has been terrified to death, and I will find who has done the deed, for let him be whom he may, he is as much her murderer as though he had plunged a dagger in her heart."

"It is so," said Mr. Smith.

"Being so, then let him beware."

Varney thought that as the father uttered these last words, he glanced in a peculiar manner at him, but he was not quite sure that such was the case.

Had he been sure, perhaps, he would have taken other steps than he did.

Little more passed during the breakfast, but when the meal was over, Sir George said,—

"Edwin, we are but dull and poor company to Mr. Smith; it will amuse him, perhaps, if you take him through the grounds, and show him the estate."

Edwin made no objection, and as the thing was put in the shape of an amusement to him, Varney could only say some civil things, and rise to go.

"I regret," he said, "to be of so much trouble."

"Not at all," said Edwin, "no trouble, sir; my own mind, God knows, wants something to distract it from too close a contemplation of its own thoughts."

"If you will accompany me in a walk over the estate, it will, perhaps, put me into better spirits."

They left the room, and when they were gone, Sir George Crofton rose and shut the door, fastening it on the inside carefully, rather to the surprise of the doctor and his son Charles, who looked at him in silence.

"Charles," he then said, "and you, doctor, I have something particular to say to you."

"What is it? What is it?"

"God forgive me if I am wrong, but I suspect our guest!"

"Mr. Smith?"

"Yes, I don't like his looks at all; now we know nothing of him but from his own report; we have searched the house right through, or at least you have, you tell me, and found nothing. He is the only stranger within our doors. Perhaps it is uncharitable to suspect him, but I cannot help it, the thought came too strongly upon me last night, as I was alone in my chamber, for me to overcome it. I have now spoken to you both frankly, and tell me what are your thoughts."

"I don't like him," said Charles.

"He is a singular man," said Dr. North.

"What—what now if he were—were—"

"Why do you hesitate, father? what would you say?"

"Go on, sir," said Dr. North, with a nod, that signified, *I know very well what you are going to say*. "Go on, sir."

"What, then, if it were really true, that there were such things, and he is a vampyre?"

Charles sprang to his feet in surprise, and said,—

"Good God! you put a frightful idea into my brain that will now never leave it. A vampyre?"

"Heaven forbid," added Sir George, "that I should say such a thing heedlessly, or that I should take upon myself to assert that such is the case; I merely throw it out as a supposition—a horrible one, I grant, but yet one that perhaps deserves some consideration."

"Get rid of him," said Dr. North.

"It is difficult after telling him he was welcome to stay, to now tell him that we want him to go. I would much prefer watching him closely, and endeavouring by such means, either to confirm or to do away entirely with my suppositions. And you can take an opportunity of speaking to Edwin upon the subject, quietly and carefully."

"I will, father."

"Then we can be all upon the alert; but above all things I charge you say nothing to Emma of the really terrific idea. Only I should say that tonight it is in the direction of her chamber that I would wish to keep the closest watch."

"And that, too, without her knowing it," said the doctor. "If she is aware of anything of the sort, there is no knowing what tricks her imagination might play her, and now, Sir George, I must say that I take the greatest interest in the matter, and will with your permission remain here until I am sent for. Poor Ringwood still remains insensible, and I take it that under the circumstances that it is really a mercy, for what a sad communication has to be made to him, when he does recover sufficiently to hear it."

"Sad, indeed."

It was now finally agreed among them that there was to be no variation whatever in their conduct towards Mr. Smith, but that after they had taken leave of him for the night, and had all gone to bed, they should each glide out of his chamber, and wait at the extreme end of the [corridor] in silence, to mark if anything should happen.

This was duly announced to Edwin, who with a shudder announced that he had his suspicions, too, of Mr. Smith, so he of course came into the scheme at once; and now they waited rather anxiously for the night to come again.

THE NIGHT WATCH.—THE SURPRISE.—THE CHASE.

Everything was now said and done that could induce a feeling in the mind of Varney, that he was perfectly welcome at the Grange, and to dispel the least idea of anything in the shape of supposition that he might have had, that he was suspected, although he had not himself by word or look betrayed such a feeling.

The day to all parties seemed a frightfully long one. Ringwood remained in the same state of unconsciousness as he had been in the day previous, and the only circumstance that served to break the monotony of the time, was the arrival of some of his friends to see him.

It is not essential to our story that we should take up space in detailing what they said and what they did; suffice it that all the grief was exhibited that was to be expected, and that finally they left the Grange with a conviction that the wounded man was in as kind hands as they could possibly wish him, and everything would be done, that kindness and skill could suggest, to recover him and preserve his life.

Probably the dreadful catastrophe that had happened in the family of the Croftons had in effect in reconciling the Ringwoods to the lesser calamity, for Dr. North gave them strong hopes of his ultimate recovery.

And so the time passed on, until the dim shadows of the evening began to creep over the landscape, and the distant trees imperceptibly mingled together in a chaotic mass. The song of the birds was over—the herds and flocks had sought their shelter for the night, and a solemn and beautiful stillness was upon the face of nature.

Assembled once more in the dining-room of the Grange, were the

Croftons—but not Emma, she was in her chamber—the doctor, and Mr. Smith.

Varney had exerted himself much to be entertaining, and yet not obtrusively so, as under the calamitous and extraordinary circumstances in which the family was placed, that would have been bad taste; but he led the conversation into the most interesting channels, and he charmed those who listened to him, in spite of themselves.

Dr. North was peculiarly pleased with so scientific a companion, and one who had travelled so much, for Varney spoke of almost every portion of the globe as familiar to him.

In this kind of way, the evening sped on, and more than once, as Varney was giving some eloquent and comprehensive description of some natural phenomenon that he had witnessed in some other clime, not only were the suspicions entertained against him forgotten, but even the grief of the family faded away for a brief space before the charm of his discourse.

At length the time for rest came.

Sir George rose, and bowing to Varney, said,—

"Do not let our example influence you, sir. We retire now."

"I shall be glad to do so," said Varney, "likewise; last night was a disturbed as well as a melancholy one for all in this house."

"It was indeed."

In another five minutes, the dining room was vacant, and all that could be heard in the house was the noise of putting up extra bars, and shooting into their places, long unused bolts in order that it should be quite beyond all doubt that no one could get into the premises.

After that, all was still.

The moon was in her last quarter now, but only at the commencement of it, so if the night proved not to be cloudy, it would be rather a brilliant one, which might, or might not be of service to those who were going to watch in the corridor the proceedings of Mr. Smith.

An hour elapsed before there was any movement whatever, and then it was Dr. North who first, with great care, emerged from his room.

He had drawn on his stockings over his shoes, so that his footsteps might not be heard, and he took his station in a dark corner by the large window we have before spoken of as lighting the corridor.

The moon was up, but it only shone in obliquely at the window, so that one side of the corridor was enveloped in the deepest gloom, while on the other the pale rays fell.

A few minutes more, for half-past eleven was the hour on which they had all agreed, and Sir George, with Edwin and Charles joined the doctor, who merely nodded to them, as they could faintly see him.

Sir George spoke in a very faint whisper, saying,—

"We are well armed."

"Good," replied the doctor, in a similar cautious tone, "but let me implore you to be careful how you use your arms. Do nothing hastily I beg of you; you don't know what cause of regret the imprudence of a moment may give rise to."

"Depend upon us, we will be very careful indeed."

"That is right."

"We had better not talk," said Charles, "these corridors carry sound sometimes too well; if we are to do any good, it must be by preserving the profoundest silence."

This advice was too practical and evidently good to be neglected, and consequently they were all as still as they could be, and stood like so many statues for the next half hour.

They heard a clock that hung in the hall below strike the hour of twelve, and when the reverberations of sound were over, a stillness even more profound than before seemed to pervade the whole house. The half hour they had waited in such silence appeared to them to be of four times the usual length, and they were glad to hear twelve strike.

Still they said nothing, for if silence before twelve o'clock was a thing to be desired, it was much more so after that hour, for it was then that the alarm of the preceding evening had taken place. Their watchfulness, and their anxiety momentarily increased.

The old clock in the hall chimed the quarter past twelve, and yet all was as still as the grave; not the smallest sound disturbed the repose of the house.

The moon had shifted round a little, so that the gloom of the corridor was not so complete as it had been, and Dr. North was aware that in another hour the spot where they all stood would be visited by some rays which would render their concealment out of the question.

But as yet all was right, and there was no need to shift their position in the least.

Suddenly Sir George Crofton laid his hand upon the arm of the doctor, and an exclamation involuntarily escaped him, but not in a loud tone.

"Hush, for God's sake," whispered the doctor.

They had all heard a slight noise, like the cautious opening of a door. They looked eagerly in the direction from whence it came, and to their surprise they found it proceed from the chamber of the dead!

Yes, the door of the room in which lay the corpse of Clara slowly opened.

"God of Heaven!" said Sir George.

"Hush—hush," again whispered the doctor, and he held him by the arm compulsively.

All was still. The door creaked upon its hinges a little, that was all.

A quarter of an hour passed, and then Sir George was about to say something, when he started as if a shock of electricity had been applied to him, for the door of Varney's room was swung wide open, and he appeared, fully dressed.

All the doors opening from the corridor creaked unless they were flung open smartly and quickly, and there could be no doubt but that Varney knew this, and hence the apparent precipitancy of his appearance.

There he stood in the moonlight, close by the threshold of his room, gazing about him. He bent himself into an attitude of intense listening, and remained in it for some time, and then he with slow sliding steps made his way towards the door of Emma's room.

His hand was actually upon the lock, when Sir George, who could stand the scene no longer, levelled a pistol he had taken from his pocket, and without giving any intimation to those who were with him of what he was going to do, he pulled the trigger.

The pistol only flashed without being fully discharged.

"How imprudent," said the doctor. "You have done it now! Follow me!"

He rushed forward, but he was too late, Varney had taken the alarm, and in a moment he regained his own room and fastened it securely on the inside.

"We must have him," cried Charles. "He cannot escape from that room. There is no other door, and the window is a good thirty feet from the garden below. Alarm the servants, we will soon open his door. It can't be very secure, for the lock was broken last night."

As he spoke, Charles made a vigorous effort to open the door, but it resisted as if it had been a part of the solid wall, while within the chamber all was perfectly still, as if Mr. Smith had quite satisfied himself by shutting out his assailants, and meant to take no further notice of them.

"This is strange," said the doctor, "but we shall soon find out what he means by it. The door must be forced as quickly as possible."

Edwin ran down stairs by his father's orders to arouse some of the men servants, besides getting some weapon or tool by the assistance of which the door might be forced, and he soon returned with several of the men, and one armed with the identical crow-bar that had been used with such effect on the preceding evening. They brought lights with them too, so that the capture of Mr. Smith appeared to be no longer a matter of doubt with such a force opposed to him.

"Now," cried Sir George, "do not mind what mischief you do, my men, so that you break open the door of that room, and quickly too."

People somehow are always glad to be engaged in anything that has a destructive look about it, and when the servants heard that they might break away at the door as much as they liked, they set about it with a vengeance that promised soon to succeed in the object.

The door yielded with a crash.

"Come on, come on. Yield yourself," cried Sir George, and he rushed into the room followed by his sons and by Dr. North.

There was no Mr. Smith there.

"Escaped," said Dr. North.

"Impossible,—impossible! and yet this open window. He must be lying dashed to pieces below, for no one could with safety drop or jump such a height. Run round to the garden some of you, at once."

"Stop," said Charles. "There is no occasion. He has had ample time to escape. Look here."

Charles pointed out the end of a thick rope, firmly fastened to the ledge of the window, and by which it was quite clear any one could safely descend into the garden, it only requiring a little nerve to do so with perfect ease.

"This has all been prepared," said Dr. North.

"Still," cried Sir George, "I will not give the affair up. Mind I offer a reward of twenty guineas to any one of my household who succeeds in catching Mr. Smith."

"Lor, sir! what has he done?" said a groom.

"Never you mind what he has done. Bring him in, and you shall have the reward."

"Very good, sir. Come on, Dick, and you Harry; let's all go, and you know it will be all the pleasanter to share the reward among us. Come on."

Thus stimulated by their companion, the servants ran out of the house into the moonlit park in search of Varney the Vampyre.

THE FUNERAL.—A STRANGE INCIDENT.

It was all very well for Sir George Crofton to offer his twenty guineas for the taking of Mr. Smith, and nothing could be more legitimate than his servants making active exertions to endeavour to earn that amount of money, but the really succeeding in doing so was quite another thing.

To be sure they went out into the park, and did the best to catch him, and being well acquainted with every turn and every pathway within it, they considered they had a fair chance of succeeding, but after their pains they were at length obliged to give up the affair as a bad job, after an hour or two's most active search.

While they were away though, there was something that occurred at the Grange which gave a great additional shock to Sir George and his sons. It will not fail to be remembered that the first door they saw move while they were keeping watch and ward in the moonlit gallery was the door of the chamber in which lay the corpse of Clara, who had met with so melancholy an end.

This circumstance recurred to them all with fearful force when they felt convinced that the now more suspected Mr. Smith had really and truly made his escape.

Upon proceeding to that room of the dead, Dr. North being first, they found some difficulty in opening the door, but upon using force they succeeded, when to their absolute horror they saw that the dead body was lying upon the floor close to the door, and that it had been the obstruction to moving it.

Dr. North would fain have spared the feelings of Sir George this affecting sight, but the baronet was so close behind him that he could not do so.

"Oh, God!" cried the father, "my child, my child."

"Take your father away, boys, for heaven's sake," said Dr. North to the two young men; "this is no sight for him to see."

It appeared too as if it was no sight for anyone to see unmoved, for both Charles and Edwin stood like statues gazing at it, and for a time incapable of motion.

"My sister—is it indeed my sister?" said Charles.

The doctor fairly closed the door upon them all, and turned them so out of the room. Then he having professionally lost all dread of the dead, lifted the body upon the bed again, and disposed of it properly, after which, without saying a word, he walked down to the dining-room.

"Tell me, tell me," said Sir George "what does all this mean?"

"Do not ask me," replied Dr. North, "I cannot tell you; I confess I do not know what advice to give you, or indeed what to say to you."

The old man rested his head upon his hands, and wept bitterly, while his two sons sat looking at each other perfectly aghast, and unable to think anything of a rational import concerning the most mysterious proceedings that had taken place.

* * * *

Let our readers then suppose that a week has passed away, and that the morning has arrived when the body of Clara is to be placed in a vault appropriated as the resting place of the Croftons, beneath the church that was close at hand.

During that time nothing whatever had been heard of Mr. Smith. He seemed to have completely disappeared from the neighbourhood as well as from the Grange-house.

Fortunately, although Sir George had offered twenty guineas for the apprehension of Mr. Smith to his servants, he had said nothing of the cause why he offered such a reward, and the neighbourhood was left to its own conjectures upon the subject. Those conjectures were of course sufficiently numerous, but it was quite agreed between Sir George, Doctor North, and the two sons that nothing more should be said upon the subject.

They of course did not wish "To fill the ear of idle curiosity" with such a tale as they might tell, but had a thousand reasons, each good and substantial of its kind, for withholding.

Young Ringwood was sufficiently recovered to be about, and to have told him the story that widowed his heart. He fell into a profound melancholy which nothing could alleviate, and as his recovery went on, he asked permission to remain at the Grange.

Sir George, and indeed all the Crofton family, gladly pressed him to remain with them as long as he would do so, for it was some alleviation of their own distress to have him about them.

He begged permission to be present at the funeral, and it is of that funeral we have now to speak, for it took place on that day of the week on which the vampyre had first taken up his dreadful residence at the old Grange-house, where all before had been so happy.

The church, as we have remarked, was not very distant, and a mournful procession it was, consisting of the funeral equipages, followed by Sir George Crofton's carriage, that at twelve o'clock in the day started to place the youngest and the fairest of the name of Crofton that had ever reposed in the family vault.

The whole neighbourhood was in a state of commotion, and by the time the funeral cortege reached the churchyard, there was not a person capable of being out, for some miles around, that was not congregated about the spot. The old church bell tolled a melancholy welcome to the procession, and the clergyman met the corpse at the entrance of the graveyard, and preceded it to the church, where it was placed by the altar while he made an impressive prayer.

This brief ceremony over, the coffin was carried to the part of one of the aisles, where upon the removal of a large stone slab, the resting-place of the Croftons was visible.

"I have not looked upon these stone steps," said Sir George, "since my poor wife went down there in the sleep of death."

"Compose yourself," whispered Dr. North, who was present. "You ought not, sir, to have been present at such a scene as this."

"Nay, it surely was my duty to follow my own child to her last resting-place."

The body was lowered into the vault, and the funeral service was read impressively over the cold and still remains of Clara.

"All is over," said the doctor.

"Yes," faltered Sir George; "all is over. Farewell, my dear child, but not a long farewell to thee; this blow has nearly stricken me into the grave."

Leaning on the arm of his son Charles, who as well as Edwin was deeply affected, the old man now allowed himself to be led from the church. He met at the door Will Stephens, the sexton, who seemed desirous of speaking to him.

"What is it, Will?"

"Will your honour have some fresh sawdust put down in the vault. It wants it, Sir George; there ain't been any put in for many a long day."

"Very well. It will be ready for me when I go. It won't be long before the vault is again opened."

"Oh, do not say that, father," said Edwin. "Do not leave us; think that if you have lost one child who loved you, you have others who ought to be as dear to you."

"That's right, Edwin," said the doctor.

Sir George made no distinct reply to this, but he pressed the hand of his son, and looked kindly upon him, to signify that he felt the full justice of what he had just said, so they had hopes that time would soon produce its usual effects upon that feeling which of all others is, while it lasts, the most poignant, at the same time that it is the most evanescent—grief for the dead.

And well it is that it should be so, otherwise we should be a world of weepers and mourners, for who is there that has not felt the pang of losing some fond heart in which we have garnered up the best affections of human nature.

Emma since her sister's death had been terribly broken down in spirit, and when they all got home to the Grange, they found her looking so ill, that the old baronet took Dr. North on one side, and said to him in tones expressive of the deepest anguish,—

"Am I to lose both my girls?"

"Oh no—no; certainly not," was the decided reply. "Why, my old friend, you used to be a man of great moral courage. Where has it all gone to now?"

"It is in the grave of my child."

"Come, come, you must for your own sake, as well as for the sake of others, who are near and dear to you, rouse yourself from this state of mental torpor, as I may call it. You can do so, and it is worthy of you to make the effort. Only think what would have been your situation if you had had but one child, and that had been snatched away from you; but you have yet three to comfort you, and yet you talk despairingly, as if every tie that bound you to the world had been suddenly burst asunder."

After this Sir George Crofton was almost ashamed to make such an exhibition of his grief, and whatever his thoughts were he kept them to himself, as well as exercising a much greater control over his voice, and the external expression of the feelings, which were still busy at his heart.

The despondency of Ringwood was great. He could not help fancy that if he had not met with the unlucky accident in the ravine, Clara would have been saved, and in some obscure way to his mind, the circumstances seemed to be connected together. He could not account either for the loss of her miniature, which he had been in the habit of wearing but which he missed upon his convalescence, so that he was irresistibly led to the conclusion that some unfriendly hands had been about him during his insensibility.

So highly did he prize the miniature, that he offered a sum of money, exceeding its intrinsic value by twenty times, for its recovery and pledged himself to make no inquiry as to how it came into the possession of the party who should restore it to him; but for all that it was not forthcoming.

The reader of this narrative knows very well in whose possession it was. Varney the Vampyre had possessed himself of it in the ravine, when he saw the young bridegroom lying insensible at his feet, and he kept it, although why he did so does not as yet appear, for surely the sight of it could only remind him of one of his victims; but then Varney had other thoughts and feelings than he used to have.

Alas, what a thousand pities it was that the ocean had presented him to the two brothers? Why did he not sink—why did not some wave hide him from their observation? What misery would have been spared to them, and to all dear to them. And what misery would have been spared to the wretched Varney himself!

It is true that he had given expression to sentiments, and declared intentions which would go far to prove that he had for ever given up and got rid of all human feelings and influences, but has he really so got rid of such feelings? It is a question which time alone can answer.

We shall soon see in his now very short career whether he is most to suffer or to inflict suffering, and what will be the result of his new principles of action—those principles which he had in the despair and the agony of his heart painted to himself as the main springs of a combined existence, he had with such vain and such fruitless perseverance strove to rid himself of. It was sad—very sad, indeed, that such a being could not die when he chose, the poor privilege of all.

[NOTE: in the original penny dreadful, the next chapter, which is not included in this edition, is entirely about the sexton, Will Stephens, preparing to visit the Crofton vault at night...unaware that a mysterious figure has broken into the family resting place...Then...]

WILL STEPHENS' VISIT TO THE FAMILY VAULT WITH THE SAW-DUST, AND WHAT HE SAW THERE.

Will Stephens waited at the ale-house much longer than he intended. To be sure the rain cleared off, but what of that? It was not a circumstance that made the ale anything worse, and so he waited to drink it with a gusto that improved each glass amazingly, and then some of those who were present—jolly topers like himself—began to laugh and to say,—

"Ah, Will, you may as well poke that bag of sawdust into some corner; you won't do anything with it tonight, old fellow, we know."

Now, some people get good-tempered and complying when they have had the drop too much, and others again, get particularly obstinate and contradictory.

Will, of the two, certainly had more pretensions to belong to the latter class than the former, so when he heard such a prophecy concerning his movements and knew it was all an assumption based upon the ale he had drank, he felt indignant.

"Not go!" he cried. "Not go. You may fancy if you please that I will not go, but you will find yourselves mistaken, I will go."

"What, so late."

"What's the odds to me. Any of you now would be frightened out of your lives to set foot in the old church at such a time as this, I know; but I'm none of the timid sort, I'm afraid of nobody living, and it ain't likely that I am now going to be afraid of anybody dead."

"Then you really will go."

The only reply that he made to this was to finish off the glass of ale that was before him, shouldering the bag of sawdust, and sally out into the open air. Will Stephens felt highly indignant and touchy about his honour, and as he had said he would go and then somebody chose to imply a doubt still, he was grievously offended.

When he got out, he found that the night was anything but an inviting one. He was still sober enough to see that, and to feel that although the heavy rain had ceased, there was a little disagreeable misty sort of vapour in the air.

He staggered at the first turning he came to, for rather an uncomfortable gust of wind blew in his face, carrying along with it such a shower of small cold rain that he was, or fancied himself to be, wet through in a moment.

"Pleasant, this," thought Will, "but I won't go back to be laughed at." As for the saw-dust he was carrying, its weight was by no means any great consideration for it was just as light as it could be.

"No, I won't go back—back indeed, not I; they would make me stand a pot of ale to a certainly if I were to go back, and besides it would be all over the parish tomorrow that Will Stephens after he got half way to the church was afraid to go any further. Confound the small rain, it pricks like pins and needles."

Nothing is more sobering than rain, and as he, Will, gradually got saturated with the small aqueous particles, the effect of the strong ale as gradually wore off, until by the time the dim, dusky outline of the church rose before him he was almost as sober as need be.

"Ah," he said, "here I am at last at any rate. I do hate this sort of rain, you can hardly make up your mind that it is raining at all, and yet somehow you get soaked before you know where you are. It's just like going through a damp cloud, that it is, and yet somehow or another, I don't much mind it; I'm earning a guinea easy enough. Ha, ha!"

This was by no means an unpleasant reflection.

"Yes," he added, "I am earning a guinea easily enough that's quite clear, but then it's not everybody who would, for a guinea, go into anybody's family vault at such a time. By-the-by, I wonder now what the time is exactly."

Scarcely had Will spoken those words when the old church-clock struck twelve.

It was a very serious, deliberate sort of clock that, and it took a long time to strike twelve, and Will listened with the greatest attention with the hope of persuading himself that it was only eleven, but there could be no mistake, twelve it was.

"Really," he said, "is it so late, well, I didn't think—"

Will stood within the porch of the church door, and he gave a sort of shiver, and then, with the bag of sawdust in his hand, he stopped to listen attentively, for he thought he heard a slight sound.

"What was that, eh? what—I thought, nay, I am sure I heard something; it's very odd—very odd indeed."

As if then to afford Will an excuse for resolving the sound to something else, the wind at this moment came in such a sudden gale round the ancient edifice, that he quite congratulated himself he was within the porch and protected from its fury; and, besides, it to his mind was a sufficing explanation of the noise he had heard.

"Some of the old doors," he muttered, "rattled by the wind, that's all. Now I suppose we shall have a clear night after all the rain. Such a gale will soon blow off the damp clouds."

Will was right. The gale, for a gale it was, blew from the north, and away went the rain clouds as if a curtain had been drawn aside by some invisible hand.

After some rummaging Will found in his pocket the key of the church; it was not the key of the principal door, but of a smaller side entrance, at which the officials, who required at all times free ingress and egress, made application. The little arched door creaked upon its hinges and then Will stood in a sort of vestibule, for another door that was never fast had to be opened before he could be fairly said to be within the church.

This second door was covered with green baize, and could be opened and shut very noiselessly, indeed. Will Stephens stood in the vestibule until he had got a small lantern out of one pocket, and some matches from another. Then, in a few moments he had a light, and once again shouldering the bag of sawdust, he pushed open the inner door, and stood in the church.

It might have been fancy—nay, he felt certain, it could be nothing else—but he thought as he opened the door that a faint sort of sigh came upon his ears.

Fancy or not, though, it was an uncomfortable thing at such an hour, and in such a place too, and he had never before heard anything of the sort upon his visits to the church, and he had visited it at all hours, many and many a time.

"It's odd," he said, "it's uncommonly odd, I never felt so uncomfortable in the church before. I—I never used to mind coming to it in the middle of the night. But now, I—eh?—what was that?" Again an odd sort of noise came upon his ears, and he dropped the bag of sawdust.

All was still again, save the regular roar of wind, as it swept round the sacred building, and although Will Stephens stood for nearly ten minutes in an attitude of listening, he heard nothing to augment his terrors. But let an impulse once be given to fear, and it will go on accumulating material from every trivial circumstance. The courage of the sexton was broken down, and there was no knowing, now, what tricks his awakened imagination might play him.

He began to wish he had not come, and from that wish, to think that he might as well go back, only shame forbade him, for it would be easily known on the morrow, that he had not placed the sawdust in the vault, and lastly, he began to think that someone might be playing him a trick.

This last supposition, probably, had more effect in raising his courage than any preceding one. Indignation took possession of him, and he no longer thought of retreating. He went forward at once, and fell over the bag of sawdust.

"Murder!" shouted Will.

The moment he did so, he recollected what it was that had occasioned his fall, and being ashamed of himself he called out impulsively, as if somebody was there to hear him,—

"No—no, it's only the sawdust. No—no."

He rose to his feet again, heartily ashamed of his own fears. Luckily, his lantern had not been broken or extinguished in his fall, and now, without another word, he prepared himself to execute the work he came to do, and leave the church to its repose as quickly as possible.

At one end of the church, the southern end, there was a large window, which might be said to light the whole of the interior, for the little windows at the sides were more ornamental than useful, being nothing but lattices; and across this window was drawn a heavy cloth curtain, so that when the sun shone too brightly upon the congregation on a summer's day, it could be wholly or partially excluded upon a sign from the clergyman.

The curtain was drawn close on the window now, at night, and Will just glanced up to it, as he walked on towards the aisle where the opening to the family vault of the Croftons was situated.

"All's right," he said, "what a fool I have been, to be sure. Upon my word I might have saved frightening myself all night, and some people would too, but that's not my way of doing business. So here we are, all right. The door on one side, so that I have just room enough to go down into the vault. Oh! when one comes to think of it, it was rather a melancholy thing, the death of such a young girl as she was, going to be married too. Well, that's the way the world goes."

The stone steps leading down to the vault were rather steep, and Will threw down the bag of sawdust first, in preference to carrying it, and then with his lantern in his hand, he commenced his own descent.

"That'll do," said Will, when he felt his feet upon the soft old sawdust that was on the floor of the vault. "That'll do—now for it, I shall soon have this job settled, and then I'll get home no faster than I can."

Some how or another, he felt very much inclined to talk; the sound of his own voice, conversing, as he might be said to be, with himself, gave him a sort of courage, and made the place not appear to be altogether so desperately lonely as it really was.

That, no doubt, was the feeling that brought forth so many indifferent remarks from Will Stephens. He held up his light to look round him, and turned gradually upon his heels as he did so.

The light shook in his hand. The hair almost stood on end on his head—his teeth chattered, and he tried to speak in vain, as he saw lying at his feet, a coffin lid.

It was new. The nails that held the blue cloth upon it, were bright, and fast—the plate shone like silver. Yes, it was the lid of the coffin of Miss Clara Crofton; but how came it off—unsecured, and lying upon the floor of the vault, while the coffin was in its proper niche?

"Gracious goodness!" gasped Will at length. "What does this mean?"

The question was easy to ask, but most difficult to answer, and he stood trembling and turning over in his mind all the most frightful explanations of what he saw, that could occur to anyone.

"Has she been buried alive? Have the body snatchers been after her? How is it—what—what has happened?"

Then it occurred to Will, that it would be just as well to look into the coffin, and see if it was tenantless or not. If it were, he thought he should know what to think, for if the dead body was there, then he could only conclude that she had been buried alive, and had had just strength enough to force open the coffin, and cast the lid of it on the floor of the vault, and then to die in that horrible place. It required almost more courage than Will could muster, to go and look into the coffin, for now that his usual indifference was completely broken down, he was as timid as any stranger to graves and vaults would have been.

But curiosity is, after all, a most exciting passion, and that lent him power.

"Yes," he said, "I—I will look in the coffin, I shall have but a poor tale to tell to Sir George Crofton, if I do not look in the coffin. I—I—have nothing to be afraid of."

He advanced with trembling steps, the light shaking in his hands as he did so. He reached the coffin, and with eyes unusually wide he looked in: it was empty.

THE APPARITION IN THE CHURCH. —WILL STEPHENS' SWOON. —THE MORNING.

For some minutes, Will Stephens continued to gaze in the empty coffin, as if there was something peculiarly fascinating in it, and most attractive, and yet nothing was in it, no vestige even of the vestments of the dead. If Clara Crofton had herself risen, and left the vault, it was quite clear she had taken with her the apparel of the grave.

Will had thought that if he found the coffin empty, all his fears would vanish, and that he should be able to come at once to the conclusion, that she had become the prey of resurrectionists. But new ideas, as he gazed at that abandoned receptacle of the dead, began to creep across him.

"I—I—don't know," he muttered, "but she may in a ghost-like kind of way be going about. I don't know whether ghosts is corpses or not. I—I wish I was out of this."

The idea of spreading the sawdust in the vault now completely left him; all he thought of was to get away, and the dread that Clara

Crofton was, perhaps, hiding somewhere, and might come suddenly out upon him with a yell, got so firm a hold of him, that several times he thought he should faint with excess of terror.

"That would be too horrible," he said, "I am sure I should go mad—mad—mad—mad."

He retreated backward to the stairs, for the coffin, empty though it was, held his gaze with a strange kind of fascinating power. He thought that if he turned round something would be sure to lay hold of him. It was a most horrifying and distressing idea that, and yet he could not conquer it.

Of course, he must turn round, it would be an awkward thing to attempt ascending the staircase short as it was, backward, so he felt the necessity of turning his back upon the vault.

"I—I will do so," he thought, "and then make such a rush up the steps, that I shall be in the church in a moment, I—I can surely do that, and—and after all it's nothing really to be afraid of—it's only a matter of imagination, after all! oh, yes, that's all, I—I will do that."

He put this notable scheme into execution by turning suddenly round and making a dash at the stairs, but as people generally do things badly when they do them in a hurry, he stumbled when about half-way and felt himself at the mercy of the whole of the supernatural world.

"Have mercy on me," he cried, "I am going. Have mercy on me."

He had struck the lantern so hard against the stone stairs that he had broken it into fragments, and now all was intense darkness around him.

He gave himself up for lost.

He lay, expecting each moment to feel some dead bony fingers clutching him, and he only groaned, thinking that surely now his last hour was come; and it is a wonder that his fancy, excited as it was, did not conjure up to him the very effect he dreaded, but it did not do so, strange to say, and he lay for full five minutes without anything occurring to add to his terrors.

Then he began gradually to recover.

"If—if," he gasped, "I could but reach the church, I—I think I should be safe. Yes, I should surely be safe in the body of the church. Have mercy on me, good ghosts; I never harmed any of you, I—I respect you very much, indeed I do. Let me go, and—I'll never say a light word of any of you again, no, never, if I were to live for a thousand years."

As he uttered these words, he crawled up the remaining stairs, and to his great satisfaction, made his way fairly into the church.

But then a new surprise, if it was not exactly a new fright, perhaps it was something of both, awaited him.

The curtain that had been, as he had observed when he was walking down the aisle, closely drawn across the large south window was now drawn on one side, so that a large portion of that window was exposed, and the north wind having chased away by this time entirely the damp clouds, the moon was sailing in a cloudless sky, and sending into the old church a glorious flood of light.

"What a change," said Will Stephens.

It was indeed a change; the church was as light as day, save in some places where shadows fell, and they, in contrast to the silvery lightness of the moonbeams, were of a jetty blackness.

But still, let the moon shine ever so brightly, there is not that distinctness and freshness of outline produced as in the direct daylight. A strange kind of hazy vapour seems to float between the eye and all objects—an indistinctness and mysteriousness of aspect, which belongs not to the sun's unreflected rays. Thus it was, that although the church was illuminated by the moon, it had a singular aspect, and would scarcely have been recognised by anyone who had only seen it by the mild searching light of day.

But of course Will Stephens the sexton knew it well, and as he wiped the perspiration from his face, he said,—

"What a relief to get out of that vault and find now that the night has turned out so fair and beautiful. I—I begin to think I have frightened myself more than I need have done—but it was that coffin-lid that did the business; I wasn't my own man after that. But now that I have got out of the vault, I feel quite different—oh, quite another thing."

Suddenly, then, it occurred to him, that the curtain had been close on the window, when he came into the church, and following upon that thought came another, namely, that it could not very well remove itself from before the casement, and that consequently some hands, mortal or ghostly, must have done that part of the business.

Here there was ample food again for all his fears, and Will Stephens almost on the instant relapsed into his former trembling and nerveless state.

"What shall I do?" he said; "It ain't all over yet. What will become of me? There's something horrid going to happen, I feel certain, and that curtain has only been drawn aside to let the moonlight come in for me to see it."

With a painful expectation of his eyes being blasted by some horrible sight, he glared round him, but he saw nothing, although the dense little mass of pews before him might have hidden many a horror.

His next movement was to turn his eyes to the gallery, and all round it he carried them until he came to the window again, but he saw nothing.

"Who knows," he muttered, "who knows after all, but that the wind, in some odd sort of way, may have blown the curtain on one side. I—I wish I had the courage to go up to the gallery, and see, but I—I don't think I should like to do that."

He hesitated. He knew that it would sound well on the morrow for him to be able to say that he went up, and yet it was rather a fearful thing.

"A—hem!" he said at length, "Is anyone here?"

As he made this inquiry, he took care to keep himself ready to make a dart out at the door into the churchyard, but as there was no response to it, he was a little encouraged. The gallery staircase was close to where he stood, and after the not unnatural hesitation of a few moments more, he approached them, and began slowly to ascend.

Nothing interrupted him, all was profoundly still, and at length he did reach the south window, and he found that the curtain was most deliberately drawn on one side, and that the window was fast, so that no vagary of the wind could have accomplished the purpose.

"Now I'll go—I'll go at once," he said, "I can't stand this any longer! I'll go and alarm the village—I'll—I'll make a disturbance of some sort."

"Awake!" said a deep, hollow voice.

Will sunk upon his knees with a groan, and mechanically his eyes wandered to the direction from whence the sound came, and he saw in a pew just beneath him, and on which the moonlight now fell brightly, a human form.

It was lying in a strange huddled up position in the pew, and a glance showed the experienced eyes of the sexton that it was arrayed in the vestments of the dead.

He tried to speak—he tried to scream—he tried to pray, but all was in vain. Intense terror froze up every faculty of his body, and he could only kneel there with his face resting upon the front of the gallery, and glare with aching eyes, that would not close for a moment, upon the scene below.

"Awake!" said a deep, strange voice again, "Awake."

It was quite clear that that voice did not come from the figure in the pew, but from someone close at hand. The sexton soon saw another form.

In the adjoining pew, standing upright as a statue, with one hand pointing upwards to the window, where came in the moonlight, was a tall figure, enveloped in a cloak. It was from the lips of that figure, that the sound came, so deeply, and so solemnly.

"Sister," it said, "be one of us—let the cold chaste moonbeams endow thee with your new, and strange, and horrible existence! Be one of us. Be one of us! Hours must yet elapse, ere the faint flash of morning will kill the moonbeams. There is time, sister. Awake, be one of us."

There was a passing cloud that swept for an instant over the face of the moon obscuring its radiance, and the figure let its arm fall to its side. But when the silvery beams streamed into the church, it again pointed to the window.

"'Tis done. She moves," he said. "I have fulfilled my mission. Ha! ha! ha!"

The laugh was so terrific and unmirthful that it froze the very blood in the veins of Will, and he thought he was surely at that moment going mad.

But still he did not close his eyes, still he moved not from the position which he had first assumed when the horrible noise met his ears.

"'Tis done," said the figure, and the arm that had been outstretched was let fall to his side.

Will Stephens looked in the pew, where he had seen what appeared to be a corpse. It had altered its position. He saw it move and wave its arms about strangely and deep sighs came from its lips. It was a dreadful sight to see, but at length it rose up in the grave clothes, and moved to the door of the pew.

The figure in the adjoining pew opened the door and stood on one side, and the revivified corpse passed out.

Slowly and solemnly it passed down the aisle. It reached the door at which Will Stephens had entered, and then it passed away from his sight. The tall figure followed closely, and Will Stephens was alone in the church.

What could he do? How could he give a sufficient alarm? Would the two horrible personages return or not? Alas! poor Will Stephens, never was an unhappy mortal sexton in such frightful tribulation before. He knelt and shook like an aspen. At length a lucky thought entered his head.

"The bell. The bell," he cried, all at once finding his voice. "To the bell."

He sprung to his feet, for what he was now about to do, did not involve the necessity of going down again into the body of the church. here was a narrow staircase at the corner of the gallery, leading to the belfry. It was up that staircase that Will now struggled and tore.

[NOTE: In the original penny dreadful, a chapter, not included in this edition, shows various people in town hearing, but ignoring, the unexpected sound of the church bells. Then…]

THE CLERGYMAN'S VISIT TO THE VAULT. — RESCUE OF THE SEXTON.

"What the devil! sounds!" Yes; that was what the parson said. With all due respect for his cloth, we cannot help recording the fact that the words at the commencement of this chapter were precisely those that came from the lips of the reverend gentleman upon the occasion of the sudden and rather alarming irruption of the beadle and the bell-ringer into his breakfast parlour at the parsonage.

"We beg your pardon, sir," said the beadle, "but—"

"Yes, sir, we beg your pardon," add the bell-ringer, "but—"

"What?" cried the parson, as he looked at the remains of his breakfast lying upon the hearth-rug in most admired disorder at his feet.

"The bell, sir—the church—the gallery—a groan—a ghost—a lot of ghosts."

Such were the incoherent words that came, thick as hail, from the beadle and the bell-ringer. In vain the clergyman strove to get to the rights of the story. He was compelled to wait until they were both very nearly tired out, and then he said,—

"Very well, I don't understand, so you may both go away again."

"But, sir—"

"But, sir—"

"If one of you will speak while the other listens I will attend, and not otherwise. This is Sunday morning, and I neither can, nor will waste any more time upon you."

Nothing is so terrible to a professed storyteller, and the beadle was something of that class, as to tell him you won't listen to him, so Mr.

Dorey at once begged that Wiggins would either allow him to tell what had happened, or tell it properly himself. Mr. Wiggins gave way, and the beadle as diffusely as possible told the tale of the bell tolling, and the visit to the church, with the awful adventure that there occurred.

"What do you think of it, sir?" he concluded by asking.

"I have no opinion formed as yet," replied the clergyman, "but I will step down to the church now, and see."

"You'll take plenty o' people with you, sir."

"Oh dear no, I shall go alone. I don't gather from what you have said that there is any danger. Your own fears, too, I am inclined to think, have much exaggerated the whole affair. I dare say it will turn out, as most of such alarms usually do, some very simple affair indeed."

The parson took his hat, and walked away to the church as coolly as possible, leaving Mr. Dorey and Mr. Wiggins to stare at each other, and to wonder at a temerity they could not have thought it possible for any human being to have practised.

But the clergyman was supported by a power of which they knew little—the power of knowledge, which enabled him at once in his own mind to divide the probable from the impossible, and therefore was it that he walked down to the church fully prepared to hear from somebody a very natural explanation of the mysterious bell-ringing in the night, which was the only circumstance that made him think that there was anything to explain, for he had heard that himself.

When he reached the sacred building, he found the door open, as the beadle and the bell-ringer had left it, and the moment he got into the body of the church, he heard a voice say,—

"Help! help! will nobody help me?"

"Yes," he replied, "of course, I will."

"Oh! thank Heaven!"

"Where are you?"

"Here, sir, I think that's your voice, Mr. Bevan."

"Ah, and I think that's your voice, Will Stephens; I thought this would turn out some very ordinary piece of business, so you are upstairs; and did you ring the bell in the night?"

"I did, sir."

"Just so—come down then."

"I'm afraid I can't, sir, without some help. I have had a very bad fall, and although, thank God, no bones are broken, I am sadly shaken and bruised, so that it is with great pain, sir, I can crawl along, and as for getting down the stairs, why—I—I rather think I couldn't by myself, if there was a hundred pound note waiting for me below, just for the trouble of fetching, sir."

"Very well, I'm coming, don't move."

Mr. Bevan ascended the staircase, and without "a bit of pride," as Will Stephens said afterwards, in telling the story, helped the bruised sexton down the gallery steps to the body of the church, and then he made him sit down on one of the forms, and tell him all that had happened, which Will did from first to last, quite faithfully, not even omitting how he had stayed rather late at the ale-house, and how terrified he had been by the curious events that took place while he was in the church, ending by his fall from the stairs leading up to the belfry.

"Will, Will," said Mr. Bevan, "the ringing of the bell is good proof that you have been in the belfry, but you will scarcely expect me to believe the remainder of your dream."

"Dream, sir?"

"Yes, to be sure. You surely don't think now, in broad daylight, that it is anything else, do you?"

"I—I don't know, sir; of course, sir, if you say it's a dream—why—why—"

"There, that will do. I will convince you that it was nothing more, or else you will go disturbing the whole neighbourhood with this story, that it is quite a mercy, I have first heard."

"Convince me, sir?"

"Yes; come with me to the vault."

Will Stephens shrunk from this proposal and his fear was so manifest, that Mr. Bevan was, at all events, convinced that he had told him nothing but what he himself believed, and accordingly he felt still more anxious to rid Will of his nervous terror.

"You surely," he said, "cannot be timid, while I am with you. Come at once, and if you do not find that the late Miss Crofton, poor girl, is quiet enough in her coffin, I promise you upon my sacred word, that I will never cease investigating this affair, and bringing it to some conclusion. Come at once, before any curious persons arrive at the church."

So urgent a request from the clergyman of the parish to Will Stephens, the sexton of the parish, almost might be said to amount to a command, so Will did not see how he could get out of it, without confessing an amount of rank cowardice that even he shrunk from.

"Well, sir," he said, "of course with you I can have no objection."

"That's right. Come along; there are means of getting a light into the vestry; wait here a moment."

Will would not wait; he stuck close by Mr. Bevan, who went into the vestry, and soon procured a candle, lighted from materials he kept there under lock and key; and they went together to the vault, the stone of which was just as it had been left when Will emerged with so much fright.

"I will go first," said Mr. Bevan.

"Thank you, sir."

The clergyman descended, and Will Stephens followed, trembling, about two stairs behind him. Little did he expect when he emerged from that vault previous to his adventures in the church, that he should revisit it again so quickly. Indeed he had made a mental resolve that nothing should induce him to go down those stairs again, and yet there he was actually descending them. So weak are the resolutions of mortals!

"Needs must," thought Will, "when the—parson, I mean, drives!"

"Come on, Will," said Mr. Bevan.

Will looked about him, but no coffin-lid was visible. There was Miss Crofton's coffin in its proper niche, with the lid on, and looking as calm and undisturbed as any respectable coffin could look. Will was amazed. He looked at the coffin, and he looked at the parson, and then he looked uncommonly foolish.

"Never mind it, Will," said Mr. Bevan, "never mind it, I say. The story need go no further. You can keep your own counsel if you like. You have come here under the influence of strong ale, and you have gone to sleep most likely in this very vault, and in your sleep, having a very vivid dream, you have walked up into the gallery, and thence into the belfry, where no doubt you did ring the bell under the influence of your dream; and then you fell down the belfry stairs, I believe, as you say you did."

"Ah!" said Will, "bless you, sir. It may be so, but—"

"You are not convinced."

"Not quite, sir,"

"Well, Will, you are quite right never to pretend to be convinced when you are not. I do not blame you for that, but in a short time, when the effect of the affair has worn off, you will entertain my opinion."

"I hope, sir, I may."

"That will do. Now the stone must be put over this vault."

"Sir, if you wouldn't mind, sir."

"What, Will?"

"Staying a moment or two, while I empty the bag of sawdust on the floor, sir, I shan't be a minute, no-- not half a minute, and then I shall have done with the vault altogether I hope, sir."

"Very well."

Will set to work, and although at any other time he would have been rather ashamed of letting Mr. Bevan see what a wonderfully small quantity of sawdust made up a guinea's worth, superior considerations now prevailed, and he would not have spared the clergyman's company on any account.

"Now I've done, sir."

"Very well, follow me."

Will did not like to ask the clergyman to follow him, so in that difficulty, for as to his remaining behind it was out of the question, he made a rush and reached the church before Mr. Bevan could ascend two of the steps.

When that gentleman did reach the church he made no remark about the precipitancy, and apparent disrespect of Will, for he put it down to its right cause, but he left the church in order to make the usual preparations for the morning service, which would now commence in an hour and a half.

Will walked home with his empty bag, for the little exercise he had had sufficed to convince him that he was not so much hurt as he thought, and that the stiffness of his limbs would soon pass away.

"It's all very well," he said to himself, "for Mr. Bevan to talk about dreams, but if that was one, nothing real, has ever, happened to me yet, that's all."

THE YOUNG LOVER'S MIDNIGHT WATCH.

Did the clergyman really think what he said? Had he no suspicions, that after all there was a something more even than he was quite willing to admit in the story told by Will Stephens? We shall see in good time, but at all events one thing is evident, that the parson thought it good sound policy, and it was, to endeavour to nip the thing in the head, and by ascribing it to a dream, put it down as a subject of speculation in the place.

He knew that nothing could be more dangerous than allowing any such story to pass current as a wonderful fact, and well he knew that in a short time, if such were the case, it would receive so many additions and so many embellishments, that the mischief it might produce upon the mind of an ignorant population might be extreme, and of a most regretful character indeed.

All this he felt honestly, and therefore Will Stephens' story was to be put down as a dream.

Now Mr . Bevan, it will be recollected, had urged Will to keep his own counsel, and to say nothing of the affair to anyone, but he had faint hopes only that Will would do that, very faint hopes indeed, for after all he, Will, was the hero of the story, and there would be something extremely gratifying in telling it, and in stating what he would have done, had not his foot slipped as he came down the narrow stairs from the old belfrey, and so completely stunned him by the fall. Mr. Bevan therefore had very few if any compunctions in adopting the course he did, which was, in the evening, when there was no service at the church, to call at the Grange, to see Sir George Crofton upon the subject.

Mr. Bevan was always a welcome guest at the Grange, and he was on those intimate and good terms with the family, that he could always call whenever he pleased, so that a mere announcement of his presence by no means had the effect of preparing Sir George for any communication.

"Ah, Mr. Bevan," he said, when the clergyman entered the room, "I am glad to see you."

"And I to see you, Sir George."

"You come to a house of mourning, sir. But that will be the case here for a long, long time. Time may and will, no doubt, do much to assuage our grief, but the blow is as yet too recent."

Tears started to the eyes of Sir George Crofton, as he made this allusion to his daughter, and he turned his head aside to hide such evidences of emotion from the parson, from whom, however, he need have expected nothing but the most friendly sympathy that one human being could bestow upon another.

Mr. Bevan was a man of refinement and consideration, and he let grief always have its way, seldom doing more than merely throw out, in the form of a suggestion for consideration as it were, that death was not the great evil it was thought to be.

In such a way he generally succeeded in bringing persons smarting under the infliction of the loss of dear friends and relations much sooner to proper sense of the subject, than if he had indulged in all the canting religious exhortations that some divines think applicable to such occasions.

Sir George Crofton was alone, for his two sons had gone for a stroll in the grounds. Ringwood who still remained with the family, was in the library, where now he passed most of his time, in trying by reading to withdraw his mind from a too painful and fixed contemplation of his loss.

He was still weak, but might be considered now quite convalescent.

"Pray be seated, Mr. Bevan," said Sir George. "Believe me, I take it very kindly of you to come so often."

"Pray dear sir, don't say another word about it—I—I am very sorry to feel myself obliged to allude to anything of an uncomfortable nature."

"Think nothing of doing so, my friend. Think nothing of it, I have a master grief which drowns all others."

"But it is concerning that master grief, sir, that I come to speak."

"Indeed!"

"Yes, sir, will you kindly hear me?"

"Certainly, certainly."

"You told me on the day following the melancholy death of your daughter, as a friend, the peculiar circumstances attendant upon that death. Now I do not mean to say that what I am going to relate to you has any connection at all with those circumstances, nor would I tell you what I come to tell at all, were I not fearful that the same story with some of the usual exaggerations of ignorance would reach you from other quarters, for it is not a matter consigned to my bosom only, or there it should remain."

"You alarm me."

"That I feared, but deeply regret. Listen to me, and remember always as you do so, that I think the whole affair is a mere dream—a disturbed slumberer's vision—nothing more."

Sir George Crofton did listen with breathless eagerness, and Mr. Bevan, without detracting anything or adding anything to the narrative of Will Stephens, told him the whole story just as Will had told it to him, concluding by saying,—

"That is all my dear sir, and I felt that my duty powerfully called upon me to be your informant upon the subject, simply that we might be forewarned against any coarse version of the story."

Sir George drew a long breath. "More horrors! More horrors!"

"Nay, why should you say that?"

"Is it not so?"

"Nay I have already given my opinion, by saying, that I look upon the whole affair as but the phantasma of dream."

"Oh! Mr. Bevan, do not trifle with me. Is that really and truly your opinion, sir, or only said from kindness to me?"

"It is the best opinion that I can come to."

"I thank you, sir; I thank you. Clara, Clara, my child, my child!"

The old man was overcome with grief, and at the interesting moment, Ringwood entered the room, with a book in his hand. He was astonished, as well he might be to see such a fearful relapse of grief on the part of Sir George Crofton, and he looked from him to Mr. Bevan, and from Mr. Bevan to him, for some few moments in silence, and then he said,—

"Surely all here have suffered enough, and there is no new calamity come upon this house."

"Tell him all," cried Sir George; "tell him all. It is fit that he should know; he is one of us now, he loved my child, and loves her memory still. I pray you, Mr. Bevan, to tell all to Ringwood, for I have not the heart to do so."

"I wonder," said Ringwood, calmly, "to hear you speak thus. I wonder to see that any new grief can come so near to that which we have already suffered. The image of my lost one fills up each crevice of my heart. I shall listen to you Mr. Bevan with respect, but my grief, I fear is selfish, and cannot feel more than its own miseries."

Ringwood seemed to imagine that what the parson had to say referred to something with which Clara had nothing to do; but when, as the story proceeded, he found how intimately connected she was with the affair, his cheek flushed for a moment, and then grew of a death-like paleness, and he sat trembling and looking in the face of Mr. Bevan, as he proceeded with his most strange relation.

When he had concluded Ringwood gave a deep groan.

"You are much affected, sir," said Mr. Bevan.

"Crushed! crushed!" was the reply. "Oh God!"

"Nay now this is not manly, sir, you feel this thing too much; if you are so crushed how can anyone expect that from you is to proceed the necessary exertion to prove that the story in all its particulars is but a falsehood?"

Ringwood caught at this idea in a moment. "Exertion from me?" he said. "What exertions would I not make to prove such a horror to be but a creation of the fancy? What would I not do! What would I not suffer? You have warned me, sir. Yes, I have a duty to do—a duty to Clara's memory; a duty to you Sir George, and a duty to myself, for did I not love her, and does not her gentle image still sit in my inmost heart enshrined? I will prove that this most monstrous story is a delusion. Bear with me, gentlemen, I must think. To-morrow you shall know more, but not until tomorrow."

He rose, and left the room.

"What does he mean," said Sir George, vacantly.

"I cannot tell you, sir; but wait until tomorrow. Perhaps by then he may have proposed some plan of action, that you or I may not think of. You will use your own discretion, about communicating the strange affair to your sons or not, sir. Upon such a point as family confidence, I never venture an opinion. Allow me to call upon you to-morrow morning, sir, when I hope to find you in better spirits."

The clergyman would not have been in such haste to leave Sir George; but as he saw Ringwood leave the room; that young man made a sign to him, that he wished to see him before he left, and accordingly Mr. Bevan was anxious to know what it was he had to say to him.

When he left Sir George, he asked a servant where Mr. Ringwood was, and being told he was in the library, Mr. Bevan, being quite familiar with the house, followed him there at once, and found him pacing that apartment in great agitation, and with disordered steps.

"Thank heaven you have come, sir," cried Ringwood, "tell me, oh, tell me, what would you advise me to do, Mr. Bevan."

"I think," replied the clergyman, "you have already half decided upon a course."

"I have, I have."

"Then follow it, if it be such a one as in its result will produce a conviction of the truth. Do not, Mr. Ringwood, allow anything to turn you aside from a course which you feel to be right; you will always find strength enough to persevere if you have that strong conviction upon your heart. What is your plan?"

"It is this night to watch in the church."

"Be it so; I will, if you like, keep watch with you."

"Oh, no, no! let me be alone. All I ask of you, sir, is to provide me with the means of getting into the sacred edifice at midnight."

"That I will do. You shall have a private key that I have for my own use; you can let yourself in without any one knowing of your presence. But do you think you have nerve enough to go alone? if you have the smallest doubt or hesitation, let me accompany you."

"No, no—I thank you, but let me go alone, and say nothing of this to Sir George. I had it in my mind when I told him I would speak to him tomorrow about what you had communicated. I would fain, if these horrors be really true, keep him in ignorance that I have verified them. But if I keep my night watch quite undisturbed, then he shall have the satisfaction of knowing that it has been so kept."

"You are right in that; I will send the key to you in the course of another hour, and remember I am at your service if you should alter your mind, and wish for company. Do not hesitate about disturbing my rest."

THE HORRORS OF THE GRAVE. —A FRIGHTFUL ADVENTURE.

One would have thought that young Ringwood might with effect and with discretion have disclosed his plan of watching in the old church to one of the brothers of Clara, but he shrunk from doing that.

In the first place he thought he should be put down as a visionary, and as one who was disposed to insult the memory of Clara by imagining that the story of the sexton could be true, and in the second place, if anything did happen, he was afraid that the feelings of the brother might clash with his.

"No," he said, "I will go alone—I will not rest again until I have thoroughly satisfied myself that this tale is but a fabrication of the fancy. Oh, Clara! can it be possible—no, no. The thought is by far too—too horrible."

It may really be considered a fortunate thing that the communication of the clergyman was made in the evening, for had it been earlier in the day, the hours of frightful anxiety which Ringwood would have endured until the night came must have been most painful.

As it was, however, the hours that would elapse ere he could venture to go to the church on his strange and melancholy errand were not many, and they passed the more quickly, that during some of them, he was making up his mind as to what he should do.

"Yes, Clara, my best beloved Clara," he said, "I will rescue your sweet memory from this horrible doubt that is cast upon it, or I will join you in the tomb. Welcome, a thousand times welcome death, rather than that I should live to think that you are—God, no—no! I cannot pronounce the dreadful word. Oh, what evil times are these, and what a world of agony do I endure. But courage, courage; let fancy sleep, I must not allow my imagination to become sufficiently excited to play me any pranks tonight. Be still my heart, and let me go upon this expedition as a spectator merely. Time enough will it be to become an actor, when I know more, if indeed there be more to know."

The clergyman sent the key, according to his promise, by a confidential servant, who had orders to ask for Mr. Ringwood and to give it into his own hands, so that the young man was fully prepared to go, when the proper time should arrive for him to start upon his expedition.

He purposely kept very much out of the way of Sir George Crofton and his two sons during the remainder of the evening, for such was the ingenuous nature of young Ringwood, and so unused was he to place any curb upon his speech, that he dreaded letting slip some information regarding his intention to keep watch in the old church that night; in such a case it would have been difficult to refuse company.

Sir George took the advice of the clergyman and said nothing to any one of the dreadful communication that had been made to him. But he could not conceal from the family and his servants, that some unusual grief was preying upon him, beyond even the sadness that had remained after the death of his daughter. He retired to rest unusually early, that he might escape their curious and inquiring glances.

The clock struck eleven.

"It is time," said Ringwood, as he sprung from his seat in his bedroom.

"It is time. For the love of thee, my Clara, I go to brave this adventure, Mine are you in death as in life. My heart is widowed, and can know no other love."

He armed himself with a pair of loaded pistols, for he made up his mind that if any trickery was at the bottom of the proceeding, the authors of such a jest should pay dearly for their temerity, and then cautiously descending from his bed-room, he crossed the dining-room, and passing through a conservatory, easily made his way out of the house, and into a flower-garden that was beyond.

He thought that if he went out of the grounds by the way of the porter's lodge, it might excite some remark, his not returning again, so he went to a part of the wall which he knew was low and rugged.

"There," he said, "I can easily climb over, and by getting into the meadows make my way into the road."

This, to a young man, was not by any means a difficult matter, and he in a few minutes more found himself quite free of the house and grounds, and making his way very rapidly towards the church, the tower of which, he could just see.

The night was again a cloudy one; although nothing had as yet fallen, the wind was uncertain, and no one could with any safety have ventured to predict whether it would be fair, or rain. Of the two, certainly, Ringwood would have preferred moonlight, for he wished in the church to be able to see well about him, without thinking of the necessity of a light.

"No," he said, as he pursued his way, "I must have no light; that would ruin all."

By the time he reached the church, he had a better opinion of the weather, and from a faint sort of halo that was in the sky, he was led to believe that the moon's light would soon be visible, and enable him to see everything that might take place.

The key that the parson had given him opened the same little door by which Will Stephens, the sexton, had entered, and there was no difficulty in turning the lock, for it was frequently used.

The young man paused for a moment, debating with himself, whether he should fasten the door securely on the inner side, or leave it open, and at last he thought, that considering all things, the latter was the best course to pursue.

"I do not wish," he said, "to stop any proceedings, so much as I wish to see what they are. There shall therefore be every facility for any one coming into the church, who may chance to have an intention so to do."

He still, it will be seen, clung a little to the hope that it was a trick.

When he pushed open the door that was covered with green baize, he found that in consequence of the cloth curtain being entirely drawn aside from before the south window, that there was not near the amount of darkness within the building that he had anticipated finding there.

When his eyes got a little accustomed to it, he could even see, dimly to be sure, but still, sufficiently to distinguish the several shapes of the well-known objects in the church. The pulpit, the communion table, the little rails before it, and some of the old monuments against the walls.

The stone slab that covered the opening to the vault of the Crofton family, had been before the commencement of the morning service properly secured, so that that entrance could be walked over with perfect safety, and Ringwood carefully ascertained that such was the fact.

"Surely, surely," he said, "it is as Mr. Bevan says. That man must have come here half stupified by ale, and have gone to sleep, The only thing that gives the slightest semblance to such a tale, is the adventure of that most mysterious man who was reclaimed from the sea."

Yes, Ringwood was right. That was the circumstance, full of dread and awful mystery as it was, which sufficed to make anything else probable, and possible.

And what had become of him? Since the time when he made his escape from the Grange, nothing had been seen or heard of him unless that were he indeed, who was in the church pointing to the moonlight when the terrified Will Stephens was there.

And yet Stephens, although he might be supposed to be in a position to know him, did not recognise him, for we do not find in his account of the affair that he made any mention of him, or insinuated any opinion even, that the Mr. Smith of the bone-house, was the same person who had played so strange a part in the church.

The reader will have his own opinion.

"Where shall I bestow myself," thought Ringwood, "I ought to be somewhere from whence I can get a good view of the whole church."

After some little consideration, and looking about him as well as the semi-darkness would permit him, he thought that he could not by any possibility do better than get into the pulpit. From there he could readily turn about in any direction from whence any noise might proceed, at the same time, that it was something like a position which could not be very well attacked except with fire arms, and if such weapons were used against him, he should have the great advantage of seeing who was his assailant.

Accordingly he ascended the pulpit stairs, and soon ensconced himself in that elevated place.

There was something very awful, and solemn, and yet beautiful about the faint view he got of the old conventicle-looking church from its pulpit, and irresistible had he chosen to resist it, there came to his lips a prayer to Heaven for its aid, its protection, and its blessing upon his enterprise.

How much calmer, and happier he felt after that. How true it is, as Prospero says, that prayer,

"Pierces so that it assaults
Mercy itself, and frees all faults."

Who is there in the wide world who has not felt the benign influence of an appeal to the great Creator of all things, under circumstances of difficulty, and of distress. Let us pity the heart, if there be such a one in existence, that is callous to such a feeling. But there are none. A reliance upon divine mercy is one of the attributes of humanity, and may not be turned aside, by even all the wickedness and the infidelity that may be arrayed against it.

"All is still," murmured Ringwood. "The stillness of the very grave is here, Oh, my Clara; methinks without a pang of mortal fear, I could converse in such an hour as this, with thy pure and unsullied spirit!"

In the enthusiasm of the moment, no doubt, Ringwood could have done so, and it is a wonder that his most excited imagination did not conjure up some apparent semblance of the being whom he loved so devotedly, and whose image he so fondly cherished, even although she had gone from him.

"Yes, my Clara," he cried, in tones of enthusiasm. "Come to me, come to me, and you will not find that in life or in death the heart that is all your own, will shrink from you!"

This species of mental exaltation was sure soon to pass away, and it did so. The sound of his own voice convinced him of the impropriety of such speeches, when he came there as an observer.

"Hush! hush!" he said. "Be still, be still."

It was evident to him that many clouds were careering over the face of the moon, for at times the church would get very dark indeed, and everything assumed a pitchy blackness, and then again a soft kind of light would steal in, and give the whole place a different aspect.

This continued for a long time, as he thought, and more than once he tried to ascertain the progress of the hours by looking at his watch, but the dim light baffled him.

"How long have I been here?" he asked himself; "I must not measure the time by my feelings, else I should call it an age."

At that moment the old church clock began to chime, and having proclaimed the four quarters past eleven, it with its deep-toned solemn bell struck the hour of twelve—Ringwood carefully counted the strokes, so that, although it was too dark to see his watch, he could not be deceived.

THE MIDNIGHT HOUR.—THE STONE SLAB. —THE VAMPIRE.

Yes, it was twelve o'clock, that mysterious hour at which it is believed by many that:

"Graves give up their dead,
And many a ghost in church-yard decay,
Rise from their cold, cold bed
To make night horrible with wild vagary."

Twelve, that hour when all that is human feels a sort of irksome dread, as if the spirits of those who have gone from the great world were too near, loading the still night air with the murky vapours of the grave. A chilliness came over Ringwood and he fancied a strange kind of light was in the church, making objects more visible than in their dim and dusky outlines they had been before.

"Why do I tremble?" he said, "why do I tremble? Clouds pass away from before the moon, that is all. Soon there may be a bright light here, and lo, all is still; I hear nothing but my own breathing; I see nothing but what is common and natural. Thank heaven, all will pass away in quiet. There will be no horror to recount—no terrific sight to chill my blood. Rest Clara, rest in Heaven."

Ten minutes passed away, and there was no alarm; how wonderfully relieved was Ringwood. Tears came to his eyes, but they were the natural tears of regret, such as he had shed before for her who had gone from him to the tomb, and left no trace behind, but in the hearts of those who loved her.

"Yes," he said, mournfully "she has gone from me, but I love her still. Still does the fond remembrance of all that she was to me, linger at my heart. She is my own, my beautiful Clara, as she ever was, and as, while life remains, to me she ever will be."

At the moment that he uttered these words a slight noise met his ears.

In an instant he sprung to his feet in the pulpit, and looked anxiously around him.

"What was that?" he said. "What was that?"

All was still again, and he was upon the point of convincing himself, that the noise was either some accidental one, or the creation of his own fancy, when it came again.

He had no doubt this time. It was a perceptible, scraping, strange sort of sound, and he turned his whole attention to the direction from whence it came. With a cold creeping chill through his frame, he saw that that direction was the one where was the family vault of the Croftons, the last home of her whom he held still in remembrance, and whose memory was so dear to him.

He felt the perspiration standing upon his brow, and if the whole world had been the recompense to him for moving away from where he was he could not have done so. All he could do was to gaze with bated breath, and distended eyes upon the aisle of the church from whence the sound came.

That something of a terrific nature was now about to exhibit itself, and that the night would not go off without some terrible and significant adventure to make it remembered he felt convinced. All he dreaded was to think for a moment what it might be.

His thoughts ran on Clara, and he murmured forth in the most agonizing accents,—

"Anything—any sight but the sight of her. Oh, no, no, no!"

But it was not altogether the sight of her that he dreaded; oh no, it was the fact that the sight of her on such an occasion would bring the horrible conviction with it, that there was some truth in the dreadful apprehension that he had of the new state of things that had ensued regarding the after-death condition of that fair girl.

The noise increased each moment, and finally there was a sudden crash.

"She comes! she comes!" gasped Ringwood.

He grasped the front of the pulpit with a frantic violence, and then slowly and solemnly there crossed his excited vision a figure all clothed in white. Yes, white flowing vestments, and he knew by their fashion that they were not worn by the living, and that it was some inhabitant of the tomb that he now looked upon.

He did not see the face. No, that for a time was hidden from him, but his heart told him who it was. Yes, it was his Clara.

It was no dream. It was no vision of a too excited fancy, for until those palpable sounds, and that most fearfully palpable form crossed his sight, he was rather inclined to go the other way, and to fancy what the sexton had reported was nothing but a delusion of his overwrought brain. Oh, that he could but for one brief moment have found himself deceived.

"Speak!" he gasped; "speak! speak!"

There was no reply.

"I conjure you, I pray you though the sound of your voice should hurl me to perdition—I implore you, speak."

All was silent, and the figure in white moved on slowly but surely towards the door of the church, but ere it passed out, it turned for a moment, as if for the very purpose of removing from the mind of Ringwood any lingering doubt as to its identity.

He then saw the face, oh, so well-known, but so pale. It was Clara Crofton!

"'Tis she! 'tis she!" was all he could say.

It seemed, too, as if some crevice in the clouds had opened at the moment, in order that he should with an absolute certainty see the countenance of that solemn figure, and then all was more than usually silent again. The door closed, and the figure was gone.

He rose in the pulpit, and clasped his hands. Irresolution seemed for a few moments to sway him to and fro, and then he rushed down into the body of the church.

"I'll follow it," he cried, "though it lead me to perdition. Yes, I'll follow it."

He made his way to the door, and even as he went he shouted,—

"Clara! Clara! Clara!"

He reached the threshold of the ancient church; he gazed around him distractedly, for he thought that he had lost all sight of the figure. No—no, even in the darkness and against the night sky, he saw it once again in its sad-looking death raiments. He dashed forward.

The moonbeams at this instant being freed from some dense clouds that had interposed between them and this world, burst forth with resplendent beauty. There was not a tree, a shrub, nor a flower, but what was made distinct and manifest, and with the church, such was the almost unprecedented lustre of the beautiful planet, that even the inscriptions upon the old tablets and tombs were distinctly visible. Such a refulgence lasted not many minutes, but while it did, it was most beautiful, and the gloom that followed it seemed doubly black.

"Stay, stay," he shouted, "yet a moment, Clara; I swear that what you are, that will I be. Take me over to the tomb with you, say but that it is your dwelling-place, and I will make it mine, and declare it a very palace of the affections."

The figure glided on.

It was in vain that he tried to keep up with it. It threaded the churchyard among the ancient tombs, with a gliding speed that soon distanced him, impeded, as he continually was, by some obstacle or another, owing to looking at the apparition he followed, instead of the ground before him.

Still, on he went, heedless whether he was conveyed, for he might be said to be dragged onward, so much were all his faculties both of mind and body intent upon following the apparition of his beloved.

Once, and once only, the figure passed, and seemed to be aware that it was followed for it flitted round an angle made by one of the walls of the church, and disappeared from his eyes.

In another moment he had turned the same point.

"Clara, Clara!" he shouted. "'Tis I—you know my voice, Clara, Clara."

She was not to be seen, and then the idea struck him that she must have re-entered the church, and he too, turned, and crossed the threshold. He lingered there for a moment or two, and the whole building echoed to the name of Clara, as with romantic eagerness, he called upon her by name to come forth to him.

Those echoes were the only reply.

Maddened—rendered desperate beyond all endurance, he went some distance into the building in search of her, and again he called.

It was in vain; she had eluded him, and with all the carefulness and all the energy and courage he had brought to bear upon that night's proceedings, he was foiled. Could anything be more agonising than this to such a man as Ringwood—he who loved her so, that he had not shrunk from her, even in death, although she had so shrunk from him.

"I will find her—I will question her," he cried. "She shall not escape me; living or dead, she shall be mine. I will wait for her, even in the tomb."

Before he carried out the intention of going actually into the vault to await her return, he thought he would take one more glance at the churchyard with the hope of seeing her there, as he could observe no indications of her presence in the church.

With this view he proceeded to the door, and emerged into the dim light. He called upon her again by name, and he thought he heard some faint sound in the church behind him. To turn and make a rush into the building was the work of a moment.

He saw something—it was black instead of white—a tall figure—it advanced towards him, and with great force, before he was aware that an attack was at all intended, it felled him to the ground.

The blow was so sudden, so unexpected, and so severe, that it struck him down in a moment before he could be aware of it. To be sure, he had arms with him, but the anxiety and agony of mind he endured that night, since seeing the apparition come from the tomb had caused him to forget them.

THE YOUNG GIRL IN THE VILLAGE, AND THE AWFUL VISIT.

It is now necessary that we draw the reader's attention to a humbler place of residence than the Grange, with its spacious chambers and lordly halls.

Situated not very far from the church, and almost close to the churchyard, upon which its little garden abutted, was a cottage, the picture of rural neatness and beauty. In the winter it was beautiful and picturesque, but in the summer time, when its porch was overrun with the woodbine and the sweet clematis, it was one of the sweetest of abodes that content and happiness could ever live in.

This cottage was inhabited by an old woman and her only child, a young girl of sixteen, beautiful as a rose, and as guileless as an angel. They contrived to live upon a small annuity that the mother had from a family in whose service she spent the best years of her life, and who, with a generosity that would be well to be abundantly and extensively imitated, would not see their old dependant want.

These two innocent and blameless persons had retired to rest at nine o'clock, their usual hour, and had slept the calm sleep of contentment until about half past one, when the mother was awakened by a loud and piercing shriek from her daughter's chamber.

To spring from her humble couch was the work of a moment. "Anna, Anna! my child, Anna!" she shrieked. As she did so, she rushed across the small stair landing which separated the two, and the only two upper rooms of the cottage, and was about to enter her daughter's room, when the door of it was opened from within, and the old dame's heart died within her, as she saw a figure upon the threshold, attired in the vestments of the grave, and opposing her entrance.

Was it a dream, or did she really see such a sight?

Aghast and trembling the mother stood, unable for a moment or two to speak, and as she fell fainting upon the landing, she thought that something passed her, but she could not be quite sure, as it was at the instant her faculties were flitting from her.

How long she lay in that seeming death she knew not, and when she recovered, it was some few minutes before recollection came back to her, and she really remembered what had so completely overpowered her.

But when her reason did resume its sway, and she recollected that it was some danger to Anna, which had first alarmed her, she called her loudly by her name.

"Anna, Anna, speak to me."

"Mother, mother," replied the young girl. "Oh, come to me."

These words supplied strength to the old woman, and rising she made her way immediately into the chamber of her daughter, whom she found in an agony of fear; a light was procured, and then Anna flung herself upon her mother's neck, and wept abundantly.

"Oh, mother, tell me, convince me that it was only a dream."

"What, my child? oh what?"

The girl trembled so much that it was only by the utmost persuasion that the following account was got from her, of the cause of her fright.

She said that she had gone to sleep as usual within a very few minutes after going to bed, that she enjoyed a calm, and uninterrupted slumber, the duration of which she had no means whatever of guessing, but she was partially awakened by a noise at the window of her room.

She instantly rose and stood looking at the window, on which a sort of shadow seemed to pass without, which alarmed her exceedingly.

Still as it did not come again, and as she certainly had not been fully awake when she sprung from her bed, she had thought it quite possible that all might be a dream, and had forborne from making any alarm upon the subject.

After some hesitation she had persuaded herself to go to bed again, and when there, although she sometimes started awake fancying she heard something, she at length yielded to sleep, and again slept, soundly for a time, until a new circumstance awakened her.

She thought she felt something touching her about the neck, and after opening her eyes, the moonlight, which at that moment happened to be very bright, disclosed to her a white figure standing by the side of her bed, the face of which figure was leaning over her, and within a very few inches of her own.

Terror at first deprived her of all power of speech or motion, but as the figure did not move, she at length gave utterance to her fears in that shriek which had come from her lips, and so much alarmed the mother.

This was all the young girl could say, with the exception that the figure when she shrieked appeared to glide away, but where to she had no means of telling, for some clouds at that moment came again over the face of the moon.

The mother was much affected and terrified, and at first she thought of calling up her neighbours, but at length as the night was considerably advanced, and the intruder gone, they agreed to let the matter rest till morning, and the mother retired to her room again.

How long it was before the shriek from her daughter's room came again she did not know, but come again it did.

Yes, again came the dreadful shriek. It was—it could be no delusion now—and the mother once more sprung from her couch to rush to the rescue of her child.

Confused and bewildered, she darted onward to the chamber, but the door was fast, nor could all her exertions suffice to open it.

"Anna, Anna!" she shouted, "speak to me. One word only, my child, my child."

All was still. The trembling mother placed her ear to the door, and she heard a strange sucking sound, as if an animal was drinking with labour and difficulty. Her head seemed to be on fire, and her senses were upon the point of leaving her, but she did manage to reach her own room. She flew to the little casement—she dashed it open.

"Help! help! help!—for the love of God, help!"

There was no reply.

Again she raised her voice in shrieking wild accents.

"Help!—murder!—help!"

"What is it?" shouted a man's voice. It was one who was going some distance to take in his fishing nets.

"Oh! thank God, some human being hears me. Come in, come in."

"How am I to get in?"

"Stay a moment, and I will come down and open the cottage door for you. For the love of mercy do not go away."

Trembling and terrified to a dreadful excess, the old woman went downstairs and let the man into the cottage, when they both proceeded up to the chamber of the daughter.

"What do you suppose is the matter?" asked the fisherman.

"Oh! I know not—I know not; but twice tonight—twice has this dreadful alarm happened. Do not leave us—oh, do not."

"I don't want to; but I should hardly think thieves would find it worth their while to come here at all for what they would get. You must have been dreaming."

"Oh, that I could think so!"

Anna's chamber was reached; and there, to the horror of the mother, she was found lying perfectly insensible on her bed, with a quantity of blood smeared about her neck.

"Why, it's a murder!" cried the fisherman; and firmly impressed with such a belief, he ran out of the house to spread an alarm.

The window of the chamber was wide open, and from that the mother now cried aloud for help; so that between her and the fisherman, such a disturbance was made all over the neighbourhood, that they were soon likely to have more assistance than could be useful.

The people living the nearest were soon roused, and they roused others, while the distracted woman, who believed Anna was dead, called for justice and for vengeance.

The alarm spread from house to house—from cottage to hall—and, in the course of half-an-hour, most of the inhabitants of the village had risen to hear the old dame's account of the horrible proceeding that had taken place that night in the cottage.

Exaggeration was out of the question. The fact itself was more than sufficient to induce the greatest amount of horror in the minds of all who heard it, and there was one, and only one, whose information enabled him to give a name to the apparition that had assaulted Anna.

That one was the schoolmaster of the place, and he, after hearing the story, said,—

"If one could persuade oneself at all of the existence of such horrors, one would suppose that a vampyre had visited the cottage."

This was a theme that was likely to be popular. The schoolmaster foolishly gave way to the vanity, and explained what a vampyre was—or was supposed and said to be; and soon the whole place was in a state of the most indescribable alarm upon the subject.

As yet the horrible news had not reached the Grange, but it was destined soon to do so; and better would it have been that anyone had at once plunged a dagger in the heart of poor Sir George Crofton than that there should be thought to be such a horrible confirmation of his worst fears.

To be sure, his daughter was not named, but he received the news with a scream of anguish, and fell insensible into the arms of his son. All was confusion. The servants ran hither and thither, not knowing what to do, and it was not until Mr. Bevan arrived that something like order was restored. He as a privileged friend assumed for the nonce a kind of dictatorship at the Grange, and gave orders, which were cheerfully and promptly obeyed. Then he desired a strictly private interview with Sir George.

It was, or course, granted to him; but the old baronet begged that Charles and Edwin might now know all. It was Emma alone from whom he wished to keep the awful truth.

THE AWFUL SUPPOSITION—A RESOLUTION.

It was with some reluctance that the clergyman spoke. "Sir," he said to the old baronet, "and you, my young gentleman, I am afraid—very much afraid, that I am doing anything but right in countenancing a supposition so utterly at variance with all my own notions and feelings; but my abhorrence of a secret impels me to speak."

"Say on, sir—say on," cried Sir George. "Perhaps we are better prepared to hear what you have to tell, than you imagine."

After this Mr. Bevan had less reluctance to speak, he said,—

"I was aware, although you all were not, that Mr. Ringwood intended to keep watch last night in the church, in order to test the truth of what had been told by Will Stephens, the sexton. I did all I could to persuade him from making the attempt, but when I found that nothing else would satisfy him, I thought it prudent to give him the means of carrying out what had become such a fixed intention with him, that to oppose it was to do far more mischief than to grant it all the aid I had in my power to do."

Sir George gave a nod of assent.

"He went there," continued Mr. Bevan, "with a private key of my own, and took his place in the church."

"I wish, sir, you had been with him," said Edwin.

"Yes," added Charles. "If you, with your cool, calm, unbiased judgment had been there, we should have been much better able to come to a correct conclusion about what occurred; for that something did occur, or was supposed by Ringwood to do so, we can well guess."

"I wish, indeed, I had been there," said Mr. Bevan, "but he begged so earnestly to be allowed to go alone, that I had not the heart to refuse him."

"And what happened, sir?"

"I will tell you. I gave him a key which admitted him to the church, by the small private entrance, at which I usually go in myself; in fact, it was my own private key, for I at times visit the church, and wish to do so, when I am not expected by those who have the ordinary charge of it."

"We have heard as much."

"No doubt. Well, then, I say I gave him that key, but it was my sympathy with his evident distress rather than my judgment which consented to do so, and I had hardly done it, when I began to busy myself with conjectures, and to deeply regret that I had yielded to him so easily. 'What if he, in his excited and grief-stricken state of mind, should come to some serious mischief?' I said to myself, 'should not I be very much to blame? Would not all prudent persons say that I did very wrong to send a man in such a condition of mind into a church at midnight, alone?' "

"Your motives and your known character, sir, would protect you," said Charles.

"I hope so," continued Mr. Bevan. "I think it would from all other charges, but imprudence; and if any great mischance had befallen Ringwood, I should not so readily have forgiven myself, as others might have been induced to forgive me."

"I understand that feeling," said Sir George.

"Well, then, with such sensations tugging at my heart, no wonder I could not rest, and so at a little after twelve, I rose, and hastily dressing myself, I left my house as noiselessly as possible, and made my way towards the church. The moon's light was at that time obscured, but every spot was so familiar to me, that I was able to go with speed, and I soon reached the venerable building. I walked round it, until I came to the door, the key of which I had given to Mr. Ringwood; it was open, but the moment I crossed the threshold, I stumbled on his insensible form."

"Go on! go on! He had seen something terrible," gasped Sir George; "I am nerved, I think, for the very worst; I pray you, sir, go on, and tell me all."

"I will, Sir George, because I feel convinced it is my duty to conceal nothing in this transaction, and because I think you had better more calmly and dispassionately, and without exaggeration, hear from me all that is to be told."

"That is a good reason, sir," said Edwin. "We should, of course, hear all from other sources, and probably, with all the aids that a feeling for the marvellous could append to it."

"That is my impression. When, then, I stumbled over a person lying just within the little private door of the church, I had no immediate means of knowing who it was; I tell you it was Ringwood, because I afterwards discovered as much. I had the means of getting a light; when I did so, I found Ringwood lying in a swoon, while at the same time, I could not but notice a large bruise upon his forehead.

"Of course, my first duty was to look after him, instead of troubling myself about his assailant, and having placed him in as convenient a posture as I could, I hurried home again, and roused up my servants. With their assistance I got him to my house, and placed him in bed."

"And did you search the church, sir?"

"I did. I went back and searched it thoroughly, but found nothing at all suspicious. Everything was in its right place, and I could not account for the affair at all, because of the wound that Ringwood had. I was most anxious to hear from him that he had had a fall."

"But—but," said Sir George, falteringly, "he told a different story."

"He did."

"A story which you will not keep from us."

"I do not feel myself justified, as I have said, in keeping it from you. This is it."

The clergyman then related to the family of the Croftons what is already known to the reader concerning the adventures of Ringwood in the old church, and which that morning, upon his recovery, Ringwood had told to him most circumstantially.

We need scarcely say that this recital was listened to with the most agonized feelings. Poor Sir George appeared to be most completely overcome by it. He trembled excessively, and could not command himself sufficiently to speak.

The two brothers looked at each other in dismay.

"Now, I pray you all to consider this matter more calmly," said Mr.

Bevan, "than you seem inclined to do."

"Calmly," gasped Sir George, "calmly."

"Yes—what evidence have we after all that the whole affair is anything more than a dream of Mr. Ringwood's?"

"Does he doubt it?"

"No—I am bound to tell you that he does not; but we may well do so for all that. He is the last person who is likely to give in to the opinion that it is a mere vision, so strangely impressed as it is upon his imagination. Recollect always that he went to the church prepared to see something."

"Oh, if we could but think it unreal," said Sir George, glancing at his sons, as if to gather their opinions of the matter from their countenances.

"I will cling to such a thought," said Charles, "until I am convinced otherwise through the medium of my own senses."

"And I," said Edwin.

"You are right," added Mr. Bevan, "I never in the whole course of my experience heard of anything of which people should be so slow of believing in, as this most uncomfortable affair. You now know all, and it is for yourselves, of course, to make whatever determination you think fit. If I might advise, it would be that you all take a short tour, perhaps on the continent for a time."

"Mr. Bevan," said Sir George, in a kindly tone, "I am greatly obliged to you. The suggestion I know springs from the very best and friendly motives; but it carries with it a strong presumption that you really do think there is something in all this affair which it would be as well to have settled in my absence."

The clergyman could not deny but that some such feeling was at the bottom of his advice; but still he would not admit that he was at all convinced of the reality of what was presumed to have happened, and a short pause in the conversation ensued, after which Sir George spoke with a solemn air of determination, saying to his sons, as well as to his friend and pastor, Mr. Bevan, "When I tell you that I have made a determination from which nothing but the hand of heaven visiting me with death shall move me, I hope no one here will try to dissuade me from carrying it out."

After such an exordium it was a difficult thing to say anything to him, so he continued,—

"My child was dear—very dear to me in life, and I have no superstitious fears concerning one who held such a place in my affections. I am resolved that tonight I will watch her poor remains, and at once convince myself of a horror that may drive me mad or take a mountain of grief and apprehension off my heart."

"Father," cried Charles, "you will allow me to accompany you."

"And me," added Edwin.

"My sons, you are both deeply interested in this matter—you would be miserable while I was gone if you were not with me. Moreover, I will not trust my own imagination entirely—we will all three go, and then we cannot be deceived. This is my most solemn resolution."

"I have only one thing to say regarding it," said Mr. Bevan, "that is, to prefer an earnest request that you will allow me to be one of the party—you shall sit in a pew of the church, that shall command a view of the whole building."

"Accompany us, Mr. Bevan, if you will," said Sir George, "but I sit in no pew."

"No pew?"

"No. But my child's coffin, in the vault where repose the remains of more than one of my race who had been dear to me in life, will I take my place."

There was an earnest resolved solemnity about Sir George's manner, which showed that he was not to be turned from his purpose, and Mr. Bevan accordingly did not attempt to do so. He had done what he scarcely expected, that is, got a consent to accompany him to the night vigil, and at all events let what would happen, he as a more disinterested party than the others, would be able, probably to interfere and prevent any disastrous circumstances from arising.

"Say nothing of what has been determined on to anyone," said Sir George, "keep it a profound secret, sir, and this night will put an end to the agony of doubt."

"Depend upon me. Will you come to my house at eleven o'clock, or shall I come here?"

"We will come to you; it is on the way."

Thus then the affair was settled, so far satisfactorily, that there was to be a watch actually now in the vault, so that there could be no delusion, no trick practised. What will be the result will be shown very shortly; in the meantime we cannot but tremble at what that attached and nearly heart-broken father may have still to go through.

The excitement too in the village was immense; for the story of the vampyre's attack upon the young girl was fresh in everybody's mouth, and it lost nothing of its real horrors by the frequency with which it was repeated, and the terror-stricken manner in which it was dilated upon.

THE GRAND CONSULTATION AT THE ALE-HOUSE.—THE AWFUL SUGGESTION.

Sir George Crofton and his family could form no idea, owing to not being in a position to know, of the state of excitement produced in the village by the mysterious and frightful attack which had been made upon the widow's daughter.

When people are very much absorbed with their own grief, they are apt to set a lighter value upon those of others, and thus it was that the family of the Croftons was so entirely taken up with what itself felt and had to do that there was little room for sympathy with others.

Mr. Bevan likewise, from his peculiar and respectable position, was not likely to be made the depository of gossiping secrets; the inhabitants of that little place were in the habit of approaching him with respect, so that, although, as we are aware, he had heard from Will Stephens, the sexton, a full and particular account of what had happened to him in the old church, and was likewise cognizant of the story of the midnight attack upon the widow's daughter, he was not fully aware of the startling effect which those circumstances had had upon the small population of that fishing village.

We are bound to believe that if he had had any idea of the real result of those operations or of what was contemplated as their result—he would have done his best to adopt some course to prevent any disastrous collision.

We, however, with all the data and materials of this most singular narrative before us, are enabled to detail to the reader facts and occurrences as they took place actually, without waiting the arrival of those periods at which they reached the knowledge of those actors in the gloomy drama of real life.

Our readers, then, will please to know that the excitement among the inhabitants of the place was of that violent and overbearing description, that all the occupations of the villagers were abandoned, and a spirit of idleness, sadly suggestive of mischief, began to be prevalent among them.

This feeling was increased by frequent visits to the ale-house, the liquor of which was well esteemed by Will Stephens, as may be readily imagined; and towards evening the large old-fashioned parlour of that place of entertainment became crowded with a motley assemblage, whose sole purpose in meeting together was to drink strong ale, and discuss the irritating and exciting subject of the appearance of the vampyre in the village.

This discussion, from being at first a sober, serious, and alarmed one, became noisy and violent; and at length a blacksmith, who was a great man in the politics of the place, and who of all things in the world most admired to hear his own voice, rose and addressed his compeers in something of a set speech.

"Listen to me," he said; "are we to have the blood sucked out of all our bodies by a lot of vampyres? Is our wives and daughters to be murdered in the middle of the night?"

"No, no, no," cried many voices; "certainly not."

"Is we to be made into victims, or isn't we? What's Sir George Crofton and his family to us? To be sure he's the landlord of some of us, and a very good landlord he is, too, as long as we pay our rent."

"Here, hear, hear."

"But there's no saying how long he might be so, if we didn't."

"Bravo, Dick!" cried the master of the place, handing the orator a pot; "bravo, Dick! take a pull at that, old fellow."

"Thank you, Muggins. Now, what I proposes is—"

"Stand on a chair, and let's all hear you."

"Thank you," said the blacksmith; and getting upon a chair, he was about to commence again, when someone advised him to get upon the table, but in an effort to accomplish that feat, he unfortunately trod upon what was a mere flap of the table, which had not sufficient power to support his weight, and down he came amid an assemblage of pots, jugs, and glasses, which made a most alarming crash.

This roused the fury of the landlord, who had no idea of being made such a sufferer in the transaction, and he accordingly began to declaim heavily at his loss. A dispute arose as to how he was to be repaid, and it was finally settled that a general subscription would be the best mode of reimbursing him. If anything was wanting to work up the feelings of the topers at the public-house to the highest pitch of aggravation, it certainly was their having to disburse for breakages a sum of money which, if liquified, would have trickled most luxuriously down their throats. They were consequently ripe and ready for anything which promised vengeance upon anybody.

The blacksmith was not discomfited by his fall. When is a man who is fond of hearing himself talk discomfited by anything? and he soon resumed his oration in the following words:—

"Is we to be put upon in this kind of way? Why, we shan't be able to sleep in our beds. All I asks is, is we to put up with it?"

"But what are we to do?" said one.

"Ah! there's the question," said the blacksmith, "I don't know exactly."

"Let's ask old Timothy Brown," said the butcher, "he's the oldest man here."

This was assented to; and accordingly the individual mentioned was questioned as to his ideas of the way of avoiding the alarming catastrophe which seemed to be impending over them. He advised them to wait patiently till the next night, and keep awake till the unwelcome nocturnal visitor made its appearance, when whoever it might visit was boldly to assail it, without any fear of the consequences to himself, till further assistance could be procured. After Timothy Brown had delivered himself of this piece of advice, a dead silence ensued among the late boisterous company. There were many dissentients, and a few who seemed in favour of a trial of the practicability of the plan. Both parties seemed to give some consideration to the proposition, and they were by far too much engaged in thinking of the advice which had been given them, to pay much attention to the quarter from whence it had emanated; more particularly, too, as from his age and infirmities, he was incapacitated from carrying it out or from giving any active assistance to those who were disposed to do so.

A great many efforts were made to get him to say more, particularly with reference to the case under consideration, as being no common one, but the octogenarian had made his effort, and he only replied to the remonstrances of those who, alternately by coaxing and bullying, strove to get information from him, by a vacant stare.

"It's of no use," said the butcher, "you'll get nothing more now from old Timothy; he's done up now, that's quite clear, and ten to one if the excitement of tonight won't go a good way towards slaughtering him before his time."

"Well, it may be so," cried the blacksmith, "but still it's good advice, and as I said before it comes to this—is we to be afraid to lay down in our beds at night, or isn't we?"

Before any reply could be made to this interrogatory, the old clock that was in the public-house parlour struck the hour of eleven, and another peal of thunder seemed to be answering to the tinkling sounds.

"It's a rough night," said one, "I thought there would be a storm before morning by the look of the sun at setting—it went down with a strange fiery redness behind a bank of clouds. I move for going home."

"Who talks of going home," cried the blacksmith, "when vampyres are abroad? Hasn't old Timothy said, that a stormy night was the very one to settle the thing in."

"No," cried another, "he did not say night at all."

"I don't care whether he said night or day; I've made up my mind to do something; there's no doubt about it but that a vampyre is about the old church. Who'll come with me and ferret it out? it will be good service done to everybody's fireside."

THE NIGHT WATCH.—THE VAULT.

It was each moment becoming a more difficult affair to carry on any conversation in the public-house parlour, for not only did the thunder each moment almost interrupt the speakers with its loud reverberations, but now and then such a tremendous gust of wind would sweep round the house that it would be quite impossible for anyone to make himself heard amidst its loud howling noise.

These were circumstances however, which greatly aided no doubt, in the getting up of a superstitious feeling in the minds of the people there assembled, which made them ripe for any proposition, which perhaps in their soberer moments they would have regarded with considerable dismay; hence when the blacksmith rushed to the door, crying,—

"Who will follow me to the old church and lay hold of the vampyre?" About half-a-dozen of the boldest and most reckless,—and be it told to their honour (if there be any honour in such an enterprise, which after all, was a grossly selfish one,) they were the worst characters in the village—started to their feet to accompany him thither.

There are many persons who waver about an enterprise, who will join it when it has a show of force, and thus was it with this affair. The moment it was found that the blacksmith's proposition had some half-dozen stout adherents, he got as many more—some of whom joined him from curiosity, and some from dread of being thought to lack courage by their companions if they held off.

There was now a sufficiently large party to make a respectable demonstration, and quite elated with his success, and caring little for the storm that was raging, the blacksmith, closely followed by the butcher, who had no objection in life to the affair, especially as he was at variance with the parson concerning the tithes of a little farm he kept, called out,—

"To the church—to the church!" and followed by the rabble, rushed forward in the direction of the sacred edifice.

* * * * *

As the hour of eleven has struck, and as the reader is aware that at that hour Sir George Crofton and his two sons, accompanied by Mr. Bevan, had agreed to go to the church on their melancholy errand, we will leave the noisy brawlers of the alehouse for the purpose of detailing the proceedings of those whose fortunes we feel more closely interested in.

The baronet was by no means wavering in his determination, notwithstanding it had been made at a time of unusual excitement, when second thoughts might have been allowed to step in, and suggest some other course of proceeding.

Now, Mr. Bevan was not without his own private hopes that such would be the case; for what he dreaded above all other things was, the truth of the affair, and that Sir George would have the horror of discovering that there was much more in the popular superstition than, without ocular demonstration, he would have been inclined to admit.

Although a man of education and of refined abilities, the evidence that had already showed itself to him of the existence at all events of some supernatural being, with powers analogous to those of the fabled vampyre, was such that he could not wholly deny, without stultifying his intellect, that there might be such things.

It is a sad circumstance when the mind is, as it were, compelled to receive undeniable evidence of a something which the judgment has the strongest general reasons for disputing, and that was precisely the position of Mr. Bevan, and a most unenviable one it was. That night's proceedings, however, in the vault, he felt must put an end to all doubts and perplexity upon the subject, and so with a fervent hope that, in some, at present inexplicable manner, the thing would be found to be a delusion, he waited more anxiously the arrival of the Croftons at the parsonage.

At half past ten o'clock, instead of eleven, for as the evening advanced, Sir George Crofton had shown such an amount of nervousness that his sons had thought it would be better to bring him to the parsonage, they arrived, and Mr. Bevan perceived at once what a remarkable effect grief and anxiety had already had upon the features of the baronet.

He was a different man to what, but a few days since, he had been, and more than ever the kind clergyman felt inclined to doubt the expediency of his being present on such an occasion, and yet how to prevent him if he were really determined, was a matter of no small difficulty.

"My dear friend," said Mr. Bevan, "will you pardon me if I make an effort now to persuade you to abandon this enterprise?"

"I can pardon the effort easily," said Sir George Crofton, "because I know it is dictated by the best of motives, but I would fain be spared it, for I am determined."

"I will say no more, but only with deep sincerity hope that you may return to your dwelling, each relieved from the load of anxiety that now oppresses you."

"I hope to Heaven it may be so."

"The night looks strange and still," said Charles, who wished to draw his father's attention as much as possible from too close a contemplation of the expedition on which they were bound.

"It does," said Edwin; "I should not be surprised at a storm, for there is every indication of some disturbance of the elements."

"Let it come," said Sir George, who fancied that in all those remarks he detected nothing but a wish to withdraw him from his enterprise;

"Let it come. I have a duty to perform, and I will do it, though Heaven's thunders should rock the very earth—the forked lightning is not launched at the father who goes to watch at the grave of his child."

Charles and Edwin, upon finding that Sir George was in the mood to make a misapplication of whatever was said to him, desisted from further remarks, but left Mr. Bevan quietly to converse with him, in a calm and unirritating manner.

It was the object of the clergyman to put off as much time as possible before proceeding to the church, so that the period to be spent in the family vault of the Croftons should be lessened as much as possible, for he felt assured that each minute there wasted would be one of great agony to the bereaved father, who would feel himself once again in such close approximation to that daughter on whom he had placed some of his dearest affections.

Sir George, however, defeated this intention, by promptly rising when his watch told him that the hour of eleven had arrived, and it was in vain to attempt to stultify him into a belief that he was wrong as regarded the time, for the church was sufficiently near for them to hear the hour of eleven pealed forth from its ancient steeple.

"Come," said Sir George, "the hour has arrived. I pray you do not delay. I know you are all anxious and fearful concerning me, but I have a spirit of resolution and firmness in this affair which shall yet stand me in good stead. I shall not shrink, as you imagine I shall shrink. Come, then, at once—it is suspense and delay which frets me, and not action."

These words enforced a better spirit into both his sons and Mr. Bevan, and in a few moments the party of four, surely sufficiently strong to overcome any unexpected obstacles, or to defeat any trickery that might be attempted to be passed off upon them, proceeded towards the church.

It will be recollected that it was just a little after that time that the storm commenced, and, in fact, the first clap of thunder, that seemed to shake the heavens, took place just as they reached the old grave-yard adjoining to the sacred building.

"There!" exclaimed Charles, "I thought that it would come."

"What matter?" said Sir George, "come on."

"Humour him in everything," said Mr. Bevan, "It is madness now to contradict him--he will not recede under any circumstances."

The natural senses of Sir George Crofton appeared to be preternaturally acute, for he turned sharply, and said quickly, but not unkindly,—

"No, he will not recede—come on."

After this, nothing was said until they reached the church door, and then while Mr. Bevan was searching in his pockets for the little key which opened the small private entrance, some vivid flashes of lightning lit up with extraordinary brilliancy the old gothic structure—the neighbouring tombs and the melancholy yew trees that waved their branches in the night air.

Perhaps the delay which ensued before Mr. Bevan could find the key, likewise arose from the wish to keep Sir George as short a time as possible within the vault, but he at length produced it, for any further delay could only be accounted for by saying that he had it not.

The small arched doorway was speedily cleared, and as another peal of thunder broke over head in awful grandeur of sound, they entered the church. Mr. Bevan took the precaution this time to close the door, so that there could be no interruption from without.

"Now, Sir George," he said, "remember your promise. You are to come away freely at the first dawn of day, and if nothing by then has occurred to strengthen the frightful supposition which, I suppose I may say, we have all indulged in, I do hope that forever this subject will be erased from your recollection."

"Be it so," said Sir George; "be it so."

Mr. Bevan then busied himself in lighting a lantern, and from beneath one of the pews, where they were hidden, he procured a couple of crowbars, with which to raise the stone that covered the entrance to the vault.

These preparations took up some little time, so that the old clock had chimed the quarter past eleven, and must have been rapidly getting on to the half-hour, before they stood in the aisle close to the vault.

"This marble slab," said Sir George, as he cast his eyes upon it, "always hitherto has been cemented in its place. Why is it not so now?"

"Is it not?" said Mr. Bevan.

"No—lend me the light."

Mr. Bevan was averse to lending him the light, but he could not very well refuse it; and when Sir George Crofton had looked more minutely at the marble slab, he saw that it had been cemented, but that the cement was torn and broken away, as if some violence had been used for the purpose of opening the vault; but whether that violence came from within or without was a matter of conjecture.

THE MADMAN.—THE VAMPYRE.

"What does this mean?" cried Sir George Crofton, excitedly.

"Hush!" said Mr. Bevan, "I pray you be calm, sir. If you are to make any discovery that will give you peace of mind, rest assured it will not be made by violence."

"You do not answer my question."

"I cannot answer it. Remember that I know no more than you do, and that, like yourselves, I am an adventurer here in search of the truth."

Sir George said no more upon that head, but with clasped hands and downcast eyes he stood in silence, while his two sons, armed with the crowbars that Mr. Bevan had provided for the occasion, proceeded to lift up the marble slab that covered the vault where lay their sister's remains.

The work was not one of great difficulty, for the slab was not very large, and as it was not cemented down, it yield at once to the powerful leverage that was brought to play against it, and in a few minutes it was placed aside, and the yawning abyss appeared before them.

"Oh! sir," said Mr. Bevan, "even now at this late hour, and when the proceedings have commenced, I pray you to pause."

"Pause!" cried Sir George, passionately, "pause for what?"

"Disturb not the dead, and let them rest in peace. Absolve your mind from the dangerous and perhaps fatal fancies that possess it, and let us say a prayer, and close again this entrance to the tomb."

The sons hesitated, and they probably would have taken the clergyman's advice, but Sir George was firm.

"No, sir," he said, "already have I suffered much in coming thus far; I will not retreat until I have effected all my purpose. I swear it, by Heaven, whose temple we now are in. You would not, Mr. Bevan, have me break such an oath."

"I would not; but I regret you made it. Since, however, it must be so, and this rash adventure is determined upon, follow me; I will lead you the way into these calm regions, where you can sleep, I trust, in peace."

Sir George Crofton made a step forward, as if he would have arrested Mr. Bevan's progress and lead the way himself, but already the clergyman had descended several steps, so he had nothing to do but to follow him.

This they all did, Sir George going immediately after him, and his two sons, with pale anxious-looking faces, as if they had a suspicion that the adventure would end in something terrific, came last, and they glanced nervously and suspiciously about them; but they said not a word, nor if they had spoken, it would have been to express great apprehension, and that was what they were ashamed to do.

Mr. Bevan carried the light, and when he felt that he was at the bottom of the stone steps, by finding that he was treading upon the sawdust that was strewn on the floor of the vault, he turned and held the lamp up at arm's length, so that his companions might see their way down the steps.

In another minute they all stood on the floor of the vault.

The light burnt with rather a faint and sickly glare, for so rapidly were noxious gases evolved in that receptacle for the dead, that notwithstanding it had been so frequently opened as it had been lately, they had again accumulated.

In a few moments, however, this was partially remedied by the air from the church above, and the light burnt more brilliantly—indeed, quite sufficiently so to enable them to look around them in the vault.

Sir George Crofton's feelings at that moment must have been of the most painful and harrowing description. He had lived long enough to be a witness of the death and the obsequies of many members of his family whom he had loved fondly, and there he stood in that chamber of death, surrounded by all the remains of those beings, the memory of whose appearance and voices came now freshly upon his mind.

Mr. Bevan could well guess the nature of the sad thoughts that transpired in the breast of the baronet, and the sons having by accident cast their eyes upon the coffin that contained the remains of their mother, regarded it in silence, while memory was busy, too, within them in conjuring up her image.

"And it has come to this," said Sir George, solemnly.

"We must all come to this," interposed Mr. Bevan; "this is indeed a place for solemn and holy thoughts—for self-examination, for self-condemnation."

"But there is peace here."

"There is—the peace that shall be eternal."

"Hark! hark!" said Charles; "what is that?"

"The wind," said Mr. Bevan; "nothing but the wind howling round and through the old belfry—you will remember that it is a boisterous night."

"Turn, turn, father."

Sir George turned and looked at Charles, who pointed in silence to the coffin which contained the corpse of his mother. The light gleamed upon the plate on which was engraved her name. Sir George's features moved convulsively as he read it, and he turned aside to hide a sudden gush of emotion that came over him.

After a few minutes, he touched Mr. Bevan on the arm, and said in a whisper,—

"Where did they place my child?"

The clergyman pointed to the narrow shelf on which was the coffin of Clara Crofton, and then Sir George, making a great effort to overcome his feelings, said,—

"Mr. Bevan, our worthy minister and friend, and you, likewise, my boys, hear me. You can guess to some extent, but not wholly—that can only be known by God—the agony that a sight of the poor remains of her who has gone from me in all the pride of her youth and beauty, must be to me; yet now that I am here I consider it to be my duty to look once again upon the face of my child—my—my lost Clara."

"Oh! father, father," said Edwin, "forego this purpose."

"You will spare us this," cried Charles.

"Repent you, sir," said Mr. Bevan, "of the wish. Let her rest in peace. The dead are sanctified."

"The dead are sanctified,—but I am her father."

"Nay, Sir George, let me implore you."

"Implore me to what, sir? Not to look upon the face of my own child? Peace—peace. It is no profanation for one who loved her as I loved her to look upon her once again. Urge me no more."

"This is in vain," said Charles.

"You are right—it is in vain."

A shriek burst from the lips of Edwin at this moment, and flinging his arms around his father, he held him back. Mr. Bevan, too, gave a cry of terror, and Charles stood with his hands clasped, as if turned to stone.

Their eyes were all bent upon Clara's coffin.

The lid moved, and a strange sound was heard from within that receptacle for the dead—the clock of the old church struck twelve—the coffin lid moved again, and then sliding on one side, it eventually fell upon the floor of the vault.

The four spectators of this scene were struck speechless for the time with terror. Then they stood gazing at the coffin as if they were so many statues.

And now the light which Mr. Bevan still for a miracle held in his trembling grasp, shone on a mass of white clothing within the coffin, and in another moment that white clothing was observed to be in motion. Slowly the dead form that was there rose up, and they all saw the pale and ghastly face.

A streak of blood was issuing from the mouth, and the eyes were open.

Sir George Crofton lifted up both his hands, and struck his head, and then he burst into a wild frightful laugh. It was the laugh of insanity.

Mr. Bevan dropped the light, and all was darkness.

"Ha, ha, ha, ha, ha!" laughed Sir George Crofton. "Ha, ha, ha, ha, ha!" and the horrible laugh was taken up by many an echo in the old church, and responded to with strange and most unearthly reverberations. "Ha, ha, ha, ha!" Oh what a dreadful sound that was coming at such a time from the lips of the father.

"Fly Edwin—oh, fly," cried Charles.

Edwin screamed twice, for he was full of horror, and then he fell on the floor of the vault in a state of insensibility.

Charles had just sense left him to spring towards the steps, and make a frantic effort to reach the church; in his hurry he fell twice, but each time rising again with a shout of despair, he resumed his efforts, and all the while the horrible laugh of his maniac father sounded in his ears, a sound which he felt that he should never forget.

By a great effort he did reach the aisle of the church, and when there, he called aloud.

"Mr. Bevan, Mr. Bevan, help—oh help! For the love of God speak. Help, help, Mr. Bevan, where are you, speak, I implore you? Am I too going mad? Oh yes, I shall—I must. What mortal intellect can stand such a scene as this. Help, help—oh, help!"

The church was suddenly lit up by a flash of light, and turning in the direction from whence it proceeded, Charles saw Mr. Bevan approaching with a light, which he had procured from the chancel, and it would appear that immediately upon dropping in his horror the light in the vault, he ran up the stairs with the intent of getting another.

"Who calls me? Who calls me?" he cried.

"I—I," said Charles. "Oh God, what a dreadful night is this."

The clergyman was trembling violently, and was very pale, but he made his way up to Charles, from whose brow the perspiration was falling in heavy drops, and then again they heard the mad Sir George laughing in the vault.

"Ha, ha, ha! ha, ha, ha! ha, ha, ha!"

"Oh God, is not that horrible?" said Charles.

"Most horrible," responded Mr. Bevan.

Bang—bang—bang! At this moment came a violent knocking at the church door, and then several voices were heard without shouting.

"The vampyre—the vampyre—the vampyre."

"What is that? What is that?" said Charles.

"Nay, I know not," replied Mr. Bevan, "I am nearly distracted already. Where is your brother? Did he not escape from the vault? Where is he? Oh, that horrible laugh. Good God! that knocking too at the church door. What can be the meaning of it? Heaven in its mercy guide us now what to do."

The reader will understand the meaning of the knocking, although those bewildered persons who heard it in the church did not. The fact is, that the party from the alehouse headed by the valiant blacksmith, and heated by their too liberal potations had just arrived at the church, and were clamouring for admission.

They had seen through one of the old pointed windows, the reflection of the light which Mr. Bevan carried, and that it was that convinced them someone was there who might if he would pay attention to the uproarious summons.

The knocking lasted with terrible effect, for the old door of the sacred edifice shook again, it seemed as if certainly it could not resist the making of such an attack.

Mr. Bevan was confounded. A horrible suspicion came across him, of what was meant by those violent demands for admission, and he shook with brutal trepidation as he conjectured what might be the effect of the proceedings of a lawless mob.

"Now Heaven help us," he said, "for we shall soon I fear be powerless."

"Good God! what mean you?" said Charles.

"I scarcely know how to explain to you all my fears. They are too dreadful to think of, but while that knocking continues, what can I think?"

"I understand! they call for my sister."

"Oh call her not now by that name. Remember, and remember with a shudder what she now is."

THE HUNT OF THE VAMPYRE.

All these occurrences which have taken a considerable time in telling, occurred as simultaneously, that although it would appear Mr. Bevan and Charles Crofton, rather neglected Sir George and Edwin who were still in the vault, they had really not had time to think of them, to say nothing of making any effort to extricate them from the frightful situation in which they were placed.

Probably, after procuring a light, Mr. Bevan would have rushed to their rescue had not that incessant knocking at the church door suggested a new and more horrible danger, still, from the evil passions of an infuriated multitude.

"Oh, Mr. Charles," he said, "if we could but get your father away from the church, there is no knowing what an amount of misery he might be spared."

"Misery, sir; surely there is no more misery in store for us—have we not suffered enough—more than enough. Oh, Mr. Bevan we have fallen upon evil times, and I dread to think what will yet be the end of those most frightful transactions."

The knocking at the church door continued violently, and Charles indicated a wish to proceed there to ascertain what it was, but Mr. Bevan stopped him, saying,—

"No, Charles—no—let them be, I hardly think they will venture to break into the sacred edifice, but whether they do or not, remember that your duty and mine, yours being the duty of a son, and mine that of a friend, should take us now to your father's vault.

"That is true, sir," said Charles, "lead on I will follow you."

Mr. Bevan, who had all the intellectual courage of a man of education, and of regular habits, led the way again to the vault, with the light in his hand. It was a great relief that the insane and horrible laugh of Sir George Crofton had ceased, the best friend of any man could almost have wished him dead, ere their ears had drunk in such horrible sounds.

The shouts and cries from without now became incessant, and it seemed as if some weapon had been procured, wherewith to hammer violently upon the church door, for the strokes were regular and incessant, and it was evident that if they continued long that frail defense against the incursions of the rabble rout without must soon give way.

The only effect, however, which these sounds had upon Mr. Bevan was to make him hasten his progress towards the vault, for anything in the shape of a collision between those who wanted to take the church by storm, and Sir George Crofton, was indeed most highly to be deprecated.

The steps were not many in number, and once again the clergyman and Charles Crofton stood upon the sawdust that covered the flooring of the vault.

At first, in consequence of the flaring of the light, the state of affairs in that dismal region could not be ascertained; but as soon as they could get a view, they found Sir George lying apparently in a state of insensibility across the coffin of his daughter Clara, while Edwin was in a swoon close to his feet.

"Sir George, Sir George," cried Mr. Bevan, "arouse yourself; it is necessary that you leave this place at once."

The baronet got up and glanced at the intruders. Charles uttered a deep groan, for the most superficial observation of his father's face was sufficient to convince him that reason had fled, and that wildness had set up his wild dominion in his brain.

"Father—father," he cried, "speak to me, and dissipate a frightful thought."

"What would you have of me," said Sir George; "I am a vampyre, and this is my tomb—you should see me in the rays of the cold moon gliding 'twixt earth and heaven, and panting for a victim. I am a vampyre."

At this moment Edwin seemed to be partially recovering, for his eyes opened as he lay upon the floor, and he looked around him with a bewildered gaze, which soon settled into one of more intelligence as memory resumed her sway, and he recollected the various circumstances that had brought him into his present position.

"Rouse yourself, Edwin, rouse yourself," cried Mr. Bevan, "you must aid us to remove your father."

"Do you talk of me?" said Sir George, "know you not that I am one of those supernatural existences known as the death and despair-dealing vampyres—it's time I took my nightly prowl to look for victims. I must have blood—I must have blood."

"Gracious Heaven! he raves," said Charles.

"Heed him not," said Mr. Bevan—"heed him not, and touch him not, so that he leave the place—when we have him once clear of the church we can procure assistance, and take him to his own home."

"Edwin," whispered Charles, "what of our sister?"

Edwin shook his head and shuddered. "I know nothing but that I saw her—oh, horrible sight, rising from her coffin, and then in a convulsion of terror my senses fled--a frightful ringing laugh came on my ears, and from that time till now, be the period long or short, I have been blessed by a death-like trance."

"Blessed indeed," said Mr. Bevan; "tarry one moment."

Sir George Crofton was ascending the steps of the vault, but his two sons paused for an instant at the request of Mr. Bevan, and then the latter approaching Clara's coffin slightly removed the lid, and was gratified as far as any feeling could be considered gratification under such circumstances, to find that the corpse occupied an ordinary position in its narrow resting place.

"All's right," he said, "let us persuade ourselves that this too has been but a dream, that we have been deceived, and that imagination has played us tricks it is accustomed to play to those who give it the rein at such hours as these—let us think and believe anything rather than that what we have seen tonight is real."

As he spoke these words, he ascended hastily the steps in pursuit of Sir George, who, by this time had alone reached the top.

The heavy strokes against the door of the church had ceased, but an odd sort of scraping, rattling sound at the lock convinced the clergyman that a workman of more skill than he who had wielded the hammer, was now at work, endeavouring to force an entrance.

"Oh, if we could but get out," he said, "by the small private entrance, all might be well; Charles, urge your father, I pray you."

Charles did so to the best of his ability, but the blacksmith who had originally incited the crowd to attack the church, in order to get possession of the body of the vampyre, had sent to his workshop for the tools of his craft, and soon quietly accomplished by skill what brute force would have been a long time about, namely, the opening of the church-door.

It was flung wide open, before Sir George Croton and his sons could reach the small private entrance, of which Mr. Bevan had the key.

The sight of the multitude of persons, for they looked such crowds in the church porch, materially increased the incipient sadness of the bereaved father.

THE FATE OF SIR GEORGE.—THE CROSS ROAD.

Sir George, when he saw the crowd of persons, seemed to have some undefined idea that they were enemies, but this would not have been productive of any serious consequences, if it had not most unfortunately happened that a most formidable weapon was within his grasp.

That weapon consisted of one of the long iron crowbars which had been successfully used by his own sons in order to force a passage to the family vault, where such horrors had been witnessed.

Suddenly, then, seizing this weapon, which, in the hands of a ferocious man was a most awful one, he swung it once round his head, and then rushed upon those he considered his foes.

He dealt but three blows, and at each of those one of the assailants fell lifeless in the church porch.

To resist, or, to attempt to contend with a man so armed, and apparently possessed of such preternatural strength, was what some of the party wished, and accordingly a free passage was left for him, and he rushed out of the church into the night air shouting for vengeance, and still at interval, accusing himself of being a vampyre, as most dangerous theme to touch upon, considering the then state of feeling in that little district.

Anxiety for the safety of Sir George induced his sons and Mr. Bevan to rush after him, regardless of all other consequences, so that the church, the vaults, and everything they contained, were left to the mercy of a mob infuriated by superstition, rendered still more desperate by the loss of three of their number in so sudden and exampled a manner.

They opposed no obstacle to the leaving of those persons, who thus for dearer considerations abandoned the old church, but they rushed with wild shouts and gesticulations into the building.

"The vampyre, the vampyre," cried the blacksmith, "death to the vampyre—death and destruction to the vampyre."

"Hurrah!" cried another, "to the vaults this way to Sir George Crofton's vault."

There seemed to be little doubt now, but that this disorderly rabble would execute summary vengeance upon the supposed nocturnal disturber of the peace of the district.

Ever and anon, too, as these shouts of discord, and of threatening vengeance, rose upon the night air, there would come the distant muttering of thunder, for the storm had not yet ceased, although its worst fury had certainly passed away.

Dark and heavy clouds were sweeping up from the horizon, and it seemed to be tolerably evident that some heavy deluge of rain would eventually settle the fury of the elements, and reconcile the discord of wind and electricity.

Several of the rioters were provided with links and matches, so that in a few moments the whole interior of the church was brilliantly illuminated, while at the same time it presented a grotesque appearance, in consequence of the unsteady and wavering flame from the links, throw myriads of dancing shadows upon the walls.

There would have been no difficulty under any ordinary circumstances in finding the entrance to the vault, where the dead of the Crofton family should have lain in peace, but now since the large flagstone that covered the entrance to that receptacle of the grave was removed, it met their observation at once.

It was strange now to perceive how, for a moment, superstition having led them on so far, the same feeling should induce them to pause, ere they ventured to make their way down these gloomy steps.

It was a critical moment, and probably if any one or two had taken a sudden panic, the whole party might have left the church with precipitation, having done a considerable amount of mischief, and yet as it is so usual with rioters, having left their principal object unaccomplished.

The blacksmith put an end to this state of indecision, for, seizing a link from the man who was nearest to him, he darted down the steps, exclaiming as he did so,—

"Whoever's afraid, need not follow me."

This was a taunt they were not exactly prepared to submit to, and the consequence was, that in a very few moments the ancient and time-honoured vault of the Crofton's was more full of the living than of the dead.

The blacksmith laid his hand upon Clara's coffin.

"Here it is," he said, "I know the very pattern of the cloth, and the fashion of the nails, I saw it at Grigson's the undertaker's before it was taken to the Grange."

"Is she there—is she there," cried half a dozen voices at once.

Even the blacksmith hesitated a moment ere he removed the lid from the receptacle of death, but when he did so, and his eyes fell upon the face of the presumed vampyre, he seemed rejoiced to find in the appearances then exhibited some sort of justification for the act of violence of which already he had been the instigator.

"Here you are," he said. "Look at the bloom upon her lips, why her cheeks are fresher and rosier than ever they were while she was alive, a vampyre my mates, this is a vampyre, or may I never break bread again; and now what's to be done."

"Burn her, burn her," cried several.

"Well," said the blacksmith, "mind it's as you like. I've brought you here, and shown you what it is, and now you can do what you like, and of course I'll lend you a hand to do it."

Anyone who had been very speculative in this affair, might have detected in these last words of the blacksmith, something like an inclination to creep out of the future consequences of what might next be done, while at the same time shame deterred him from exactly leaving his companions in the lurch.

After some suggestions then, and some argumentation as to the probability or possibility of interruption—the coffin itself, was with its sad and wretched occupant, lifted from the niche where it should have remained until that awful day when the dead shall rise for judgement, and carried up the steps into the graveyard, but scarcely had they done so, when the surcharged clouds burst over their heads, and the rain came down in perfect torrents.

The deluge was of so frightful, and continuous a character, that they shrank back again beneath the shelter of the church porch, and there waited until its first fury had passed away.

Such an even down storm seldom lasts long in our climate, and the consequence was that in about ten minutes the shower had so far subsided that although a continuous rain was falling it bore but a very distant comparison to what had taken place.

"How are we to burn the body on such a night as this?"

"Aye, how indeed," said another; "you could not so much as kindle a fire, and if you did, it would not live many minutes."

"I'll tell you what to do at once," said one who had as yet borne but a quiet part in the proceedings; I'll tell you what to do at once, for I saw it done myself; a vampyre is quite as secure buried in a cross-road with a stake through its body, as if you burned it in all the fires in the world; come on, the rain won't hinder you doing that."

This was a suggestion highly approved of, and the more so as there was a cross road close at hand, so that the deed would be done quick, and the parties dispersed to their respective homes, for already the exertion they had taken, and the rain that had fallen, had had a great effect in sobering them.

And even now the perilous and disgusting operation of destroying the body, by fire or any other way, might have been abandoned, had any one of the party suggested such a course—but the dread of a future imputation of cowardice kept all silent.

Once more the coffin was raised by four of the throng, and carried through the churchyard, which was now running in many little rivulets, in consequence of the rain. The crossroad was not above a quarter of a mile from the spot, and while those who were disengaged from carrying the body, were hurrying away to get spades and mattocks, the others walked through the rain, and finally paused at the place they though suitable for that ancient superstitious rite, which it was thought would make the vampyre rest in peace.

It is hard to suppose that Sir George Crofton, his sons, and Mr. Bevan were all deceived concerning these symptoms of vitality which they had observed in the corpse of Clara; but certainly now, there was no appearance of anything of the kind, and the only suspicious circumstances appeared to be the blood upon the lips, and the very fresh-like appearance of the face.

If it were really a fact that the attack of Varney the Vampyre upon this fair young girl had converted her into one of those frightful existences, and that she had been about to leave her tomb for the purpose of seeking a repast of blood, it would appear that the intention had been checked and frustrated by the presence of Sir George and his party in the vault.

At last a dozen men now arrived well-armed with spades and picks, and they commenced the work of digging a deep, rather than a capacious, grave in silence.

A gloomy and apprehensive spirit seemed to come over the whole assemblage, and the probability is that this was chiefly owing to the fact that they now encountered no opposition, and that they were permitted unimpeded to accomplish a purpose which had never yet been attempted within the memory of any of the inhabitants of the place.

The grave was dug, and about two feet depth of soil was thrown in a huge mound upon the surface; the coffin was lowered, and there lay the corpse within that receptacle of poor humanity, unimprisoned by any lid for that had been left in the vault, and awaiting the doom which they had decreed upon it, but which they now with a shuddering horror shrunk from performing.

A hedge-stake with a sharp point had been procured, and those who held it looked around them with terrified countenances, while the few links that had not been extinguished by the rain, shed a strange and lurid glare upon all objects.

"It must be done," said the blacksmith, "don't let it be said that we got thus far and then were afraid."

"Do it then yourself," said the man that held the stake, "I dare not."

"Aye, do," cried several voices; "you brought us here, why don't you do it—are you afraid after all your boasting."

"Afraid—afraid of the dead; I'm not afraid of any of you that are alive, and it's not likely I'm going to be afraid of a dead body; you're a pretty set of cowards. I've no animosity against the girl, but I want that we shall all sleep in peace, and that our wives and children should not be disturbed nocturnally in their blessed repose. I'll do it if none of you'll do it, and then you may thank me afterwards for the act, although I suppose if I get into trouble I shall have you all turn tail upon me."

"No, we won't—no, we won't."

"Well, well, here goes, whether you do or not. I—I'll do it directly."

"He shrinks," cried one.

"No," said another; "he'll do it—now for it, stand aside."

"Stand aside yourself—do you want to fall into the grave."

The blacksmith shuddered as he held the stake in an attitude to pierce the body, and even up to that moment it seemed to be a doubtful case, whether he would be able to accomplish his purpose or not; at length, when they all thought he was upon the point of abandoning his design, and casting the stake away, he thrust it with tremendous force through the body and the back of the coffin.

The eyes of the corpse opened wide—the hands were clenched, and a shrill, piercing shriek came from the lips—a shriek that was answered by as many as there were persons present, and then with pallid fear upon their countenances they rushed headlong from the spot.

THE SOLITARY MAN. —VARNEY'S DESPAIR.

There lay the dead, alone, in that awful grave, dabbled in blood, and the victim of the horrible experiment that had been instituted to lay a vampire. The rain still fell heavily. Oh, surely, pitying Heaven sent those drops to wash out the remembrance of such a deed.

The grave slowly began to be a pool of water; it rose up the sides of the coffin, and in a few minutes, nothing more of the ghastly and the terrible contents of that grave could have been seen.

Before that took place, a man of tall stature and solemn gait stepped up and stood upon the brink of the little excavation.

For a time he was as still as that sad occupant of the little space of earth that served her for a resting place, but at length in a tone of deep anguish he spoke,—

"And has it come to this?" he said, "is this my work? Oh, horror! Horror unspeakable. Is this some hideous dream or a reality of tragedy, so far transcending all I looked for, that if I had tears I should shed them now; but I have none. A hundred years ago that fount was dry. I thought that I had steeled my heart against all gentle impulses; that I had crushed—aye, completely crushed dove-eyed pity in my heart, but it is not so, and still sufficient of my once-human feelings clings to me to make me grieve for thee, Clara Crofton, thou victim!"

We need not tell our readers now, that it was no other than Varney the Vampyre himself from whom these words came.

After thus, then, giving such fervent utterance to the sad feeling that had overcome him, he stood for a time silent, and then glancing around him as well as he could by the dim light, he found the spades, by the aid of which the grave had been dug, and which the men had in their great flight left behind them.

Seizing one, he commenced, with an energy and perseverance that was well adapted to accomplish the object, to fill up the grave.

"You shall now rest in peace," he said.

In the course of about ten minutes the grave was levelled completely, so that there were no signs or indications of any one having been there interred.

The rain was still falling, and notwithstanding that circumstance, he continued at his work, until he had stamped down the earth to a perfect level; and then, even, as if he was still further anxious to thoroughly destroy any indication of the deed that had been done, he took the loose earth that was superfluous, and scattered it about.

"This done," he said, "surely you will now know peace."

He cast down the spade with which he had been working, and lingered for a few brief moments. Suddenly he started, for he heard, or thought he heard, an approaching footstep.

His first impulse appeared to be to fly, but that he soon corrected, and folding his arms solemnly across his breast, he waited for the man that was now evidently making speed towards that spot.

In a few moments more he saw the dusky outline of the figure, and then Mr. Bevan, the clergyman, stood before him.

Mr. Bevan did not at the moment recognize in the form before him the man who had been the guest of Sir George Crofton, and from whom it was supposed had sprung all the mischief and horror that had fallen upon the family, at the Grange.

"Who are you?" he cried; "can you give me information of an outrage that has been committed hereabouts."

"Much," said Varney.

"Ah! I know the voice. Are you not he who was rescued from the sea by the two sons of Sir George Crofton?"

"Well."

"Now I know you, and I am glad to have met with you."

"You will try to kill me?"

"No, no—peace is my profession."

"Ah! you are the priest of this place. Well, sir, what would you with me?"

"I would implore you to tell me if it be really true that—that—"

Mr. Bevan paused, for he disliked to show that the fear that it might be true there were such creatures as vampyres, had taken so strong a hold of him.

"Proceed," said Varney.

"I will. Are you then a vampyre?"

"A strange question for one living man to put to another! Are you?"

"You are inclined to trifle with me. But I implore you to answer me. I am perhaps the only man in all this neighbourhood to whom you can give an answer in the affirmative with safety."

"And why so?"

"Because I question not the decrees of Heaven. If it seems fit to the great Ruler of Heaven and of earth that there should be ever such horrible creatures as vampyres, ought I his creature to question it?"

"You ought not—you ought not. I have heard much from priests, but from your lips I hear sound reason. I am a vampyre."

Mr. Bevan shrunk back, and shook for a moment, as he said in a low faltering tone,—

"For how long—have you—"

"You would know how long I have endured such a state of existence. I will tell you that I have a keen remembrance of being hunted through the streets of London in the reign of Henry the Fourth."

"Henry the Fourth?"

"Yes, I have seen all the celebrities of this and many other lands from that period. More than once have I endeavoured to cast off this horrible existence, but it is my destiny to remain in it. I was picked up by the brothers Crofton after one of my attempts to court death. They have been repaid."

"Horribly!"

"I cannot help it—I am what I am."

There was a strange and mournful solemnity about the tones of Varney that went to the heart of Mr. Bevan, and after a few moments pause, he said,—

"You greatly, very greatly awake my interest. Do not leave me. Ask yourself if there is anything that I can do to alleviate your destiny. Have you tried prayer?"

"Prayer?"

"Yes. Oh! there is great virtue in prayer."

"I pray? What for should I pray but for that death which whenever it seems to be in my grasp has then flitted from me in mockery, leaving me still a stranded wretch upon the shores of this world. Perhaps you have at times fancied you have suffered some great amount of mental agony. Perhaps you have stood by the bed-side of dying creatures, and heard them howl their hopelessness of Heaven's mercy, but you cannot know—you cannot imagine—what I have suffered."

As he spoke, he turned away, but Mr. Bevan followed him, saying,—

"Remain—remain, I implore you."

"Remain—and wherefore?"

"I will be your friend—it is my duty to be such; remain, and you shall if you wish it, have an asylum in my house. If you will not pray yourself, to Heaven, I will pray for you, and in time to come you will have some hope. Oh, believe me, earnest prayer is not in vain."

"My friend!"

"Yes, your friend; I am, I ought to be the friend of all who are unhappy."

"And is there really one human being who does not turn from me in horror and disgust? Oh, sir, you jest."

"No—on my soul, that which I say I mean. Come with me now, and you shall if you please, remain in secret in my house—no one shall know you are with me—from the moment that you cross the threshold you shall hope for happier days."

The vampyre paused, and it was evident that he was deeply affected by what Mr. Bevan said to him, for his whole frame shook.

GLOSSARY

B———: For the Bannerworth family, whom Varney threatens for the first 126 chapters.

Baize: Fabric.

Dissentients: People who think a different way, who disagree.

Dr. Chillingworth: An opponent of Varney during his time with the Bannerworths.

"Knit up the ravelled sleeve of care": From Shakespeare's *Macbeth,* Act 2, Scene 2.

Peculiarly: In the sense of "in particular."

"Pierces so that it assaults / Mercy itself, and frees all faults.": From the epilogue of Shakespeare's *The Tempest*, spoken by the wizard Prospero.

Resurrectionists: A common nickname for body snatchers. In the early 19th century, dissection was a highly restricted practice, and "Resurrectionists" would sometimes bring fresh cadavers to doctors and medical students.
"That strong conviction upon your heart": Because of a typographical error in the original 1847 text, there is no word to end the sentence after "your." "Heart" is, therefore, a conjecture.
Topers: Drinkers.

AFTERWORD

Clara Crofton's victimization is so horrific, it serves as the final turning point of the long penny dreadful story. Sir Francis Varney, sickened by what he has done to Clara, and moved by Bevans's offer, gives up his evil un-life, writes some autobiographical notes, and travels to Naples to leap into the fires of Mt. Vesuvius. Varney is finally destroyed, and the saga comes to an end.

Clara's story seems like the exact opposite of vampirism as female empowerment. Silent until her final scream, Clara is terrified and completely alone—she flees both those who love and those who hate her. Does she avoid her fiancée and family to keep from attacking them? The story doesn't say, any more than it tells us whether the undead Clara has the power of speech.

But notice that Varney doesn't summon Clara back from the dead as his "slave" or "bride," but as a "sister" in what would presumably be a growing family. Given time, it has to be assumed that Clara would grow accustomed to her new state, and regain the ability to talk and walk among humans the way Varney does.

But she never gets the chance. Varney neglects her, leaving her to the mercy of a monster far worse than a vampire: a mob.

And on that note, it's interesting to see how the villagers who pursue Clara are portrayed. A little more than a century earlier, official reports of "real" vampires in Serbia described communities gathering together to dig up and stake the monsters. The villagers were quite willing to go ahead without official assistance, but their first impulse was to the authorities, secular and religious, for assistance. And they expected to be taken seriously. A hundred and twenty years later, an English writer pictures the early Victorian "lower classes" as a drunken rabble. Unlike the Central European villagers, the Englishmen don't seek help from any legal authority.

Now, the mob pursuing Clara Crofton is, in fact, hunting down a supernatural serial killer who is guaranteed to strike again; they are protecting themselves from a genuine threat to everyone in their community, and seek to "lay" the vampire (as one would "lay" a ghost or evil spirit) in the only way such creatures can be dealt with. Nevertheless, the mob is condemned, individually and collectively, by the narrator. Trapped in her coffin, Clara seems like the helpless victim of a lynch mob...or a fatal gang rape.

However, if they had *enlisted the help of a policeman, a judge, or even the Croftons and Dr. Bevan, would the end result have been any different? Clara would still end up screaming as someone drove a stake through her heart. (Contrast what happens to Clara with the fate of Lucy in* Dracula*—but Lucy is destroyed by the individualized heroes of that novel, who stake her for the same reason Thalaba stakes Oneiza: to save her soul.)*

There is a long British tradition of sympathy for the underdog, and so sympathy here goes out to the hunted criminal. There may be something else to it, though: Clara, the beautiful daughter of a Baronet, has murdered the lower-class Anna. This is, in a way, just one more commoner victimized by an aristocrat—one of countless examples. But in this case, as in a dream, the commoners get their revenge. Did that idea—that regular people would rise up against their "betters"—fill the middle-class author of Varney *with horror?*

The fear of mob violence, of the common people getting out of control, is also part of the backdrop of the next story. It, too, features an English vampire.

But the author is Russian.

ALICE

I stood still before her, and tried to speak; but the voice died away in my throat, though it was no longer fear exactly I felt.

Different cultures and languages have different ideas of what sounds exotic. For the Russian Ivan Turgenev, who was also fluent in French, German, Spanish and English, a mysterious ghostly vampire, floating through both space and time, could have no more romantic, evocative name than...Alice.

To English readers, the name seems so common—or maybe, so linked with Lewis Carroll's slightly later heroine—that some texts and commentary opt for the slightly more enigmatic "Ellis." But we'll go with the queen of Russian-into-English translators, Constance Garnett, and call her Alice.

Alice's conception seems to owe a lot to Russian folklore about supernatural women who exhaust their male victims by giving them flying piggy-back rides over the Russian countryside by moonlight. But Alice isn't Russian—she is, probably, English, although she remains ultimately mysterious, and, in the end, unknowable.

The story was written in 1863 and first published in 1864, in the premiere issue of Fyodor Dostoevsky's literary magazine Epoch.

PHANTOMS

Ivan Turgenev

Translated by Constance Garnett

'One instant . . . and the fairy tale is over,
And once again the actual fills the soul . . . '
— A. FET.

I

For a long time I could not get to sleep, and kept turning from side to side. "Confound this foolishness about table-turning!" I thought. "It simply upsets one's nerves." . . . Drowsiness began to overtake me at last. . . .

Suddenly it seemed to me as though there were the faint and plaintive sound of a harp-string in the room.

I raised my head. The moon was low in the sky, and looked me straight in the face. White as chalk lay its light upon the floor. . . . The strange sound was distinctly repeated.

I leaned on my elbow. A faint feeling of awe plucked at my heart. A minute passed, another. . . . Somewhere, far away, a cock crowed; another answered still more remote.

I let my head sink back on the pillow. "See what one can work oneself up to," I thought again . . . "there's a singing in my ears."

After a little while I fell asleep—or I thought I fell asleep. I had an extraordinary dream. I fancied I was lying in my room, in my bed—and was not asleep, could not even close my eyes. And again I heard the sound. . . . I turned over. . . . The moonlight on the floor began softly to lift, to rise up, to round off slightly above. . . . Before me, impalpable as mist, a white woman was standing motionless.

"Who are you?" I asked with an effort.

A voice made answer, like the rustle of leaves: "It is I… I . . . I have come for you."

"For me? But who are you?"

"Come by night to the edge of the wood where there stands an old oak tree. I will be there."

I tried to look closely into the face of the mysterious woman—and suddenly I gave an involuntary shudder: there was a chilly breath upon me. And then I was not lying down, but sitting up in my bed; and where, as I fancied, the phantom had stood, the moonlight lay in a long streak of white upon the floor.

II

The day passed somehow. I tried, I remember, to read, to work . . . everything was a failure. The night came. My heart was throbbing within me, as though it expected something. I lay down, and turned with my face to the wall.

"Why did you not come?" sounded a distinct whisper in the room. I looked round quickly.

Again she . . . again the mysterious phantom. Motionless eyes in a motionless face, and a gaze full of sadness.

"Come!" I heard the whisper again.

"I will come," I replied with instinctive horror. The phantom bent slowly forward, and undulating faintly like smoke, melted away altogether. And again the moon shone white and untroubled on the smooth floor.

III

I passed the day in unrest. At supper I drank almost a whole bottle of wine, and all but went out on to the steps; but I turned back and flung myself into my bed. My blood was pulsing painfully.

Again the sound was heard. . . . I started, but did not look round. All at once I felt that someone had tight hold of me from behind, and was whispering in my very ear: "Come, come, come . . ."

Trembling with terror, I moaned out: "I will come!" and sat up.

A woman stood stooping close to my very pillow. She smiled dimly and vanished. I had time, though, to make out her face. It seemed to me I had seen her before — but where, when? I got up late, and spent the whole day wandering about the country. I went to the old oak at the edge of the forest, and looked carefully all around.

Towards evening I sat at the open window in my study. My old housekeeper set a cup of tea before me, but I did not touch it. . . . I kept asking myself in bewilderment: "Am not I going out of my mind?" The sun had just set: and not the sky alone was flushed with red; the whole atmosphere was suddenly filled with an almost unnatural purple. The leaves and grass never stirred, stiff as though freshly coated with varnish. In their stony rigidity, in the vivid sharpness of their outlines, in this combination of intense brightness and death-like stillness, there was something weird and mysterious. A rather large grey bird suddenly flew up without a sound and settled on the very window sill. . . . I looked at it, and it looked at me sideways with its round, dark eye. "Were you sent to remind me, then?" I wondered.

At once the bird fluttered its soft wings, and without a sound — as before — flew away. I sat a long time still at the window, but I was no longer a prey to uncertainty. I had, as it were, come within the enchanted circle, and I was borne along by an irresistible though gentle force, as a boat is borne along by the current long before it reaches the waterfall. I started up at last. The purple had long vanished from the air, the colors were darkened, and the enchanted silence was broken. There was the flutter of a gust of wind, the moon came out brighter and brighter in the sky that was growing bluer, and soon the leaves of the trees were weaving patterns of black and silver in her cold beams. My old housekeeper came into the study with a lighted candle, but there was a draught from the window and the flame went out. I could restrain myself no longer. I jumped up, clapped on my cap, and set off to the corner of the forest, to the old oak-tree.

IV

This oak had, many years before, been struck by lightning; the top of the tree had been shattered, and was withered up, but there was still life left in it for centuries to come. As I was coming up to it, a cloud passed over the moon: it was very dark under its thick branches. At first I noticed nothing special; but I glanced on one side, and my heart fairly failed me—a white figure was standing motionless beside a tall bush between the oak and the forest. My hair stood upright on my head, but I plucked up my courage and went towards the forest.

Yes, it was she, my visitor of the night. As I approached her, the moon shone out again. She seemed all, as it were, spun out of half-transparent, milky mist—through her face I could see a branch faintly stirring in the wind; only the hair and eyes were a little dark, and on one of the fingers of her clasped hands a slender ring shone with a gleam of pale gold. I stood still before her, and tried to speak; but the voice died away in my throat, though it was no longer fear exactly I felt. Her eyes were turned upon me; their gaze expressed neither distress nor delight, but a sort of lifeless attention. I waited to see whether she would utter a word, but she remained motionless and speechless, and still gazed at me with her deathly intent eyes. Dread came over me again.

"I have come!" I cried at last with an effort. My voice sounded muffled and strange to me.

"I love you," I heard her whisper.

"You love me!" I repeated in amazement.

"Give yourself up to me," was whispered to me again in reply.

"Give myself up to you! But you are a phantom; you have no body even." A strange animation came upon me. "What are you—smoke, air, vapor? Give myself up to you! Answer me first, Who are you? Have you lived upon the earth? Whence have you come?"

"Give yourself up to me. I will do you no harm. Only say two words: 'Take me.' "

I looked at her. "What is she saying?" I thought. "What does it all mean? And how can she take me? Shall I try?"

"Very well," I said, and unexpectedly loudly, as though some one had given me a push from behind; "take me!"

I had hardly uttered these words when the mysterious figure, with a sort of inward laugh, which set her face quivering for an instant, bent forward, and stretched out her arms wide apart. . . I tried to dart away, but I was already in her power. She seized me, my body rose a foot from the ground, and we both floated smoothly and not too swiftly over the wet, still grass.

V

At first I felt giddy, and instinctively I closed my eyes. . . . A minute later I opened them again. We were floating as before; but the forest was now nowhere to be seen. Under us stretched a plain, spotted here and there with dark patches. With horror I felt that we had risen to a fearful height.

"I am lost; I am in the power of Satan," flashed through me like lightning. Till that instant the idea of a temptation of the evil one, of the possibility of perdition, had never entered my head. We still whirled on, and seemed to be mounting higher and higher.

"Where will you take me?" I moaned at last.

"Where you like," my companion answered. She clung close to me; her face was almost resting upon my face. But I was scarcely conscious of her touch.

"Let me sink down to the earth, I am giddy at this height."

"Very well; only shut your eyes and hold your breath."

I obeyed, and at once felt that I was falling like a stone flung from the hand . . . the air whistled in my ears. When I could think again, we were floating smoothly once more just above the earth, so that we caught our feet in the tops of the tall grass.

"Put me on my feet," I began. "What pleasure is there in flying? I'm not a bird."

"I thought you would like it. We have no other pastime."

"You? Then what are you?"

There was no answer.

"You don't dare to tell me that?"

The plaintive sound which had awakened me the first night quivered in my ears. Meanwhile we were still, scarcely perceptibly, moving in the damp night air.

"Let me go!" I said. My companion moved slowly away, and I found myself on my feet. She stopped before me and again folded her hands. I grew more composed and looked into her face; as before it expressed submissive sadness.

"Where are we?" I asked. I did not recognize the country about me.

"Far from your home, but you can be there in an instant."

"How can that be done? by trusting myself to you again?"

"I have done you no harm and will do you none. Let us fly till dawn, that is all. I can bear you away wherever you fancy—to the ends of the earth. Give yourself up to me! Say only: 'Take me!' "

"Well . . . take me!"

She again pressed close to me, again my feet left the earth— and we were flying.

VI

"Which way?" she asked me.

"Straight on, keep straight on."

"But here is a forest."

"Lift us over the forest, only slower."

We darted upwards like a wild snipe flying up into a birch-tree, and again flew on in a straight line. Instead of grass, we caught glimpses of tree-tops just under our feet. It was strange to see the forest from above, its bristling back lighted up by the moon. It looked like some huge slumbering wild beast, and accompanied us with a vast unceasing murmur, like some inarticulate roar. In one place we crossed a small glade; intensely black was the jagged streak of shadow along one side of it. Now and then there was the plaintive cry of a hare below us; above us the owl hooted, plaintively too; there was a scent in the air of mushrooms, buds, and dawn-flowers; the moon fairly flooded everything on all sides with its cold, hard light; the Pleiades gleamed just over our heads. And now the forest was left behind; a streak of fog stretched out across the open country; it was the river. We flew along one of its banks, above the bushes, still and weighed down with moisture. The river's waters at one moment glimmered with a flash of blue, at another flowed on in darkness, as it were, in wrath. Here and there a delicate mist moved strangely over the water, and the water-lilies' cups shone white in maiden pomp with every petal open to its full, as though they knew their safety out of reach. I longed to pick one of them, and behold, I found myself at once on the river's surface. . . . The damp air struck me an angry blow in the face, just as I broke the thick stalk of a great flower. We began to fly across from bank to bank, like the water-fowl we were continually waking up and chasing before us. More than once we chanced to swoop down on a family of wild ducks, settled in a circle on an open spot among the reeds, but they did not stir; at most one of them would thrust out its neck from under its wing, stare at us, and anxiously poke its beak away again in its fluffy feathers, and another faintly quacked, while its body twitched a little all over. We startled one heron; it flew up out of a willow bush, brandishing its legs and fluttering its wings with clumsy eagerness: it struck me as remarkably like a German. There was not the splash of a fish to be heard, they too were asleep.

I began to get used to the sensation of flying, and even to find a pleasure in it; any one will understand me, who has experienced flying in dreams. I proceeded to scrutinize with close attention the strange being, by whose good offices such unlikely adventures had befallen me.

VII

She was a woman with a small un-Russian face. Greyish-white, half-transparent, with scarcely marked shades, she reminded one of the alabaster figures on a vase lighted up within, and again her face seemed familiar to me.

"Can I speak with you?" I asked.

"Speak."

"I see a ring on your finger; you have lived then on the earth, you have been married?"

I waited . . . There was no answer.

"What is your name, or, at least, what was it?"

"Call me Alice."

"Alice! That's an English name! Are you an Englishwoman? Did you know me in former days?"

"No."

"Why is it then you have come to me?"

"I love you."

"And are you content?"

"Yes; we float, we whirl together in the fresh air."

"Alice!" I said all at once, "You are perhaps a sinful, condemned soul?"

My companion's head bent towards me. "I don't understand you," she murmured.

"I adjure you in God's name. . . . " I was beginning.

"What are you saying?" she put in in perplexity. "I don't understand."

I fancied that the arm that lay like a chilly girdle about my waist softly trembled. . . .

"Don't be afraid," said Alice, "don't be afraid, my dear one!" Her face turned and moved towards my face. . . . I felt on my lips a strange sensation, like the faintest prick of a soft and delicate sting. . . . Leeches might prick so in mild and drowsy mood.

VIII

I glanced downwards. We had now risen again to a considerable height. We were flying over some provincial town I did not know, situated on the side of a wide slope. Churches rose up high among the dark mass of wooden roofs and orchards; a long bridge stood out black at the bend of a river; everything was hushed, buried in slumber. The very crosses and cupolas seemed to gleam with a silent brilliance; silently stood the tall posts of the wells beside the round tops of the willows; silently the straight whitish road darted arrow-like into one end of the town, and silently it ran out again at the opposite end on to the dark waste of monotonous fields.

"What town is this?" I asked.

"X. . . ."

"X . . . in Y . . . province?"

"Yes."

"I'm a long distance indeed from home!"

"Distance is not for us."

"Really?" I was fired by a sudden recklessness. "Then take me to South America!"

"To America I cannot. It's daylight there by now."

"And we are night-birds. Well, anywhere, where you can, only far, far away."

"Shut your eyes and hold your breath," answered Alice, and we flew along with the speed of a whirlwind. With a deafening noise the air rushed into my ears. We stopped, but the noise did not cease. On the contrary, it changed into a sort of menacing roar, the roll of thunder . . .

"Now you can open your eyes," said Alice.

IX

I obeyed . . . Good God, where was I?

Overhead, ponderous, smoke-like storm-clouds; they huddled, they moved on like a herd of furious monsters . . . and there below, another monster; a raging, yes, raging, sea . . . The white foam gleamed with spasmodic fury, and surged up in hillocks upon it, and hurling up shaggy billows, it beat with a sullen roar against a huge cliff, black as pitch. The howling of the tempest, the chilling gasp of the storm-rocked abyss, the weighty splash of the breakers, in which from time to time one fancied something like a wail, like distant cannon-shots, like a bell ringing—the tearing crunch and grind of the shingle on the beach, the sudden shriek of an unseen gull, on the murky horizon the disabled hulk of a ship—on every side death, death and horror. . . . Giddiness overcame me, and I shut my eyes again with a sinking heart. . . .

"What is this? Where are we?"

"On the south coast of the Isle of Wight opposite the Blackgang cliff where ships are so often wrecked," said Alice, speaking this time with peculiar distinctness, and as it seemed to me with a certain malignant pleasure. . . .

"Take me away, away from here . . . home! home!" I shrank up, hid my face in my hands . . . I felt that we were moving faster than before; the wind now was not roaring or moaning, it whistled in my hair, in my clothes . . . I caught my breath . . .

"Stand on your feet now," I heard Alice's voice saying. I tried to master myself, to regain consciousness . . . I felt the earth under the soles of my feet, and I heard nothing, as though everything had swooned away about me . . . only in my temples the blood throbbed irregularly, and my head was still giddy with a faint ringing in my ears. I drew myself up and opened my eyes.

X

We were on the bank of my pond. Straight before me there were glimpses through the pointed leaves of the willows of its broad surface with threads of fluffy mist clinging here and there upon it. To the right a field of rye shone dimly; on the left stood up my orchard trees, tall, rigid, drenched it seemed in dew . . . The breath of the morning was already upon them. Across the pure grey sky stretched like streaks of smoke, two or three slanting clouds; they had a yellowish tinge, the first faint glow of dawn fell on them; one could not say whence it came; the eye could not detect on the horizon, which was gradually growing lighter, the spot where the sun was to rise. The stars had disappeared;

nothing was astir yet, though everything was already on the point of awakening in the enchanted stillness of the morning twilight.

"Morning! see, it is morning!" cried Alice in my ear. "Farewell till tomorrow."

I turned round . . . Lightly rising from the earth, she floated by, and suddenly she raised both hands above her head. The head and hands and shoulders glowed for an instant with warm, corporeal light; living sparks gleamed in the dark eyes; a smile of mysterious tenderness stirred the reddening lips. . . . A lovely woman had suddenly arisen before me. . . . But as though dropping into a swoon, she fell back instantly and melted away like vapor.

I remained passive.

When I recovered myself and looked round me, it seemed to me that the corporeal, pale-rosy colour that had flitted over the figure of my phantom had not yet vanished, and was enfolding me, diffused in the air. . . . It was the flush of dawn. All at once I was conscious of extreme fatigue and turned homewards. As I passed the poultry-yard, I heard the first morning cackling of the geese (no birds wake earlier than they do); along the roof at the end of each beam sat a rook, and they were all busily and silently pluming themselves, standing out in sharp outline against the milky sky. From time to time they all rose at once, and after a short flight, settled again in a row, without uttering a caw. . . . From the wood close by came twice repeated the drowsy, fresh chuck-chuck of the black-cock, beginning to fly into the dewy grass, overgrown by brambles. . . . With a faint tremor all over me I made my way to my bed, and soon fell into a sound sleep.

XI

The next night, as I was approaching the old oak, Alice moved to meet me, as if I were an old friend. I was not afraid of her as I had been the day before, I was almost rejoiced at seeing her; I did not even attempt to comprehend what was happening to me; I was simply longing to fly farther to interesting places.

Alice's arm again twined about me, and we took flight again.

"Let us go to Italy," I whispered in her ear.

"Wherever you wish, my dear one," she answered solemnly and slowly, and slowly and solemnly she turned her face towards me. It struck me as less transparent than on the eve; more womanlike and more imposing; it recalled to me the being I had had a glimpse of in the early dawn at parting.

"This night is a great night," Alice went on. "It comes rarely —when seven times thirteen . . ."

At this point I could not catch a few words.

"Tonight we can see what is hidden at other times."

"Alice!" I implored, "but who are you, tell me at last?"

Silently she lifted her long white hand. In the dark sky, where her finger was pointing, a comet flashed, a reddish streak among the tiny stars.

"How am I to understand you?" I began, "Or, as that comet floats between the planets and the sun, do you float among men . . . or what?"

But Alice's hand was suddenly passed before my eyes. . . . It was as though a white mist from the damp valley had fallen on me. . . .

"To Italy! to Italy!" I heard her whisper. "This night is a great night!"

XII

The mist cleared away from before my eyes, and I saw below me an immense plain. But already, by the mere breath of the warm soft air upon my cheeks, I could tell I was not in Russia; and the plain, too, was not like our Russian plains. It was a vast dark expanse, apparently desert and not overgrown with grass; here and there over its whole extent gleamed pools of water, like broken pieces of looking-glass; in the distance could be dimly descried a noiseless motionless sea. Great stars shone bright in the spaces between the big beautiful clouds; the murmur of thousands, subdued but never-ceasing, rose on all sides, and very strange was this shrill but drowsy chorus, this voice of the darkness and the desert. . . .

"The Pontine marshes," said Alice. "Do you hear the frogs? do you smell the sulphur?"

"The Pontine marshes. . . ." I repeated, and a sense of grandeur and of desolation came upon me. "But why have you brought me here, to this gloomy forsaken place? Let us fly to Rome instead."

"Rome is near," answered Alice. . . . "Prepare yourself!"

We sank lower, and flew along an ancient Roman road. A bullock slowly lifted from the slimy mud its shaggy monstrous head, with short tufts of bristles between its crooked backward-bent horns. It turned the whites of its dull malignant eyes askance, and sniffed a heavy snorting breath into its wet nostrils, as though scenting us.

"Rome, Rome is near . . ." whispered Alice. "Look, look in front. . .."

I raised my eyes.

What was the blur of black on the edge of the night sky? Were these the lofty arches of an immense bridge? What river did it span? Why was it broken down in parts? No, it was not a bridge, it was an ancient aqueduct. All around was the holy ground of the Campagna, and there, in the distance, the Albanian hills, and their peaks and the grey ridge of the old aqueduct gleamed dimly in the beams of the rising moon. . . .

We suddenly darted upwards, and floated in the air before a deserted ruin. No one could have said what it had been: sepulchre, palace, or castle. . . . Dark ivy encircled it all over in its deadly clasp, and below gaped yawning a half-ruined vault. A heavy underground smell rose in my face from this heap of tiny closely-fitted stones, whence the granite facing of the wall had long crumbled away.

"Here," Alice pronounced, and she raised her hand: "Here! call aloud three times running the name of the mighty Roman!"

"What will happen?"

"You will see."

I wondered. "Divus Caius Julius Caesar!" I cried suddenly; "Divus Caius Julius Caesar!" I repeated deliberately; "Caesar!"

XIII

The last echoes of my voice had hardly died away, when I heard. . . .

It is difficult to say what I did hear. At first there reached me a confused din the ear could scarcely catch, the endlessly-repeated clamor of the blare of trumpets, and the clapping of hands. It seemed that somewhere, immensely far away, at some fathomless depth, a multitude innumerable was suddenly astir, and was rising up, rising up in agitation, calling to one another, faintly, as if muffled in sleep, the suffocating sleep of ages. Then the air began moving in dark currents over the ruin. . . . Shades began flitting before me, myriads of shades, millions of outlines, the rounded curves of helmets, the long straight lines of lances; the moonbeams were broken into momentary gleams of blue upon these helmets and lances, and all this army, this multitude, came closer and closer, and grew, in more and more rapid movement. . . . An indescribable force, a force fit to set the whole world moving, could be felt in it; but not one figure stood out clearly. . . . And suddenly I fancied a sort of tremor ran all round, as if it were the rush and rolling apart of some huge waves. . . . "Caesar, Caesar venit!" sounded voices, like the leaves of a forest when a storm has suddenly broken upon it . . . a muffled shout thundered through the multitude, and a pale stern head, in a wreath of laurel, with downcast eyelids, the head of the emperor, began slowly to rise out of the ruin. . . .

There is no word in the tongue of man to express the horror which clutched at my heart. . . . I felt that were that head to raise its eyes, to part its lips, I must perish on the spot! "Alice!" I moaned, "I won't, I can't, I don't want Rome, coarse, terrible Rome. . . . Away, away from here!"

"Coward!" she whispered, and away we flew. I just had time to hear behind me the iron voice of the legions, like a peal of thunder . . . then all was darkness.

XIV

"Look round," Alice said to me, "and don't fear."

I obeyed—and, I remember, my first impression was so sweet that I could only sigh. A sort of smoky-grey, silvery-soft, half-light, half-mist, enveloped me on all sides. At first I made out nothing: I was dazzled by this azure brilliance; but little by little began to emerge the outlines of beautiful mountains and forests; a lake lay at my feet, with stars quivering in its depths, and the musical plash of waves. The fragrance of orange flowers met me with a rush, and with it—and also as it were with a rush—came floating the pure powerful notes of a woman's young voice. This fragrance, this music, fairly drew me downwards, and I began to sink . . . to sink down towards a magnificent marble palace, which stood, invitingly white, in the midst of a wood of cypress. The music flowed out from its wide open windows, the waves of the lake, flecked with the pollen of flowers, splashed upon its walls, and just opposite, all clothed in the dark green of orange flowers and laurels, enveloped in shining mist, and studded with statues, slender columns, and the porticoes of temples, a lofty round island rose out of the water. . . .

"Isola Bella!" said Alice. . . . "Lago Maggiore. . . . "

I murmured only "Ah!" and continued to drop. The woman's voice sounded louder and clearer in the palace; I was irresistibly drawn towards it. . . . I wanted to look at the face of the singer, who, in such music, gave voice to such a night. We stood still before the window.

In the center of a room, furnished in the style of Pompeii, and more like an ancient temple than a modern drawing-room, surrounded by Greek statues, Etruscan vases, rare plants, and precious stuffs, lighted up by the soft radiance of two lamps enclosed in crystal globes, a young woman was sitting at the piano. Her head slightly bowed and her eyes half-closed, she sang an Italian melody; she sang and smiled, and at the same time her face wore an expression of gravity, almost of sternness . . . a token of perfect rapture! She smiled . . . and Praxiteles' Faun, indolent, youthful as she, effeminate, and voluptuous, seemed to smile back at her from a corner, under the branches of an oleander, across the delicate smoke that curled upwards from a bronze censer on an antique tripod. The beautiful singer was alone. Spell-bound by the music, her beauty, the splendor and sweet fragrance of the night, moved to the heart by the picture of this youthful, serene, and untroubled happiness, I utterly forgot my companion, I forgot the strange way in which I had become a witness of this life, so remote, so completely apart from me, and I was on the point of tapping at the window, of speaking. . . .

I was set trembling all over by a violent shock — just as though I had touched a galvanic battery. I looked round. . . . The face of Alice was — for all its transparency — dark and menacing; there was a dull glow of anger in her eyes, which were suddenly wide and round. . . .

"Away!" she murmured wrathfully, and again whirling and darkness and giddiness. . . . Only this time not the shout of legions, but the voice of the singer, breaking on a high note, lingered in my ears. . . .

We stopped. The high note, the same note was still ringing and did not cease to ring in my ears, though I was breathing quite a different air, a different scent . . . a breeze was blowing upon me, fresh and invigorating, as though from a great river, and there was a smell of hay, smoke and hemp. The long-drawn-out note was followed by a second, and a third, but with an expression so unmistakable, a trill so familiar, so peculiarly our own, that I said to myself at once: "That's a Russian singing a Russian song!" and at that very instant everything grew clear about me.

XV

We found ourselves on a flat riverside plain. To the left, newly-mown meadows, with rows of huge hayricks, stretched endlessly till they were lost in the distance; to the right extended the smooth surface of a vast mighty river, till it too was lost in the distance. Not far from the bank, big dark barges slowly rocked at anchor, slightly tilting their slender masts, like pointing fingers. From one of these barges came floating up to me the sounds of a liquid voice, and a fire was burning in it, throwing a long red light that danced and quivered on the water. Here and there, both on the river and in the fields, other lights were glimmering, whether close at hand or far away, the eye could not distinguish; they shrank together, then suddenly lengthened out into great blurs of light; grasshoppers innumerable kept up an unceasing churr, persistent as the frogs of the Pontine marshes; and across the cloudless, but dark lowering sky floated from time to time the cries of unseen birds.

"Are we in Russia?" I asked of Alice.

"It is the Volga," she answered.

We flew along the river-bank. "Why did you tear me away from there, from that lovely country?" I began. "Were you envious, or was it jealousy in you?"

The lips of Alice faintly stirred, and again there was a menacing light in her eyes. . . . But her whole face grew stony again at once.

"I want to go home," I said.

"Wait a little, wait a little," answered Alice. "Tonight is a great night. It will not soon return. You may be a spectator. . . . Wait a little."

And we suddenly flew across the Volga in a slanting direction, keeping close to the water's surface, with the low impetuous flight of swallows before a storm. The broad waves murmured heavily below us, the sharp river breeze beat upon us with its strong cold wing . . . the high right bank began soon to rise up before us in the half-darkness. Steep mountains appeared with great ravines between. We came near to them.

"Shout: 'Lads, to the barges!' " Alice whispered to me. I remembered the terror I had suffered at the apparition of the Roman phantoms. I felt weary and strangely heavy, as though my heart were ebbing away within me. I wished not to utter the fatal words; I knew beforehand that in response to them there would appear, as in the wolves' valley of the Freischütz, some monstrous thing; but my lips parted against my will, and in a weak forced voice I shouted, also against my will: "Lads, to the barges!"

XVI

At first all was silence, even as it was at the Roman ruins, but suddenly I heard close to my very ear a coarse bargeman's laugh, and with a moan something dropped into the water and a gurgling sound followed. . . . I looked round: no one was anywhere to be seen, but from the bank the echo came bounding back, and at once from all sides rose a deafening din. There was a medley of everything in this chaos of sound: shouting and whining, furious abuse and laughter, laughter above everything; the plash of oars and the cleaving of hatchets, a crash as of the smashing of doors and chests, the grating of rigging and wheels, and the neighing of horses, and the clang of the alarm bell and the clink of chains, the roar and crackle of fire, drunken songs and quick, gnashing chatter, weeping inconsolable, plaintive despairing prayers, and shouts of command, the dying gasp and the reckless whistle, the guffaw and the thud of the dance. . . . "Kill them! Hang them! Drown them! rip them up! bravo! bravo! Don't spare them!" could be heard distinctly; I could even hear the hurried breathing of men panting. And meanwhile all around, as far as the eye could reach, nothing could be seen, nothing was changed; the river rolled by mysteriously, almost sullenly, the very bank seemed more deserted and desolate—and that was all.

I turned to Alice, but she put her finger to her lips. . . .

"Stepan Timofeitch! Stepan Timofeitch is coming!" was shouted noisily all round; "he is coming, our father, our ataman, our bread-giver!" As before I saw nothing but it seemed to me as though a huge body were moving straight at me. . . . "Frolka! where art thou, dog?" thundered an awful voice. "Set fire to every corner at once—and to the hatchet with them, the white-handed scoundrels!"

I felt the hot breath of the flame close by, and tasted the bitter savor of the smoke; and at the same instant something warm like blood spurted over my face and hands. . . . A savage roar of laughter broke out all round. . . .

I lost consciousness, and when I came to myself, Alice and I were gliding along beside the familiar bushes that bordered my wood, straight towards the old oak. . . .

"Do you see the little path?" Alice said to me, "where the moon shines dimly and where are two birch-trees overhanging? Will you go there?"

But I felt so shattered and exhausted that I could only say in reply: "Home! home!"

"You are at home," replied Alice.

I was in fact standing at the very door of my house—alone. Alice had vanished. The yard-dog was about to approach, he scanned me suspiciously—and with a bark ran away.

With difficulty I dragged myself up to my bed and fell asleep without undressing.

XVII

All the following morning my head ached, and I could scarcely move my legs; but I cared little for my bodily discomfort; I was devoured by regret, overwhelmed with vexation.

I was excessively annoyed with myself. "Coward!" I repeated incessantly; "Yes—Alice was right. What was I frightened of? how could I miss such an opportunity? . . . I might have seen Cæsar himself—and I was senseless with terror, I whimpered and turned away, like a child at the sight of the rod. Razin, now—that's another matter. As a nobleman and landowner . . . though, indeed, even then what had I really to fear? Coward! coward!" . . .

"But wasn't it all a dream?" I asked myself at last. I called my housekeeper.

"Marfa, what o'clock did I go to bed yesterday— do you remember?"

"Why, who can tell, master? . . . Late enough, surely. Before it was quite dark you went out of the house; and you were tramping about in your bedroom when the night was more than half over. Just on morning—yes. And this is the third day it's been the same. You've something on your mind, it's easy to see."

"Aha-ha!" I thought. "Then there's no doubt about the flying. Well, and how do I look today?" I added aloud.

"How do you look? Let me have a look at you. You've got thinner a bit. Yes, and you're pale, master; to be sure, there's not a drop of blood in your face."

I felt a slight twinge of uneasiness. . . . I dismissed Marfa.

"Why, going on like this, you'll die, or go out of your mind, perhaps," I reasoned with myself, as I sat deep in thought at the window. "I must give it all up. It's dangerous. And now my heart beats so strangely. And when I fly, I keep feeling as though some one were sucking at it, or as it were drawing something out of it — as the spring sap is drawn out of the birch-tree, if you stick an axe into it. I'm sorry, though. And Alice too. . . . She is playing cat and mouse with me . . . still she can hardly wish me harm. I will give myself up to her for the last time—and then. . . . But if she is drinking my blood? That's awful. Besides, such rapid locomotion cannot fail to be injurious; even in England, I'm told, on the railways, it's against the law to go more than one hundred miles an hour. . . ."

So I reasoned with myself—but at ten o'clock in the evening, I was already at my post before the old oak-tree.

XVIII

The night was cold, dull, grey; there was a feeling of rain in the air. To my amazement, I found no one under the oak; I walked several times round it, went up to the edge of the wood, turned back again, peered anxiously into the darkness. . . . All was emptiness. I waited a little, then several times I uttered the name, Alice, each time a little louder, . . . but she did not appear. I felt sad, almost sick at heart; my previous apprehensions vanished; I could not resign myself to the idea that my companion would not come back to me again.

"Alice! Alice! come! Can it be you will not come?" I shouted, for the last time.

A crow, who had been waked by my voice, suddenly darted upwards into a tree-top close by, and catching in the twigs, fluttered his wings.....But Alice did not appear.

With downcast head, I turned homewards. Already I could discern the black outlines of the willows on the pond's edge, and the light in my window peeped out at me through the apple-trees in the orchard—peeped at me, and hid again, like the eye of some man keeping watch on me—when suddenly I heard behind me the faint swish of the rapidly parted air, and something at once embraced and snatched me upward, as a buzzard pounces on and snatches up a quail. . . . It was Alice sweeping down upon me. I felt her cheek against my cheek, her enfolding arm about my body, and like a cutting cold her whisper pierced to my ear, "Here I am." I was frightened and delighted both at once. . . . We flew at no great height above the ground.

"You did not mean to come today?" I said.

"And you were dull without me? You love me? Oh, you are mine!"

The last words of Alice confused me. . . . I did not know what to say.

"I was kept," she went on; "I was watched."

"Who could keep you?"

"Where would you like to go?" inquired Alice, as usual not answering my question.

"Take me to Italy—to that lake, you remember."

Alice turned a little away, and shook her head in refusal. At that point I noticed for the first time that she had ceased to be transparent. And her face seemed tinged with color; there was a faint glow of red over its misty whiteness. I glanced at her eyes. . . and felt a pang of dread; in those eyes something was astir—with the slow, continuous, malignant movement of the benumbed snake, twisting and turning as the sun begins to thaw it.

"Alice," I cried, "who are you? Tell me who you are."

Alice simply shrugged her shoulders.

I felt angry . . . I longed to punish her; and suddenly the idea occurred to me to tell her to fly with me to Paris. "That's the place for you to be jealous," I thought. "Alice," I said aloud, "you are not afraid of big towns—Paris, for instance?"

"No."

"Not even those parts where it is as light as in the boulevards?"

"It is not the light of day."

"Good; then take me at once to the Boulevard des Italiens."

Alice wrapped the end of her long hanging sleeve about my head. I was at once enfolded in a sort of white vapor full of the drowsy fragrance of the poppy. Everything disappeared at once; every light, every sound, and almost consciousness itself. Only the sense of being alive remained, and that was not unpleasant.

Suddenly the vapor vanished; Alice took her sleeve from my head, and I saw at my feet a huge mass of closely—packed buildings, brilliant light, movement, noisy traffic. . . . I saw Paris.

XIX

I had been in Paris before, and so I recognized at once the place to which Alice had directed her course. It was the Garden of the Tuileries with its old chestnut-trees, its iron railings, its fortress moat, and its brutal-looking Zouave sentinels. Passing the palace, passing the Church of St. Roche, on the steps of which the first Napoleon for the first time shed French blood, we came to a halt high over the Boulevard des Italiens, where the third Napoleon did the same thing and with the same success. Crowds of people, dandies young and old, workmen in blouses, women in gaudy dresses, were thronging on the pavements; the gilded restaurants and cafés were flaring with lights; omnibuses, carriages of all sorts and shapes, moved to and fro along the boulevard; everything was bustle, everything was brightness, wherever one chanced to look. . . . But, strange to say, I had no inclination to forsake my pure dark airy height. I had no inclination to get nearer to this human ant-hill. It seemed as though a hot, heavy, reddish vapor rose from it, half-fragrance, half-stench; so many lives were flung struggling in one heap together there. I was hesitating. . . . But suddenly, sharp as the clang of iron bars, the voice of a harlot of the streets floated up to me; like an insolent tongue, it was thrust out, this voice; it stung me like the sting of a viper. At once I saw in imagination the strong, heavy-jawed, greedy, flat Parisian face, the mercenary eyes, the paint and powder, the frizzed hair, and the nosegay of gaudy artificial flowers under the high-pointed hat, the polished nails like talons, the hideous crinoline. . . . I could fancy too one of our sons of the steppes running with pitiful eagerness after the doll put up for sale. . . . I could fancy him with clumsy coarseness and violent stammering, trying to imitate the manners of the waiters at Véfour's, mincing, flattering, wheedling . . . and a feeling of loathing gained possession of me. . . . "No," I thought, "here Alice has no need to be jealous. . . ."

Meanwhile I perceived that we had gradually begun to descend. . . . Paris was rising to meet us with all its din and odor. . . .

"Stop," I said to Alice. "Are you not stifled and oppressed here?"

"You asked me to bring you here yourself."

"I am to blame, I take back my word. Take me away, Alice, I beseech you. To be sure, here is Prince Kulmametov hobbling along the boulevard; and his friend, Serge Varaksin, waves his hand to him, shouting: 'Ivan Stepanitch, *allons souper*, make haste, *zhay angazha Rigolbouche* itself!' Take me away from these furnished apartments and *maisons dorées*, from the Jockey Club and the Figaro, from close-shaven military heads and varnished barracks, from sergents-de-ville with Napoleonic beards, and from glasses of muddy absinthe, from gamblers playing dominoes at the cafés, and gamblers on the Bourse, from red ribbons in button-holes, from M. de Four, inventor of "matrimonial specialities," and the gratuitous consultations of Dr. Charles Albert, from liberal lectures and government pamphlets, from Parisian comedies and Parisian operas, from Parisian wit and Parisian ignorance. . . . Away! away! away!"

"Look down," Alice answered; "you are not now in Paris."

I lowered my eyes. . . . It was true. A dark plain, intersected here and there by the whitish lines of roads, was rushing rapidly by below us, and only behind us on the horizon, like the reflection of an immense conflagration, rose the great glow of the innumerable lights of the capital of the world.

XX

Again a veil fell over my eyes. . . . Again I lost consciousness. The veil was withdrawn at last. What was it down there below? What was this park, with avenues of lopped lime-trees, with isolated fir-trees of the shape of parasols, with porticoes and temples in the Pompadour style, with statues of satyrs and nymphs of the Bernini school, with rococo tritons in the midst of meandering lakes, closed in by low parapets of blackened marble? Wasn't it Versailles? No, it was not Versailles. A small palace, also rococo, peeped out behind a clump of bushy oaks. The moon shone dimly, shrouded in mist, and over the earth there was, as it were spread out, a delicate smoke. The eye could not decide what it was, whether moonlight or fog. On one of the lakes a swan was asleep; its long back was white as the snow of the frost-bound steppes, while glow-worms gleamed like diamonds in the bluish shadow at the base of a statue.

"We are near Mannheim," said Alice; "this is the Schwetzingen garden."

"We are in Germany," I thought, and I fell to listening. All was silence, except somewhere, secluded and unseen, the splash and babble of falling water. It seemed continually to repeat the same words: "Aye, aye, aye, for aye, aye." And all at once I fancied that in the very centre of one of the avenues, between clipped walls of green, a cavalier came tripping along in red-heeled boots, a gold-braided coat, with lace ruffs at his wrists, a light steel rapier at his thigh, smilingly offering his arm to a lady in a powdered wig and a gay chintz. . . . Strange, pale faces. . . . I tried to look into them. . . . But already everything had vanished, and as before there was nothing but the babbling water.

"Those are dreams wandering," whispered Alice; "yesterday there was much—oh, much—to see; today, even the dreams avoid man's eye. Forward! forward!"

We soared higher and flew farther on. So smooth and easy was our flight that it seemed that we moved not, but everything moved to meet us. Mountains came into view, dark, undulating, covered with forest; they rose up and swam towards us. . . . And now they were slipping by beneath us, with all their windings, hollows, and narrow glades, with gleams of light from rapid brooks among the slumbering trees at the bottom of the dales; and in front of us more mountains sprung up again and floated towards us. . . . We were in the heart of the Black Forest.

Mountains, still mountains . . . and forest, magnificent, ancient, stately forest. The night sky was clear; I could recognise some kinds of trees, especially the splendid firs, with their straight white trunks. Here and there on the edge of the forest, wild goats could be seen; graceful and alert, they stood on their slender legs and listened, turning their heads prettily and pricking up their great funnel-shaped ears. A ruined tower, sightless and gloomy, on the crest of a bare cliff, laid bare its crumbling turrets; above the old forgotten stones, a little golden star was shining peacefully. From a small almost black lake rose, like a mysterious wail, the plaintive croak of tiny frogs. I fancied other notes, long-drawn-out, languid like the strains of an Æolian harp. . . . Here we were in the home of legend! The same delicate moonlight mist, which had struck me in Schwetzingen, was shed here on every side, and the farther away the mountains, the thicker was this mist. I counted up five, six, ten different tones of shadow at different heights on the mountain slopes, and over all this realm of varied silence the moon queened it pensively. The air blew in soft, light currents. I felt myself a lightness at heart, and, as it were, a lofty calm and melancholy. . . .

"Alice, you must love this country!"

"I love nothing."

"How so? Not me?"

"Yes . . . you!" she answered indifferently.

It seemed to me that her arm clasped my waist more tightly than before.

"Forward! forward!" said Alice, with a sort of cold fervor.

"Forward!" I repeated.

XXI

A loud, thrilling cry rang out suddenly over our heads, and was at once repeated a little in front.

"Those are belated cranes flying to you, to the north," said Alice; "Would you like to join them?"

"Yes, yes! raise me up to them."

We darted upwards and in one instant found ourselves beside the flying flock.

The big handsome birds (there were thirteen of them) were flying in a triangle, with slow sharp flaps of their hollow wings; with their heads and legs stretched rigidly out, and their breasts stiffly pressed forward, they pushed on persistently and so swiftly that the air whistled about them. It was marvelous at such a height, so remote from all things living, to see such passionate, strenuous life, such unflinching will, untiringly cleaving their triumphant way through space. The cranes now and then called to one another, the foremost to the hindmost; and there was a certain pride, dignity, and invincible faith in these loud cries, this converse in the clouds. "We shall get there, be sure, hard though it be," they seemed to say, cheering one another on. And then the thought came to me that men, such as these birds—in Russia—nay, in the whole world, are few.

"We are flying towards Russia now," observed Alice. I noticed now, not for the first time, that she almost always knew what I was thinking of. "Would you like to go back?"

"Let us go back . . . or no! I have been in Paris; take me to Petersburg."

"Now?"

"At once....Only wrap my head in your veil, or it will go ill with me."

Alice raised her hand . . . but before the mist enfolded me, I had time to feel on my lips the contact of that soft, dull sting....

XXII

"Li-i-isten!" sounded in my ears a long drawn out cry. "Li-i-isten!" was echoed back with a sort of desperation in the distance. "Li-i-isten!" died away somewhere far, far away. I started. A tall golden spire flashed on my eyes; I recognized the fortress of St. Peter and St. Paul.

A northern, pale night! But was it night at all? Was it not rather a pallid, sickly daylight? I never liked Petersburg nights; but this time the night seemed even fearful to me; the face of Alice had vanished completely, melted away like the mist of morning in the July sun, and I saw her whole body clearly, as it hung, heavy and solitary on a level with the Alexander column. So here was Petersburg! Yes, it was Petersburg, no doubt. The wide empty grey streets; the greyish-white, and yellowish-grey and greyish-lilac houses, covered with stucco, which was peeling off, with their sunken windows, gaudy sign-boards, iron canopies over steps, and wretched little green-grocer's shops; the façades, inscriptions, sentry-boxes, troughs; the golden cap of St. Isaac's; the senseless motley Bourse; the granite walls of the fortress, and the broken wooden pavement; the barges loaded with hay and timber; the smell of dust, cabbage, matting, and hemp; the stony-faced dvorniks in sheepskin coats, with high collars; the cab-drivers, huddled up dead asleep on their decrepit cabs—yes, this was Petersburg, our northern Palmyra. Everything was visible; everything was clear — cruelly clear and distinct — and everything was mournfully sleeping, standing out in strange huddled masses in the dull clear air. The flush of sunset — a hectic flush — had not yet gone, and would not be gone till morning from the white starless sky; it was reflected on the silken surface of the Neva, while faintly gurgling and faintly moving, the cold blue waves hurried on. . . .

"Let us fly away," Alice implored.

And without waiting for my reply, she bore me away across the Neva, over the palace square to Liteiny Street. Steps and voices were audible beneath us; a group of young men, with worn faces, came along the street talking about dancing-classes. "Sub-lieutenant Stolpakov's seventh!" shouted suddenly a soldier, standing half-asleep on guard at a pyramid of rusty bullets; and a little farther on, at an open window in a tall house, I saw a girl in a creased silk dress, without cuffs, with a pearl net on her hair, and a cigarette in her mouth. She was reading a book with reverent attention; it was a volume of the works of one of our modern Juvenals.

"Let us fly away!" I said to Alice.

One instant more, and there were glimpses below us of the rotting pine copses and mossy bogs surrounding Petersburg. We bent our course straight to the south; sky, earth, all grew gradually darker and darker. The sick night; the sick daylight; the sick town—all were left behind us.

XXIII

We flew more slowly than usual, and I was able to follow with my eyes the immense expanse of my native land gradually unfolding before me, like the unrolling of an endless panorama. Forests, copses, fields, ravines, rivers—here and there villages and churches—and again fields and forests and copses and ravines. . . . Sadness came over me, and a kind of indifferent dreariness. And I was not sad and dreary simply because it was Russia I was flying over. No. The earth itself, this flat surface which lay spread out beneath me; the whole earthly globe, with its populations, multitudinous, feeble, crushed by want, grief and diseases, bound to a clod of pitiful dust; this brittle, rough crust, this shell over the fiery sands of our planet, overspread with the mildew we call the organic, vegetable kingdom; these human flies, a thousand times paltrier than flies; their dwellings glued together with filth, the pitiful traces of their tiny, monotonous bustle, of their comic struggle with the unchanging and inevitable, how revolting it all suddenly was to me. My heart turned slowly sick, and I could not bear to gaze longer on these trivial pictures, on this vulgar show. . . . Yes, I felt dreary, worse than dreary. Even pity I felt nothing of for my brother men: all feelings in me were merged in one which I scarcely dare to name: a feeling of loathing, and stronger than all and more than all within me was the loathing—for myself.

"Cease," whispered Alice, "cease, or I cannot carry you. You have grown heavy."

"Home," I answered her in the very tone in which I used to say the word to my coachman, when I came out at four o'clock at night from some Moscow friends, where I had been talking since dinner-time of the future of Russia and the significance of the commune. "Home," I repeated, and closed my eyes.

XXIV

But I soon opened them again. Alice seemed huddling strangely up to me; she was almost pushing against me. I looked at her and my blood froze at the sight. One who has chanced to behold on the face of another a sudden look of intense terror, the cause of which he does not suspect, will understand me. By terror, overmastering terror, the pale features of Alice were drawn and contorted, almost effaced. I had never seen anything like it even on a living human face. A lifeless, misty phantom, a shade . . . and this deadly horror. . . .

"Alice, what is it?" I said at last.

"She . . . she . . ." she answered with an effort. "She."

"She? Who is she?"

"Do not utter her name, not her name," Alice faltered hurriedly. "We must escape, or there will be an end to everything, and forever. . . . Look, over there!"

I turned my head in the direction in which her trembling hand was pointing, and discerned something . . . something horrible indeed.

This something was the more horrible that it had no definite shape. Something bulky, dark, yellowish-black, spotted like a lizard's belly, not a storm-cloud, and not smoke, was crawling with a snake-like motion over the earth. A wide rhythmic undulating movement from above downwards, and from below upwards, an undulation recalling the malignant sweep of the wings of a vulture seeking its prey; at times an indescribably revolting grovelling on the earth, as of a spider stooping over its captured fly. . . . Who are you, what are you, menacing mass?

Under her influence, I saw it, I felt it — all sank into nothingness, all was dumb. . . . A putrefying, pestilential chill came from it. At this chill breath the heart turned sick, and the eyes grew dim, and the hair stood up on the head. It was a power moving; that power which there is no resisting, to which all is subject, which, sightless, shapeless, senseless, sees all, knows all, and like a bird of prey picks out its victims, like a snake, stifles them and stabs them with its frozen sting. . . .

"Alice! Alice!" I shrieked like one in frenzy. "It is death! death itself!"

The wailing sound I had heard before broke from Alice's lips; this time it was more like a human wail of despair, and we flew. But our flight was strangely and alarmingly unsteady; Alice turned over in the air, fell, rushed from side to side like a partridge mortally wounded, or trying to attract a dog away from her young. And meanwhile in pursuit of us, parting from the indescribable mass of horror, rushed sort of long undulating tentacles, like outstretched arms, like talons. . . . Suddenly a huge shape, a muffled figure on a pale horse, sprang up and flew upwards into the very heavens. . . . Still more fearfully, still more desperately Alice struggled. "She has seen! All is over! I am lost!" I heard her broken whisper. "Oh, I am miserable! I might have profited, have won life . . . and now. . . . Nothingness, nothingness!" It was too unbearable. . . . I lost consciousness.

XXV

When I came to myself, I was lying on my back in the grass, feeling a dull ache all over me, as from a bad bruise. The dawn was beginning in the sky: I could clearly distinguish things. Not far off, alongside a birch copse, ran a road planted with willows: the country seemed familiar to me. I began to recollect what had happened to me, and shuddered all over directly my mind recalled the last, hideous apparition. . . .

"But what was Alice afraid of?" I thought. "Can she too be subject to that power? Is she not immortal? Can she too be in danger of annihilation, dissolution? How is it possible?"

A soft moan sounded close by me. I turned my head. Two paces from me lay stretched out motionless a young woman in a white gown, with thick disordered tresses, with bare shoulders. One arm was thrown behind her head, the other had fallen on her bosom. Her eyes were closed, and on her tightly shut lips stood a fleck of crimson stain. Could it be Alice? But Alice was a phantom, and I was looking upon a living woman. I crept up to her, bent down. . . .

"Alice, is it you?" I cried. Suddenly, slowly quivering, the wide eyelids rose; dark piercing eyes were fastened upon me, and at the same instant lips too fastened upon me, warm, moist, smelling of blood . . . soft arms twined tightly round my neck, a burning, full heart pressed convulsively to mine. "Farewell, farewell forever!" the dying voice uttered distinctly, and everything vanished.

I got up, staggering like a drunken man, and passing my hands several times over my face, looked carefully about me. I found myself near the high road, a mile and a half from my own place. The sun had just risen when I got home.

All the following nights I awaited—and I confess not without alarm—the appearance of my phantom; but it did not visit me again. I even set off one day, in the dusk, to the old oak, but nothing took place there out of the common. I did not, however, overmuch regret the discontinuance of this strange acquaintance. I reflected much and long over this inexplicable, almost unintelligible phenomenon; and I am convinced that not only science cannot explain it, but that even in fairy tales and legends nothing like it is to be met with. What was Alice, after all? An apparition, a restless soul, an evil spirit, a sylphide, a vampire, or what? Sometimes it struck me again that Alice was a woman I had known at some time or other, and I made tremendous efforts to recall where I had seen her. . . . Yes, yes, I thought sometimes, directly, this minute, I shall remember. . . In a flash everything had melted away again like a dream.

Yes, I thought a great deal, and, as is always the way, came to no conclusion. The advice or opinion of others I could not bring myself to invite; fearing to be taken for a madman. I gave up all reflection upon it at last; to tell the truth, I had no time for it. For one thing, the emancipation had come along with the redistribution of property, etc.; and for another, my own health failed; I suffered with my chest, with sleeplessness, and a cough. I got thin all over. My face was yellow as a dead man's. The doctor declares I have too little blood, calls my illness by the Greek name, "anæmia," and is sending me to Gastein. The arbitrator swears that without me there's no coming to an understanding with the peasants. Well, what's one to do?

But what is the meaning of the piercingly-pure, shrill notes, the notes of an harmonica, which I hear directly any one's death is spoken of before me? They keep growing louder, more penetrating. . . . And why do I shudder in such anguish at the mere thought of annihilation?

GLOSSARY

Aeolian Harp: A stringed instrument that makes music when the wind moves the strings. Aeolus was the Greek god of the winds.
A.Fet: Afanasy Afanasyevich Fet, (1820-1892), Russian poet.
Ataman: A Cossack leader.
Black Forest: In Eastern Germany.
Commune: People living and working together under full equality—an idea that was gaining ground in Russian intellectual circles.
Dvornik: An "outdoor man," anything from a doorman to a groundskeeper. In Petersburg, probably a doorman.
Emancipation: The freeing of the serfs in 1861 by order of the Tsar.
Fortress of St. Peter and St. Paul: 18th century fortress in St. Petersburg. Political prisoners were kept there and it was known as the "Russian Bastille." Currently a museum.
Frolka: Nickname for Frol Razin, brother of Stepan (below).
Gastein: A health spa in Salzburg, Austria, famous for its hot springs.
Juvenal: An ancient Roman satirist.
Maison Doree: "The Gilded House," a famous Parisian restaurant. It closed in 1902.
Neva: Main river in St. Petersburg.
Palmyra: Ancient city in Syria, once an important cultural hub.
Praxitiles: Most famous of ancient Greek sculptors (395-330 BC).
Rigol-bouche: Turgenev has his faux-Western Russians speaking bad French, trying to go to the home of Rigolboche—the stage name of Amelia Marguerite Badel, (popular circa 1858-1861) an entertainer who invented the can-can.
"Seven times thirteen…": A hint at some mystical order or connection. Any reader would know that 7 is a lucky number and 13 an unlucky one, and accept that some kind of magical/astrological spell or rule is being invoked. However, 7 x 13 = 91, which, in the numerology of the Kabbalah, is a number closely associated with God and the word "Amen." Other numerological systems also apply some significance to the number in terms of new life or new opportunities. The narrator

doesn't hear the rest of Alice's explanation, so we don't know, and are probably not intended to know, whether she's talking about a cycle of 91 nights, or weeks, or months, or years—or, frankly, whether Turgenev had any specific numerology in mind.

Stepan Timofeitch Razin: Cossack leader of a major anti-government populist rebellion in 1670-1671. Also known as "Stenka" Razin.

Sylphide: a spirit of the air, invented by the 16th century Swiss physician/alchemist Paracelsus; featured in the ballet *La Sylphide.*

Véfour's: Le Grand Véfour, Parisian restaurant opened in 1784 as the *Café de Chartres*; bought and renamed by Jean Véfour in 1820; closed from 1905-1947, then reopened and still in business today.

Zouave: Infantryman, usually an Algerian serving French colonial masters from 1830 to 1962.

AFTERWORD

The story was controversial. Although Dostoevsky told Turgenev that **Phantoms** ***had "an excess of reality...the reality is the anguish of a developed and conscious being, living in our time," which is the sort of thing an author might take as praise, he privately wrote to his brother that it "contains a lot of trash."***

Alice herself is fascinatingly obscure. Like every other vampire in this book, Alice is remarkably beautiful. Like many of her sisters between these pages, she is devoted to her human beloved—but beyond that, Alice is a mystery. While there are hints as to her origins and desires, nothing can be pinned down. Turgenev himself wrote to a puzzled friend, "I understand Alice as little as you."

Alice's flights are brilliantly described—especially for the 19th century,

when only a handful of people had even been up in a hot air balloon. Her avoidance of natural sunlight is much stronger than the occasional aversion to bright daylight exhibited by some of the earlier undead. The idea that sunlight is instantly fatal to vampires wouldn't become a standard notion until the 20th century (and seems to have been invented for the 1922 Dracula film adaptation Nosferatu*). But Alice is a creature entirely of the night. However, she doesn't seem to come out of a grave, and she isn't affected by Christian incantations. She doesn't even seem to know what they are. The lack of these vampire tropes makes her seem more a denizen of dreams than graveyards.*

Around the same time as Phantoms, *Paul Féval was experimenting with the vampire theme in France. He wrote three vampire stories between 1856 and 1867, although they were not widely known outside of France and have only recently been translated as* The Vampire Countess, Knightshade, *and* The Vampire City.

The Vampire Countess *might seem like a natural addition to this collection…but, aside from the lack of an available English translation, Féval's Countess Addhema is excluded for her very non-traditional vampirism: rather than sucking blood, she retains her youth by scalping young women and putting their hair on her bald head.*

The next story is about a far more recognizable vampire. It's a classic of Gothic fiction, a tale of vampire passion…which, in this case, is not entirely unrequited…

CARMILLA

It was like the ardour of a lover; it embarrassed me; it was hateful and yet overpowering; and with gloating eyes she drew me to her, and her hot lips travelled along my cheek in kisses; and she would whisper, almost in sobs, "You are mine, you shall be mine, you and I are one forever."

Carmilla is the most famous female vampire in literature, although she had to wait almost a century to become really popular. One of the last creations of the Anglo-Irish writer Sheridan Le Fanu, sometimes called "The Father of the Victorian ghost story," Carmilla *was first serialized in an English magazine called* The Dark Blue *from late 1871 to early 1872. It was reprinted in 1872 in a collection of five stories titled* In a Glass Darkly. *The stories either feature or have supposedly been collected by Dr. Martin Hesselius, a character who has been called literature's first occult detective. After the Prologue to* Carmilla, *though, Dr. Hesselius plays no part in the story of a young woman who encounters a distant relative with a vague past and a mysterious present.*

The great male vampires of the 19th century, Lord Ruthven and Varney, are English, as are Clara Crofton and Alice—and the Lady Bright is Scottish. Lilith and Oneiza are Middle Eastern, the Bride of Corinth is Greek, Aurelie and Brunhilda are German; but Carmilla lives in Styria, in southeastern Austria, and the setting is a Gothic castle among the deep woods. Le Fanu found novelty by going back to the sources of vampire lore. He set his story in Central Europe, in the general region where the vampire superstitions took root. It's clear that Le Fanu read about Arnold Paul and other "real-life" vampires. (*See* Volume I.) Carmilla *feels authentic to the folklore and is, in fact, very much a model for the "classic" vampire story. His heroine Laura, however, is from the West, with an English heritage. She is a modern woman traveling to an unfamiliar realm.*

Did Bram Stoker read Carmilla? *There's no hard evidence, but many critics feel he probably did. As a young man, Stoker was interested in ghost stories, so he was most likely aware of the work of another Anglo-Irish writer from the generation just before his. Stoker was in his mid-20's when* Carmilla *was first published. Plus, there are elements in* Dracula's Guest, *the last story in this anthology, that seem to be influenced by* Carmilla. *But Le Fanu's Gothic tale of passion and the undead can stand on its own, and retains its power after a century and a half...*

CARMILLA

Sheridan Le Fanu

PROLOGUE

Upon a paper attached to the Narrative which follows, Doctor Hesselius has written a rather elaborate note, which he accompanies with a reference to his Essay on the strange subject which the MS illuminates.

This mysterious subject he treats in that Essay with his usual learning and acumen, and with remarkable directness and condensation. It will form but one volume of the series of that extraordinary man's collected papers.

As I publish the case, in these volumes, simply to interest the "laity," I shall forestall the intelligent lady, who relates it, in nothing; and, after due consideration, I have determined, therefore, to abstain from presenting any *precis* of the learned Doctor's reasoning, or extract from his statement on a subject which he describes as "involving, not improbably, some of the profoundest arcana of our dual existence, and its intermediates."

I was anxious, on discovering this paper, to re-open the correspondence commenced by Doctor Hesselius, so many years before, with a person so clever and careful as his informant seems to have been. Much to my regret, however, I found that she had died in the interval.

She, probably, could have added little to the Narrative which she communicates in the following pages, with, so far as I can pronounce, such a conscientious particularity.

CHAPTER I:

AN EARLY FRIGHT

In Styria, we, though by no means magnificent people, inhabit a castle, or *schloss.* A small income, in that part of the world, goes a great way. Eight or nine hundred a year does wonders. Scantily enough ours would have answered among wealthy people at home. My father is English, and I bear an English name, although I never saw England. But here, in this lonely and primitive place, where everything is so marvellously cheap, I really don't see how ever so much more money would at all materially add to our comforts, or even luxuries.

My father was in the Austrian service, and retired upon a pension and his patrimony, and purchased this feudal residence, and the small estate on which it stands, a bargain.

Nothing can be more picturesque or solitary. It stands on a slight eminence in a forest. The road, very old and narrow, passes in front of its drawbridge, never raised in my time, and its moat, stocked with perch and sailed over by many swans, and floating on its surface white fleets of water-lilies. Over all this the schloss shows its many-windowed front; its towers, and its Gothic chapel. The forest opens in an irregular and very picturesque glade before its gate, and at the right a steep Gothic bridge carries the road over a stream that winds in deep shadow through the wood.

I have said that this is a very lonely place. Judge whether I say truth. Looking from the hall door towards the road, the forest in which our castle stands extends fifteen miles to the right, and twelve to the left. The nearest inhabited village is about seven of your English miles to the left. The nearest inhabited schloss of any historic associations, is that of old General Spielsdorf, nearly twenty miles away to the right.

I have said "the nearest inhabited village," because there is, only three miles westward, that is to say in the direction of General Spielsdorf's schloss, a ruined village, with its quaint little church, now roofless, in the aisle of which are the mouldering tombs of the proud family of Karnstein, now extinct, who once owned the equally desolate chateau which, in the thick of the forest, overlooks the silent ruins of the town.

Respecting the cause of the desertion of this striking and melancholy spot, there is a legend which I shall relate to you another time.

I must tell you now, how very small is the party who constitute the inhabitants of our castle. I don't include servants, or those dependants who occupy rooms in the buildings attached to the schloss. Listen, and wonder! My father, who is the kindest man on earth, but growing old; and I, at the date of my story, only nineteen. Eight years have passed since then. I and my father constituted the family at the schloss. My mother, a Styrian lady, died in my infancy, but I had a good- natured governess, who had been with me from, I might almost say, my infancy. I could not remember the time when her fat, benignant face was not a familiar picture in my memory. This was Madame Perrodon, a native of Berne, whose care and good nature in part supplied to me the loss of my mother, whom I do not even remember, so early I lost her. She made a third at our little dinner party. There was a fourth, Mademoiselle De Lafontaine, a lady such as you term, I believe, a "finishing governess." She spoke French and German, Madame Perrodon French and broken English, to which my father and I added English, which, partly to prevent its becoming a lost language among us, and partly from patriotic motives, we spoke every day. The consequence was a Babel, at which strangers used to laugh, and which I shall make no attempt to reproduce in this narrative. And there were two or three young lady friends besides, pretty nearly of my own age, who were occasional visitors, for longer or shorter terms; and these visits I sometimes returned.

These were our regular social resources; but of course there were chance visits from "neighbours" of only five or six leagues distance. My life was, notwithstanding, rather a solitary one, I can assure you.

My gouvernantes had just so much control over me as you might conjecture such sage persons would have in the case of a rather spoiled girl, whose only parent allowed her pretty nearly her own way in everything.

The first occurrence in my existence, which produced a terrible impression upon my mind, which, in fact, never has been effaced, was one of the very earliest incidents of my life which I can recollect. Some people will think it so trifling that it should not be recorded here. You will see, however, by-and-by, why I mention it. The nursery, as it was called, though I had it all to myself, was a large room in the upper story of the castle, with a steep oak roof. I can't have been more than six years old, when one night I awoke, and looking round the room from my bed, failed to see the nursery-maid. Neither was my nurse there; and I thought myself alone. I was not frightened, for I was one of those happy children who are studiously kept in ignorance of ghost stories, of fairy tales, and of all such lore as makes us cover up our heads when the door creaks suddenly, or the flicker of an expiring candle makes the shadow of a bed-post dance upon the wall, nearer to our faces. I was vexed and insulted at finding myself, as I conceived, neglected, and I began to whimper, preparatory to a hearty bout of roaring; when to my surprise, I saw a solemn, but very pretty face looking at me from the side of the bed. It was that of a young lady who was kneeling, with her hands under the coverlet. I looked at her with a kind of pleased wonder, and ceased whimpering. She caressed me with her hands, and lay down beside me on the bed, and drew me towards her, smiling; I felt immediately delightfully soothed, and fell asleep again. I was wakened by a sensation as if two needles ran into my breast very deep at the same moment, and I cried loudly. The lady started back, with her eyes fixed on me, and then slipped down upon the floor, and, as I thought, hid herself under the bed.

I was now for the first time frightened, and I yelled with all my might and main. Nurse, nursery-maid, housekeeper, all came running in, and hearing my story, they made light of it, soothing me all they could meanwhile. But, child as I was, I could perceive that their faces were pale with an unwonted look of anxiety, and I saw them look under the bed, and about the room, and peep under tables and pluck open cupboards; and the housekeeper whispered to the nurse: "Lay your hand along that hollow in the bed; someone did lie there, so sure as you did not; the place is still warm."

I remember the nursery-maid petting me, and all three examining my chest, where I told them I felt the puncture, and pronouncing that there was no sign visible that any such thing had happened to me.

The housekeeper and the two other servants who were in charge of the nursery remained sitting up all night; and from that time a servant always sat up in the nursery until I was about fourteen.

I was very nervous for a long time after this. A doctor was called in; he was pallid and elderly. How well I remember his long saturnine face, slightly pitted with small-pox, and his chestnut wig. For a good while, every second day, he came and gave me medicine, which of course I hated.

The morning after I saw this apparition I was in a state of terror, and could not bear to be left alone, daylight though it was, for a moment.

I remember my father coming up and standing at the bedside, and talking cheerfully, and asking the nurse a number of questions, and laughing very heartily at one of the answers; and patting me on the shoulder, and kissing me, and telling me not to be frightened, that it was nothing but a dream and could not hurt me.

But I was not comforted, for I knew the visit of the strange woman was not a dream; and I was awfully frightened.

I was a little consoled by the nursery-maid's assuring me that it was she who had come and looked at me, and lain down beside me in the bed, and that I must have been half-dreaming not to have known her face. But this, though supported by the nurse, did not quite satisfy me.

I remember, in the course of that day, a venerable old man, in a black cassock, coming into the room with the nurse and housekeeper, and talking a little to them, and very kindly to me; his face was very sweet and gentle, and he told me they were going to pray, and joined my hands together, and desired me to say, softly, while they were praying, "Lord, hear all good prayers for us, for Jesus' sake." I think these were the very words, for I often repeated them to myself, and my nurse used for years to make me say them in my prayers.

I remember so well the thoughtful sweet face of that white-haired old man, in his black cassock, as he stood in that rude, lofty, brown room, with the clumsy furniture of a fashion three hundred years old about him, and the scanty light entering its shadowy atmosphere through the small lattice. He kneeled, and the three women with him, and he prayed aloud with an earnest quavering voice for what appeared to me a long time. I forget all my life preceding that event, and for some time after it is all obscure also, but the scenes I have just described stand out vivid as the isolated pictures of the phantasmagoria surrounded by darkness.

CHAPTER II: A GUEST

I am now going to tell you something so strange that it requires all your faith in my veracity to believe my story. It is not only true, nevertheless, but truth of which I have been an eye-witness.

It was a sweet summer evening, and my father asked me, as he sometimes did, to take a little ramble with him along that beautiful forest vista which I have mentioned as lying in front of the schloss.

"General Spielsdorf cannot come to us so soon as I had hoped," said my father, as we pursued our walk.

He was to have paid us a visit of some weeks, and we had expected his arrival next day. He was to have brought with him a young lady, his niece and ward, Mademoiselle Rheinfeldt, whom I had never seen, but whom I had heard described as a very charming girl, and in whose society I had promised myself many happy days. I was more disappointed than a young lady living in a town, or a bustling neighbourhood can possibly imagine. This visit, and the new acquaintance it promised, had furnished my day-dream for many weeks.

"And how soon does he come?" I asked.

"Not till autumn. Not for two months, I dare say," he answered. "And I am very glad now, dear, that you never knew Mademoiselle Rheinfeldt."

"And why?" I asked, both mortified and curious.

"Because the poor young lady is dead," he replied. "I quite forgot I had not told you, but you were not in the room when I received the General's letter this evening."

I was very much shocked. General Spielsdorf had mentioned in his first letter, six or seven weeks before, that she was not so well as he would wish her, but there was nothing to suggest the remotest suspicion of danger.

"Here is the General's letter," he said, handing it to me. "I am afraid he is in great affliction; the letter appears to me to have been written very nearly in distraction."

We sat down on a rude bench, under a group of magnificent lime-trees. The sun was setting with all its melancholy splendour behind the sylvan horizon, and the stream that flows beside our home, and passes under the steep old bridge I have mentioned, wound through many a group of noble trees, almost at our feet, reflecting in its current the fading crimson of the sky. General Spielsdorf's letter was so extraordinary, so vehement, and in some places so self-contradictory, that I read it twice over—the second time aloud to my father—and was still unable to account for it, except by supposing that grief had unsettled his mind. It said,

> *I have lost my darling daughter, for as such I loved her. During the last days of dear Bertha's illness I was not able to write to you. Before then I had no idea of her danger. I have lost her, and now learn all, too late. She died in the peace of innocence, and in the glorious hope of a blessed futurity. The fiend who betrayed our infatuated hospitality has done it all. I thought I was receiving into my house innocence, gaiety, a charming companion for my lost Bertha. Heavens! what a fool have I been! I thank God my child died without a suspicion of the cause of her sufferings. She is gone without so much as conjecturing the nature of her illness, and the accursed passion of the agent of all this misery. I devote my remaining days to*

tracking and extinguishing a monster. I am told I may hope to accomplish my righteous and merciful purpose. At present there is scarcely a gleam of light to guide me. I curse my conceited incredulity, my despicable affectation of superiority, my blindness, my obstinacy—all—too late. I cannot write or talk collectedly now. I am distracted. So soon as I shall have a little recovered, I mean to devote myself for a time to enquiry, which may possibly lead me as far as Vienna. Sometime in the autumn, two months hence, or earlier if I live, I will see you--that is, if you permit me; I will then tell you all that I scarce dare put upon paper now. Farewell. Pray for me, dear friend.

In these terms ended this strange letter. Though I had never seen Bertha Rheinfeldt my eyes filled with tears at the sudden intelligence; I was startled, as well as profoundly disappointed.

The sun had now set, and it was twilight by the time I had returned the General's letter to my father.

It was a soft clear evening, and we loitered, speculating upon the possible meanings of the violent and incoherent sentences which I had just been reading. We had nearly a mile to walk before reaching the road that passes the schloss in front, and by that time the moon was shining brilliantly.

At the drawbridge we met Madame Perrodon and Mademoiselle De Lafontaine, who had come out, without their bonnets, to enjoy the exquisite moonlight.

We heard their voices gabbling in animated dialogue as we approached. We joined them at the drawbridge, and turned about to admire with them the beautiful scene.

The glade through which we had just walked lay before us. At our left the narrow road wound away under clumps of lordly trees, and was lost to sight amid the thickening forest. At the right the same road crosses the steep and picturesque bridge, near which stands a ruined tower which once guarded that pass; and beyond the bridge an abrupt eminence rises, covered with trees, and showing in the shadows some grey ivy-clustered rocks.

Over the sward and low grounds a thin film of mist was stealing, like smoke, marking the distances with a transparent veil; and here and there we could see the river faintly flashing in the moonlight.

No softer, sweeter scene could be imagined. The news I had just heard made it melancholy; but nothing could disturb its character of profound serenity, and the enchanted glory and vagueness of the prospect.

My father, who enjoyed the picturesque, and I, stood looking in silence over the expanse beneath us. The two good governesses, standing a little way behind us, discoursed upon the scene, and were eloquent upon the moon.

Madame Perrodon was fat, middle-aged, and romantic, and talked and sighed poetically. Mademoiselle De Lafontaine, in right of her father, who was a German, assumed to be psychological, metaphysical, and something of a mystic, now declared that when the moon shone with a light so intense it was well known that it indicated a special spiritual activity. The effect of the full moon in such a state of brilliancy was manifold. It acted on dreams, it acted on lunacy, it acted on nervous people; it had marvellous physical influences connected with life. Mademoiselle related that her cousin, who was mate of a merchant ship, having taken a nap on deck on such a night, lying on his back, with his face full in the light of the moon, had wakened, after a dream of an old woman clawing him by the cheek, with his features horribly drawn to one side; and his countenance had never quite recovered its equilibrium.

"The moon, this night," she said, "is full of odylic and magnetic influence—and see, when you look behind you at the front of the schloss, how all its windows flash and twinkle with that silvery splendour, as if unseen hands had lighted up the rooms to receive fairy guests."

There are indolent states of the spirits in which, indisposed to talk ourselves, the talk of others is pleasant to our listless ears; and I gazed on, pleased with the tinkle of the ladies' conversation.

"I have got into one of my moping moods to-night," said my father, after a silence, and quoting Shakespeare, whom, by way of keeping up our English, he used to read aloud, he said:

"In truth I know not why I am so sad:
It wearies me; you say it wearies you;
But how I got it—came by it—

"I forget the rest. But I feel as if some great misfortune were hanging over us. I suppose the poor General's afflicted letter has had something to do with it."

At this moment the unwonted sound of carriage wheels and many hoofs upon the road, arrested our attention.

They seemed to be approaching from the high ground overlooking the bridge, and very soon the equipage from that point. Two horsemen first crossed the bridge, then came a carriage drawn by four horses, and two men rode behind.

It seemed to be the travelling carriage of a person of rank; and we were all immediately absorbed in watching that unusual spectacle. It became, in a few moments, greatly more interesting, for just as the carriage had passed the summit of the steep bridge, one of the leaders, taking fright, communicated his panic to the rest, and after a plunge or two, the whole team broke into a wild gallop together, and dashing between the horsemen who rode in front, came thundering along the road towards us with the speed of a hurricane.

The excitement of the scene was made more painful by the clear, long-drawn screams of a female voice from the carriage window.

We all advanced in curiosity and horror; my father in silence, the rest with various ejaculations of terror.

Our suspense did not last long. Just before you reach the castle drawbridge, on the route they were coming, there stands by the roadside a magnificent lime-tree, on the other side stands an ancient stone cross, at sight of which the horses, now going at a pace that was perfectly frightful, swerved so as to bring the wheel over the projecting roots of the tree.

I knew what was coming. I covered my eyes, unable to see it out, and turned my head away; at the same moment I heard a cry from my lady-friends, who had gone on a little.

Curiosity opened my eyes, and I saw a scene of utter confusion. Two of the horses were on the ground, the carriage lay upon its side with two wheels in the air; the men were busy removing the traces, and a lady, with a commanding air and figure, had got out, and stood with clasped hands, raising the handkerchief that was in them every now and then to her eyes. Through the carriage door was now lifted a young lady, who appeared to be lifeless. My dear old father was already beside the eider lady, with his hat in his hand, evidently tendering his aid and the resources of his schloss. The lady did not appear to hear him, or to have eyes for anything but the slender girl who was being placed against the slope of the bank.

I approached; the young lady was apparently stunned, but she was certainly not dead. My father, who piqued himself on being something of a physician, had just had his fingers to her wrist and assured the lady, who declared herself her mother, that her pulse, though faint and irregular, was undoubtedly still distinguishable. The lady clasped her hands and looked upward, as if in a momentary transport of gratitude; but immediately she broke out again in that theatrical way which is, I believe, natural to some people.

She was what is called a fine-looking woman for her time of life, and must have been handsome; she was tall, but not thin, and dressed in black velvet, and looked rather pale, but with a proud and commanding countenance, though now agitated strangely.

"Was ever being so born to calamity?" I heard her say, with clasped hands, as I came up. "Here am I, on a journey of life and death, in prosecuting which to lose an hour is possibly to lose all. My child will not have recovered sufficiently to resume her route for who can say how long. I must leave her; I cannot, dare not, delay. How far on, sir, can you tell, is the nearest village? I must leave her there; and shall not see my darling, or even hear of her till my return, three months hence."

I plucked my father by the coat, and whispered earnestly in his ear: "Oh! papa, pray ask her to let her stay with us—it would be so delightful. Do, pray."

"If Madame will entrust her child to the care of my daughter, and of her good gouvernante, Madame Perrodon, and permit her to remain as our guest, under my charge, until her return, it will confer a distinction and an obligation upon us, and we shall treat her with all the care and devotion which so sacred a trust deserves."

"I cannot do that, sir, it would be to task your kindness and chivalry too cruelly," said the lady, distractedly.

"It would, on the contrary, be to confer on us a very great kindness at the moment when we most need it. My daughter has just been disappointed by a cruel misfortune, in a visit from which she had long anticipated a great deal of happiness. If you confide this young lady to our care it will be her best consolation. The nearest village on your route is distant, and affords no such inn as you could think of placing your daughter at; you cannot allow her to continue her journey for any considerable distance without danger. If, as you say, you cannot suspend your journey, you must part with her to-night, and nowhere could you do so with more honest assurances of care and tenderness than here."

There was something in this lady's air and appearance so distinguished, and even imposing, and in her manner so engaging, as to impress one, quite apart from the dignity of her equipage, with a conviction that she was a person of consequence.

By this time the carriage was replaced in its upright position, and the horses, quite tractable, in the traces again.

The lady threw on her daughter a glance which I fancied was not quite so affectionate as one might have anticipated from the beginning of the scene; then she beckoned slightly to my father, and withdrew two or three steps with him out of hearing; and talked to him with a fixed and stern countenance, not at all like that with which she had hitherto spoken.

I was filled with wonder that my father did not seem to perceive the change, and also unspeakably curious to learn what it could be that she was speaking, almost in his ear, with so much earnestness and rapidity. Two or three minutes at most I think she remained thus employed, then she turned, and a few steps brought her to where her daughter lay, supported by Madame Perrodon. She kneeled beside her for a moment and whispered, as Madame supposed, a little benediction in her ear; then hastily kissing her she stepped into her carriage, the door was closed, the footmen in stately liveries jumped up behind, the outriders spurred on, the postillions cracked their whips, the horses plunged and broke suddenly into a furious canter that threatened soon again to become a gallop, and the carriage whirled away, followed at the same rapid pace by the two horsemen in the rear.

CHAPTER III:
WE COMPARE NOTES

We followed the cortege with our eyes until it was swiftly lost to sight in the misty wood; and the very sound of the hoofs and the wheels died away in the silent night air. Nothing remained to assure us that the adventure had not been an illusion of a moment but the young lady, who just at that moment opened her eyes. I could not see, for her face was turned from me, but she raised her head, evidently looking about her, and I heard a very sweet voice ask complainingly, "Where is mamma?"

Our good Madame Perrodon answered tenderly, and added some comfortable assurances. I then heard her ask: "Where am I? What is this place?" and after that she said, "I don't see the carriage; and Matska, where is she?"

Madame answered all her questions in so far as she understood them; and gradually the young lady remembered how the misadventure came about, and was glad to hear that no one in, or in attendance on, the carriage was hurt; and on learning that her mamma had left her here, till her return in about three months, she wept.

I was going to add my consolations to those of Madame Perrodon when Mademoiselle De Lafontaine placed her hand on my arm, saying: "Don't approach, one at a time is as much as she can at present converse with; a very little excitement would possibly overpower her now."

As soon as she is comfortably in bed, I thought, I will run up to her room and see her.

My father in the meantime had sent a servant on horseback for the physician, who lived about two leagues away; and a bed-room was being prepared for the young lady's reception.

The stranger now rose, and leaning on Madame's arm walked slowly over the drawbridge and into the castle gate.

In the hall, servants waited to receive her, and she was conducted forthwith to her room.

The room we usually sat in as our drawing-room is long, having four windows, that looked over the moat and drawbridge, upon the forest scene I have just described. It is furnished in old carved oak, with large carved cabinets, and the chairs are cushioned with crimson Utrecht velvet. The walls are covered with tapestry, and surrounded with great gold frames, the figures being as large as life, in ancient and very curious costume, and the subjects represented are hunting, hawking, and generally festive. It is not too stately to be extremely comfortable; and here we had our tea, for with usual patriotic leanings my father insisted that the beverage should make its appearance regularly with our coffee and chocolate.

We sat here this night, and with candles lighted, were talking over the adventure of the evening.

Madame Perrodon and Mademoiselle De Lafontaine were both of our party. The young stranger had hardly lain down in her bed when she sank into a deep sleep; and those ladies had left her in the care of a servant.

"How do you like our guest?" I asked, as soon as Madam entered. "Tell me all about her."

"I like her extremely," answered Madame, "She is, I almost think, the prettiest creature I ever saw; about your age, and so gentle and nice."

"She is absolutely beautiful," threw in Mademoiselle, who had peeped for a moment into the stranger's room.

"And such a sweet voice!" added Madame Perrodon.

"Did you remark a woman in the carriage, after it was set up again, who did not get out," inquired Mademoiselle, "but only looked from the window?"

"No, we had not seen her."

Then she described a hideous black woman, with a sort of coloured turban on her head, who was gazing all the time from the carriage window, nodding and grinning derisively towards the ladies, with gleaming eyes and large white eye-balls, and her teeth set as if in fury.

"Did you remark what an ill-looking pack of men the servants were?" asked Madame.

"Yes," said my father, who had just come in, "ugly, hang-dog looking fellows, as ever I beheld in my life. I hope they mayn't rob the poor lady in the forest. They are clever rogues, however; they got everything to rights in a minute."

"I dare say they are worn out with too long travelling," said Madame. "Besides looking wicked, their faces were so strangely lean, and dark, and sullen. I am very curious, I own; but I dare say the young lady will tell us all about it to-morrow, if she is sufficiently recovered."

"I don't think she will," said my father, with a mysterious smile, and a little nod of his head, as if he knew more about it than he cared to tell us.

This made me all the more inquisitive as to what had passed between him and the lady in the black velvet, in the brief but earnest interview that had immediately preceded her departure.

We were scarcely alone, when I entreated him to tell me. He did not need much pressing.

"There is no particular reason why I should not tell you. She expressed a reluctance to trouble us with the care of her daughter, saying she was in delicate health, and nervous, but not subject to any kind of seizure—she volunteered that—nor to any illusion; being, in fact, perfectly sane."

"How very odd to say all that!" I interpolated. "It was so unnecessary."

"At all events it was said," he laughed, "and as you wish to know all that passed, which was indeed very little, I tell you. She then said, 'I am making a long journey of vital importance'—she emphasized the word—'rapid and secret; I shall return for my child in three months; in the meantime, she will be silent as to who we are, whence we come, and whither we are travelling.' That is all she said. She spoke very pure French. When she said the word 'secret,' she paused for a few seconds, looking sternly, her eyes fixed on mine. I fancy she makes a great point of that. You saw how quickly she was gone. I hope I have not done a very foolish thing, in taking charge of the young lady."

For my part, I was delighted. I was longing to see and talk to her; and only waiting till the doctor should give me leave. You, who live in towns, can have no idea how great an event the introduction of a new friend is, in such a solitude as surrounded us.

The doctor did not arrive till nearly one o'clock; but I could no more have gone to my bed and slept, than I could have overtaken, on foot, the carriage in which the princess velvet had driven away.

When the physician came down to the drawing-room, it was to report very favourably upon his patient. She was now sitting up, her pulse quite regular, apparently perfectly well. She sustained no injury, and the little shock to her nerves passed away quite harmlessly. There could be no harm certainly in my seeing her, if we both wished it; and, with permission, I sent, forthwith, to know whether she would allow me to visit her for a few minutes in her room.

The servant returned immediately to say that she desired nothing more.

You may be sure I was not long in availing myself of this permission.

Our visitor lay in one of the handsomest rooms in the schloss. It was, perhaps, a little stately. There was a sombre piece of tapestry opposite the foot of the bed, representing Cleopatra with the asp to her bosom; and other solemn classic scenes were displayed, a little faded, upon the other walls. But there was gold carving, and rich and varied colour enough in the other decorations of the room, to more than redeem the gloom of the old tapestry.

There were candles at the bed-side. She was sitting up; her slender pretty figure enveloped in the soft silk dressing gown, embroidered with flowers, and lined with thick quilted silk, which her mother had thrown over her feet as she lay upon the ground.

What was it that, as I reached the bed-side and had just begun my little greeting, struck me dumb in a moment, and made me recoil a step or two from before her? I will tell you.

I saw the very face which had visited me in my childhood at night, which remained so fixed in my memory, and on which I had for so many years so often ruminated with horror, when no one suspected of what I was thinking.

It was pretty, even beautiful; and when I first beheld it, wore the same melancholy expression. But this almost instantly lighted into a strange fixed smile of recognition. There was a silence of fully a minute, and then at length she spoke; I could not. "How wonderful!" she exclaimed, "Twelve years ago, I saw your face in a dream, and it has haunted me ever since."

"Wonderful indeed?" I repeated, overcoming with an effort the horror that had for a time suspended my utterances. "Twelve years ago, in vision or reality, I certainly saw you. I could not forget your face. It has remained before my eyes ever since."

Her smile had softened. Whatever I had fancied strange in it was gone, and it and her dimpling cheeks were now delightfully pretty and intelligent.

I felt reassured, and continued more in the vein which hospitality indicated, to bid her welcome, and to tell her how much pleasure her accidental arrival had given us all, and especially what a happiness it was to me.

I took her hand as I spoke. I was a little shy, as lonely people are, but the situation made me eloquent, and even bold. She pressed my hand, she laid hers upon it, and her eyes glowed, as, looking hastily into mine, she smiled again, and blushed.

She answered my welcome very prettily. I sat down beside her, still wondering; and she said: "I must tell you my vision about you; it is so very strange that you and I should have had, each of the other so vivid a dream, that each should have seen, I you and you me, looking as we do now, when of course we both were mere children. I was a child, about six years old, and I awoke from a confused and troubled dream, and found myself in a room, unlike my nursery, wainscoted clumsily in some dark wood, and with cupboards and bedsteads, and chairs, and benches placed about it. The beds were, I thought, all empty, and the room itself without anyone but myself in it; and I, after looking about me for some time, and admiring especially an iron candlestick, with two branches, which I should certainly know again, crept under one of the beds to reach the window; but as I got from under the bed, I heard someone crying; and looking, up, while I was still upon my knees, saw you—most assuredly you—as I see you now; a beautiful young lady, with golden hair and large blue eyes, and lips—your lips—you, as you are here. Your looks won me; I climbed on the bed and put arms about you, and I think we both fell asleep. I was aroused by a scream; you were sitting up screaming. I was frightened, and slipped down upon the ground, and, it seemed to me, lost consciousness for a moment; and when I came to myself, I was again in my nursery at home. Your face I have never forgotten since. I could not be misled by mere resemblance. You *are* the lady whom I then saw."

It was now my turn to relate my corresponding vision, which I did, to the undisguised wonder of my acquaintance.

"I don't know which should be most afraid of the other," she said, again smiling. "If you were less pretty I think I would be very much afraid of you, but being as you are, and you and I both so young, I feel only that I have made your acquaintance twelve years ago, and have already a right to intimacy; at all events it does seem as if we were from our earliest childhood, to be friends. I wonder you feel as strangely drawn towards me as I do to you; I never had a friend—shall I find one now?" She sighed, and fine dark eyes gazed passionately on me.

Now the truth is, I felt rather unaccountably towards the beautiful stranger. I did feel, as she said, "drawn towards her," but there was also something of repulsion. In this feeling, however, the sense of attraction immensely prevailed. She interested and won me; she was so beautiful and so indescribably engaging.

I perceived now something of langour and exhaustion stealing over her, and hastened to bid her good night.

"The doctor thinks," I added, "that you ought to have a maid to sit up with you to-night; one of ours is waiting, and you will find her a very useful and quiet creature."

"How kind of you, but I could not sleep, I never could with an attendant in the room. I shan't require any assistance—and, shall I confess my weakness, I am haunted with a terror of robbers. Our house was robbed once, and two servants murdered, so I always lock my door. It has become a habit—and you look so kind I know you will forgive me. I see there is a key in the lock."

She held me close in her pretty arms for a moment and whispered in my ear, "Good night, darling, it is very hard to part with you, but good-night; to-morrow, but not early, I shall see you again."

She sank back on the pillow with a sigh, and her fine eyes followed me with a fond and melancholy gaze, and she murmured again, "Good-night, dear friend."

Young people like, and even love, on impulse. I was flattered by the evident, though as yet undeserved, fondness she showed me. I liked the confidence with which she at once received me. She was determined that we should be very near friends.

Next day came and we met again. I was delighted with my companion; that is to say, in many respects.

Her looks lost nothing in daylight—she was certainly the most beautiful creature I had ever seen, and the unpleasant remembrance of the face presented in my early dream, had lost the effect of the first unexpected recognition.

She confessed that she had experienced a similar shock on seeing me, and precisely the same faint antipathy that had mingled with my admiration of her. We now laughed together over our momentary horrors.

CHAPTER IV: HER HABITS—A SAUNTER

I told you that I was charmed with her in most particulars. There were some that did not please me so well. I shall begin by describing her. She was above the middle height of women. She was slender, and wonderfully graceful. Except that her movements were languid—very languid—indeed, there was nothing in her appearance to indicate an invalid. Her complexion was rich and brilliant; her features were small and beautifully formed; her eyes large, dark, and lustrous; her hair was quite wonderful, I never saw hair so magnificently thick and long when it was down about her shoulders; I have often placed my hands under it, and laughed with wonder at its weight. It was exquisitely fine and soft, and in colour a rich very dark brown, with something of gold. I loved to let it down, tumbling with its own weight, as, in her room, she lay back in her chair talking in her sweet low voice, I used to fold and braid it, and spread it out and play with it. Heavens! If I had but known all!

I said there were particulars which did not please me. I have told you that her confidence won me the first night I saw her; but I found that she exercised with respect to herself, her mother, her history, everything in fact connected with her life, plans, and people, an ever wakeful reserve. I dare say I was unreasonable, perhaps I was wrong; I dare say I ought to have respected the solemn injunction laid upon my father by the stately lady in black velvet. But curiosity is a restless and unscrupulous passion, and no one girl can endure, with patience, that hers should be baffled by another. What harm could it do anyone to tell me what I so ardently desired to know? Had she no trust in my good sense or honour? Why would she not believe me when I assured her, so solemnly, that I would not divulge one syllable of what she told me to any mortal breathing?

There was a coldness, it seemed to me, beyond her years, in her, smiling melancholy persistent refusal to afford me the least ray of light. I cannot say we quarrelled upon this point, for she would not quarrel upon any. It was, of course, very unfair of me to press her, very ill-bred, but I really could not help it; and I might just as well have let it alone.

What she did tell me amounted, in my unconscionable estimation, to nothing. It was all summed up in three very vague disclosures:

First—Her name was Carmilla.

Second—Her family was very ancient and noble.

Third—Her home lay in the direction of the west.

She would not tell me the name of her family, nor their armorial bearings, nor the name of their estate, nor even that of the country they lived in.

You are not to suppose that I worried her incessantly on these subjects. I watched for opportunity, and rather insinuated than urged my inquiries. Once or twice, indeed, I did attack her more directly. But no matter what my tactics, utter failure was invariably the result. Reproaches and caresses were all lost upon her. But I must add this, that her evasion was conducted with so pretty a melancholy and deprecation, with so many, and even passionate declarations of her liking for me, and trust in my honour, and with so many promises that I should at last know all, that I could not find it in my heart long to be offended with her.

She used to place her pretty arms about my neck, draw me to her, and laying her cheek to mine, murmur with her lips near my ear, "Dearest, your little heart is wounded; think me not cruel because I obey the irresistible law of my strength and weakness; if your dear heart is wounded, my wild heart bleeds with yours. In the rapture of my enormous humiliation I live in your warm life, and you shall die—die, sweetly die—into mine. I cannot help it; as I draw near to you, you, in your turn, will draw near to others, and learn the rapture of that cruelty, which yet is love; so, for a while, seek to know no more of me and mine, but trust me with all your loving spirit."

And when she had spoken such a rhapsody, she would press me more closely in her trembling embrace, and her lips in soft kisses gently glowed upon my cheek.

Her agitations and her language were unintelligible to me.

From these foolish embraces, which were not of very frequent occurrence, I must allow, I used to wish to extricate myself; but my energies seemed to fail me. Her murmured words sounded like a lullaby in my ear, and soothed my resistance into a trance, from which I only seemed to recover myself when she withdrew her arms.

In these mysterious moods I did not like her. I experienced a strange tumultuous excitement that was pleasurable, ever and anon, mingled with a vague sense of fear and disgust. I had no distinct thoughts about her while such scenes lasted, but I was conscious of a love growing into adoration, and also of abhorrence. This I know is paradox, but I can make no other attempt to explain the feeling.

I now write, after an interval of more than ten years, with a trembling hand, with a confused and horrible recollection of certain occurrences and situations, in the ordeal through which I was unconsciously passing; though with a vivid and very sharp remembrance of the main current of my story. But, I suspect, in all lives there are certain emotional scenes, those in which our passions have been most wildly and terribly roused, that are of all others the most vaguely and dimly remembered.

Sometimes after an hour of apathy, my strange and beautiful companion would take my hand and hold it with a fond pressure, renewed again and again; blushing softly, gazing in my face with languid and burning eyes, and breathing so fast; that her dress rose and fell with the tumultuous respiration. It was like the ardour of a lover; it embarrassed me; it was hateful and yet overpowering; and with gloating eyes she drew me to her, and her hot lips travelled along my cheek in kisses; and she would whisper, almost in sobs, "You are mine, you shall be mine, you and I are one forever." Then she had thrown herself back in her chair, with her small hands over her eyes, leaving me trembling.

"Are we related," I used to ask; "what can you mean by all this? I remind you perhaps of someone whom you love; but you must not, I hate it; I don't know you—I don't know myself when you look so and talk so."

She used to sigh at my vehemence, then turn away and drop my hand.

Respecting these very extraordinary manifestations I strove in vain to form any satisfactory theory—I could not refer them to affectation or trick. It was unmistakably the momentary breaking out of suppressed instinct and emotion. Was she, notwithstanding her mother's volunteered denial, subject to brief visitations of insanity; or was there here a disguise and a romance? I had read in old story books of such things. What if a boyish lover had found his way into the house, and sought to persecute his suit in masquerade, with the assistance of a clever old adventuress? But there were many things against this hypothesis, highly interesting as it was to my vanity.

I could boast of no little attentions such as masculine gallantry delights to offer. Between these passionate moments there were long intervals of common-place, of gaiety, of brooding melancholy, during which, except that I detected her eyes so full of melancholy fire, following me, at times I might have seen as nothing to her. Except in these brief periods of mysterious excitement her ways were girlish; and there was always a langour about her, quite incompatible with a masculine system in a state of health.

In some respects her habits were odd. Perhaps not so singular in the opinion of a town lady like you, as they appeared to us rustic people. She used to come down very late, generally not till one o'clock. She would then take a cup of chocolate, but eat nothing; we then went out for a walk, which was a mere saunter, and she seemed, almost immediately, exhausted, and either returned to the schloss or sat on one of benches that were placed, here and there, among the trees. This was a bodily langour in which her mind did not sympathize. She was always an animated talker, and very intelligent.

She sometimes alluded for a moment to her own home, or mentioned an adventure or situation, or an early recollection, which indicated a people of strange manners, and described customs of which we knew nothing. I gathered from these chance hints that her native country was much more remote than I had at first fancied.

As we sat thus one afternoon under the trees a funeral passed us by. It was that of a pretty young girl, whom I had often seen, the daughter of one of the rangers of the forest. The poor man was walking behind the coffin of his darling; she was his only child, and he looked quite heartbroken. Peasants walking two-and-two came behind, they were singing a funeral hymn.

I rose to mark my respect as they passed, and joined in the hymn they were very sweetly singing.

My companion shook me a little roughly, and I turned surprised.

She said brusquely, "Don't you perceive how discordant that is?"

"I think it very sweet, on the contrary," I answered, vexed at the interruption, and very uncomfortable, lest the people who composed the little procession should observe and resent what was passing.

I resumed, therefore, instantly, and was again interrupted. "You pierce my ears," said Carmilla, almost angrily, and stopping her ears with her tiny fingers. "Besides, how can you tell that your religion and mine are the same; your forms wound me, and I hate funerals. What a fuss! Why you must die—everyone must die; and all are happier when they do. Come home."

"My father has gone on with the clergyman to the churchyard. I thought you knew she was to be buried to day."

"She? I don't trouble my head about peasants. I don't know who she is," answered Carmilla, with a flash from her fine eyes.

"She is the poor girl who fancied she saw a ghost a fortnight ago, and has been dying ever since, till yesterday, when she expired."

"Tell me nothing about ghosts. I shan't sleep tonight if you do."

"I hope there is no plague or fever coming; all this looks very like it," I continued. "The swineherd's young wife died only a week ago, and she thought something seized her by the throat as she lay in her bed, and nearly strangled her. Papa says such horrible fancies do accompany some forms of fever. She was quite well the day before. She sank afterwards, and died before a week."

"Well, *her* funeral is over, I hope, and her hymn sung; and our ears shan't be tortured with that discord and jargon. It has made me nervous. Sit down here, beside me; sit close; hold my hand; press it hard—hard—harder."

We had moved a little back, and had come to another seat.

She sat down. Her face underwent a change that alarmed and even terrified me for a moment. It darkened, and became horribly livid; her teeth and hands were clenched, and she frowned and compressed her lips, while she stared down upon ground at her feet, and trembled all over with a continued shudder as irrepressible as ague. All her energies seemed strained to suppress a fit, with which she was then breathlessly tugging; and at length a low convulsive cry of suffering broke from her, and gradually the hysteria subsided. "There! That comes of strangling people with hymns!" she said at last. "Hold me, hold me still. It is passing away."

And so gradually it did; and perhaps to dissipate the sombre impression which the spectacle had left upon me, she became unusually animated and chatty; and so we got home.

This was the first time I had seen her exhibit any definable symptoms of that delicacy of health which her mother had spoken of. It was the first time, also, I had seen her exhibit anything like temper.

Both passed away like a summer cloud; and never but once afterwards did I witness on her part a momentary sign of anger. I will tell you how it happened.

She and I were looking out of one of the long drawing-room windows, when there entered the court-yard, over the draw- bridge, a figure of a wanderer whom I knew very well. He used to visit the schloss generally twice a year.

It was the figure of a hunchback, with the sharp lean features that generally accompany deformity. He wore a pointed black beard, and he was smiling from ear to ear, showing his white fangs. He was dressed in buff, black, and scarlet, and crossed with more straps and belts than I could count, from which hung all manner of things. Behind, he carried a magic-lantern, and two boxes, which I well knew, in one of which was a salamander, and in the other a mandrake. These monsters used to make my father laugh. They were compounded of parts of monkeys, parrots, squirrels, fish, and hedgehogs, dried and stitched together with great neatness and startling effect. He had a fiddle, a box of conjuring apparatus, a pair of foils and masks attached to his belt several other mysterious cases dangling about him, and a black staff with copper ferrules in his hand. His companion was a rough spare dog that followed at his heels, but stopped short suspiciously at the drawbridge, and in a little while began to howl dismally.

In the meantime, the mountebank, standing in the midst of the courtyard, raised his grotesque hat, and made us a very ceremonious bow, paying his compliments very volubly in execrable French, and German not much better. Then, disengaging his fiddle, he began to scrape a lively air, to which he sang with a merry discord, dancing with ludicrous airs and activity, that made me laugh, in spite of the dog's howling.

Then he advanced to the window with many smiles and salutations, and his hat in his left hand, his fiddle under his arm, and with a fluency that never took breath he gabbled a long advertisement of all his accomplishments, and the resources of the various arts which he placed at our service, and the curiosities and entertainments which it was in his power, at our bidding, to display.

"Will your ladyships be pleased to buy an amulet against the *oupire*, which is going like the wolf, I hear, through these woods," he said, dropping his hat on the pavement. "They are dying of it right and left, and here is a charm that never fails; only pinned to the pillow, and you may laugh in his face."

These charms consisted of oblong slips of vellum, with cabalistic ciphers and diagrams upon them.

Carmilla instantly purchased one, and so did I.

He was looking up, and we were smiling down upon him, amused; at least, I can answer for myself. His piercing black eye, as he looked up in our faces, seemed to detect something that fixed for a moment his curiosity.

In an instant he unrolled a leather case, full of all manner of odd little steel instruments.

"See here, my lady," he said, displaying it, and addressing me, "I profess, among other things less useful, the art of dentistry. Plague take the dog!" he interpolated. "Silence, beast! He howls so that your ladyships can scarcely hear a word. Your noble friend, the young lady at your right, has the sharpest tooth, long, thin, pointed, like an awl, like a needle; ha, ha! With my sharp and long sight, as I look up, I have seen it distinctly; now if it happens to hurt the young lady, and I think it must, here am I, here are my file, my punch, my nippers; I will make it round and blunt, if her ladyship pleases; no longer the tooth of a fish, but of a beautiful young lady as she is. Hey? Is the young lady displeased? Have I been too bold? Have I offended her?"

The young lady, indeed, looked very angry as she drew back from the window.

"How dares that mountebank insult us so? Where is your father? I shall demand redress from him. My father would have had the wretch tied up to the pump, and flogged with a cart-whip, and burnt to the bones with the castle brand!"

She retired from the window a step or two, and sat down, and had hardly lost sight of the offender, when her wrath subsided as suddenly as it had risen, and she gradually recovered her usual tone, and seemed to forget the little hunchback and his follies.

My father was out of spirits that evening. On coming in he told us that there had been another case very similar to the two fatal ones which had lately occurred. The sister of a young peasant on his estate, only a mile away, was very ill, had been, as she described it, attacked very nearly in the same way, and was now slowly but steadily sinking.

"All this," said my father, "is strictly referable to natural causes. These poor people infect one another with their superstitions, and so repeat in imagination the images of terror that have infested their neighbours."

"But that very circumstance frightens one horribly," said Carmilla.

"How so?" inquired my father.

"I am so afraid of fancying I see such things; I think it would be as bad as reality."

"We are in God's hands; nothing can happen without His permission, and all will end well for those who love Him. He is our faithful creator; He has made us all, and will take care of us."

"Creator! Nature!" said the young lady in answer to my gentle father. "And this disease that invades the country is natural Nature. All things proceed from Nature—don't they? All things in the heaven, in the earth, and under the earth, act and live as Nature ordains? I think so."

"The doctor said he would come here today," said my father, after a silence. "I want to know what he thinks about it, and what he thinks we had better do."

"Doctors never did me any good," said Carmilla.

"Then you have been ill?" I asked.

"More ill than ever you were," she answered.

"Long ago?"

"Yes, a long time. I suffered from this very illness; but I forget all but my pain and weakness, and they were not so bad as are suffered in other diseases."

"You were very young then?"

"I dare say; let us talk no more of it. You would not wound a friend?" She looked languidly in my eyes, and passed her arm round my waist lovingly, and led me out of the room. My father was busy over some papers near the window.

"Why does your papa like to frighten us?" said the pretty girl, with a sigh and a little shudder.

"He doesn't, dear Carmilla, it is the very furthest thing from his mind."

"Are you afraid, dearest?"

"I should be very much if I fancied there was any real danger of my being attacked as those poor people were."

"You are afraid to die?"

"Yes, everyone is."

"But to die as lovers may—to die together, so that they may live together. Girls are caterpillars while they live in the world, to be finally butterflies when the summer comes; but in the meantime there are grubs and larvae, don't you see—each with their peculiar propensities, necessities and structure. So says Monsieur Buffon, in his big book, in the next room."

Later in the day the doctor came and was closeted with papa for some time. He was a skillful man, of sixty and upwards He wore powder, and shaved his pale face as smooth as a pumpkin. He and papa emerged from the room together, and heard papa laugh, and say as they came out:

"Well. I do wonder at a wise man like you. What do you say to hippogriffs and dragons?"

The doctor was smiling, and made answer, shaking his head:

"Nevertheless life and death are mysterious states, and we know little of the resources of either."

And so they walked on, and I heard no more. I did not then know what the doctor had been broaching, but I think I guess of it now.

CHAPTER V:
A WONDERFUL LIKENESS

This evening there arrived from Gratz the grave, dark-faced son of the picture cleaner, with a horse and cart laden with two large packing cases, having many pictures in each. It was a journey of ten leagues, and whenever a messenger arrived at the schloss from our little capital of Gratz, we used to crowd about him in the hall, to hear the news.

This arrival created in our secluded quarters quite a sensation. The cases remained in the hall, and the messenger was taken charge of by the servants till he had eaten his supper. Then with assistants, and armed with hammer, ripping-chisel, and turnscrew, he met us in the hall, where we had assembled to witness the unpacking of the cases.

Carmilla sat looking listlessly on, while one after the other the old pictures, nearly all portraits, which had undergone the process of renovation, were brought to light. My mother was of an old Hungarian family, and most of these pictures, which were about to be restored to their places, had come to us through her.

My father had a list in his hand, from which he read, as the artist rummaged out the corresponding numbers. I don't know that the pictures were very good, but they were, undoubtedly, very old, and some of them very curious also. They had, for the most part, the merit of being now seen by me, I may say, for the first time; for the smoke and dust of time had all but obliterated them.

"There is a picture that I have not seen yet," said my father. "In one corner, at the top of it, is the name, as well as I could read, 'Marcia Karnstein,' and the date '1698,' and I am curious to see how it has turned out."

I remembered it; it was a small picture, about a foot and a half high, and nearly square, without a frame; but it was so blackened by age that I could not make it out.

The artist now produced it, with evident pride. It was quite beautiful; it was startling; it seemed to live. It was the effigy of Carmilla!

"Carmilla, dear, here is an absolute miracle. Here you are, living, smiling, ready to speak, in this picture. Isn't it beautiful, papa? And see, even the little mole on her throat."

My father laughed, and said "Certainly it is a wonderful likeness," but he looked away, and to my surprise seemed but little struck by it, and went on talking to the picture cleaner, who was also something of an artist, and discoursed with intelligence about the portraits or other works, which his art had just brought into light and colour, while I was more and more lost in wonder the more I looked at the picture.

"Will you let me hang this picture in my room, papa?" I asked.

"Certainly, dear," said he, smiling, "I'm very glad you think it so like. It must be prettier even than I thought it, if it is."

The young lady did not acknowledge this pretty speech, did not seem to hear it. She was leaning back in her seat, her fine eyes under their long lashes gazing on me in contemplation, and she smiled in a kind of rapture.

"And now you can read quite plainly the name that is written in the corner. It is not Marcia; it looks as if it was done in gold. The name is Mircalla, Countess Karnstein, and this is a little coronet over it, and underneath AD 1698. I am descended from the Karnsteins; that is, mamma was."

"Ah?" said the lady, languidly, "so am I, I think, a very long descent, very ancient. Are there any Karnsteins living now?"

"None who bear the name, I believe. The family were ruined, I believe, in some civil wars, long ago, but the ruins of the castle are only about three miles away."

"How interesting," she said, languidly. "But see what beautiful moonlight!" She glanced through the hall-door, which stood a little open. "Suppose you take a little ramble round the court, and look down at the road and river."

"It is so like the night you came to us," I said.

She sighed, smiling.

She rose, and each with her arm about the other's waist, we walked out upon the pavement.

In silence, slowly we walked down to the drawbridge, where the beautiful landscape opened before us.

"And so you were thinking of the night I came here?" she almost whispered. "Are you glad I came?"

"Delighted, dear Carmilla," I answered.

"And you asked for the picture you think like me, to hang in your room," she murmured with a sigh, as she drew her arm closer about my waist, and let her pretty head sink upon my shoulder.

"How romantic you are, Carmilla," I said. "Whenever you tell me your story, it will be made up chiefly of some one great romance."

She kissed me silently.

"I am sure, Carmilla, you have been in love; that there is, at this moment, an affair of the heart going on."

"I have been in love with no one, and never shall," she whispered, "unless it should be with you."

How beautiful she looked in the moonlight!

Shy and strange was the look with which she quickly hid her face in my neck and hair, with tumultuous sighs, that seemed almost to sob, and pressed in mine a hand that trembled.

Her soft cheek was glowing against mine. "Darling, darling," she murmured, "I live in you; and you would die for me, I love you so."

I started from her.

She was gazing on me with eyes from which all fire, all meaning had flown, and a face colourless and apathetic.

"Is there a chill in the air, dear?" she said drowsily. "I almost shiver; have I been dreaming? Let us come in. Come; come; Come in."

"You look ill, Carmilla; a little faint. You certainly must take some wine," I said.

"Yes, I will. I'm better now. I shall be quite well in a few minutes. Yes, do give me a little wine," answered Carmilla, as we approached the door. "Let us look again for a moment; it is the last time, perhaps, I shall see the moonlight with you."

"How do you feel now, dear Carmilla? Are you really better?" I asked.

I was beginning to take alarm, lest she should have been stricken with the strange epidemic that they said had invaded the country about us.

"Papa would be grieved beyond measure," I added, "if he thought you were ever so little ill, without immediately letting us know. We have a very skillful doctor near this, the physician who was with papa today."

"I'm sure he is. I know how kind you all are; but, dear child, I am quite well again. There is nothing ever wrong with me, but a little weakness. People say I am languid; I am incapable of exertion; I can scarcely walk as far as a child of three years old; and every now and then the little strength I have falters, and I become as you have just seen me. But after all I am very easily set up again; in a moment I am perfectly myself. See how I have recovered."

So, indeed, she had; and she and I talked a great deal, and very animated she was; and the remainder of that evening passed without any recurrence of what I called her infatuations. I mean her crazy talk and looks, which embarrassed, and even frightened me.

But there occurred that night an event which gave my thoughts quite a new turn, and seemed to startle even Carmilla's languid nature into momentary energy.

CHAPTER VI:
A VERY STRANGE AGONY

When we got into the drawing-room, and had sat down to our coffee and chocolate, although Carmilla did not take any, she seemed quite herself again, and Madame, and Mademoiselle De Lafontaine, joined us, and made a little card party, in the course of which papa came in for what he called his "dish of tea."

When the game was over he sat down beside Carmilla on the sofa, and asked her, a little anxiously, whether she had heard from her mother since her arrival. She answered "No."

He then asked whether she knew where a letter would reach her at present. "I cannot tell," she answered ambiguously, "but I have been thinking of leaving you; you have been already too hospitable and too kind to me. I have given you an infinity of trouble, and I should wish to take a carriage to-morrow, and post in pursuit of her; I know where I shall ultimately find her, although I dare not yet tell you."

"But you must not dream of any such thing," exclaimed my father, to my great relief. "We can't afford to lose you so, and I won't consent to your leaving us, except under the care of your mother, who was so good as to consent to your remaining with us till she should herself return. I should be quite happy if I knew that you heard from her; but this evening the accounts of the progress of the mysterious disease that has invaded our neighbourhood, grow even more alarming; and my beautiful guest, I do feel the responsibility, unaided by advice from your mother, very much. But I shall do my best; and one thing is certain, that you must not think of leaving us without her distinct direction to that effect. We should suffer too much in parting from you to consent to it easily."

"Thank you, sir, a thousand times for your hospitality," she answered, smiling bashfully. "You have all been too kind to me; I have seldom been so happy in all my life before, as in your beautiful chateau, under your care, and in the society of your dear daughter."

So he gallantly, in his old-fashioned way, kissed her hand, smiling and pleased at her little speech.

I accompanied Carmilla as usual to her room, and sat and chatted with her while she was preparing for bed.

"Do you think," I said at length, "that you will ever confide fully in me?"

She turned round smiling, but made no answer, only continued to smile on me.

"You won't answer that?" I said. "You can't answer pleasantly; I ought not to have asked you."

"You were quite right to ask me that, or anything. You do not know how dear you are to me, or you could not think confidence too great to look for. But I am under vows, half so awfully, and I dare not tell my story yet, even to you. The time is very near when you shall know everything. You will think me cruel, very selfish, but love is always selfish; the more ardent the more selfish. How jealous I am you cannot know. You must come with me, loving me, to death; or else hate me and still come with me, and hating me through death and after. There is no such word as indifference in my apathetic nature."

"Now, Carmilla, you are going to talk your wild nonsense again," I said hastily.

"Not I, silly little fool as I am, and full of whims and fancies; for your sake I'll talk like a sage. Were you ever at a ball?"

"No; how you do run on. What is it like? How charming it must be."

"I almost forget, it is years ago."

I laughed.

"You are not so old. Your first ball can hardly be yet."

"I remember everything about it—with an effort. I see it all, as divers see what is going on above them, through a medium, dense, rippling, but transparent. There occurred that night what has confused the picture, and made its colours faint. I was all but assassinated in my bed, wounded here," she touched her breast, "and never was the same since."

"Were you near dying?"

"Yes, very—a cruel love—strange love, that would have taken my life. Love will have its sacrifices. No sacrifice without blood. Let us go to sleep now; I feel so lazy. How can I get up just now and lock my door?" She was lying with her tiny hands buried in her rich wavy hair, under her cheek, her little head upon the pillow, and her glittering eyes followed me wherever I moved, with a kind of shy smile that I could not decipher. I bid her good-night, and crept from the room with an uncomfortable sensation.

I often wondered whether our pretty guest ever said her prayers. I certainly had never seen her upon her knees. In the morning she never came down until long after our family prayers were over, and at night she never left the drawing room to attend our brief evening prayers in the hall.

If it had not been that it had casually come out in one of our careless talks that she had been baptized, I should have doubted her being a Christian. Religion was a subject on which I had never heard her speak a word. If I had known the world better, this particular neglect or antipathy would not have so much surprised me.

The precautions of nervous people are infectious, and persons of a like temperament are pretty sure, after a time, to imitate them. I had adopted Carmilla's habit of locking her bed-room door, having taken into my head all her whimsical alarms about midnight invaders and prowling assassins. I had also adopted her precaution of making a brief search through her room, to satisfy herself that no lurking assassin or robber was "ensconced."

These wise measures taken, I got into my bed and fell asleep. A light was burning in my room. This was an old habit, of very early date, and which nothing could have tempted me to dispense with.

Thus fortified I might take my rest in peace. But dreams come through stone walls, light up dark rooms, or darken light ones, and their persons make their exits and their entrances as they please, and laugh at locksmiths. I had a dream that night that was the beginning of a very strange agony.

I cannot call it a nightmare, for I was quite conscious of being asleep. But I was equally conscious of being in my room, and lying in bed, precisely as I actually was. I saw, or fancied I saw, the room and its furniture just as I had seen it last, except that it was very dark, and I saw something moving round the foot of the bed, which at first I could not accurately distinguish. But I soon saw that it was a sooty-black animal that resembled a monstrous cat. It appeared to me about four or five feet long, for it measured fully the length of the hearthrug as it passed over it; and it continued toing and froing with the lithe sinister restlessness of a beast in a cage. I could not cry out, although as you may suppose, I was terrified. Its pace was growing faster, and the room rapidly darker and darker, and at length so dark that I could no longer see anything of it but its eyes. I felt it spring lightly on the bed. The two broad eyes approached my face, and suddenly I felt a stinging pain as if two large needles darted, an inch or two apart, deep into my breast. I waked with a scream. The room was lighted by the candle that burnt there all through the night, and I saw a female figure standing at the foot of the bed, a little at the right side. It was in a dark loose dress, and its hair was down and covered its shoulders. A block of stone could not have been more still. There was not the slightest stir of respiration. As I stared at it, the figure appeared to have changed its place, and was now nearer the door; then, close to it, the door opened, and it passed out.

I was now relieved, and able to breathe and move. My first thought was that Carmilla had been playing me a trick, and that I had forgotten to secure my door. I hastened to it, and found it locked as usual on the inside. I was afraid to open it—I was horrified. I sprang into my bed and covered my head up in the bed-clothes, and lay there more dead than alive till morning.

CHAPTER VII: DESCENDING

It would be vain my attempting to tell you the horror with which, even now, I recall the occurrence of that night. It was no such transitory terror as a dream leaves behind it. It seemed to deepen by time, and communicated itself to the room and the very furniture that had encompassed the apparition.

I could not bear next day to be alone for a moment. I should have told papa, but for two opposite reasons. At one time I thought he would laugh at my story, and I could not bear its being treated as a jest; and at another, I thought he might fancy that I had been attacked by the mysterious complaint which had invaded our neighbourhood. I had myself no misgivings of the kind, and as he had been rather an invalid for some time, I was afraid of alarming him.

I was comfortable enough with my good-natured companions, Madame Perrodon, and the vivacious Mademoiselle La Fontaine. They both perceived that I was out of spirits and nervous, and at length I told them what lay so heavy at my heart.

Mademoiselle laughed, but I fancied that Madame Perrodon looked anxious.

"By-the-by," said Mademoiselle, laughing, "the long limetree walk, behind Carmilla's bedroom-window, is haunted?

"Nonsense!" exclaimed Madame, who probably thought the theme rather inopportune, "and who tells that story, my dear?"

"Martin says that he came up twice, when the old yard-gate was being repaired, before sunrise, and twice saw the same female figure walking down the lime-tree avenue."

"So he well might, as long as there are cows to milk in the river fields," said Madame.

"I daresay; but Martin chooses to be frightened, and never did I see fool more frightened."

"You must not say a word about it to Carmilla, because she can see down that walk from her room window," I interposed, "and she is, if possible, a greater coward than I."

Carmilla came down rather later than usual that day.

"I was so frightened last night," she said, so soon as were together, "and I am sure I should have seen something dreadful if it had not been for that charm I bought from the poor little hunchback whom I called such hard names. I had a dream of something black coming round my bed, and I awoke in a perfect horror, and I really thought, for some seconds, I saw a dark figure near the chimney-piece, but I felt under my pillow for my charm, and the moment my fingers touched it, the figure disappeared, and I felt quite certain, only that I had it by me, that something frightful would have made its appearance, and, perhaps, throttled me, as it did those poor people we heard of."

"Well, listen to me," I began, and recounted my adventure, at the recital of which she appeared horrified.

"And had you the charm near you?" she asked, earnestly.

"No, I had dropped it into a china vase in the drawing room, but I shall certainly take it with me to-night, as you have so much faith in it."

At this distance of time I cannot tell you, or even understand, how I overcame my horror so effectually as to lie alone in my room that night. I remember distinctly that I pinned the charm to my pillow. I fell asleep almost immediately, and slept even more soundly than usual all night.

Next night I passed as well. My sleep was delightfully deep and dreamless. But I wakened with a sense of lassitude and melancholy, which, however, did not exceed a degree that was almost luxurious.

"Well, I told you so," said Carmilla, when I described my quiet sleep. "I had such delightful sleep myself last night; I pinned the charm to the breast of my night-dress. It was too far away the night before. I am quite sure it was all fancy, except the dreams. I used to think that evil spirits made dreams, but our doctor told me it is no such thing. Only a fever passing by, or some other malady, as they often do, he said, knocks at the door, and not being able to get in, passes on, with that alarm."

"And what do you think the charm is?" said I.

"It has been fumigated or immersed in some drug, and is an antidote against the malaria," she answered.

"Then it acts only on the body?"

"Certainly; you don't suppose that evil spirits are frightened by bits of ribbon, or the perfumes of a druggist's shop? No, these complaints, wandering in the air, begin by trying the nerves, and so infect the brain, but before they can seize upon you, the antidote repels them. That I am sure is what the charm has done for us. It is nothing magical, it is simply natural."

I should have been happier if I could have quite agreed with Carmilla, but I did my best, and the impression was a little losing its force.

For some nights I slept profoundly; but still every morning I felt the same lassitude, and a languor weighed upon me all day. I felt myself a changed girl. A strange melancholy was stealing over me, a melancholy that I would not have interrupted. Dim thoughts of death began to open, and an idea that I was slowly sinking took gentle, and, somehow, not unwelcome, possession of me. If it was sad, the tone of mind which this induced was also sweet. Whatever it might be, my soul acquiesced in it. I would not admit that I was ill, I would not consent to tell my papa, or to have the doctor sent for.

Carmilla became more devoted to me than ever, and her strange paroxysms of languid adoration more frequent. She used to gloat on me with increasing ardour the more my strength and spirits waned. This always shocked me like a momentary glare of insanity.

Without knowing it, I was now in a pretty advanced stage of the strangest illness under which mortal ever suffered. There was an unaccountable fascination in its earlier symptoms that more than reconciled me to the incapacitating effect of that stage of the malady. This fascination increased for a time, until it reached a certain point, when gradually a sense of the horrible mingled itself with it, deepening, as you shall hear, until it discoloured and perverted the whole state of my life.

The first change I experienced was rather agreeable. It was very near the turning point from which began the descent to Avernus.

Certain vague and strange sensations visited me in my sleep. The prevailing one was of that pleasant, peculiar cold thrill which we feel in bathing, when we move against the current of a river. This was soon accompanied by dreams that seemed interminable, and were so vague that I could never recollect their scenery and persons, or any one connected portion of their action. But they left an awful impression, and a sense of exhaustion, as if I had passed through a long period of great mental exertion and danger. After all these dreams there remained on waking a remembrance of having been in a place very nearly dark, and of having spoken to people whom I could not see; and especially of one clear voice, of a female's, very deep, that spoke as if at a distance, slowly, and producing always the same sensation of indescribable solemnity and fear. Sometimes there came a sensation as if a hand was drawn softly along my cheek and neck. Sometimes it was as if warm lips kissed me, and longer and more lovingly as they reached my throat, but there the caress fixed itself. My heart beat: faster, my breathing rose and fell rapidly and full drawn; a sobbing, that rose into a sense of strangulation, and turned into a dreadful convulsion, in which my senses left me and I became unconscious.

It was now three weeks since the commencement of this unaccountable state. My sufferings had, during the last week, told upon my appearance. I had grown pale, my eyes were dilated and darkened underneath, and the languor which I had long felt began to display itself in my countenance.

My father asked me often whether I was ill; but, with an obstinacy which now seems to me unaccountable, I persisted in assuring him that I was quite well.

In a sense this was true. I had no pain, I could complain of no bodily derangement. My complaint seemed to be one of the imagination, or the nerves, and, horrible as my sufferings were, I kept them, with a morbid reserve, very nearly to myself.

It could not be that terrible complaint which the peasants called the oupire, for I had now been suffering for three weeks, and they were seldom ill for much more than three days, when death put an end to their miseries.

Carmilla complained of dreams and feverish sensations, but by no means of so alarming a kind as mine. I say that mine were extremely alarming. Had I been capable of comprehending my condition, I would have invoked aid and advice on my knees. The narcotic of an unsuspected influence was acting upon me, and my perceptions were benumbed.

I am going to tell you now of a dream that led immediately to an odd discovery.

One night, instead of the voice I was accustomed to hear in the dark, I heard one, sweet and tender, and at the same time terrible, which said, "Your mother warns you to beware of the assassin." At the same time a light unexpectedly sprang up, and I saw Carmilla, standing, near the foot of my bed, in her white nightdress, bathed, from her chin to her feet, in one great stain of blood.

I wakened with a shriek, possessed with the one idea that Carmilla was being murdered. I remember springing from my bed, and my next recollection is that of standing in the lobby, crying for help.

Madame and Mademoiselle came scurrying out of their rooms in alarm; a lamp burned always on the lobby, and seeing me, they soon learned the cause of my terror.

I insisted on our knocking at Carmilla's door. Our knocking was unanswered. It soon became a pounding and an uproar. We shrieked her name, but all was vain.

We all grew frightened, for the door was locked. We hurried back, in panic, to my room. There we rang the bell long and furiously. If my father's room had been at that side of the house, we would have called him up at once to our aid. But, alas! he was quite out of hearing, and to reach him involved an excursion for which we none of us had courage.

Servants, however, soon came running up the stairs; I had got on my dressing-gown and slippers meanwhile, and my companions were already similarly furnished. Recognizing the voices of the servants in the lobby, we sallied out together; and having renewed, as fruitlessly, our summons at Carmilla's door, I ordered the men to force the lock. They did so, and we stood, holding our lights aloft, in the doorway, and so stared into the room.

We called her by name; but there was still no reply. We looked round the room. Everything was undisturbed. It was exactly in the state in which I had left it on bidding her goodnight. But Carmilla was gone.

CHAPTER VIII: SEARCH

At sight of the room, perfectly undisturbed except for our violent entrance, we began to cool a little, and soon recovered our senses sufficiently to dismiss the men. It had struck Mademoiselle that possibly Carmilla had been wakened by the uproar at her door, and in her first panic had jumped from her bed, and hid herself in a press, or behind a curtain, from which she could not, of course, emerge until the majordomo and his myrmidons had withdrawn. We now recommenced our search, and began to call her by name again.

It was all to no purpose. Our perplexity and agitation increased. We examined the windows, but they were secured. I implored of Carmilla, if she had concealed herself, to play this cruel trick no longer--to come out, and to end our anxieties. It was all useless. I was by this time convinced that she was not in the room, nor in the dressing-room, the door of which was still locked on this side. She could not have passed it. I was utterly puzzled. Had Carmilla discovered one of those secret passages which the old house-keeper said were known to exist in the schloss, although the tradition of their exact situation had been lost. A little time would, no doubt, explain all—utterly perplexed as, for the present, we were.

It was past four o'clock, and I preferred passing the remaining hours of darkness in Madame's room. Daylight brought no solution of the difficulty.

The whole household, with my father at its head, was in a state of agitation next morning. Every part of the chateau was searched. The grounds were explored. Not a trace of the missing lady could be discovered. The stream was about to be dragged; my father was in distraction; what a tale to have to tell the poor girl's mother on her return. I, too, was almost beside myself, though my grief was quite of a different kind.

The morning was passed in alarm and excitement. It was now one o'clock, and still no tidings. I ran up to Carmilla's room, and found her standing at her dressing-table. I was astounded. I could not believe my eyes. She beckoned me to her with her pretty finger, in silence. Her face expressed extreme fear.

I ran to her in an ecstasy of joy; I kissed and embraced her again and again. I ran to the bell and rang it vehemently, to bring others to the spot, who might at once relieve my father's anxiety.

"Dear Carmilla, what has become of you all this time? We have been in agonies of anxiety about you," I exclaimed. "Where have you been? How did you come back?"

"Last night has been a night of wonders," she said.

"For mercy's sake, explain all you can."

"It was past two last night," she said, "when I went to sleep as usual in my bed, with my doors locked, that of the dressing room, and that opening upon the gallery. My sleep was uninterrupted, and, so far as I know, dreamless; but I awoke just now on the sofa in the dressing-room there, and I found the door between the rooms open, and the other door forced. How could all this have happened without my being wakened? It must have been accompanied with a great deal of noise, and I am particularly easily wakened; and how could I have been carried out of my bed without my sleep having been interrupted, I whom the slightest stir startles?"

By this time, Madame, Mademoiselle, my father, and a number of the servants were in the room. Carmilla was, of course, overwhelmed with inquiries, congratulations, and welcomes. She had but one story to tell, and seemed the least able of all the party to suggest any way of accounting for what had happened.

My father took a turn up and down the room, thinking. I saw Carmilla's eye follow him for a moment with a sly, dark glance.

When my father had sent the servants away, Mademoiselle having gone in search of a little bottle of valerian and sal volatile, and there being no one now in the room with Carmilla, except my father, Madame, and myself, he came to her thoughtfully, took her hand very kindly, led her to the sofa, and sat down beside her.

"Will you forgive me, my dear, if I risk a conjecture, and ask a question?"

"Who can have a better right?" she said. "Ask what you please, and I will tell you everything. But my story is simply one of bewilderment and darkness. I know absolutely nothing. Put any question you please. But you know, of course, the limitations mamma has placed me under."

"Perfectly, my dear child. I need not approach the topics on which she desires our silence. Now, the marvel of last night consists in your having been removed from your bed and your room, without being wakened, and this removal having occurred apparently while the windows were still secured, and the two doors locked upon the inside. I will tell you my theory, and first ask you a question."

Carmilla was leaning on her hand dejectedly; Madame and I were listening breathlessly.

"Now, my question is this. Have you ever been walking in your sleep?"

"Never, since I was very young indeed."

"But you did walk in your sleep when you were young?"

"Yes; I know I did. I have been told so often by my nurse." My father smiled and nodded.

"Well, what has happened is this. You got up in your sleep, unlocked the door, not leaving the key, as usual, in the lock, but taking it out and locking it on the outside; you again took the key out, and carried it away with you to some one of the five-and-twenty rooms on this floor, or perhaps up-stairs or down-stairs. There are so many rooms and closets, so much heavy furniture, and such accumulations of lumber, that it would require a week to search this old house thoroughly. Do you see, now, what I mean?"

"I do, but not all," she answered.

"And how, papa, do you account for her finding herself on the sofa in the dressing-room, which we had searched so carefully?"

"She came there after you had searched it, still in her sleep, and at last awoke spontaneously, and was as much surprised to find herself where she was as anyone else. I wish all mysteries were as easily and innocently explained as yours, Carmilla," he said, laughing. "And so we may congratulate ourselves on the certainty that the most natural explanation of the occurrence is one that involves no drugging, no tampering with locks, no burglars, or poisoners, or witches—nothing that need alarm Carmilla, or anyone else, for our safety."

Carmilla was looking charmingly. Nothing could be more beautiful than her tints. Her beauty was, I think, enhanced by that graceful languor that was peculiar to her. I think my father was silently contrasting her looks with mine, for he said:

"I wish my poor Laura was looking more like herself," and he sighed.

So our alarms were happily ended, and Carmilla restored to her friends.

CHAPTER IX: THE DOCTOR

As Carmilla would not hear of an attendant sleeping in her room, my father arranged that a servant should sleep outside her door, so that she could not attempt to make another such excursion without being arrested at her own door.

That night passed quietly; and next morning early, the doctor, whom my father had sent for without telling me a word about it, arrived to see me. Madame accompanied me to the library; and there the grave little doctor, with white hair and spectacles, whom I mentioned before, was waiting to receive me.

I told him my story, and as I proceeded he grew graver and graver.

We were standing, he and I, in the recess of one of the windows, facing one another. When my statement was over, he leaned with his shoulders against the wall, and with his eyes fixed on me earnestly, with an interest in which was a dash of horror.

After a minute's reflection, he asked Madame if he could see my father.

He was sent for accordingly, and as he entered, smiling, he said:

"I dare say, doctor, you are going to tell me that I am an old fool for having brought you here; I hope I am."

But his smile faded into shadow as the doctor, with a very grave face, beckoned him to him.

He and the doctor talked for some time in the same recess where I had just conferred with the physician. It seemed an earnest and argumentative conversation. The room is very large, and I and Madame stood together, burning with curiosity, at the further end. Not a word could we hear, however, for they spoke in a very low tone, and the deep recess of the window quite concealed the doctor from view, and very nearly my father, whose foot, arm, and shoulder only could we see; and the voices were, I suppose, all the less audible for the sort of closet which the thick wall and window formed.

After a time my father's face looked into the room; it was pale, thoughtful, and, I fancied, agitated.

"Laura, dear, come here for a moment. Madame, we shan't trouble you, the doctor says, at present."

Accordingly I approached, for the first time a little alarmed; for, although I felt very weak, I did not feel ill; and strength, one always fancies, is a thing that may be picked up when we please.

My father held out his hand to me, as I drew near, but he was looking at the doctor, and he said: "It certainly is very odd; I don't understand it quite. Laura, come here, dear; now attend to Doctor Spielsberg, and recollect yourself."

"You mentioned a sensation like that of two needles piercing the skin, somewhere about your neck, on the night when you experienced your first horrible dream. Is there still any soreness?"

"None at all," I answered.

"Can you indicate with your finger about the point at which you think this occurred?"

"Very little below my throat—here," I answered. I wore a morning dress, which covered the place I pointed to.

"Now you can satisfy yourself," said the doctor. "You won't mind your papa's lowering your dress a very little. It is necessary, to detect a symptom of the complaint under which you have been suffering."

I acquiesced. It was only an inch or two below the edge of my collar.

"God bless me!—so it is," exclaimed my father, growing pale.

"You see it now with your own eyes," said the doctor, with a gloomy triumph.

"What is it?" I exclaimed, beginning to be frightened. "Nothing, my dear young lady, but a small blue spot, about the size of the tip of your little finger; and now," he continued, turning to papa, "the question is, what is best to be done?"

"Is there any danger?" I urged, in great trepidation.

"I trust not, my dear," answered the doctor. "I don't see why you should not recover. I don't see why you should not begin immediately to get better. That is the point at which the sense of strangulation begins?"

"Yes," I answered.

"And—recollect as well as you can—the same point was a kind of center of that thrill which you described just now, like the current of a cold stream running against you?"

"It may have been; I think it was."

"Ay, you see?" he added, turning to my father. "Shall I say a word to Madame?"

"Certainly," said my father.

He called Madame to him, and said:

"I find my young friend here far from well. It won't be of any great consequence, I hope; but it will be necessary that some steps be taken, which I will explain by-and-by; but in the meantime, Madame, you will be so good as not to let Miss Laura be alone for one moment. That is the only direction I need give for the present. It is indispensable."

"We may rely upon your kindness, Madame, I know," added my father. Madame satisfied him eagerly.

"And you, dear Laura, I know you will observe the doctor's direction. I shall have to ask your opinion upon another patient, whose symptoms slightly resemble those of my daughter, that have just been detailed to you--very much milder in degree, but I believe quite of the same sort. She is a young lady—our guest; but as you say you will be passing this way again this evening, you can't do better than take your supper here, and you can then see her. She does not come down till the afternoon."

"I thank you," said the doctor. "I shall be with you, then, at about seven this evening."

And then they repeated their directions to me and to Madame, and with this parting charge my father left us, and walked out with the doctor; and I saw them pacing together up and down between the road and the moat, on the grassy platform in front of the castle, evidently absorbed in earnest conversation.

The doctor did not return. I saw him mount his horse there, take his leave, and ride away eastward through the forest.

Nearly at the same time I saw the man arrive from Dranfeld with the letters, and dismount and hand the bag to my father.

In the meantime, Madame and I were both busy, lost in conjecture as to the reasons of the singular and earnest direction which the doctor and my father had concurred in imposing. Madame, as she afterwards told me, was afraid the doctor apprehended a sudden seizure, and that, without prompt assistance, I might either lose my life in a fit, or at least be seriously hurt.

This interpretation did not strike me; and I fancied, perhaps luckily for my nerves, that the arrangement was prescribed simply to secure a companion, who would prevent my taking too much exercise, or eating unripe fruit, or doing any of the fifty foolish things to which young people are supposed to be prone.

About half-an-hour after my father came in—he had a letter in his hand—and said:

"This letter has been delayed; it is from General Spielsdorf. He might have been here yesterday, he may not come till tomorrow, or he may be here today."

He put the open letter into my hand; but he did not look pleased, as he used when a guest, especially one so much loved as the General, was coming. On the contrary, he looked as if he wished him at the bottom of the Red Sea. There was plainly something on his mind which he did not choose to divulge.

"Papa, darling, will you tell me this?" said I, suddenly laying my hand on his arm, and looking, I am sure, imploringly in his face.

"Perhaps," he answered, smoothing my hair caressingly over my eyes. "Does the doctor think me very ill?"

"No, dear; he thinks, if right steps are taken, you will be quite well again, at least, on the high road to a complete recovery, in a day or two," he answered, a little drily. "I wish our good friend, the General, had chosen any other time; that is, I wish you had been perfectly well to receive him."

"But do tell me, papa," I insisted, "what does he think is the matter with me?"

"Nothing; you must not plague me with questions," he answered, with more irritation than I ever remember him to have displayed before; and seeing that I looked wounded, I suppose, he kissed me, and added, "You shall know all about it in a day or two; that is, all that I know. In the meantime you are not to trouble your head about it."

He turned and left the room, but came back before I had done wondering and puzzling over the oddity of all this; it was merely to say that he was going to Karnstein, and had ordered the carriage to be ready at twelve, and that I and Madame should accompany him; he was going to see the priest who lived near those picturesque grounds, upon business, and as Carmilla had never seen them, she could follow, when she came down, with Mademoiselle, who would bring materials for what you call a picnic, which might be laid for us in the ruined castle.

At twelve o'clock, accordingly, I was ready, and not long after, my father, Madame and I set out upon our projected drive.

Passing the drawbridge we turned to the right, and followed the road over the steep Gothic bridge, westward, to reach the deserted village and ruined castle of Karnstein.

No sylvan drive can be fancied prettier. The ground breaks into gentle hills and hollows, all clothed with beautiful woods, totally destitute of the comparative formality which artificial planting and early culture and pruning impart.

The irregularities of the ground often lead the road out of its course, and cause it to wind beautifully round the sides of broken hollows and the steeper sides of the hills, among varieties of ground almost inexhaustible.

Turning one of these points, we suddenly encountered our old friend, the General, riding towards us, attended by a mounted servant. His portmanteaus were following in a hired wagon, such as we term a cart.

The General dismounted as we pulled up, and, after the usual greetings, was easily persuaded to accept the vacant seat in the carriage, and send his horse on with his servant to the schloss.

CHAPTER X: BEREAVED

It was about ten months since we had last seen him; but that time had sufficed to make an alteration of years in his appearance. He had grown thinner; something of gloom and anxiety had taken the place of that cordial serenity which used to characterize his features. His dark blue eyes, always penetrating, now gleamed with a sterner light from under his shaggy grey eyebrows. It was not such a change as grief alone usually induces, and angrier passions seemed to have had their share in bringing it about.

We had not long resumed our drive, when the General began to talk, with his usual soldierly directness, of the bereavement, as he termed it, which he had sustained in the death of his beloved niece and ward; and he then broke out in a tone of intense bitterness and fury, inveighing against the "hellish arts" to which she had fallen a victim, and expressing, with more exasperation than piety, his wonder that Heaven should tolerate so monstrous an indulgence of the lusts and malignity of hell.

My father, who saw at once that something very extraordinary had befallen, asked him, if not too painful to him, to detail the circumstances which he thought justified the strong terms in which he expressed himself.

"I should tell you all with pleasure," said the General, "but you would not believe me."

"Why should I not?" he asked.

"Because," he answered testily, "you believe in nothing but what consists with your own prejudices and illusions. I remember when I was like you, but I have learned better."

"Try me," said my father; "I am not such a dogmatist as you suppose. Besides which, I very well know that you generally require proof for what you believe, and am, therefore, very strongly pre-disposed to respect your conclusions."

"You are right in supposing that I have not been led lightly into a belief in the marvelous—for what I have experienced is marvellous—and I have been forced by extraordinary evidence to credit that which ran counter, diametrically, to all my theories. I have been made the dupe of a preternatural conspiracy."

Notwithstanding his professions of confidence in the General's penetration, I saw my father, at this point, glance at the General, with, as I thought, a marked suspicion of his sanity.

The General did not see it, luckily. He was looking gloomily and curiously into the glades and vistas of the woods that were opening before us.

"You are going to the ruins of Karnstein?" he said. "Yes, it is a lucky coincidence; do you know I was going to ask you to bring me there to inspect them. I have a special object in exploring. There is a ruined chapel, ain't there, with a great many tombs of that extinct family?"

"So there are—highly interesting," said my father. "I hope you are thinking of claiming the title and estates?"

My father said this gaily, but the General did not recollect the laugh, or even the smile, which courtesy exacts for a friend's joke; on the contrary, he looked grave and even fierce, ruminating on a matter that stirred his anger and horror.

"Something very different," he said, gruffly. "I mean to unearth some of those fine people. I hope, by God's blessing, to accomplish a pious sacrilege here, which will relieve our earth of certain monsters, and enable honest people to sleep in their beds without being assailed by murderers. I have strange things to tell you, my dear friend, such as I myself would have scouted as incredible a few months since."

My father looked at him again, but this time not with a glance of suspicion—with an eye, rather, of keen intelligence and alarm.

"The house of Karnstein," he said, "has been long extinct a hundred years at least. My dear wife was maternally descended from the Karnsteins. But the name and title have long ceased to exist. The castle is a ruin; the very village is deserted; it is fifty years since the smoke of a chimney was seen there; not a roof left."

"Quite true. I have heard a great deal about that since I last saw you; a great deal that will astonish you. But I had better relate everything in the order in which it occurred," said the General. "You saw my dear ward—my child, I may call her. No creature could have been more beautiful, and only three months ago none more blooming."

"Yes, poor thing! when I saw her last she certainly was quite lovely," said my father. "I was grieved and shocked more than I can tell you, my dear friend; I knew what a blow it was to you."

He took the General's hand, and they exchanged a kind pressure. Tears gathered in the old soldier's eyes. He did not seek to conceal them. He said:

"We have been very old friends; I knew you would feel for me, childless as I am. She had become an object of very near interest to me, and repaid my care by an affection that cheered my home and made my life happy. That is all gone. The years that remain to me on earth may not be very long; but by God's mercy I hope to accomplish a service to mankind before I die, and to subserve the vengeance of Heaven upon the fiends who have murdered my poor child in the spring of her hopes and beauty!"

"You said, just now, that you intended relating everything as it occurred," said my father. "Pray do; I assure you that it is not mere curiosity that prompts me."

By this time we had reached the point at which the Drunstall road, by which the General had come, diverges from the road which we were travelling to Karnstein.

"How far is it to the ruins?" inquired the General, looking anxiously forward.

"About half a league," answered my father. "Pray let us hear the story you were so good as to promise."

CHAPTER XI: THE STORY

"With all my heart," said the General, with an effort; and after a short pause in which to arrange his subject, he commenced one of the strangest narratives I ever heard.

"My dear child was looking forward with great pleasure to the visit you had been so good as to arrange for her to your charming daughter." Here he made me a gallant but melancholy bow. "In the meantime we had an invitation to my old friend the Count Carlsfeld, whose schloss is about six leagues to the other side of Karnstein. It was to attend the series of fetes which, you remember, were given by him in honour of his illustrious visitor, the Grand Duke Charles."

"Yes; and very splendid, I believe, they were," said my father.

"Princely! But then his hospitalities are quite regal. He has Aladdin's lamp. The night from which my sorrow dates was devoted to a magnificent masquerade. The grounds were thrown open, the trees hung with coloured lamps. There was such a display of fireworks as Paris itself had never witnessed. And such music—music, you know, is my weakness—such ravishing music! The finest instrumental band, perhaps, in the world, and the finest singers who could be collected from all the great operas in Europe. As you wandered through these fantastically illuminated grounds, the moon-lighted chateau throwing a rosy light from its long rows of windows, you would suddenly hear these ravishing voices stealing from the silence of some grove, or rising from boats upon the lake. I felt myself, as I looked and listened, carried back into the romance and poetry of my early youth.

"When the fireworks were ended, and the ball beginning, we returned to the noble suite of rooms that were thrown open to the dancers. A masked ball, you know, is a beautiful sight; but so brilliant a spectacle of the kind I never saw before.

"It was a very aristocratic assembly. I was myself almost the only 'nobody' present.

"My dear child was looking quite beautiful. She wore no mask. Her excitement and delight added an unspeakable charm to her features, always lovely. I remarked a young lady, dressed magnificently, but wearing a mask, who appeared to me to be observing my ward with extraordinary interest. I had seen her, earlier in the evening, in the great hall, and again, for a few minutes, walking near us, on the terrace under the castle windows, similarly employed. A lady, also masked, richly and gravely dressed, and with a stately air, like a person of rank, accompanied her as a chaperone. Had the young lady not worn a mask, I could, of course, have been much more certain upon the question whether she was really watching my poor darling. I am now well assured that she was.

"We were now in one of the salons. My poor dear child had been dancing, and was resting a little in one of the chairs near the door; I was standing near. The two ladies I have mentioned had approached, and the younger took the chair next to my ward; while her companion stood beside me, and for a little time addressed herself, in a low tone, to her charge.

"Availing herself of the privilege of her mask, she turned to me, and in the tone of an old friend, and calling me by my name, opened a conversation with me, which piqued my curiosity a good deal. She referred to many scenes where she had met me—at Court, and at distinguished houses. She alluded to little incidents which I had long ceased to think of, but which, I found, had only lain in abeyance in my memory, for they instantly started into life at her touch.

"I became more and more curious to ascertain who she was, every moment. She parried my attempts to discover very adroitly and pleasantly. The knowledge she showed of many passages in my life seemed to me all but unaccountable; and she appeared to take a not unnatural pleasure in foiling my curiosity, and in seeing me flounder, in my eager perplexity, from one conjecture to another.

"In the meantime the young lady, whom her mother called by the odd name of Millarca, when she once or twice addressed her, had, with the same ease and grace, got into conversation with my ward.

She introduced herself by saying that her mother was a very old acquaintance of mine. She spoke of the agreeable audacity which a mask rendered practicable; she talked like a friend; she admired her dress, and insinuated very prettily her admiration of her beauty. She amused her with laughing criticisms upon the people who crowded the ballroom, and laughed at my poor child's fun. She was very witty and lively when she pleased, and after a time they had grown very good friends, and the young stranger lowered her mask, displaying a remarkably beautiful face. I had never seen it before, neither had my dear child. But though it was new to us, the features were so engaging, as well as lovely, that it was impossible not to feel the attraction powerfully. My poor girl did so. I never saw anyone more taken with another at first sight, unless, indeed, it was the stranger herself, who seemed quite to have lost her heart to her.

"In the meantime, availing myself of the license of a masquerade, I put not a few questions to the eider lady.

" 'You have puzzled me utterly,' I said, laughing. 'Is that not enough? Won't you, now, consent to stand on equal term, and do me the kindness to remove your mask?'

" 'Can any request be more unreasonable?' she replied. 'Ask a lady to yield an advantage! Beside, how do you know you should recognize me? Years make changes.'

" 'As you see,' I said, with a bow, and, I suppose, melancholy little laugh.

" 'As philosophers tell us,' she said; 'and how do you know that a sight of my face would help you?'

" 'I should take chance for that,' I answered. 'It is trying to make yourself out an old woman; your figure betrays you.'

" 'Years, nevertheless, have passed since I saw you, since you saw me, for that is what I am considering. Millarca, there, is my daughter; I cannot then be young, even in opinion of people whom time has taught to be indulgent, I may not like to be compared with what you remember. You have no mask to remove. You can offer me nothing in exchange.'

" 'My petition is to your pity, to remove it.'

" 'And mine to yours, to let it stay where it is,' she replied.

" 'Well, then, at least you will tell me whether you are French or German; you speak both languages so perfectly.'

" 'I don't think I shall tell you that, General; you intend a surprise, and are meditating the particular point of attack.'

" 'At all events, you won't deny this,' I said, 'that being honoured by your permission to converse, I ought to know how to address you. Shall I say Madame la Comtesse?'

"She laughed, and she would, no doubt, have met me with another evasion—if, indeed, I can treat any occurrence in an interview every circumstance of which was pre-arranged, as I now believe, with the profoundest cunning, as liable to be modified by accident.

" 'As to that,' she began; but she was interrupted, almost as she opened her lips, by a gentleman, dressed in black, who looked particularly elegant and distinguished, with this drawback, that his face as the most deadly pale I ever saw, except in death. He was in no masquerade—in the plain evening dress of a gentleman; and he said, without a smile, but with a courtly and unusually low bow:

" 'Will Madame la Comtesse permit me to say a very few words which may interest her?'

"The lady turned quickly to him, and touched her lip in token of silence; she then said to me, 'Keep my place for me, General; I shall return when I have said a few words.'

"And with this injunction, playfully given, she walked a little aside with the gentleman in black, and talked for some minutes, apparently very earnestly. They then walked away slowly together in the crowd, and I lost them for some minutes.

"I spent the interval in cudgelling my brains for a conjecture as to the identity of the lady who seemed to remember me so kindly, and I was thinking of turning about and joining in the conversation between my pretty ward and the Countess's daughter, and trying whether, by the time she returned, I might not have a surprise in store for her, by having her name, title, chateau, and estates at my fingers' ends. But at this moment she returned, accompanied by the pale man in black, who said:

" 'I shall return and inform Madame la Comtesse when her carriage is at the door.' He withdrew with a bow."

CHAPTER XII:
A PETITION

" 'Then we are to lose Madame la Comtesse, but I hope only for a few hours,' I said, with a low bow.

" 'It may be that only, or it may be a few weeks. It was very unlucky his speaking to me just now as he did. Do you now know me?'

"I assured her I did not.

" 'You shall know me,' she said, 'but not at present. We are older and better friends than, perhaps, you suspect. I cannot yet declare myself. I shall in three weeks pass your beautiful schloss, about which I have been making enquiries. I shall then look in upon you for an hour or two, and renew a friendship which I never think of without a thousand pleasant recollections. This moment a piece of news has reached me like a thunderbolt. I must set out now, and travel by a devious route, nearly a hundred miles, with all the dispatch I can possibly make. My perplexities multiply. I am only deterred by the compulsory reserve I practice as to my name from making a very singular request of you. My poor child has not quite recovered her strength. Her horse fell with her, at a hunt which she had ridden out to witness, her nerves have not yet recovered the shock, and our physician says that she must no account exert herself for some time to come. We came here, in consequence, by very easy stages—hardly six leagues a day. I must now travel day and night, on a mission of life and death—a mission the critical and momentous nature of which I shall be able to explain to you when we meet, as I hope we shall, in a few weeks, without the necessity of any concealment.'

"She went on to make her petition, and it was in the tone of a person from whom such a request amounted to conferring, rather than seeking a favour. This was only in manner, and, as it seemed, quite unconsciously. Than the terms in which it was expressed, nothing could be more deprecatory. It was simply that I would consent to take charge of her daughter during her absence.

"This was, all things considered, a strange, not to say, an audacious request. She in some sort disarmed me, by stating and admitting everything that could be urged against it, and throwing herself entirely upon my chivalry. At the same moment, by a fatality that seems to have predetermined all that happened, my poor child came to my side, and, in an undertone, besought me to invite her new friend, Millarca, to pay us a visit. She had just been sounding her, and thought, if her mamma would allow her, she would like it extremely.

"At another time I should have told her to wait a little, until, at least, we knew who they were. But I had not a moment to think in. The two ladies assailed me together, and I must confess the refined and beautiful face of the young lady, about which there was something extremely engaging, as well as the elegance and fire of high birth, determined me; and, quite overpowered, I submitted, and undertook, too easily, the care of the young lady, whom her mother called Millarca.

"The Countess beckoned to her daughter, who listened with grave attention while she told her, in general terms, how suddenly and peremptorily she had been summoned, and also of the arrangement she had made for her under my care, adding that I was one of her earliest and most valued friends.

"I made, of course, such speeches as the case seemed to call for, and found myself, on reflection, in a position which I did not half like.

"The gentleman in black returned, and very ceremoniously conducted the lady from the room.

"The demeanour of this gentleman was such as to impress me with the conviction that the Countess was a lady of very much more importance than her modest title alone might have led me to assume.

"Her last charge to me was that no attempt was to be made to learn more about her than I might have already guessed, until her return. Our distinguished host, whose guest she was, knew her reasons.

" 'But here,' she said, 'neither I nor my daughter could safely remain for more than a day. I removed my mask imprudently for a moment, about an hour ago, and, too late, I fancied you saw me. So I resolved to seek an opportunity of talking a little to you. Had I found that you had seen me, I should have thrown myself on your high sense of honour to keep my secret for some weeks. As it is, I am satisfied that you did not see me; but if you now suspect, or, on reflection, should suspect, who I am, I commit myself, in like manner, entirely to your honour. My daughter will observe the same secrecy, and I well know that you will, from time to time, remind her, lest she should thoughtlessly disclose it.'

"She whispered a few words to her daughter, kissed her hurriedly twice, and went away, accompanied by the pale gentleman in black, and disappeared in the crowd.

" 'In the next room,' said Millarca, 'there is a window that looks upon the hall door. I should like to see the last of mamma, and to kiss my hand to her.'

"We assented, of course, and accompanied her to the window. We looked out, and saw a handsome old-fashioned carriage, with a troop of couriers and footmen. We saw the slim figure of the pale gentleman in black, as he held a thick velvet cloak, and placed it about her shoulders and threw the hood over her head. She nodded to him, and just touched his hand with hers. He bowed low repeatedly as the door closed, and the carriage began to move.

" 'She is gone,' said Millarca, with a sigh.

“ ‘She is gone,’ I repeated to myself, for the first time—in the hurried moments that had elapsed since my consent—reflecting upon the folly of my act.

“ ‘She did not look up,’ said the young lady, plaintively.

“ ‘The Countess had taken off her mask, perhaps, and did not care to show her face,’ I said; ‘And she could not know that you were in the window.’

“She sighed, and looked in my face. She was so beautiful that I relented. I was sorry I had for a moment repented of my hospitality, and I determined to make her amends for the unavowed churlishness of my reception.

“The young lady, replacing her mask, joined my ward in persuading me to return to the grounds, where the concert was soon to be renewed. We did so, and walked up and down the terrace that lies under the castle windows. Millarca became very intimate with us, and amused us with lively descriptions and stories of most of the great people whom we saw upon the terrace. I liked her more and more every minute. Her gossip, without being ill-natured, was extremely diverting to me, who had been so long out of the great world. I thought what life she would give to our sometimes lonely evenings at home.

“This ball was not over until the morning sun had almost reached the horizon. It pleased the Grand Duke to dance till then, so loyal people could not go away, or think of bed.

“We had just got through a crowded salon, when my ward asked me what had become of Millarca. I thought she had been by her side, and she fancied she was by mine. The fact was, we had lost her.

“All my efforts to find her were vain. I feared that she had mistaken, in the confusion of a momentary separation from us, other people for her new friends, and had, possibly, pursued and lost them in the extensive grounds which were thrown open to us.

“Now, in its full force, I recognized a new folly in my having undertaken the charge of a young lady without so much as knowing her name; and lettered as I was by promises, of the reasons for imposing which I knew nothing, I could not even point my inquiries by saying that the missing young lady was the daughter of the Countess who had taken her departure a few hours before.

"Morning broke. It was clear daylight before I gave up my search. It was not till near two o'clock next day that we heard anything of my missing charge. At about that time a servant knocked at my niece's door, to say that he had been earnestly requested by a young lady, who appeared to be in great distress, to make out where she could find the General Baron Spielsdorf and the young lady his daughter, in whose charge she had been left by her mother.

"There could be no doubt, notwithstanding the slight inaccuracy, that our young friend had turned up; and so she had. Would to heaven we had lost her!

"She told my poor child a story to account for her having failed to recover us for so long. Very late, she said, she had got to the housekeeper's bedroom in despair of finding us, and had then fallen into a deep sleep which, long as it was, had hardly sufficed to recruit her strength after the fatigues of the ball.

"That day Millarca came home with us. I was only too happy, after all, to have secured so charming a companion for my dear girl."

CHAPTER XIII:
THE WOOD-MAN

"There soon, however, appeared some drawbacks. In the first place, Millarca complained of extreme languor—the weakness that remained after her late illness—and she never emerged from her room till the afternoon was pretty far advanced. In the next place, it was accidentally discovered, although she always locked her door on the inside, and never disturbed the key from its place till she admitted the maid to assist at her toilet, that she was undoubtedly sometimes absent from her room in the very early morning, and at various times later in the day, before she wished it to be understood that she was stirring. She was repeatedly seen from the windows of the schloss, in the first faint grey of the morning, walking through the trees, in an easterly direction, and looking like a person in a trance. This convinced me that she walked in her sleep. But this hypothesis did not solve the puzzle. How did she pass out from her room, leaving the door locked on the inside? How did she escape from the house without unbarring door or window? In the midst of my perplexities, an anxiety of a far more urgent kind presented itself.

"My dear child began to lose her looks and health, and that in a manner so mysterious, and even horrible, that I became thoroughly frightened.

"She was at first visited by appalling dreams; then, as she fancied, by a spectre, sometimes resembling Millarca, sometimes in the shape of a beast, indistinctly seen, walking round the foot of her bed, from side to side. Lastly came sensations. One, not unpleasant, but very peculiar, she said, resembled the flow of an icy stream against her breast. At a later time, she felt something like a pair of large needles pierce her, a little below the throat, with a very sharp pain. A few nights after, followed a gradual and convulsive sense of strangulation; then came unconsciousness."

I could hear distinctly every word the kind old General was saying, because by this time we were driving upon the short grass that spreads on either side of the road as you approach the roofless village which had not shown the smoke of a chimney for more than half a century.

You may guess how strangely I felt as I heard my own symptoms so exactly described in those which had been experienced by the poor girl who, but for the catastrophe which followed, would have been at that moment a visitor at my father's chateau. You may suppose, also, how I felt as I heard him detail habits and mysterious peculiarities which were, in fact, those of our beautiful guest, Carmilla!

A vista opened in the forest; we were on a sudden under the chimneys and gables of the ruined village, and the towers and battlements of the dismantled castle, round which gigantic trees are grouped, overhung us from a slight eminence.

In a frightened dream I got down from the carriage, and in silence, for we had each abundant matter for thinking; we soon mounted the ascent, and were among the spacious chambers, winding stairs, and dark corridors of the castle.

"And this was once the palatial residence of the Karnsteins," said the old General at length, as from a great window he looked out across the village, and saw the wide, undulating expanse of forest. "It was a bad family, and here its bloodstained annals were written," he continued. "It is hard that they should, after death, continue to plague the human race with their atrocious lusts. That is the chapel of the Karnsteins, down there."

He pointed down to the grey walls of the Gothic building, partly visible through the foliage, a little way down the steep. "And I hear the axe of a woodman," he added, "busy among the trees that surround it; he possibly may give us the information of which I am in search, and point out the grave of Mircalla, Countess of Karnstein. These rustics preserve the local traditions of great families, whose stories die out among the rich and titled so soon as the families themselves become extinct."

"We have a portrait, at home, of Mircalla, the Countess Karnstein; should you like to see it?" asked my father.

"Time enough, dear friend," replied the General. "I believe that I have seen the original; and one motive which has led me to you earlier than I at first intended, was to explore the chapel which we are now approaching."

"What! see the Countess Mircalla," exclaimed my father; "Why, she has been dead more than a century!"

"Not so dead as you fancy, I am told," answered the General.

"I confess, General, you puzzle me utterly," replied my father, looking at him, I fancied, for a moment with a return of the suspicion I detected before. But although there was anger and detestation, at times, in the old General's manner, there was nothing flighty.

"There remains to me," he said, as we passed under the heavy arch of the Gothic church—for its dimensions would have justified its being so styled—"but one object which can interest me during the few years that remain to me on earth, and that is to wreak on her the vengeance which, I thank God, may still be accomplished by a mortal arm."

"What vengeance can you mean?" asked my father, in increasing amazement.

"I mean, to decapitate the monster," he answered, with a fierce flush, and a stamp that echoed mournfully through the hollow ruin, and his clenched hand was at the same moment raised, as if it grasped the handle of an axe, while he shook it ferociously in the air.

"What?" exclaimed my father, more than ever bewildered.

"To strike her head off."

"Cut her head off!"

"Aye, with a hatchet, with a spade, or with anything can cleave through her murderous throat. You shall hear," he answered, trembling with rage. And hurrying forward he said: "That beam will answer for a seat; your dear child is fatigued; let her be seated, and I will, in a few sentences, close my dreadful story."

The squared block of wood, which lay on the grass-grown pavement of the chapel, formed a bench on which I was very glad to seat myself, and in the meantime the General called to the woodman, who had been removing some boughs which leaned upon the old walls; and, axe in hand, the hardy old fellow stood before us.

He could not tell us anything of these monuments; but there was an old man, he said, a ranger of this forest, at present sojourning in the house of the priest, about two miles away, who could point out every monument of the old Karnstein family; and, for a trifle, he undertook to bring him back with him, if we would lend him one of our horses, in little more than half-an-hour.

"Have you been long employed about this forest?" asked my father of the old man.

"I have been a woodman here," he answered in his patois, "under the forester, all my days; so has my father before me, and so on, as many generations as I can count up. I could show you the very house in the village here, in which my ancestors lived."

"How came the village to be deserted?" asked the General.

"It was troubled by revenants, sir; several were tracked to their graves, there detected by the usual tests, and extinguished in the usual way, by decapitation, by the stake, and by burning; but not until many of the villagers were killed.

"But after all these proceedings according to law," he continued, "—so many graves opened, and so many vampires deprived of their horrible animation—the village was not relieved. But a Moravian nobleman, who happened to be travelling this way, heard how matters were, and being skilled—as many people are in his country—in such affairs, he offered to deliver the village from its tormentor. He did so thus: There being a bright moon that night, he ascended, shortly after sunset, the tower of the chapel here, from whence he could distinctly see the churchyard beneath him; you can see it from that window. From this point he watched until he saw the vampire come out of his grave, and placed near it the linen clothes in which he had been folded, and then glided away towards the village to plague its inhabitants.

"The stranger, having seen all this, came down from the steeple, took the linen wrappings of the vampire, and carried them up to the top of the tower, which he again mounted. When the vampire returned from his prowlings and missed his clothes, he cried furiously to the Moravian, whom he saw at the summit of the tower, and who, in reply, beckoned him to ascend and take them. Whereupon the vampire, accepting his invitation, began to climb the steeple, and so soon as he had reached the battlements, the Moravian, with a stroke of his sword, clove his skull in twain, hurling him down to the church-yard, whither, descending by the winding stairs, the stranger followed and cut his head off, and next day delivered it and the body to the villagers, who duly impaled and burnt them.

"This Moravian nobleman had authority from the then head of the family to remove the tomb of Mircalla, Countess Karnstein, which he did effectually, so that in a little while its site was quite forgotten."

"Can you point out where it stood?" asked the General, eagerly.

The forester shook his head and smiled.

"Not a soul living could tell you that now," he said; "besides, they say her body was removed; but no one is sure of that either."

Having thus spoken, as time pressed, he dropped his axe and departed, leaving us to hear the remainder of the General's strange story.

CHAPTER XIV: THE MEETING

"My beloved child," he resumed, "was now growing rapidly worse. The physician who attended her had failed to produce the slightest impression upon her disease, for such I then supposed it to be. He saw my alarm, and suggested a consultation. I called in an abler physician, from Gratz. Several days elapsed before he arrived. He was a good and pious, as well as a learned man. Having seen my poor ward together, they withdrew to my library to confer and discuss. I, from the adjoining room, where I awaited their summons, heard these two gentlemen's voices raised in something sharper than a strictly philosophical discussion. I knocked at the door and entered. I found the old physician from Gratz maintaining his theory. His rival was combating it with undisguised ridicule, accompanied with bursts of laughter. This unseemly manifestation subsided and the altercation ended on my entrance.

" 'Sir,' said my first physician, 'my learned brother seems to think that you want a conjuror, and not a doctor.'

" 'Pardon me,' said the old physician from Gratz, looking displeased, 'I shall state my own view of the case in my own way another time. I grieve, Monsieur le General, that by my skill and science I can be of no use. Before I go I shall do myself the honour to suggest something to you.'

"He seemed thoughtful, and sat down at a table and began to write. Profoundly disappointed, I made my bow, and as I turned to go, the other doctor pointed over his shoulder to his companion who was writing, and then, with a shrug, significantly touched his forehead.

"This consultation, then, left me precisely where I was. I walked out into the grounds, all but distracted. The doctor from Gratz, in ten or fifteen minutes, overtook me. He apologized for having followed me, but said that he could not conscientiously take his leave without a few words more. He told me that he could not be mistaken; no natural disease exhibited the same symptoms; and that death was already very near. There remained, however, a day, or possibly two, of life. If the fatal seizure were at once arrested, with great care and skill her strength might possibly return. But all hung now upon the confines of the irrevocable. One more assault might extinguish the last spark of vitality which is, every moment, ready to die.

"'And what is the nature of the seizure you speak of?' I entreated.

"'I have stated all fully in this note, which I place in your hands upon the distinct condition that you send for the nearest clergyman, and open my letter in his presence, and on no account read it till he is with you; you would despise it else, and it is a matter of life and death. Should the priest fail you, then, indeed, you may read it.'

"He asked me, before taking his leave finally, whether I would wish to see a man curiously learned upon the very subject, which, after I had read his letter, would probably interest me above all others, and he urged me earnestly to invite him to visit him there; and so took his leave.

"The ecclesiastic was absent, and I read the letter by myself. At another time, or in another case, it might have excited my ridicule. But into what quackeries will not people rush for a last chance, where all accustomed means have failed, and the life of a beloved object is at stake?

"Nothing, you will say, could be more absurd than the learned man's letter. It was monstrous enough to have consigned him to a madhouse. He said that the patient was suffering from the visits of a vampire! The punctures which she described as having occurred near the throat, were, he insisted, the insertion of those two long, thin, and sharp teeth which, it is well known, are peculiar to vampires; and there could be no doubt, he added, as to the well-defined presence of the small livid mark which all concurred in describing as that induced by the demon's lips, and every symptom described by the sufferer was in exact conformity with those recorded in every case of a similar visitation.

"Being myself wholly skeptical as to the existence of any such portent as the vampire, the supernatural of the good doctor furnished, in my opinion, but another learning and intelligence oddly associated with some one hallucination. I was so miserable, however, that, rather try nothing, I acted upon the instructions of the letter.

"I concealed myself in the dark dressing-room, that upon the poor patient's room, in which a candle was burning, and watched there till she was fast asleep. I stood at the door, peeping through the small crevice, my sword laid on the table beside me, as my directions prescribed, until, a little after one, I saw a large black object, very ill-defined, crawl, as it seemed to me, over the foot of the bed, and swiftly spread itself up to the poor girl's throat, where it swelled, in a moment, into a great, palpitating mass.

"For a few moments I had stood petrified. I now sprang forward, with my sword in my hand. The black creature suddenly contracted toward the foot of the bed, glided over it, and, standing on the floor about a yard below the foot of the bed, with a glare of skulking ferocity and horror fixed on me, I saw Millarca. Speculating I know not what, I struck at her instantly with my sword; but I saw her standing near the door, unscathed. Horrified, I pursued, and struck again. She was gone; and my sword flew to shivers against the door.

"I can't describe to you all that passed on that horrible night. The whole house was up and stirring. The spectre Millarca was gone. But her victim was sinking fast, and before the morning dawned, she died."

The old General was agitated. We did not speak to him. My father walked to some little distance, and began reading the inscriptions on the tombstones; and thus occupied, he strolled into the door of a side-chapel to prosecute his researches. The General leaned against the wall, dried his eyes, and sighed heavily. I was relieved on hearing the voices of Carmilla and Madame, who were at that moment approaching. The voices died away.

In this solitude, having just listened to so strange a story, connected, as it was, with the great and titled dead, whose monuments were mouldering among the dust and ivy round us, and every incident of which bore so awfully upon my own mysterious case—in this haunted spot, darkened by the towering foliage that rose on every side, dense and high above its noiseless walls—a horror began to steal over me, and my heart sank as I thought that my friends were, after all, not about to enter and disturb this *triste* and ominous scene.

The old General's eyes were fixed on the ground, as he leaned with his hand upon the basement of a shattered monument.

Under a narrow, arched doorway, surmounted by one of those demoniacal grotesques in which the cynical and ghastly fancy of old Gothic carving delights, I saw very gladly the beautiful face and figure of Carmilla enter the shadowy chapel.

I was just about to rise and speak, and nodded smiling, in answer to her peculiarly engaging smile; when with a cry, the old man by my side caught up the woodman's hatchet, and started forward. On seeing him a brutalized change came over her features. It was an instantaneous and horrible transformation, as she made a crouching step backwards. Before I could utter a scream, he struck at her with all his force, but she dived under his blow, and unscathed, caught him in her tiny grasp by the wrist. He struggled for a moment to release his arm, but his hand opened, the axe fell to the ground, and the girl was gone.

He staggered against the wall. His grey hair stood upon his head, and a moisture shone over his face, as if he were at the point of death.

The frightful scene had passed in a moment. The first thing I recollect after, is Madame standing before me, and impatiently repeating again and again, the question, "Where is Mademoiselle Carmilla?"

I answered at length, "I don't know—I can't tell—she went there," and I pointed to the door through which Madame had just entered, "only a minute or two since."

"But I have been standing there, in the passage, ever since Mademoiselle Carmilla entered; and she did not return."

She then began to call "Carmilla," through every door and passage and from the windows, but no answer came.

"She called herself Carmilla?" asked the General, agitated.

"Carmilla, yes," I answered.

"Aye," he said; "that is Millarca. That is the same who long ago was called Mircalla, Countess Karnstein. Depart from this accursed ground, my poor child, as quickly as you can. Drive to the clergyman's house, and stay there till we come. Begone! May you never behold Carmilla more; you will not find her here."

CHAPTER XV: ORDEAL AND EXECUTION

As he spoke one of the strangest-looking men I ever beheld, entered the chapel at the door through which Carmilla had made her entrance and her exit. He was tall, narrow-chested, stooping, with high shoulders, and dressed in black. His face was brown and dried in with deep furrows; he wore an oddly shaped hat with a broad leaf. His hair, long and grizzled, hung on his shoulders. He wore a pair of gold spectacles, and walked slowly, with an odd shambling gait, with his face sometimes turned up to the sky, and sometimes bowed down toward the ground, and seemed to wear a perpetual smile; his long thin arms were swinging, and his lank hands, in old black gloves ever so much too wide for them, waving and gesticulating in utter abstraction.

"The very man? exclaimed the General, advancing with manifest delight. "My dear Baron, how happy I am to see you, I had no hope of meeting you so soon." He signed to my father, who had by this time returned, leading the fantastic old gentleman, whom he called the

Baron, to meet him. He introduced him formally, and they at once entered into earnest conversation. The stranger took a roll of paper from his pocket, and spread it on the worn surface of a tomb that stood by. He had a pencil case in his fingers, with which he traced imaginary lines from point to point on the paper, which from their often glancing from it, together, at certain points of the building, I concluded to be a plan of the chapel. He accompanied, what I may term, his lecture, with occasional readings from a dirty little book, whose yellow leaves were closely written over.

They sauntered together down the side aisle, opposite to the spot where I was standing, conversing as they went; then they began measuring distances by paces, and finally they all stood together, facing a piece of the side-wall, which they began to examine with great minuteness; pulling off the ivy that clung over it, and rapping the plaster with the ends of their sticks, scraping here, and knocking there. At length they ascertained the existence of a broad marble tablet, with letters carved in relief upon it.

With the assistance of the woodman, who soon returned, a monumental inscription, and carved escutcheon were disclosed. They proved to be those of the long lost monument of Mircalla, Countess Karnstein.

The old General, though not I fear given to the praying mood, raised his hands and eyes to heaven, in mute thanksgiving for some moments.

"Tomorrow," I heard him say, "the commissioner will be here, and the inquisition will be held according to law."

Then turning to the old man with the gold spectacles, whom I have described, he shook him warmly by both hands and said:

"Baron, how can I thank you? How can we all thank you? You will have delivered this region from a plague that has scourged its inhabitants for more than a century. The horrible enemy, thank God, is at last tracked."

My father led the stranger aside, and the General followed. I knew that he had led them out of hearing, that he might relate my case, and I saw them glance often quickly at me, and the discussion proceeded.

My father came to me, kissed me again and again, and leading me from the chapel, said:

"It is time to return, but before we go home, we must add to our party the good priest, who lives but a little way from this; and persuade him to accompany us to the schloss."

In this quest we were successful: and I was glad, being unspeakably fatigued when we reached home. But my satisfaction was changed to dismay, on discovering that there were no tidings of Carmilla. Of the scene that had occurred in the ruined chapel, no explanation was offered to me, and it was clear that it was a secret which my father for the present determined to keep from me.

The sinister absence of Carmilla made the remembrance of the scene more horrible to me. The arrangements for that night were singular. Two servants, and Madame were to sit up in my room that night; and the ecclesiastic with my father kept watch in the adjoining dressing-room.

The priest had performed certain solemn rites that night, the purport of which I did not understand any more than I comprehended the reason of this extraordinary precaution taken for my safety during sleep.

I saw all clearly a few days later.

The disappearance of Carmilla was followed by the discontinuance of my nightly sufferings.

You have heard, no doubt, of the appalling superstition that prevails in Upper and Lower Styria, in Moravia, Silesia, in Turkish Servia, in Poland, even in Russia; the superstition, so we must call it, of the Vampire.

If human testimony, taken with every care and solemnity, judicially, before commissions innumerable, each consisting of many members, all chosen for integrity and intelligence, and constituting reports more voluminous perhaps than exist upon any one other class of cases, is worth anything, it is difficult to deny, or even to doubt the existence of such a phenomenon as the Vampire. For my part I have heard no theory by which to explain what I myself have witnessed and experienced, other than that supplied by the ancient and well-attested belief of the country.

The next day the formal proceedings took place in the Chapel of Karnstein. The grave of the Countess Mircalla was opened; and the General and my father recognized each his perfidious and beautiful guest, in the face now disclosed to view. The features, though a hundred and fifty years had passed since her funeral, were tinted with the warmth of life. Her eyes were open; no cadaverous smell exhaled from the coffin. The two medical men, one officially present, the other on the part of the promoter of the inquiry, attested the marvellous fact, that there was a faint but appreciable respiration, and a corresponding action of the heart. The limbs were perfectly flexible, the flesh elastic; and the leaden coffin floated with blood, in which to a depth of seven inches, the body lay immersed. Here then, were all the admitted signs and proofs of vampirism. The body, therefore, in accordance with the ancient practice, was raised, and a sharp stake driven through the heart of the vampire, who uttered a piercing shriek at the moment, in all respects such as might escape from a living person in the last agony. Then the head was struck off, and a torrent of blood flowed from the severed neck. The body and head were next placed on a pile of wood, and reduced to ashes, which were thrown upon the river and borne away, and that territory has never since been plagued by the visits of a vampire.

My father has a copy of the report of the Imperial Commission, with the signatures of all who were present at these proceedings, attached in verification of the statement. It is from this official paper that I have summarized my account of this last shocking scene.

CHAPTER XVI: CONCLUSION

I write all this you suppose with composure. But far from it; I cannot think of it without agitation. Nothing but your earnest desire so repeatedly expressed, could have induced me to sit down to a task that has unstrung my nerves for months to come, and reinduced a shadow of the unspeakable horror which years after my deliverance continued to make my days and nights dreadful, and solitude insupportably terrific.

Let me add a word or two about that quaint Vordenburg, to whose curious lore we were indebted for discovery of the Countess Mircalla's grave.

He had taken up his abode in Gratz, where, living upon mere pittance, which was all that remained to him of princely estates of his family, in Upper Styria, he himself to the minute and laborious investigation of the marvellously authenticated tradition of Vampirism. He had at his fingers' ends all the great and little works upon the *Magia Posthuma, Phlegon de Mirabilibus, Augustinus cura pro Mortuis, Philosophicae et Christianae Cogitationes de Vampiris* by John Christofer Harenberg; and a thousand others, among which I remember only a few of those which he lent to my father. He had a voluminous digest of all the judicial cases, from which he had extracted a system of principles that appear to govern—some always, and others occasionally only—the condition of the vampire. I may mention, in passing, that the deadly pallor attributed to that sort of revenants, is a mere melodramatic fiction. They present, in the grave, and when they show themselves in human society, the appearance of healthy life. When disclosed to light in their coffins, they exhibit all the symptoms that are enumerated as those which proved the vampire-life of the long-dead Countess Karnstein.

How they escape from their graves and return to them for certain hours every day, without displacing the clay or leaving any trace of disturbance in the state of the coffin or the cerements, has always been admitted to be utterly inexplicable. The amphibious existence of the vampire is sustained by daily renewed slumber in the grave. Its horrible lust for living blood supplies the vigour of its waking existence. The vampire is prone to be fascinated with an engrossing vehemence, resembling the passion of love, by particular persons. In pursuit of these it will exercise inexhaustible patience and stratagem, for access to a particular object may be obstructed in a hundred ways. It will never desist until it has satiated its passion, and drained the very life of its coveted victim. But it will, in these cases, husband and protract its murderous enjoyment with the refinement of an epicure, and heighten it by the gradual approaches of an artful courtship. In these cases it seems to yearn for something like sympathy and consent. In ordinary ones it goes direct to its object, overpowers with violence, and strangles and exhausts often at a single feast.

The vampire is, apparently, subject, in certain situations, to special conditions. In the particular instance of which I have given you a relation, Mircalla seemed to be limited to a name which, if not her real one, should at least reproduce, without the omission or addition of a single letter, those, as we say, anagrammatically, which compose it. Carmilla did this; so did Millarca.

My father related to the Baron Vordenburg, who remained with us for two or three weeks after the expulsion of Carmilla, the story about the Moravian nobleman and the vampire at Karnstein churchyard, and then he asked the Baron how he had discovered the exact position of the long-concealed tomb of the Countess Mircalla? The Baron's grotesque features puckered up into a mysterious smile; he looked down, still smiling, on his worn spectacle-case and fumbled with it. Then looking up, he said:

"I have many journals, and other papers, written by that remarkable man; the most curious among them is one treating of the visit of which you speak, to Karnstein. The tradition, of course, discolours and distorts a little. He might have been termed a Moravian nobleman, for he had changed his abode to that territory, and was, beside, a noble. But he was, in truth, a native of Upper Styria. It is enough to say that in very early youth he had been a passionate and favoured lover of the beautiful Mircalla, Countess Karnstein. Her early death plunged him into inconsolable grief. It is the nature of vampires to increase and multiply, but according to an ascertained and ghostly law.

"Assume, at starting, a territory perfectly free from that pest. How does it begin, and how does it multiply itself? I will tell you. A person, more or less wicked, puts an end to himself. A suicide, under certain circumstances, becomes a vampire. That spectre visits living people in their slumbers; they die, and almost invariably, in the grave, develop into vampires. This happened in the case of the beautiful Mircalla, who was haunted by one of those demons. My ancestor, Vordenburg, whose title I still bear, soon discovered this, and in the course of the studies to which he devoted himself, learned a great deal more.

"Among other things, he concluded that suspicion of vampirism would probably fall, sooner or later, upon the dead Countess, who in life had been his idol. He conceived a horror, be she what she might, of her remains being profaned by the outrage of a posthumous execution. He has left a curious paper to prove that the vampire, on its expulsion from its amphibious existence, is projected into a far more horrible life; and he resolved to save his once beloved Mircalla from this.

"He adopted the stratagem of a journey here, a pretended removal of her remains, and a real obliteration of her monument. When age had stolen upon him, and from the vale of years he looked back on the scenes he was leaving, he considered, in a different spirit, what he had done, and a horror took possession of him. He made the tracings and notes which have guided me to the very spot, and drew up a confession of the deception that he had practised. If he had intended any further action in this matter, death prevented him; and the hand of a remote descendant has, too late for many, directed the pursuit to the lair of the beast."

We talked a little more, and among other things he said was this:

"One sign of the vampire is the power of the hand. The slender hand of Mircalla closed like a vice of steel on the General's wrist when he raised the hatchet to strike. But its power is not confined to its grasp; it leaves a numbness in the limb it seizes, which is slowly, if ever, recovered from."

The following Spring my father took me on a tour through Italy. We remained away for more than a year. It was long before the terror of recent events subsided; and to this hour the image of Carmilla returns to memory with ambiguous alternations—sometimes the playful, languid, beautiful girl; sometimes the writhing fiend I saw in the ruined church; and often from a reverie I have started, fancying I heard the light step of Carmilla at the drawing-room door.

GLOSSARY

"…a hundred and fifty years had passed since her funeral": Carmilla's (or Mircalla's or Millarca's) portrait was painted from life in 1698; so the events of the story can take place no earlier than 1848. Laura writes her memoir ten years later, perhaps 1858, at the age of thirty. By 1871, when the first part of the story was serialized, the introduction states that Laura is dead.

Amphibious: Le Fanu doesn't mean that vampires can breathe underwater; he means that they survive in two environments, above and below ground.

"..a town lady like you": It seems, from this aside in Chapter IV, that Laura is writing her memoir to a female acquaintance.

Augustinus cura pro Mortuis, De cura pro mortuis gerenda, "On the Care of the Dead," was written by the 5th-century Saint, Augustine of Hippo. The text emphases the importance of proper burial procedures, and includes accounts of the dead visiting people in dreams.

Avernus: Hades/Hell.

Buffon: Georges Louis Lederc de Buffon (1707-88), French naturalist, cosmologist and mathematician. He devised a system for classifying animals and influenced 19th century biologists.

Cabalistic ciphers: Magical symbols.

"First ball": This may indicate that Carmilla appears to be under 18, too young to make her first official public appearance at a ball.

"Formal proceedings": Le Fanu goes back to the records of 18th century sources like the Arnold Paul case in Dom Calmet's *Dissertations on the Revenants and Vampires of Hungary, Bohemia, Moravia and Silesia*, Calmet, 1746.

Gouvernantes: Governesses.

Grand Duke Charles: Possibly Charles II, Grand Duke of Mecklenburg-Strelitz (a German province) from 1794 to 1816; or Charles, Grand Duke of Baden (another German province) from 1811 to 1818; perhaps even Charles Augustus, Duke of Saxe-Weimar-Eisenach (yet another German region) from 1757-1828.

Gratz: Or Graz, a university town and the capital of Styria.

"How they escape from their graves…has always been admitted to be utterly inexplicable:" A question that Dom Calmet worried over in his seminal *Dissertations on the Revenants and Vampires of Hungary, Bohemia, Moravia and Silesia* (1746). As noted elsewhere, most writers avoided the question, either by never having their vampires need to return to their graves, or by having them buried in aristocratic above-ground tombs, and coffins that they could presumably lift open from the inside with their vampiric strength.

"In truth I know not why I am so sad": The opening lines of Shakespeare's *The Merchant of Venice.*

Leaf: Irish-English slang for hat-brim.

Magia Posthuma: "Posthumous Magic," a short book by Karl Ferdinand von Schertz, written in Latin and published in Olmutz, Moravia (now Omuluc, part of the Czech Republic) in 1704 (although, oddly, the book has "1706" on its title page). It describes a woman named Maevia who, although buried with all appropriate Catholic rites, returned four day after her burial as a "spectrum" or spectre—sometimes in the form of a man, sometimes as a cat (a form Carmilla takes). Maevia did not suck blood, but she attacked humans, cows, and horses, "grasping their throats, and compressing their stomachs, so as to suffocate them." No one seems to have died, but the spectre's victims were weakened or exhausted to a state of near death. Sometimes she tied cows' tails together, which sounds like the work of a folklorish sprite, or maybe some local boys. The attacks went on for several months; von Schertz doesn't say how they ended. , nor does he give an exact date or location for the events. Maevia did not bite her victims or suck their blood; but the story was quoted by Calmet (although he misquotes von Schertz in saying the spectre appeared as a dog, rather than a cat.).

Matska: a "feminine diminutive," used for a Czech or Polish servant.

Moravian: From Moravia, formerly an Austrian province, now part of the Czech Republic.

MS: manuscript.

Odylic ... influence: a mysterious force, which sensitive persons can detect, supposedly flowing through all through nature, a part of magnetism, hypnotism and chemical reactions. The idea was promoted by the scientist/philosopher Baron Karl von Reichenbach (1788-1869).
Oupire: vampire. Slavic variant of Czech and Russian "upir" or "upyr," Polish "upior" and Magyar "vampyr."
Patois: Local dialect, usually of the common people of a region or country.
Philosophicae et Christianae Cogitationes de Vampiris by John Christofer Harenberg: "Christian Philosophy and Thoughts About the Vampire," by Johann Christoph Harenberg. The 1733 book was written in German, as *Vernünftige und Christliche Gedancken über die Vampirs, oder Bluhtsaugende Todten (Reasonable and Written Thoughts About Vampires, or Bloodsucking Dead),* but somehow got a Latin title in Calmet's book, which Le Fanu used.
Press: A wardrobe.
Revenants and Vampires of Hungary, Bohemia, Moravia and Silesia (1746, see below) to have the final destruction of Carmilla officially performed by the local authorities—followed by a signed report.
Rheinfeldt: It may just be a coincidence that a vampiric victim in Le Fanu has a name so similar to Stoker's madman, Renfield. Possibly, Stoker remembered the name, consciously or unconsciously.
Schloss: German for "castle."
Styria: Austrian province, on the Hungarian border.
"The deadly pallor attributed to that sort of revenants, is a mere melodramatic fiction":
Valerian ... sal volatile: valerian is a sedative, *sal volatile* (volatile salt, or smelling-salts) is a restorative.
Servia: Serbia; under Turkish rule at the time of the story.
Silesia: North-east of Bohemia and Moravia.

AFTERWORD

Carmilla and her reputation slept in a tomb for decades, known only to specialists in the genre. Le Fanu's reputation was revived by critics in the 1920's.

In 1940, CBS radio's Columbia Workshop *updated Le Fanu's story to then-contemporary New York. But Carmilla's true resurrection as a cultural force came almost a century after her first publication: personified by Ingrid Pitt in the 1970 Hammer film* The Vampire Lovers. *The film, a reasonably faithful adaptation of Le Fanu, spawned several sequels. Since then, Carmilla has been adopted as the iconic lesbian vampire, and is constantly being adapted in every medium, from fanfic sequels to videogames* (Castlevania) *to webisodes. Carmilla isn't a household name, at least not in many households; but she has a secure niche in the second or third tier of popular culture, with critics ranking her tale just behind* Dracula *(and sometimes ahead of it) among 19th century vampire stories*

Strangely, after Le Fanu, female vampires in literature retreated more and more to the edges of stories. In the last quarter of the 19th century—when Victorian fantastic literature gave us Dr. Jekyll and Mr. Hyde, the Invisible Man, Dorian Gray, and Count Dracula himself—female vampires were rare, and when they did appear, they were rarely more than one-dimensional threats.

The complex female vampires of the first two-thirds of the century, righteous, avenging, angry, anguished, loving, tortured—were mostly forgotten. The new, modern vampire lady had all the sexuality of her older sisters, but with none of their heart. At most, they were symbols of The Other, incarnations of darkness, sensuality, and appetite, in a time when those things were not considered to be positives.

Tastes had changed. Maybe it was a reaction to women's growing demand for voting rights and other forms of equality. And it wasn't just that all vampire fiction had been written by men—as the next story demonstrates: It's a well-crafted narrative where the female vampire is a very real danger but only a shadowy personality. Ironically, it's probably the first vampire story written by a woman...

VESPERTILIA

…she slowly approached and laid her head upon his shoulder, the outstretched arms clasped themselves closely around her, so that her face was hidden upon his neck…

The next story is, arguably, the only major vampire story in English written between Carmilla *and* Dracula. A Mystery of the Campagna, *a skilfully-constructed and atmospheric tale of gradually building suspense and horror, was published in the British magazine* Unwin's Christmas Annual for 1887.

The byline, Von Degen, was the nom de plume *of the American writer Anne Crawford (1846-1912). Crawford's mother was the sister of Julia Ward Howe, a social activist who wrote the lyrics to* The Battle Hymn of the Republic. *Her father sculpted statue of Freedom on the U.S. Capitol. Despite this patriotic heritage, Crawford was born in Rome and married a German Baron, becoming the Baroness von Rabe.*

Arts and literature were part of Crawford's heritage; she was an amateur painter, and her younger sister Mary and younger brother Francis both became novelists. They each wrote stories of horror and the supernatural—Francis even wrote about a female vampire (who is named only The Thing), in the short story For The Blood Is The Life, *but that was in 1911, in the post-Dracula era, and therefore beyond the scope of this book.*

Crawford published under a pseudonym, in part to avoid potential social disapproval—after all, should the Baroness von Rabe really be writing tales of the undead?

Crawford sets her story in and around Rome, an area she knew very well. Her knowledge of painting is also put to good use. In constructing her tale. Crawford uses the device of two separate first-person narrators—an earlier version of Bram Stoker's novel with its multiple narrators.

While Sheridan Le Fanu wrote Carmilla *from the first-person perspective of a young woman, both of Crawford's narrators in* A Mystery of the Campagna *are men; and Crawford's male personae are entirely convincing. The climactic confrontation with the vampire is perfectly presented from the perspective of a late-Victorian man.*

A MYSTERY OF THE CAMPAGNA

Von Degen
(Anne Crawford, Baroness von Rabe)

I.
MARTIN DETAILLE'S ACCOUNT OF WHAT HAPPENED AT THE VIGNA MARZIALI

MARCELLO's voice is pleading with me now, perhaps because after years of separation I have met an old acquaintance who had a part in his strange story. I have a longing to tell it, and have asked Monsieur Sutton to help me. He noted down the circumstances at the time, and he is willing to join his share to mine, that Marcello may be remembered.

One day, it was in spring, he appeared in my little studio among the laurels and green alleys of the Villa Medici. "Come, *mon enfant*," he said, "put up your paints;" and he unceremoniously took my palette out of my hand. "I have a cab waiting outside, and we are going in search of a hermitage." He was already washing my brushes as he spoke, and this softened my heart, for I hate to do it myself. Then he pulled off my velvet jacket and took down my respectable coat from a nail on the wall. I let him dress me like a child. We always did his will, and he knew it, and in a moment we were sitting in the cab, driving through the Via

Sifitina on our way to the Porta San Giovanni, whither he had directed the coachman to go.

I must tell my story as I can, for though I have been told by my comrades, who cannot know very well, that I can speak good English, writing it is another thing. Monsieur Sutton has asked me to use his tongue, because he has so far forgotten mine that he will not trust himself in it, though he has promised to correct my mistakes, that what I have to tell you may not seem ridiculous, and make people laugh when they read of Marcello. I tell him I wish to write this for my countrymen, not his; but he reminds me that Marcello had many English friends who still live, and that the English do not forget as we do. It is of no use to reason with him, for neither do they yield as we do, and so I have consented to his wish. I think he has a reason which he does not tell me, but let it go. I will translate it all into my own language for my own people. Your English phrases seem to me to be always walking sideways, or trying to look round the corner or stand upon their heads, and they have as many little tails as a kite. I will try not to have recourse to my own language, but he must pardon me if I forget myself. He may be sure I do not do it to offend him. Now that I have explained so much, let me go on.

When we had passed out of the Porta San Giovanni, the coachman drove as slowly as he liked. The pay is more outside the gates, and they always pretend then that their horses are tired, and creep as slowly as possible; but Marcello was never practical. How could he be, I ask you, with an opera in his head? So we crawled along, and he gazed dreamily before him. At last, when we had reached the part where the little villas and vineyards begin, he began to look about him.

You all know how it is out there; iron gates with rusty names or initials over them, and beyond them straight walks bordered with roses and lavender leading up to a forlorn little casino, with trees and a wilderness behind it sloping down to the Campagna, lonely enough to be murdered in and no one to hear you cry. We stopped at several of these gates and Marcello stood looking in, but none of the places were to his taste. He seemed not to doubt that he might have whatever pleased him, but nothing did so. He would jump out and run to the gate, and return saying, "The shape of those windows would disturb my inspiration," or, "That yellow paint would make me fail my duet in the second Act;" and once he liked the air of the house well enough, but there were marigolds growing in the walk, and he hated them. So we drove on and on, until I thought we should find nothing more to reject. At last we came to one which suited him, though it was terribly lonely, and I should have fancied it very *agaçant* to live so far away from the world with nothing but those melancholy olives and green oaks—ilexes, you call them—for company.

"I shall live here and become famous!" he said decidedly, as he pulled the iron rod which rang a great bell inside. We waited, and then he rang again very impatiently and stamped his foot.

"No one lives here, *mon vieux*! Come, it is getting late, and it is so damp out here, and you know that the damp for a tenor voice——" He stamped his foot again and interrupted me angrily.

"Why, then, have you got a tenor? You are stupid! A bass would be more sensible; nothing hurts it. But you have not got one, and you call yourself my friend! Go home without me."

How could I, so far on foot?

"Go and sing your lovesick songs to your lean English misses! They will thank you with a cup of abominable tea, and you will be in Paradise! This is *my* Paradise, and I shall stay until the angel comes to open it!"

He was very cross and unreasonable, and those were just the times when one loved him most, so I waited and enveloped my throat in my pocket-handkerchief and sang a passage or two just to prevent my voice from becoming stiff in that damp air.

"Be still! silence yourself!" he cried. "I cannot hear if anyone is coming."

Someone came at last, a rough-looking sort of keeper, or *guardiano* as they are called there, who looked at us as though he thought we were mad. One of us certainly was, but it was not I. Marcello spoke pretty good Italian, with a French accent, it is true, but the man understood him, especially as he held his purse in his hand. I heard him say a great many impetuously persuasive things all in a breath, then he slipped a gold piece into the *guardiano's* horny hand, and the two turned toward the house, the man shrugging his shoulders in a resigned sort of way, and Marcello called out to me over his shoulder—

"Go home in the cab, or you will be late for your horrible English party! I am going to stay here tonight." *Ma foi*! I took his permission and left him; for a tenor voice is as tyrannical as a jealous woman. Besides, I was furious, and yet I laughed. His was the artist temperament, and appeared to us by turns absurd, sublime, and intensely irritating; but this last never for long, and we all felt that were we more like him our pictures would be worth more. I had not got as far as the city gate when my temper had cooled, and I began to reproach myself for leaving him in that lonely place with his purse full of money, for he was not poor at all, and tempting the dark *guardiano* to murder him. Nothing could be easier than to kill him in his sleep and bury him away somewhere under the olive trees or in some old vault of a ruined catacomb, so common on the borders of the Campagna. There were sure to be a hundred such convenient places. I stopped the coachman and told him to turn back, but he shook his head and said something about having to be in the Piazza of St. Peter at eight o'clock. His horse began to go lame, as though he had understood his master and were his accomplice. What could I do? I said to myself that it was fate, and let him take me back to the Villa Medici, where I had to pay him a pretty sum for our crazy expedition, and then he rattled off, the horse not lame at all, leaving me bewildered at this strange afternoon.

I did not sleep well that night, though my tenor song had been applauded, and the English misses had caressed me much. I tried not to think of Marcello, and he did not trouble me much until I went to bed; but then I could not sleep, as I have told you. I fancied him already murdered, and being buried in the darkness by the *guardiano*. I saw the man dragging his body, with the beautiful head thumping against the stones, down dark passages, and at last leaving it all bloody and covered with earth under a black arch in a recess, and coming back to count the gold pieces. But then again I fell asleep, and dreamed that Marcello was standing at the gate and stamping his foot; and then I slept no more, but got up as soon as the dawn came, and dressed myself and went to my studio at the end of the laurel walk. I took down my painting-jacket, and remembered how he had pulled it off my shoulders. I took up the brushes he had washed for me; they were only half cleaned after all, and stiff with paint and soap. I felt glad to be angry with him, and *sacré*d a little, for it made me sure that he was yet alive if I could scold at him. Then I pulled out my study of his head for my picture of Mucius Scævola holding his hand in the flame, and then I forgave him; for who could look upon that face and not love it?

I worked with the fire of friendship in my brush, and did my best to endow the features with the expression of scorn and obstinacy I had seen at the gate. It could not have been more suitable to my subject! Had I seen it for the last time? You will ask me why I did not leave my work and go to see if anything had happened to him, but against this there were several reasons. Our yearly exhibition was not far off and my picture was barely painted in, and my comrades had sworn that it would not be ready. I was expecting a model for the King of the Etruscans; a man who cooked chestnuts in the Piazza Hontanara, and who had consented to stoop to sit to me as a great favor; and then, to tell the truth, the morning was beginning to dispel my fancies. I had a good northern light to work by, with nothing sentimental about it, and I was not fanciful by nature; so when I sat down to my easel I told myself that I had been a fool, and that Marcello was perfectly safe: the smell of the paints helping me to feel practical again. Indeed, I thought every moment that he would come in, tired of his caprice already, and even was preparing and practising a little lecture for him. Someone knocked at my door, and I cried "*Entrez!*" thinking it was he at last; but no, it was Pierre Magnin.

"There is a curious man, a man of the country, who wants you," he said. "He has your address on a dirty piece of paper in Marcello's handwriting, and a letter for you, but he won't give it up. He says he must see 'il Signor Martino.' He'd make a superb model for a murderer!

Come and speak to him, and keep him while I get a sketch of his head."

I followed Magnin through the garden, and outside—for the porter had not allowed him to enter—I found the *guardiano* of yesterday. He showed his white teeth, and said "Good day, signore," like a Christian; and here in Rome he did not look half so murderous, only a stupid, brown, country fellow. He had a rough peasant-cart waiting, and he had tied up his shaggy horse to a ring in the wall. I held out my hand for the letter and pretended to find it difficult to read, for I saw Magnin standing with his sketch-book in the shadow of the entrance-hall. The note said this—I have it still, and I will copy it. It was written in pencil on a leaf torn from his pocket-book:

> "*Mon vieux*! I have passed a good night here, and the man will keep me as long as I like. Nothing will happen to me, except that I shall be divinely quiet, and I have already a famous *motif* in my head. Go to my lodgings and pack up some clothes and all my manuscripts, with plenty of music paper and a few bottles of Bordeaux, and give them to my messenger. Be quick about it!
>
> "Fame is preparing to descend upon me! If you care to see me, do not come before eight days. The gate will not be opened if you come sooner. The *guardiano* is my slave, and he has instructions to kill any intruder who in the guise of a friend tries to get in uninvited. He will do it, for he has confessed to me that he has murdered three men already."

(Of course this was a joke. I knew Marcello's way.)

> "When you come, go to the *poste restante* and fetch my letters. Here is my card to legitimate you. Don't forget pens and a bottle of ink!

Your MARCELLO."

There was nothing for it but to jump into the cart, tell Magnin, who had finished his sketch, to lock up my studio, and go bumping off to obey these commands. We drove to his lodgings in the Via del Governo Vecchio, and there I made a bundle of all that I could think of; the landlady hindering me by a thousand questions about when the signore would return. He had paid for the rooms in advance, so she had no need to be anxious about her rent. When I told her where he was she shook her head, and talked a good deal about the bad air out there, and said "Poor signorino!" in a melancholy way, as though he were already buried, and looked mournfully after us from the window when we drove away. She irritated me, and made me feel superstitious. At the corner of the Via del Tritone I jumped down and gave the man a franc out of pure sentimentality, and cried after him, "Greet the signore!" but he did not hear me, and jogged away stupidly while I was longing to be with him. Marcello was a cross to us sometimes, but we loved him always.

The eight days went by sooner than I had thought they would, and Thursday came, bright and sunny, for my expedition. At one o'clock I descended into the Piazza di Spagna, and made a bargain with a man who had a well-fed horse, remembering how dearly Marcello's want of good sense had cost me a week ago, and we drove off at a good pace to the Vigna Marziali, as I was almost forgetting to say that it was called. My heart was beating, though I did not know why I should feel so much emotion. When we reached the iron gate the *guardiano* answered my ring directly, and I had no sooner set foot in the long flower-walk than I saw Marcello hastening to meet me.

"I knew you would come," he said, drawing my arm within his, and so we walked toward the little gray house, which had a sort of portico and several balconies, and a sun-dial on its front. There were grated windows down to the ground floor, and the place, to my relief, looked safe and habitable. He told me that the man did not sleep there, but in a little hut down toward the Campagna, and that he, Marcello, locked himself in safely every night, which I was also relieved to know.

"What do you get to eat?" said I.

"Oh, I have goat's flesh, and dried beans and polenta, with pecorino cheese, and there is plenty of black bread and sour wine," he answered smilingly. "You see, I am not starved."

"Do not overwork yourself, *mon vieux*," I said; "you are worth more than your opera ever will be."

"Do I look overworked?" he said, turning his face to me in the broad, out-door light. He seemed a little offended at my saying that about his opera, and I was foolish to do it.

I examined his face critically, and he looked at me half defiantly. "No, not yet," I answered rather unwillingly, for I could not say that he did; but there was a restless, inward look in his eyes, and an almost imperceptible shadow lay around them. It seemed to me as though the full temples had grown slightly hollow, and a sort of faint mist lay over his beauty, making it seem strange and far off. We were standing before the door, and he pushed it open, the *guardiano* following us with slow, loud-resounding steps.

"Here is my Paradise," said Marcello, and we entered the house, which was like all the others of its kind. A hall, with stucco bas-reliefs, and a stairway adorned with antique fragments, gave access to the upper rooms. Marcello ran up the steps lightly, and I heard him lock a door somewhere above and draw out the key, then he came and met me on the landing.

"This," he said, "is my work-room," and he threw open a low door. The key was in the lock, so this room could not be the one I heard him close. "Tell me I shall not write like an angel here!" he cried. I was so dazzled by the flood of bright sunshine after the dusk of the passage, that I blinked like an owl at first, and then I saw a large room, quite bare except for a rough table and chair, the chair covered with manuscript music.

"You are looking for the furniture," he said, laughing; "it is outside. Look here!" and he drew me to a rickety door of worm-eaten wood and coarse greenish glass, and flung it open on to a rusty iron balcony. He was right; the furniture was outside: that is to say, a divine view met my eyes. The Sabine Mountains, the Alban Hills, the broad Campagna, with its medieval towers and ruined aqueducts, and the open plain to the sea. All this glowing and yet calm in the sunlight. No wonder he could write there! The balcony ran round the corner of the house, and to the right I looked down upon an alley of ilexes, ending in a grove of tall laurel trees—very old, apparently. There were bits of sculpture and some ancient sarcophagi standing gleaming among them, and even from so high I could hear a little stream of water pouring from an antique mask into a long, rough trough. I saw the brown *guardiano* digging at his cabbages and onions, and I laughed to think that I could fancy him a murderer! He had a little bag of relics, which dangled to and fro over his sun-burned breast, and he looked very innocent when he sat down upon an old column to eat a piece of black bread with an onion which he had just pulled out of the ground, slicing it with a knife not at all like a dagger. But I kept my thoughts to myself, for Marcello would have laughed at them. We were standing together, looking down at the man as he drank from his hands at the running fountain, and Marcello now leaned down over the balcony, and called out a long "*Ohé!*" The lazy *guardiano* looked up, nodded, and then got up slowly from the stone where he had been half-kneeling to reach the jet of water.

"We are going to dine," Marcello explained. "I have been waiting for you." Presently we heard the man's heavy tread upon the stairs, and he entered bearing a strange meal in a basket.

There came to light pecorino cheese made from ewe's milk, black bread of the consistency of a stone, a great bowl of salad apparently composed of weeds, and a sausage which filled the room with a strong smell of garlic. Then he disappeared and came back with a dish full of ragged-looking goat's flesh cooked together with a mass of smoking polenta, and I am not sure that there was not oil in it.

"I told you I lived well, and now you see!" said Marcello. It was a terrible meal, but I had to eat it, and was glad to have some rough, sour wine to help me, which tasted of earth and roots. When we had finished, I said, "And your opera! How are you getting on?"

"Not a word about that!" he cried. "You see how I have written," and he turned over a heap of manuscript; "but do not talk to me about it. I will not lose my ideas in words." This was not like Marcello, who loved to discuss his work, and I looked at him astonished.

"Come," he said, "we will go down into the garden, and you shall tell me about the comrades. What are they doing? Has Magnin found a model for his Clytemnestra?"

I humored him, as I always did, and we sat upon a stone bench behind the house, looking toward the laurel grove, talking of the pictures and the students. I wanted to walk down the ilex alley, but he stopped me.

"If you are afraid of the damp, don't go down there," he said; "the place is like a vault. Let us stay here and be thankful for this heavenly view."

"Well, let us stay here," I answered, resigned as ever. He lit a cigar and offered me one in silence. If he did not care to talk, I could be still too. From time to time he made some indifferent observation, and I answered it in the same tone. It almost seemed to me as though we, the old heart-comrades, had become strangers who had not known each other a week, or as though we had been so long apart that we had grown away from each other. There was something about him which escaped me. Yes, the few days of solitude had indeed put years and a sort of shyness, or rather ceremony, between us! It did not seem natural to me now to clap him on the back, and make the old, harmless jokes at him. He must have felt the constraint, too, for we were like children who had looked forward to a game and did not know what to play at.

At six o'clock I left him. It was not like parting with Marcello. I felt rather as though I should find my old friend in Rome that evening, and here only left a shadowy likeness of him. He accompanied me to the gate, and pressed my hand, and for a moment the true Marcello looked out of his eyes; but we called out no last words to each other as I drove away. I had only said, "Let me know when you want me;" and he had said, "*Merci*!" and all the way back to Rome I felt a chill upon me, his hand had been so cold, and I thought and thought what could be the matter with him.

That evening I spoke out my anxiety to Pierre Magnin, who shook his head and declared that malaria fever must be taking hold of him, and that people often began to show it by being a little odd.

"He must not stay there! We must get him away as soon as possible," I cried.

"We know Marcello, and that nothing can make him stir against his will," said Pierre. "Let him alone, and he will get tired of his whim. It will not kill him to have a touch of malaria, and some evening he will turn up among us merry as ever."

But he did not. I worked hard at my picture and finished it, but for a few touches, and he had not yet appeared. Perhaps it was the extreme application, perhaps the sitting out in that damp place, for I insist upon tracing it to something more material than emotion. Well, whatever it was, I fell ill; more ill than I had ever been in my life. It was almost twilight when it overtook me, and I remember it distinctly, though I forget what happened afterward, or, rather, I never knew, for I was found by Magnin quite unconscious, and he has told me that I remained so for some time, and then became delirious, and talked of nothing but Marcello. I have told you that it was very nearly twilight; but just at the moment when the sun is gone the colors show in their true value. Artists know this, and I was putting last touches here and there to my picture, and especially to my head of Mucius Scævola, or, rather, Marcello.

The rest of the picture came out well enough; but that head, which should have been the principal one, seemed faded and sunk in. The face appeared to grow paler and paler, and to recede from me; a strange veil spread over it, and the eyes seemed to close. I am not easily frightened, and I know what tricks some peculiar methods of color will play by certain lights, for the moment I spoke of had gone, and the twilight grayness had set in; so I stepped back to look well at it. Just then the lips, which had become almost white, opened a little, and sighed! An illusion, of course. I must have been very ill and quite delirious already, for to my imagination it was a real sigh, or, rather, a sort of exhausted gasp. Then it was that I fainted, I suppose, and when I came to myself I was in my bed, with Magnin and Monsieur Sutton standing by me, and a Sœur de Charité moving softly about among medicine bottles, and speaking in whispers. I stretched out my hands, and they were thin and yellow, with long, pale nails; and I heard Magnin's voice, which sounded very far away, say, "*Dieu merci*!" And now Monsieur Sutton will tell you what I did not know until long afterward.

MARTIN DETAILLE.

II.
ROBERT SUTTON'S ACCOUNT OF WHAT HAPPENED AT THE VIGNA MARZIALI

I am attached to Detaille, and was very glad to be of use to him, but I never fully shared his admiration for Marcello Souvestre, though I appreciated his good points. He was certainly very promising—I must say that. But he was an odd, flighty sort of fellow, not of the kind which we English care to take the trouble to understand. It is my business to write stories, but not having need of such characters I have never particularly studied them. As I say, I was glad to be of use to Detaille, who is a thorough good fellow, and I willingly gave up my work to go and sit by his bedside. Magnin knew that I was a friend of his, and very properly came to me when he found that Detaille's illness was a serious one and likely to last for a long time. I found him perfectly delirious, and raving about Marcello.

"Tell me what the *motif* is! I know it is a *Marche Funèbre*!" And here he would sing a peculiar melody, which, as I have a knack at music, I noted down, it being like nothing I had heard before. The Sister of

Charity looked at me with severe eyes; but how could she know that all is grist for our mill, and that observation becomes with us a mechanical habit? Poor Detaille kept repeating this curious melody over and over, and then would stop and seem to be looking at his picture, crying that it was fading away.

"Marcello! Marcello! You are fading too! Let me come to you!" He was as weak as a baby, and could not have moved from his bed unless in the strength of delirium.

"I cannot come!" he went on; "they have tied me down." And here he made as though he were trying to gnaw through a rope at his wrists, and then burst into tears. "Will no one go for me and bring me a word from you? Ah! if I could know that you are alive!"

Magnin looked at me. I knew what he was thinking. He would not leave his comrade, but I must go. I don't mind acknowledging that I did not undertake this unwillingly. To sit by Detaille's bedside and listen to his ravings enervated me, and what Magnin wanted struck me as troublesome but not uninteresting to one of my craft, so I agreed to go. I had heard all about Marcello's strange seclusion from Magnin and Detaille himself, who lamented over it openly in his simple way at supper at the Academy, where I was a frequent guest.

I knew that it would be useless to ring at the gate of the Vigna Marziali. Not only should I not be admitted, but I should arouse Marcello's anger and suspicion, for I did not for a moment believe that he was not alive, though I thought it very possible that he was becoming a little crazy, as his countrymen are so easily put off their balance. Now, odd people are oddest late in the day and at evening-time. Their nerves lose the power of resistance then, and the real man gets the better of them. So I determined to try to discover something at night, reflecting also that I should be safer from detection then. I knew his liking for wandering about when he ought to be in his bed, and I did not doubt that I should get a glimpse of him, and that was really all I needed.

My first step was to take a long walk out of the Porta San Giovanni, and this I did in the early morning, tramping along steadily until I came to an iron gate on the right of the road with "Vigna Marziali" over it; and then I walked straight on, never stopping until I had reached a little bushy lane running down toward the Campagna to the right. It was pebbly, and quite shut in by luxuriant ivy and elder bushes, and it bore deep traces of the last heavy rains. These had evidently been effaced by no foot-prints, so I concluded that it was little used. Down this path I made my way cautiously, looking behind and before me, from a habit contracted in my lonely wanderings in the Abruzzi. I had a capital revolver with me—an old friend—and I feared no man; but I began to feel a dramatic interest in my undertaking, and determined that it should not be crossed by any disagreeable surprises. The lane led me further down the plain than I had reckoned upon, for the bushy edge shut out the view; and when I had got to the bottom and faced round, the Vigna Marziali was lying quite far to my left. I saw at a glance that behind the gray casino an alley of ilexes ended in a laurel grove; then there were plantations of kitchen-stuff, with a sort of thatched cabin in their midst, probably that of the gardener. I looked about for a kennel, but saw none, so there was no watch-dog. At the end of this primitive kitchen garden was a broad patch of grass, bounded by a fence, which I could take at a spring. Now, I knew my way, but I could not resist tracing it out a little farther. It was well that I did so, for I found just within the fence a sunken stream, rather full at the time, in consequence of the rains, too deep to wade and too broad to jump. It struck me that it would be easy enough to take a board from the fence and lay it over for a bridge. I measured the breadth with my eye, and decided that the board would span it; then I went back as I had come, and returned to find Detaille still raving.

As he could understand nothing, it seemed to me rather a fool's errand to go off in search of comfort for him; but a conscious moment might come, and, moreover, I began to be interested in my undertaking; and so I agreed with Magnin that I should go and take some food and rest and return to the Vigna that night. I told my landlady that I was going into the country and should return the next day, and I went to Nazarri's and laid in a stock of sandwiches and filled my flask with something they called sherry, for, though I was no great wine-drinker, I feared the night-chill.

It was about seven o'clock when I started, and I retraced my morning's steps exactly. As I reached the lane, it occurred to me that it was still too light for me to pass unobserved over the stream, and I made a place for myself under the hedge and lay down, quite screened by the thick curtain of tangled overhanging ivy.

I must have been out of training, and tired by the morning's walk, for I fell asleep. When I awoke it was night; the stars were shining, a dank mist made its way down my throat, and I felt stiff and cold. I took a pull at my flask, finding it nasty stuff, but it warmed me. Then I rang my repeater, which struck a quarter to eleven, got up and shook myself free of the leaves and brambles, and went on down the lane. When I got to the fence I sat down and thought the thing over. What did I expect to discover? What *was* there to discover? Nothing! Nothing but that Marcello was alive; and that was no discovery at all, for I felt sure of it. I was a fool, and had let myself be allured by the mere stage nonsense and mystery of the business, and a mouse would creep out of this mountain of precautions! Well, at least, I could turn it to account by describing my own absurd behavior in some story yet to be written, and, as it was not enough for a chapter, I would add to it by further experience. "Come along!" I said to myself. "You're an ass, but it may prove instructive." I raised the top board from the fence noiselessly. There was a stile just there, and the boards were easily moved. I laid down my bridge with some difficulty and stepped carefully across, and made my way to the laurel grove as quickly and noiselessly as possible.

There all was thick darkness, and my eyes only grew slowly accustomed to it. After all there was not much to see; some stone seats in a semicircle, and some fragments of columns set upright with antique busts upon them. Then a little to the right a sort of arch, with apparently some steps descending into the ground, probably the entrance to some discovered branch of a catacomb. In the midst of the inclosure, not a very large one, stood a stone table, deeply fixed in the earth. No one was there; of that I felt certain, and I sat down, having now got used to the gloom, and fell to eat my sandwiches, for I was desperately hungry.

Now that I had come so far, was nothing to take place to repay me for my trouble? It suddenly struck me that it was absurd to expect Marcello to come out to meet me and perform any mad antics he might be meditating there before my eyes for my especial satisfaction. Why I had supposed that something would take place in the grove I do not know, except that this seemed a fit place for it. I would go and watch the house, and if I saw a light anywhere I might be sure that he was within. Any fool might have thought of that, but a novelist lays the scene of his drama and expects his characters to slide about in the grooves like puppets. It is only when mine surprise me that I feel they are alive. When I reached the end of the ilex alley I saw the house before me. There were more cabbages and onions after I had left the trees, and I saw that in this open space I could easily be perceived by any one standing on the balcony above. As I drew back again under the ilexes, a window above, not the one on the balcony, was suddenly lighted up; but the light did not remain long, and presently a gleam shone through the glass oval over the door below.

I had just time to spring behind the thickest trunk near me when the door opened. I took advantage of its creaking to creep up the slanting tree like a cat, and lie out upon a projecting branch.

As I expected, Marcello came out. He was very pale, and moved mechanically like a sleep-walker. I was shocked to see how hollow his face had become, as he held the candle still lighted in his hand, and it cast deep shadows on his sunken cheeks and fixed eyes, which burned wildly and seemed to see nothing. His lips were quite white, and so drawn that I could see his gleaming teeth. Then the candle fell from his hand, and he came slowly and with a curiously regular step on into the darkness of the ilexes, I watching him from above. But I scarcely think he would have noticed me had I been standing in his path. When he had passed, I let myself down and followed him. I had taken off my shoes, and my tread was absolutely noiseless; moreover, I felt sure he would not turn round.

On he went with the same mechanical step until he reached the grove. There I knelt behind an old sarcophagus at the entrance, and waited. What would he do? He stood perfectly still, not looking about him, but as though the clock-work within him had suddenly stopped. I felt that he was becoming psychologically interesting, after all. Suddenly he threw up his arms as men do when they are mortally wounded on the battle-field, and I expected to see him fall at full length. Instead of this, he made a step forward.

I looked in the same direction and saw a woman, who must have concealed herself there while I was waiting before the house, come from out of the gloom, and as she slowly approached and laid her head upon his shoulder, the outstretched arms clasped themselves closely around her, so that her face was hidden upon his neck.

So this was the whole matter, and I had been sent off on a wild-goose chase to spy out a common love-affair! His opera and his seclusion for the sake of work, his tyrannical refusal to see Detaille unless he sent for him—all this was but a mask to a vulgar intrigue which, for reasons best known to himself, could not be indulged in in the city. I was thoroughly angry! If Marcello passed his time mooning about in that damp hole all night, no wonder that he looked so wretchedly ill, and seemed half mad! I knew very well that Marcello was no saint. Why should he be? But I had not taken him for a fool! He had had plenty of romantic episodes, and as he was discreet without being uselessly mysterious no one had ever unduly pried into them, nor should we have done so now. I said to myself that that mixture of French and Italian blood was at the bottom of it; French flimsiness and light-headedness and Italian love of cunning! I looked back upon all the details of my mysterious expedition. I suppose at the root of my anger lay a certain dramatic disappointment at not finding him lying murdered, and I despised myself for all the trouble I had taken to this ridiculous end: just to see him holding a woman in his arms. I could not see her face, and her figure was enveloped from head to foot in something long and dark; but I could make out that she was tall and slender, and that a pair of white hands gleamed from her drapery. As I was looking intently, for all my indignation, the couple moved on, and still clinging to one another descended the steps. So even the solitude of the lonely laurel grove could not satisfy Marcello's insane love of secrecy! I kept still awhile; then I stole to where they had disappeared, and listened; but all was silent, and I cautiously struck a match and peered down. I could see the steps for a short distance below me, and then the darkness seemed to rise and swallow them. It must be a catacomb, as I had imagined, or an old Roman bath, perhaps, which Marcello had made comfortable enough, no doubt, and as likely as not they were having a nice little cold supper there. My empty stomach told me that I could have forgiven him even then could I have shared it. I was in truth frightfully hungry as well as angry, and sat down on one of the stone benches to finish my sandwiches.

The thought of waiting to see this love-sick pair return to upper earth never for a moment occurred to me. I had found out the whole thing, and a great humbug it was! Now I wanted to get back to Rome before my temper had cooled, and to tell Magnin on what a fool's errand he had sent me. If he liked to quarrel with me, all the better!

All the way home I composed cutting French speeches, but they suddenly cooled and petrified like a gust of lava from a volcano when I discovered that the gate was closed. I had never thought of getting a pass, and Magnin ought to have warned me. Another grievance against the fellow! I enjoyed my resentment, and it kept me warm as I patrolled up and down. There are houses, and even small eating-shops, outside the gate, but no light was visible, and I did not care to attract attention by pounding at the doors in the middle of the night; so I crept behind a bit of wall. I was getting used to hiding by this time, and made myself as comfortable as I could with my ulster, took another pull at my flask, and waited. At last the gate was opened and I slipped through, trying not to look as though I had been out all night like a bandit. The guard looked at me narrowly, evidently wondering at my lack of luggage. Had I had a knapsack I might have been taken for some innocently mad English tourist indulging in the mistaken pleasure of trudging in from Fractal or Albano; but a man in an ulster, with his hands in his pockets, sauntering in at the gate of the city at break of day as though returning from a stroll, naturally puzzled the officials, who looked after me and shrugged their shoulders.

Luckily I found an early cab in the Piazza of the Lateran, for I was dead beat, and was soon at my lodgings in the Via della Croce, where my landlady let me in very speedily. Then at last I had the comfort of throwing off my clothes, all damp with the night dew, and turning in. My wrath had cooled to a certain point, and I did not fear to lower its temperature too greatly by yielding to an overwhelming desire for sleep. An hour or two could make no great difference to Magnin—let him fancy me still hanging about the Vigna Marziali! Sleep I must have, no matter what he thought. I slept long, and was awakened at last by my landlady, Sora Nanna, standing over me, and saying, "There is a signore who wants you."

"It is I, Magnin!" said a voice behind her. "I could not wait for you to come!" He looked haggard with anxiety and watching.

"Detaille is raving still," he went on, "only worse than before. Speak, for Heaven's sake! Why don't you tell me something?" And he shook me by the arm as though he thought I was still asleep.

"Have you nothing to say? You must have seen something! Did you see Marcello?"

"Oh! yes, I saw him."

"Well?"

"Well, he was very comfortable—quite alive. He had a woman's arms around him."

I heard my door violently slammed to, a ferocious "*Sacré gamin*!" and then steps springing down the stairs. I felt perfectly happy at having made such an impression, and turned and resumed my broken sleep with almost a kindly feeling toward Magnin, who was at that moment probably tearing up the Spanish Scalinata two steps at a time, and making himself horribly hot. It could not help Detaille, poor fellow! He could not understand my news. When I had slept long enough I got up, refreshed myself with a bath and something to eat, and went off to see Detaille. It was not his fault that I had been made a fool of, so I felt sorry for him.

I found him raving just as I had left him the day before, only worse, as Magnin said. He persisted in continually crying, "Marcello, take care! no one can save you!" in hoarse, weak tones, but with the regularity of a knell, keeping up a peculiar movement with his feet, as though he were weary with a long road, but must press forward to his goal. Then he would stop and break into childish sobs.

"My feet are so sore," he murmured, piteously, "and I am so tired! But I will come! They are following me, but I am strong!" Then a violent struggle with his invisible pursuers, in which he would break off into that singing of his, alternating with the warning cry. The singing voice was quite another from the speaking one. He went on and on, repeating the singular air which he had himself called a Funeral March, and which had become intensely disagreeable to me. If it was one indeed, it surely was intended for no Christian burial. As he sang, the tears kept trickling down his cheeks, and Magnin sat wiping them away as tenderly as a woman. Between his song he would clasp his hands, feebly enough, for he was very weak when the delirium did not make him violent, and cry in heart-rending tones, "Marcello, I shall never see you again! Why did you leave us?" At last, when he stopped for a moment, Magnin left his side, beckoning the Sister to take it, and drew me into the other room, closing the door behind him.

"Now tell me exactly how you saw Marcello," said he; so I related my whole absurd experience—forgetting, however, my personal irritation, for he looked too wretched and worn for anybody to be angry with him. He made me repeat several times my description of Marcello's face and manner as he had come out of the house. That seemed to make more impression upon him than the love business.

"Sick people have strange intuitions," he said, gravely; "and I persist in thinking that Marcello is very ill and in danger. *Tenez!*" And here he broke off, went to the door, and called "*Ma sœur!*" under his breath. She understood, and after having drawn the bed-clothes straight, and once more dried the trickling tears, she came noiselessly to where we stood, the wet handkerchief still in her hand. She was a singularly tall and strong-looking woman, with piercing black eyes and a self-controlled manner. Strange to say, she bore the adopted name of Claudius, instead of a more feminine one.

"*Ma sœur*," said Magnin, "at what o'clock was it that he sprang out of bed and we had to hold him for so long?"

"Half-past eleven and a few minutes," she answered promptly. Then he turned to me.

"At what time did Marcello come out into the garden?"

"Well, it might have been half-past eleven," I answered, unwillingly. "I should say that three quarters of an hour might possibly have passed since I rang my repeater. Mind you, I won't swear it!" I hate to have people try to prove mysterious coincidences, and this was just what they were attempting.

"Are you sure of the hour, *ma sœur*?" I asked, a little tartly. She looked at me calmly with her great, black eyes, and said:

"I heard the Trinità dei Monti strike the half-hour just before it happened."

"Be so good as to tell Monsieur Sutton exactly what took place," said Magnin.

"One moment, monsieur;" and she went swiftly and softly to Detaille, raised him on her strong arm, and held a glass to his lips, from which he drank mechanically. Then she came and stood where she could watch him through the open door.

"He hears nothing," she said, as she hung the handkerchief to dry over a chair; and then she went on. "It was half-past eleven, and my patient had been very uneasy—that is to say, more so even than before. It might have been four or five minutes after the clock had finished striking that he became suddenly quite still and then began to tremble all over, so that the bed shook with him." She spoke admirable English, as many of the Sisters do, so I need not translate, but will give her own words.

"He went on trembling until I thought he was going to have a fit, and told Monsieur Magnin to be ready to go for the doctor, when just then the trembling stopped, he became perfectly stiff, his hair stood up upon his head, and his eyes seemed coming out of their sockets, though he could see nothing, for I passed the candle before them. All at once he sprang out of his bed and rushed to the door. I did not know he was so strong. Before he got there I had him in my arms, for he has become very light, and I carried him back to bed again, though he was struggling like a child. Monsieur Magnin came in from the next room just as he was trying to get up again, and we held him down until it was past, but he screamed Monsieur Souvestre's name for a long time after that. Afterward he was very cold and exhausted, of course, and I gave him some beef-tea, though it was not the hour for it."

"I think you had better tell the Sister all about it," said Magnin, turning to me. "It is best that the nurse should know everything."

"Very well," said I; "though I do not think it's much in her line." She answered me herself: "Everything which concerns our patients is our business. Nothing shocks us." Thereupon she sat down and thrust her hands into her long sleeves, prepared to listen. I repeated the whole affair as I had done to Magnin. She never took her brilliant eyes from off my face, and listened as coolly as though she had been a doctor hearing an account of a difficult case, though to me it seemed almost sacrilege to be describing the behavior of a love-stricken youth to a Sister of Charity.

"What do you say to that, *ma sœur*?" asked Magnin, when I had done.

"I say nothing, monsieur. It is sufficient that I know it;" and she withdrew her hands from her sleeves, took up the handkerchief, which was dry by this time, and returned quietly to her place at the bedside.

"I wonder if I have shocked her, after all?" I said to Magnin.

"Oh, no," he answered. "They see many things, and a *sœur* is as abstract as a confessor; they do not allow themselves any personal feelings. I have seen Sœur Claudius listen perfectly unmoved to the most abominable ravings, only crossing herself beneath her cape at the most hideous blasphemies. It was last summer when poor Justin Revol died. You were not here."

Magnin put his hand to his forehead.

"You are looking ill yourself," I said . "Go and try to sleep, and I will stay."

"Very well," he answered; "but I cannot rest unless you promise to remember everything he says, that I may hear it when I wake;" and he threw himself down upon the hard sofa like a sack, and was asleep in a moment; and I, who had felt so angry with him but a few hours ago, put a cushion under his head and made him comfortable.

I sat down in the next room and listened to Detaille's monotonous ravings, while Sœur Claudius read in her book of prayers. It was getting dusk, and several of the academicians stole in and stood over the sick man and shook their heads. They looked around for Magnin, but I pointed to the other room with my finger on my lips, and they nodded and went away on tiptoe.

It required no effort of memory to repeat Detaille's words to Magnin when he woke, for they were always the same. We had another Sister that night, and as Sœur Claudius was not to return till the next day at midday, I offered to share the watch with Magnin, who was getting very nervous and exhausted, and who seemed to think that some such attack might be expected as had occurred the night before. The new Sister was a gentle, delicate-looking little woman, with tears in her soft brown eyes as she bent over the sick man, and crossed herself from time to time, grasping the crucifix which hung from the beads at her waist. Nevertheless she was calm and useful, and as punctual as Sœur Claudius herself in giving the medicines.

The doctor had come in the evening, and prescribed a change in these. He would not say what he thought of his patient, but only declared that it was necessary to wait for a crisis. Magnin sent for some supper, and we sat over it together in silence, neither of us hungry. He kept looking at his watch.

"If the same thing happens to-night, he will die!" said he, and laid his head on his arms.

"He will die in a most foolish cause, then," I said, angrily, for I thought he was going to cry, as those Frenchmen have a way of doing, and I wanted to irritate him by way of a tonic; so I went on—

"It would be dying for a *vaurien* who is making an ass of himself in a ridiculous business which will be over in a week! Souvestre may get as much fever as he likes! only don't ask me to come and nurse him."

"It is not the fever," said he slowly, "it is a horrible nameless dread that I have; I suppose it is listening to Detaille that makes me nervous. Hark!" he added, "it strikes eleven. We must watch!"

"If you really expect another attack you had better warn the Sister," I said; so he told her in a few words what might happen.

"Very well, monsieur," she answered, and sat down quietly near the bed, Magnin at the pillow, and I near him. No sound was to be heard but Detaille's ceaseless lament.

And now, before I tell you more, I must stop to entreat you to believe me. It will be almost impossible for you to do so, I know, for I have laughed myself at such tales, and no assurances would have made me credit them. But I, Robert Sutton, swear that this thing happened. More I cannot do. It is the truth. We had been watching Detaille intently. He was lying with closed eyes, and had been very restless. Suddenly he became quite still, and then began to tremble, exactly as Sœur Claudius had described. It was a curious, uniform trembling, apparently in every fibre, and his iron bedstead shook as though strong hands were at its head and foot. Then came the absolute rigidity she had also described, and I do not exaggerate when I say that not only did his short-cropped hair seem to stand erect, but that it literally did so. A lamp cast the shadow of his profile against the wall to the left of his bed, and as I looked at the immovable outline which seemed painted on the wall, I saw the hair slowly rise until the line where it joined the forehead was quite a different one—abrupt instead of a smooth sweep. His eyes opened wide and were frightfully fixed, then as frightfully strained, but they certainly did not see us.

We waited breathlessly for what might follow. The little Sister was standing close to him, her lips pressed together and a little pale, but very calm. "Do not be frightened, *ma sœur*," whispered Magnin; and she answered in a business-like tone, "No, monsieur," and drew still nearer to her patient, and took his hands, which were stiff as those of a corpse, between her own to warm them. I laid mine upon his heart; it was beating so imperceptibly that I almost thought it had stopped, and as I leaned my face to his lips I could feel no breath issue from them. It seemed as though the rigor would last forever.

Suddenly, without any transition, he hurled himself with enormous force, and literally at one bound, almost into the middle of the room, scattering us aside like leaves in the wind. I was upon him in a moment, grappling with him with all my strength, to prevent him from reaching the door. Magnin had been thrown backward against the table, and I heard the medicine bottles crash with his fall. He had flung back his hand to save himself, and rushed to help me with the blood dropping from a cut in his wrist. The little Sister sprang to us, Detaille had thrown her violently back upon her knees, and now, with a nurse's instinct, she tried to throw a shawl over his bare breast. We four must have made a strange group!

Four? *We were five*! Marcello Souvestre stood before us, just within the door! We all saw him, for he was there. His bloodless face was turned toward us unmoved; his hands hung by his side as white as his face; only his eyes had life in them; they were fixed on Detaille.

"Thank God, you have come at last!" I cried. "Don't stand there like a fool! Help us, can't you?" But he never moved. I was furiously angry, and, leaving my hold, sprang upon him to drag him forward. My outstretched hands struck hard against the door, and I felt a thing like a spider's web envelop me. It seemed to draw itself over my mouth and eyes, and to blind and choke me, and then to flutter and tear and float from me.

Marcello was gone!

Detaille had slipped from Magnin's hold, and lay in a heap upon the floor, as though his limbs were broken. The Sister was trembling violently as she knelt over him and tried to raise his head. We gazed at one another, stooped and lifted him in our arms, and carried him back to his bed, while Sœur Marie quietly collected the broken phials.

"You saw it, *ma sœur*?" I heard Magnin whisper hoarsely.

"Yes, monsieur!" she only answered, in a trembling voice, holding on to her crucifix. Then she said, in a professional tone: "Will monsieur let me bind up his wrist?" And though her fingers trembled and his hand was shaking, the bandage was an irreproachable one.

Magnin went into the next room, and I heard him throw himself heavily into a chair. Detaille seemed to be sleeping. His breath came regularly; his eyes were closed with a look of peace about the lids, his hands lying in a natural way upon the quilt. He had not moved since we laid him there. I went softly to where Magnin was sitting in the dark. He did not move, but only said, "Marcello is dead!"

"He is either dead or dying," I answered, "and we must go to him."

"Yes," Magnin whispered, "we must go to him, but we shall not reach him."

"We will go as soon as it is light," I said, and then we were still again. When the morning came at last he went and found a comrade to take his place, and only said to Sœur Marie, "It is not necessary to speak of this night;" and at her quiet "You are right, monsieur," we felt that we could trust her. Detaille was still sleeping. Was this the crisis the doctor had expected? Perhaps; but surely not in such fearful form. I insisted upon my companion having some breakfast before we started, and I breakfasted myself, but I cannot say I tasted what passed between my lips.

We engaged a closed carriage, for we did not know what we might bring home with us, though neither of us spoke out his thoughts. It was early morning still when we reached the Vigna Marziali, and we had not exchanged a word all the way. I rang at the bell, while the coachman looked on curiously. It was answered promptly by the *guardiano*, of whom Detaille has already told you.

"Where is the signore?" I asked through the gate.

"*Chi lo sa*?" he answered. "He is here, of course; he has not left the Vigna. Shall I call him?"

"*Call him*?" I knew that no mortal voice could reach Marcello now, but I tried to fancy he was still alive.

"No," I said. "Let us in. We want to surprise him; he will be pleased."

The man hesitated, but he finally opened the gate, and we entered, leaving the carriage to wait outside. We went straight to the house; the door at the back was wide open. There had been a gale in the night, and it had torn some leaves and bits of twigs from the trees and blown them into the entrance-hall. They lay scattered across the threshold, and were evidence that the door had remained open ever since they had fallen. The *guardiano* left us, probably to escape Marcello's anger at having let us in, and we went up the stairs unhindered, Magnin foremost, for he knew the house better than I, from Detaille's description. He had told him about the corner room with the balcony, and we pretended that Marcello might be there, absorbed betimes in his work, but we did not call him.

He was not there. His papers were strewn over the table as though he had been writing, but the inkstand was dry and full of dust; he could not have used it for days. We went silently into the other chambers. Perhaps he was still asleep? But, no! We found his bed untouched, so he could not have lain in it that night. The rooms were all unlocked but one, and this closed door made our hearts beat. Marcello could scarcely be there, however, for there was no key in the lock; I saw the daylight shining through the key-hole. We called his name, but there came no answer. We knocked loudly, still no sign from within; so I put my shoulder to the door, which was old and cracked in several places, and succeeded in bursting it open.

Nothing was there but a sculptor's modeling-stand, with something upon it covered with a white cloth, and the modeling-tools on the floor. At the sight of the cloth, still damp, we drew a deep breath. It could not have hung there for many hours, certainly not for twenty-four. We did not raise it. "He would be vexed," said Magnin, and I nodded, for it is accounted almost a crime in the artist's world to unveil a sculptor's work behind his back. We expressed no surprise at the fact of his modeling; a ban seemed to lie upon our tongues. The cloth hung tightly to the object beneath it, and showed us the outline of a woman's head and rounded bust, and so veiled we left her. There was a little winding stair leading out of the passage, and we climbed it, to find ourselves in a sort of belvedere, commanding a superb view. It was a small, open terrace, on the roof of the house, and we saw at a glance that no one was there.

We had now been all over the casino, which was small and simply built, being evidently intended only for short summer use. As we stood leaning over the balustrade we could look down into the garden. No one was there but the *guardiano*, lying among his cabbages with his arms behind his head, half asleep. The laurel grove had been in my mind from the beginning, only it had seemed more natural to go to the house first. Now we descended the stairs silently and directed our steps thither.

As we approached it, the *guardiano* came toward us lazily.

"Have you seen the signore?" he asked, and his stupidly placid face showed me that he, at least, had no hand in his disappearance.

"No, not yet," I answered, "but we shall come across him somewhere, no doubt. Perhaps he has gone to take a walk, and we will wait for him. What is this?" I went on, trying to seem careless. We were standing now by the little arch, of which you know.

"This?" said he; "I have never been down there, but they say it is something old. Do the signori want to see it? I will fetch a lantern."

I nodded, and he went off to his cabin. I had a couple of candles in my pocket, for I had intended to explore the place, should we not find Marcello. It was there that he had disappeared that night, and my thoughts had been busy with it; but I kept my candles concealed, reflecting that they would give our search an air of premeditation which would excite curiosity.

"When did you see the signore last?" I asked, when he had returned with the lantern.

"I brought him his supper yesterday evening."

"At what o'clock?"

"It was the Ave Maria, signore," he replied. "He always sups then."

It would be useless to put any further questions. He was evidently utterly unobserving, and would lie to please us.

"Let me go first," said Magnin, taking the lantern. We set our feet upon the steps; a cold air seemed to fill our lungs and yet to choke us, and a thick darkness lay beneath. The steps, as I could see by the light of my candle, were modern, as well as the vaulting above them. A tablet was let into the wall, and in spite of my excitement I paused to read it, perhaps because I was glad to delay whatever awaited us below.

It ran thus:

"Questo antico sepolcro Romano scoprì il Conte Marziali nell anno 1853, e piamente conservato."

In plain English:

"Count Marziali discovered this ancient Roman sepulcher in the year 1853, and piously preserved it."

I read it more quickly than it has taken time to write here, and hurried after Magnin, whose footsteps sounded faintly below me. As I hastened, a draught of cold air extinguished my candle, and I was trying to make my way down by feeling along the wall, which was horribly dark and clammy, when my heart stood still at a cry from far beneath me—a cry of horror!

"Where are you?" I shouted; but Magnin was calling my name, and could not hear me. "I am here. I am in the dark!"

I was making haste as fast as I could, but there were several turnings.

"I have found him!" came up from below.

"Alive?" I shouted. No answer.

One last short flight brought me face to face with the gleam of the lantern. It came from a low doorway, and within stood Magnin, peering into the darkness. I knew by his face, as he held the light high above him, that our fears were realized.

Yes, Marcello was there. He was lying stretched upon the floor, staring at the ceiling, dead, and already stiff, as I could see at a glance. We stood over him saying not a word, then I knelt down and felt of him, for mere form's sake, and said, as though I had not known it before, "He has been dead for some hours."

Since yesterday evening," said Magnin, in a horror –stricken voice, yet with a certain satisfaction in it, as though to say, "You see, I was right."

Marcello was lying with his head slightly thrown back, no contortions in his handsome features; rather the look of a person who has quietly died of exhaustion—who has slipped unconsciously from life to death. His collar was thrown open and a part of his breast, of a ghastly white, was visible. Just over the heart was a small spot.

"Give me the lantern," I whispered, as I stooped over it. It was a very little spot, of a faint purplish-brown, and must have changed color within the night.

I examined it intently, and should say that the blood had been sucked to the surface, and then a small prick or incision made. The slight subcutaneous effusion led me to this conclusion. One tiny drop of coagulated blood closed the almost imperceptible wound. I probed it with the end of one of Magnin's matches. It was scarcely more than skin-deep, so it could not be the stab of a stiletto, however slender, or the track of a bullet. Still, it was strange, and with one impulse we turned to see if no one were concealed there, or if there were no second exit. It would be madness to suppose that the murderer, if there was one, would remain by his victim. Had Marcello been making love to a pretty contadina, and was this some jealous lover's vengeance? But it was not a stab. Had one drop of poison in the little wound done this deadly work?

We peered about the place, and I saw that Magnin's eyes were blinded by tears and his face as pale as that upturned one on the floor, whose lids I had vainly tried to close. The chamber was low, and beautifully ornamented with stucco bas-reliefs, in the manner of the well-known one not far from there upon the same road. Winged genii, griffins, and arabesques, modeled with marvelous lightness, covered the walls and ceiling. There was no other door than the one we had entered by. In the center stood a marble sarcophagus, with the usual subjects sculptured upon it, on the one side Hercules conducting a veiled figure, on the other a dance of nymphs and fauns. A space in the middle contained the following inscription, deeply cut in the stone, and still partially filled with red pigment:

D.M. VESPERTILIAE. ΤΟ ΠΤΗΝΟΕΙΔΗ ΑΙΜΑΤΟΣ
Q. FLAVIVS. VIX. IPSE. SOSPE.
MONPOVIT.

"What is this?" whispered Magnin. It was only a pickaxe and a long crowbar, such as the country people use in hewing out their blocks of "tufa," and his foot had struck against them. Who could have brought them here? They must belong to the *guardiano* above, but he said that he had never come here, and I believed him, knowing the Italian horror of darkness and lonely places; but what had Marcello wanted with them? It did not occur to us that archaeological curiosity could have led him to attempt to open the sarcophagus, the lid of which had evidently never been raised, thus justifying the expression, "piously preserved."

As I rose from examining the tools my eyes fell upon the line of mortar where the cover joined to the stone below, and I noticed that some of it had been removed, perhaps with the pickaxe which lay at my feet. I tried it with my nails and found that it was very crumbly. Without a word I took the tool in my hand, Magnin instinctively following my movements with the lantern. What impelled us I do not know. I had myself no thought, only an irresistible desire to see what was within. I saw that much of the mortar had been broken away, and lay in small fragments upon the ground, which I had not noticed before. It did not take long to complete the work. I snatched the lantern from Magnin's hand and set it upon the ground, where it shone full upon Marcello's dead face, and by its light I found a little break between the two masses of stone and managed to insert the end of my crowbar, driving it in with a blow of the pickaxe. The stone chipped and then cracked a little. Magnin was shivering.

"What are you going to do?" he said, looking around at where Marcello lay.

"Help me!" I cried, and we two bore with all our might upon the crowbar. I am a strong man, and I felt a sort of blind fury as the stone refused to yield. What if the bar should snap? With another blow I drove it in still further, then using it as a lever, we weighed upon it with our outstretched arms until every muscle was at its highest tension. The stone moved a little, and, almost fainting, we stopped to rest.

From the ceiling hung the rusty remnant of an iron chain which must once have held a lamp. To this, by scrambling upon the sarcophagus,

I contrived to make fast the lantern.

"Now!" said I, and we heaved again at the lid. It rose, and we alternately heaved and pushed until it lost its balance and fell with a thundering crash upon the other side; such a crash that the walls seemed to shake, and I was for a moment utterly deafened, while little pieces of stucco rained upon us from the ceiling. When we had paused to recover from the shock we leaned over the sarcophagus and looked in.

The light shone full upon it, and we saw—how is it possible to tell? We saw lying there, amid folds of moldering rags, the body of a woman, perfect as in life, with faintly rosy face, soft crimson lips, and a breast of living pearl, which seemed to heave as though stirred by some delicious dream. The rotten stuff swathed about her was in ghastly contrast to this lovely form, fresh as the morning! Her hands lay stretched at her side, the pink palms were turned a little outward, her eyes were closed as peacefully as those of a sleeping child, and her long hair, which shone red-golden in the dim light from above, was wound around her head in numberless finely plaited tresses, beneath which little locks escaped in rings upon her brow. I could have sworn that the blue veins on that divinely perfect bosom held living blood!

We were absolutely paralyzed, and Magnin leaned gasping over the edge as pale as death, paler by far than this living, almost smiling face to which his eyes were glued. I do not doubt that I was as pale as he at this inexplicable vision. As I looked, the red lips seemed to grow redder. They were redder! The little pearly teeth showed between them. I had not seen them before, and now a clear ruby drop trickled down to her rounded chin and from there slipped sideways and fell upon her neck. Horror-struck I gazed upon the living corpse, till my eyes could not bear the sight any longer. As I looked away my glance fell once more upon the mysterious inscription, half Latin, half Greek, and the awful meaning of the words flashed upon me suddenly as I read them this second time. "To Vespertilia"—that was in Latin, and even the Latin name of the woman suggested a thing of evil flitting in the dusk. But the full horror of the nature of that thing had been veiled to

Roman eyes under the Greek, "The blood-drinker, the vampire woman." And Flavius—her lover—*vix ipse sospes*, "himself hardly saved" from that deadly embrace, had buried her here, and set a seal upon her sepulcher, trusting to the weight of stone and the strength of clinging mortar to imprison forever the beautiful monster he had loved.

"Infamous murderess!" I cried, "You have killed Marcello!" and a sudden, vengeful calm came over me.

"Give me the pickaxe," I said to Magnin. I can hear myself saying it still. He picked it up and handed it to me as in a dream; he seemed little better than an idiot, and the beads of sweat were shining on his forehead. I took my knife, and from the long wooden handle of the pickaxe I cut a fine, sharp stake. Then I clambered, scarcely feeling any repugnance, over the side of the sarcophagus, my feet among the folds of Vespertilia's decaying winding-sheet, which crushed like ashes beneath my boot.

I looked for one moment at that white breast, but only to choose the loveliest spot, where the network of azure veins shimmered like veiled turquoises, and then with one blow I drove the pointed stake deep down through the breathing snow and stamped it in with my heel.

An awful shriek, so ringing and horrible that I thought my ears must have burst; but even then I felt neither fear nor horror. There are times when these cannot touch us. I stooped and gazed once again at the face, now undergoing a fearful change—fearful and final!

"Foul vampire!" I said quietly in my concentrated rage. "You will do no more harm now!" And then, without looking back upon her cursed face, I clambered out of the horrible tomb.

We raised Marcello, and slowly carried him up the steep stairs—a difficult task, for the way was narrow and he was so stiff. I noticed that the steps were ancient up to the end of the second flight; above, the modern passage was somewhat broader. When we reached the top, the *guardiano* was lying upon one of the stone benches; he did not mean us to cheat him out of his fee. I gave him a couple of francs.

"You see that we have found the signore," I tried to say in a natural voice. "He is very weak, and we will carry him to the carriage." I had thrown my handkerchief over Marcello's face, but the man knew as well as I that he was dead. Those stiff feet told their own story, but Italians are timid of being involved in such affairs. They have a childish dread of the police, and he only answered, "Poor signorino! He is very ill; it is better to take him to Rome," and kept cautiously clear of us as we went up to the ilex alley with our icy burden, and he did not go to the gate with us, not liking to be observed by the coachman, who was dozing on his box. With difficulty we got Marcello's corpse into the carriage, the driver turning to look at us suspiciously. I explained we had found our friend very ill, and at the same time slipped a gold piece into his hand, telling him to drive to the Via del Governo Vecchio. He pocketed the money, and whipped his horses into a trot, while we sat supporting the stiff body, which swayed like a broken doll at every pebble in the road. When we reached the Via del Governo Vecchio at last, no one saw us carry him into the house. There was no step before the door, and we drew up so close to it that it was possible to screen our burden from sight. When we had brought him into his room and laid him upon his bed, we noticed that his eyes were closed; from the movement of the carriage, perhaps, though that was scarcely possible. The landlady behaved very much as I had expected her to do, for, as I told you, I know the Italians. She pretended, too, that the signore was very ill, and made a pretense of offering to fetch a doctor, and when I thought it best to tell her that he was dead, declared that it must have happened that very moment, for she had seen him look at us and close his eyes again. She had always told him that he ate too little and that he would be ill. Yes, it was weakness and that bad air out there which had killed him; and then he worked too hard. When she had successfully established this fiction, which we were glad enough to agree to—for neither did we wish for the publicity of an inquest—she ran out and fetched a gossip to come and keep her company.

So died Marcello Souvestre, and so died Vespertilia the blood-drinker at last.

There is not much more to tell. Marcello lay calm and beautiful upon his bed, and the students came and stood silently looking at him, then knelt down for a moment to say a prayer, crossed themselves, and left him forever.

We hastened to the Villa Medici, where Detaille was sleeping, and Sister Claudius watching him with a satisfied look on her strong face. She rose noiselessly at our entrance, and came to us at the threshold. "He will recover," said she, softly. She was right. When he awoke and opened his eyes he knew us directly, and Magnin breathed a devout "Thank God!"

"Have I been ill, Magnin?" he asked very feebly.

"You have had a little fever," answered Magnin, promptly; "but it is over now. Here is Monsieur Sutton come to see you."

"Has Marcello been here?" was the next question.

Magnin looked at him very steadily.

"No," he only said, letting his face tell the rest.

"Is he dead, then?" Magnin only bowed his head.

"Poor friend!" Detaille murmured to himself, then closed his heavy eyes and slept again.

A few days after Marcello's funeral we went to the fatal Vigna Marziali to bring back the objects which had belonged to him. As I laid the manuscript score of the opera carefully together, my eye fell upon a passage which struck me as the identical one which Detaille had so constantly sung in his delirium, and which I had noted down. Strange to say, when I reminded him of it later, it was perfectly new to him, and he declared that Marcello had not let him examine his manuscript. As for the veiled bust in the other room, we left it undisturbed, and to crumble away unseen.

GLOSSARY

Agaçant: French for "annoying."

Belvedere: From the Italian "Fair View," a terrace or other architectural structure designed to let people look out on a beautiful view or scene.

Chi lo sa?: Italian for "Who knows?"

Clytemnestra: Wife of Agamemnon (leader of the Greeks in the Trojan War). She killed him when he came home, because he had sacrificed their daughter to get a favorable wind to sail to Troy.

Dieu Merci!: French for "Thank God!"

Entrez!: French for "Enter," "Come in."

Ma foi!: "My faith!" A mild curse to express exasperation.

Marche Funèbre: French for funeral march.

Ma soeur: French for "my sister."

Merci: French for "Thank you."

Mon enfant: French for "My baby" or "my child" – a French term of endearment.

Mon vieux: Literally, "my old." In other words, French for "my old friend."

Motif: Dominant artistic idea.

Mucius Scævola: Livy tells the story of the young Roman patriot Gaius Mucius, who tried to assassinate the enemy king of the Etruscans during a war in 508 BC. Mucius killed the wrong person and was caught; he showed his contempt for danger and the enemy king by thrusting his right hand into a sacrificial fire and holding it there. The enemy king was so impressed he let Mucius go back to Rome and started peace negotiations. Mucius was thereafter nicknamed Scaevola, or "left-handed."

Ohe: Italian for "Hey, you!"

Poste restante: French for the "General Delivery" part of a post office where mail is held for pick-up.

"*Sacré gamin!*": French; literally, "sacred boy," but an expression meaning, "What a kid!" or "That's a hell of boy!"

Sœur de Charité: French for "Sister of Mercy," a nun helping in medical matters. The Sisters of Mercy were first formed in Ireland in the 1830's.
Tenez: French for "Hold."
Trinità dei Monti: A Renaissance church in Rome; the reference is to the church's bells.
Tufa: A type of limestone.
Ulster: A man's long coat, often belted.
Vaurien: French for "scoundrel," "rascal," "good-for-nothing."
Vigna: Italian for vineyard.

AFTERWORD

Despite her very thorough destruction, Vespertilia had an interesting literary afterlife.

In 1895, seven years after this story and two years before **Dracula,** ***the English poet Rosamund Marriott Watson published a poem about a young man who meets the shade of a woman long dead. (Like Crawford, Watson assumes the identity of a male first-person narrator.)***

The ghostly woman is named Vespertilia.

Is Watson's Vespertilia supposed to be the same as Crawford's creation? She seems like a ghost, but is she in fact a vampire? The name seems too unusual for it to simply be a coincidence. And although the setting of the poem is somewhere in the British Isles, not Italy, Watson's Vespertilia says she loved a man who sailed a "beaked galley", i.e. someone from ancient Roman times. It seems likely that Watson at least took the name from the earlier story, and perhaps re-imagined the vampire in more sympathetic terms. We can feel for her—but who and what she is remain just out of reach.

We don't know whether Crawford ever knew about Watson's poem; if she did, there's no record of any protest.

VESPERTILIA

Rosamund Marriott Watson

In the late autumn's dusky-golden prime,
When sickles gleam and rusts the idle plough,
The time of apples dropping from the bough,
And yellow leaves on sycamore and lime;
O'er grassy uplands far above the sea
Often at twilight would my footsteps fare,
And oft I met a stranger-woman there

Who stayed and spake with me:
Hard by the ancient barrow smooth and green.
Whose rounded burg swells dark upon the sky
Lording it high o'er dusky dell and dene.

We wandered — she and I.
Ay, many a time as came the evening hour
And the red moon rose up behind the sheaves,
I found her straying by that barren bower.
Her fair face glimmering like a white wood-flower
That gleams through withered leaves,
Her mouth was redder than the pimpernel,
Her eyes seemed darker than the purple air
'Neath brows half hidden — I remember well —
'Mid mists of cloudy hair.

And all about her breast, around her head,
Was wound a wide veil shadowing cheek and chin.
Woven like the ancient grave-gear of the dead:
A twisted clasp and pin

Confined her long blue mantle's heavy fold
Of splendid tissue dropping to decay,
Faded like some rich raiment worn of old.
With rents and tatters gaping to the day.
Her sandals wrought about with threads of gold,
Scarce held together still, so worn were they,
Yet sewn with winking gems of green and blue,
And pale as pearls her naked feet shone through.

And all her talk was of some outland rare.
Where myrtles blossom by the blue sea's rim,
And life is ever good and sunny and fair;
"Long since," she sighed, "I sought this island grey —
Here, where the winds moan and the sun is dim.
When his beaked galleys cleft the ocean spray,
For love I followed him."

Once, as we stood, we heard the nightingale
Pipe from a thicket on the sheer hillside.
Breathless she hearkened, still and marble-pale.
Then turned to me with strange eyes open wide —
"Now I remember ! . . . Now I know !" said she,
"Love will be life . . . ah, Love *is* Life!" she cried,
"And thou — thou lovest me?"

I took her chill hands gently in mine own,
"Dear, but no love is mine to give," I said,
"My heart is colder than the granite stone
That guards my true-love in her grassy bed;
My faith and troth are hers, and hers alone,
Are hers . . . and she is dead."

Weeping, she drew her veil about her face,
And faint her accents were and dull with pain;

"Poor Vespertilia! gone her days of grace,
Now doth she plead for love — and plead in vain:
None praise her beauty now, or woo her smile!

"Ah, hadst thou loved me but a little while,
I might have lived again."

Then slowly as a wave along the shore
She glided from me to yon sullen mound;
My frozen heart, relenting, smote me sore —

Too late — I searched the hollow slopes around,
Swiftly I followed her, but nothing found.
Nor saw nor heard her more.

And now, alas, my true-love's memory
Even as a dream of night-time half-forgot.

Fades faint and far from me,
And all my thoughts are of the stranger still,

Yea, though I loved her not:
I loved her not — and yet — I fain would see
Upon the wind-swept hill
Her dark veil fluttering in the autumn breeze;
Fain would I hear her changeful voice awhile.
Soft as the wind of spring-tide in the trees,
And watch her slow, sweet smile.

Ever the thought of her abides with me
Unceasing as the murmur of the sea;

When the round moon is low and night-birds flit.
When sink the stubble-fires with smouldering flame,

Over and o'er the sea-wind sighs her name,
And the leaves whisper it.

"Poor Vespertilia," sing the grasses sere,
"Poor Vespertilia," moans the surf-beat shore;
Almost I feel her very presence near —
Yet she comes nevermore.

GLOSSARY

Barrow: In rural England, a mound of earth over a corpse.
Dene: A valley.

AFTERWORD

One final note: the name "Vespertilia" is connected to "vesper," or evening...which led to Vespertilionidae ***becoming the family name for over 300 species of night-flying bats. So "vespertilian" means "bat-like"...***

THE WOMAN WHO DID NOT CARE

A fool there was and his goods he spent,
(Even as you or I!)
Honour and faith and a sure intent
(And it wasn't the least what the lady meant)

1897 is the most significant year in vampire fiction. It is, of course, the year Bram Stoker's Dracula *was published in England...but that was in May, and while the novel was a success, it didn't match the immediate cultural impact of something that happened a few weeks earlier, in April...something that would affect the way women and vampires were viewed for the next three decades.*

There was a painter in London named Philip Burne-Jones, son of the Pre-Raphaelite painter Edward Burne-Jones. Philip had just ended a love affair with the striking raven-haired Mrs. Patrick Campbell, one of the greatest actresses of her day. Philip turned his bitterness into a painting of a smiling woman perched like a triumphant predator over an unconscious, bare-chested man. The painting was called The Vampire. *(The idea and composition seem to be inspired by Henry Fuseli's 1781* The Nightmare. *Strangely,* The Vampire *in its original form seems to have disappeared into thin air or a private collection; a black and white print is reproduced at the beginning of this section.)*

Burne-Jones had a cousin who was a writer, and this cousin composed a poem as a promotional tie-in for the painting. The cousin was Rudyard Kipling, already world-famous for novels like The Man Who Would Be King *and* The Jungle Book, *and for poems like* Gunga Din. *Kipling's poem was also called* The Vampire...

THE VAMPIRE

Rudyard Kipling

A FOOL there was and he made his prayer
(Even as you or I!)
To a rag and a bone and a hank of hair,
(We called her the woman who did not care),
But the fool he called her his lady fair—
(Even as you or I!)

Oh, the years we waste and the tears we waste,
And the work of our head and hand
Belong to the woman who did not know
(And now we know that she never could know)
And did not understand!

A fool there was and his goods he spent,
(Even as you or I!)
Honour and faith and a sure intent
(And it wasn't the least what the lady meant),
But a fool must follow his natural bent
(Even as you or I!)

Oh, the toil we lost and the spoil we lost
And the excellent things we planned
Belong to the woman who didn't know why
(And now we know that she never knew why)
And did not understand!

The fool was stripped to his foolish hide,
(Even as you or I!)
Which she might have seen when she threw him aside--
(But it isn't on record the lady tried)
So some of him lived but the most of him died--
(Even as you or I!)

And it isn't the shame and it isn't the blame
That stings like a white-hot brand—
It's coming to know that she never knew why
(Seeing, at last, she could never know why)
And never could understand.

GLOSSARY

Hank: A looped or coiled bundle of something, such as hair.

AFTERWORD

Even in 1897, a lot of people felt that this was misogynistic; but after Kipling's poem, a woman who used her feminine wiles and sex appeal to drain a man of his money and, eventually, his will to live, was a "vampire."

Kipling's poem was turned into a play in 1909, A Fool There Was, ***and the 1915 movie version stars the actress who was the silent era's queen of the femme fatales, Theda Bara. Theda plays "The Vampire," a woman who drives men mad, yet is snubbed by a society woman at a resort. In revenge, Theda steals the woman's husband and reduces him to a drug-addicted wreck. ("So some of him lived but the most of him died.")***

After Theda Bara, "vampire" was often shortened to "vamp," which was both a noun and a verb (as in, "She was vamping around" or "She decided to vamp him," or "According to the newspapers, mothers worry that their sons are being vamped at parties.")

It wasn't until 1931, and the indelible impression Bela Lugosi made in the movie version of Dracula, *that the public's primary image of the vampire would once again be a man—a tall, pale man in evening dress, with a flowing cape and a Central European accent. The "vamp" became as obsolete as the flapper.*

In the movies, at least until Hammer's Carmilla films of the 1970's, female vampires, once symbols of empowered women, were usually reduced to the sexy slave-brides of the master vampire, who often neglected to feed her properly, leading her to make a batline for the neck of the unsuspecting hero—before being dispatched with a cross and a phallic stake.

There was one major exception, however—and it was inspired by a chapter that never made it into Dracula...

COUNTESS DOLINGEN

"Tell me, Johann, what is tonight?"
He crossed himself…

In 1936, Universal Pictures released a sequel to their 1931 Dracula, *called* Dracula's Daughter. *It turned out that, somehow, the Count had a daughter living in England—a tall, black-haired aristocrat played by Gloria Holden. As Countess Zaleska, Holden struggled with her vampire nature, not wanting to drink blood but succumbing to her addiction and seducing a young woman in a famous scene.*

According to the film's opening credits, it's "Based on a work by Bram Stoker." That "work" is the following story, Dracula's Guest.

It's been said that this was originally an early chapter of Dracula, allegedly cut from the book before it publication in 1897. Stoker, the story goes, was persuaded by his publisher to cut the chapter in order to keep the book from being too long. In fact, it seems more like an early draft of what became Jonathan Harker's journey to Dracula's castle. Stoker's widow had it published in 1914, two years after her husband's death, and it's survived as an odd little footnote to the more famous work.

It's a very effective mini-adventure, and there is a female vampire—although she's nothing like the character Gloria Holden played. The story and movie really have almost nothing in common. Still, the movie is worth watching and the story is well worth reading…

DRACULA'S GUEST

Bram Stoker

When we started for our drive the sun was shining brightly on Munich, and the air was full of the joyousness of early summer. Just as we were about to depart, Herr Delbruck (the *maitre d'hotel* of the Quatre Saisons, where I was staying) came down bareheaded to the carriage and, after wishing me a pleasant drive, said to the coachman, still holding his hand on the handle of the carriage door, "Remember you are back by nightfall. The sky looks bright but there is a shiver in the north wind that says there may be a sudden storm. But I am sure you will not be late." Here he smiled and added, "For you know what night it is."

Johann answered with an emphatic, "*Ja, mein Herr*," and, touching his hat, drove off quickly. When we had cleared the town, I said, after signalling to him to stop:

"Tell me, Johann, what is tonight?"

He crossed himself, as he answered laconically: "*Walpurgis nacht*." Then he took out his watch, a great, old-fashioned German silver thing as big as a turnip and looked at it, with his eyebrows gathered together and a little impatient shrug of his shoulders. I realized that this was his way of respectfully protesting against the unnecessary delay and sank back in the carriage, merely motioning him to proceed. He started off rapidly, as if to make up for lost time. Every now and then the horses seemed to throw up their heads and sniff the air suspiciously. On such occasions I often looked round in alarm. The road was pretty bleak, for we were traversing a sort of high windswept plateau. As we drove, I saw a road that looked but little used and which seemed to dip through a little winding valley. It looked so inviting that, even at the risk of offending him, I called Johann to stop--and when he had pulled up, I told him I would like to drive down that road. He made all sorts of excuses and frequently crossed himself as he spoke. This somewhat piqued my curiosity, so I asked him various questions. He answered fencingly and repeatedly looked at his watch in protest.

Finally I said, "Well, Johann, I want to go down this road. I shall not ask you to come unless you like; but tell me why you do not like to go, that is all I ask." For answer he seemed to throw himself off the box, so quickly did he reach the ground. Then he stretched out his hands appealingly to me and implored me not to go. There was just enough of English mixed with the German for me to understand the drift of his talk. He seemed always just about to tell me something--the very idea of which evidently frightened him; but each time he pulled himself up saying, *"Walpurgis nacht!"*

I tried to argue with him, but it was difficult to argue with a man when I did not know his language. The advantage certainly rested with him, for although he began to speak in English, of a very crude and broken kind, he always got excited and broke into his native tongue—and every time he did so, he looked at his watch. Then the horses became restless and sniffed the air. At this he grew very pale, and, looking around in a frightened way, he suddenly jumped forward, took them by the bridles, and led them on some twenty feet. I followed and asked why he had done this. For an answer he crossed himself, pointed to the spot we had left, and drew his carriage in the direction of the other road, indicating a cross, and said, first in German, then in English, "Buried him—him what killed themselves."

I remembered the old custom of burying suicides at cross roads: "Ah! I see, a suicide. How interesting!" But for the life of me I could not make out why the horses were frightened.

Whilst we were talking, we heard a sort of sound between a yelp and a bark. It was far away; but the horses got very restless, and it took Johann all his time to quiet them. He was pale and said, "It sounds like a wolf—but yet there are no wolves here now."

"No?" I said, questioning him. "Isn't it long since the wolves were so near the city?"

"Long, long," he answered, "in the spring and summer; but with the snow the wolves have been here not so long."

Whilst he was petting the horses and trying to quiet them, dark clouds drifted rapidly across the sky. The sunshine passed away, and a breath of cold wind seemed to drift over us. It was only a breath, however, and more of a warning than a fact, for the sun came out brightly again.

Johann looked under his lifted hand at the horizon and said, "The storm of snow, he comes before long time." Then he looked at his watch again, and, straightway holding his reins firmly--for the horses were still pawing the ground restlessly and shaking their heads--he climbed to his box as though the time had come for proceeding on our journey.

I felt a little obstinate and did not at once get into the carriage.

"Tell me," I said, "about this place where the road leads," and I pointed down.

Again he crossed himself and mumbled a prayer before he answered, "It is unholy."

"What is unholy?" I enquired.

"The village."

"Then there is a village?"

"No, no. No one lives there hundreds of years."

My curiosity was piqued, "But you said there was a village."

"There was."

"Where is it now?"

Whereupon he burst out into a long story in German and English, so mixed up that I could not quite understand exactly what he said. Roughly I gathered that long ago, hundreds of years, men had died there and been buried in their graves; but sounds were heard under the clay, and when the graves were opened, men and women were found rosy with life and their mouths red with blood. And so, in haste to save their lives (aye, and their souls!--and here he crossed himself) those who were left fled away to other places, where the living lived and the dead were dead and not—not something. He was evidently afraid to speak the last words. As he proceeded with his narration, he grew more and more excited. It seemed as if his imagination had got hold of him, and he ended in a perfect paroxysm of fear--white-faced, perspiring, trembling, and looking round him as if expecting that some dreadful presence would manifest itself there in the bright sunshine on the open plain.

Finally, in an agony of desperation, he cried, "*Walpurgis nacht*!" and pointed to the carriage for me to get in.

All my English blood rose at this, and standing back I said, "You are afraid, Johann--you are afraid. Go home, I shall return alone, the walk will do me good." The carriage door was open. I took from the seat my oak walking stick—which I always carry on my holiday excursions—and closed the door, pointing back to Munich, and said, "Go home, Johann—*Walpurgis nacht* doesn't concern Englishmen."

The horses were now more restive than ever, and Johann was trying to hold them in, while excitedly imploring me not to do anything so foolish. I pitied the poor fellow, he was so deeply in earnest; but all the same I could not help laughing. His English was quite gone now. In his anxiety he had forgotten that his only means of making me understand was to talk my language, so he jabbered away in his native German. It began to be a little tedious. After giving the direction, "Home!" I turned to go down the cross road into the valley.

With a despairing gesture, Johann turned his horses towards Munich. I leaned on my stick and looked after him. He went slowly along the road for a while, then there came over the crest of the hill a man tall and thin. I could see so much in the distance. When he drew near the horses, they began to jump and kick about, then to scream with terror. Johann could not hold them in; they bolted down the road, running away madly. I watched them out of sight, then looked for the stranger; but I found that he, too, was gone.

With a light heart I turned down the side road through the deepening valley to which Johann had objected. There was not the slightest reason, that I could see, for his objection; and I daresay I tramped for a couple of hours without thinking of time or distance and certainly without seeing a person or a house. So far as the place was concerned, it was desolation itself. But I did not notice this particularly till, on turning a bend in the road, I came upon a scattered fringe of wood; then I recognized that I had been impressed unconsciously by the desolation of the region through which I had passed.

I sat down to rest myself and began to look around. It struck me that it was considerably colder than it had been at the commencement of my walk--a sort of sighing sound seemed to be around me with, now and then, high overhead, a sort of muffled roar. Looking upwards I noticed that great thick clouds were drafting rapidly across the sky from north to south at a great height. There were signs of a coming storm in some lofty stratum of the air. I was a little chilly, and, thinking that it was the sitting still after the exercise of walking, I resumed my journey.

The ground I passed over was now much more picturesque. There were no striking objects that the eye might single out, but in all there was a charm of beauty. I took little heed of time, and it was only when the deepening twilight forced itself upon me that I began to think of how I should find my way home. The air was cold, and the drifting of clouds high overhead was more marked. They were accompanied by a sort of faraway rushing sound, through which seemed to come at intervals that mysterious cry which the driver had said came from a wolf. For a while I hesitated. I had said I would see the deserted village, so on I went and presently came on a wide stretch of open country, shut in by hills all around. Their sides were covered with trees which spread down to the plain, dotting in clumps the gentler slopes and hollows which showed here and there. I followed with my eye the winding of the road and saw that it curved close to one of the densest of these clumps and was lost behind it.

As I looked there came a cold shiver in the air, and the snow began to fall. I thought of the miles and miles of bleak country I had passed, and then hurried on to seek shelter of the wood in front. Darker and darker grew the sky, and faster and heavier fell the snow, till the earth before and around me was a glistening white carpet the further edge of which was lost in misty vagueness. The road was here but crude, and when on the level its boundaries were not so marked as when it passed through the cuttings; and in a little while I found that I must have strayed from it, for I missed underfoot the hard surface, and my feet sank deeper in the grass and moss. Then the wind grew stronger and blew with ever-increasing force, till I was fain to run before it. The air became icy-cold, and in spite of my exercise I began to suffer. The snow was now falling so thickly and whirling around me in such rapid eddies that I could hardly keep my eyes open. Every now and then the heavens were torn asunder by vivid lightning, and in the flashes I could see ahead of me a great mass of trees, chiefly yew and cypress all heavily coated with snow.

I was soon amongst the shelter of the trees, and there in comparative silence I could hear the rush of the wind high overhead. Presently the blackness of the storm had become merged in the darkness of the night. By-and-by the storm seemed to be passing away, it now only came in fierce puffs or blasts. At such moments the weird sound of the wolf appeared to be echoed by many similar sounds around me.

Now and again, through the black mass of drifting cloud, came a straggling ray of moonlight which lit up the expanse and showed me that I was at the edge of a dense mass of cypress and yew trees. As the snow had ceased to fall, I walked out from the shelter and began to investigate more closely. It appeared to me that, amongst so many old foundations as I had passed, there might be still standing a house in which, though in ruins, I could find some sort of shelter for a while. As I skirted the edge of the copse, I found that a low wall encircled it, and following this I presently found an opening. Here the cypresses formed an alley leading up to a square mass of some kind of building. Just as I caught sight of this, however, the drifting clouds obscured the moon, and I passed up the path in darkness. The wind must have grown colder, for I felt myself shiver as I walked; but there was hope of shelter, and I groped my way blindly on.

I stopped, for there was a sudden stillness. The storm had passed; and, perhaps in sympathy with nature's silence, my heart seemed to cease to beat. But this was only momentarily; for suddenly the moonlight broke through the clouds showing me that I was in a graveyard and that the square object before me was a great massive tomb of marble, as white as the snow that lay on and all around it. With the moonlight there came a fierce sigh of the storm which appeared to resume its course with a long, low howl, as of many dogs or wolves. I was awed and shocked, and I felt the cold perceptibly grow upon me till it seemed to grip me by the heart. Then while the flood of moonlight still fell on the marble tomb, the storm gave further evidence of renewing, as though it were returning on its track. Impelled by some sort of fascination, I approached the sepulchre to see what it was and why such a thing stood alone in such a place. I walked around it and read, over the Doric door, in German—

COUNTESS DOLINGEN OF GRATZ

IN STYRIA

SOUGHT AND FOUND DEATH

1801

On the top of the tomb, seemingly driven through the solid marble—for the structure was composed of a few vast blocks of stone—was a great iron spike or stake. On going to the back I saw, graven in great Russian letters: *"The dead travel fast."*

There was something so weird and uncanny about the whole thing that it gave me a turn and made me feel quite faint. I began to wish, for the first time, that I had taken Johann's advice. Here a thought struck me, which came under almost mysterious circumstances and with a terrible shock. This was Walpurgis Night!

Walpurgis Night was when, according to the belief of millions of people, the devil was abroad--when the graves were opened and the dead came forth and walked. When all evil things of earth and air and water held revel. This very place the driver had specially shunned. This was the depopulated village of centuries ago. This was where the suicide lay; and this was the place where I was alone—unmanned, shivering with cold in a shroud of snow with a wild storm gathering again upon me! It took all my philosophy, all the religion I had been taught, all my courage, not to collapse in a paroxysm of fright.

And now a perfect tornado burst upon me. The ground shook as though thousands of horses thundered across it; and this time the storm bore on its icy wings, not snow, but great hailstones which drove with such violence that they might have come from the thongs of Balearic slingers—hailstones that beat down leaf and branch and made the shelter of the cypresses of no more avail than though their stems were standing corn. At the first I had rushed to the nearest tree; but I was soon fain to leave it and seek the only spot that seemed to afford refuge, the deep Doric doorway of the marble tomb. There, crouching against the massive bronze door, I gained a certain amount of protection from the beating of the hailstones, for now they only drove against me as they ricocheted from the ground and the side of the marble.

As I leaned against the door, it moved slightly and opened inwards. The shelter of even a tomb was welcome in that pitiless tempest and I was about to enter it when there came a flash of forked lightning that lit up the whole expanse of the heavens. In the instant, as I am a living man, I saw, as my eyes turned into the darkness of the tomb, a beautiful woman with rounded cheeks and red lips, seemingly sleeping on a bier. As the thunder broke overhead, I was grasped as by the hand of a giant and hurled out into the storm. The whole thing was so sudden that, before I could realize the shock, moral as well as physical, I found the hailstones beating me down. At the same time I had a strange, dominating feeling that I was not alone. I looked towards the tomb. Just then there came another blinding flash which seemed to strike the iron stake that surmounted the tomb and to pour through to the earth, blasting and crumbling the marble, as in a burst of flame. The dead woman rose for a moment of agony while she was lapped in the flame, and her bitter scream of pain was drowned in the thundercrash. The last thing I heard was this mingling of dreadful sound, as again I was seized in the giant grasp and dragged away, while the hailstones beat on me and the air around seemed reverberant with the howling of wolves. The last sight that I remembered was a vague, white, moving mass, as if all the graves around me had sent out the phantoms of their sheeted dead, and that they were closing in on me through the white cloudiness of the driving hail.

Gradually there came a sort of vague beginning of consciousness, then a sense of weariness that was dreadful. For a time I remembered nothing, but slowly my senses returned. My feet seemed positively racked with pain, yet I could not move them. They seemed to be numbed. There was an icy feeling at the back of my neck and all down my spine, and my ears, like my feet, were dead yet in torment; but there was in my breast a sense of warmth which was by comparison delicious. It was as a nightmare--a physical nightmare, if one may use such an expression; for some heavy weight on my chest made it difficult for me to breathe.

This period of semi-lethargy seemed to remain a long time, and as it faded away I must have slept or swooned. Then came a sort of loathing, like the first stage of seasickness, and a wild desire to be free of something—I knew not what. A vast stillness enveloped me, as though all the world were asleep or dead—only broken by the low panting as of some animal close to me. I felt a warm rasping at my throat, then came a consciousness of the awful truth which chilled me to the heart and sent the blood surging up through my brain. Some great animal was lying on me and now licking my throat. I feared to stir, for some instinct of prudence bade me lie still; but the brute seemed to realize that there was now some change in me, for it raised its head. Through my eyelashes I saw above me the two great flaming eyes of a gigantic wolf. Its sharp white teeth gleamed in the gaping red mouth, and I could feel its hot breath fierce and acrid upon me.

For another spell of time I remembered no more. Then I became conscious of a low growl, followed by a yelp, renewed again and again. Then seemingly very far away, I heard a "Holloa! holloa!" as of many voices calling in unison. Cautiously I raised my head and looked in the direction whence the sound came, but the cemetery blocked my view. The wolf still continued to yelp in a strange way, and a red glare began to move round the grove of cypresses, as though following the sound. As the voices drew closer, the wolf yelped faster and louder. I feared to make either sound or motion. Nearer came the red glow over the white pall which stretched into the darkness around me. Then all at once from beyond the trees there came at a trot a troop of horsemen bearing torches. The wolf rose from my breast and made for the cemetery. I saw one of the horsemen (soldiers by their caps and their long military cloaks) raise his carbine and take aim. A companion knocked up his arm, and I heard the ball whiz over my head. He had evidently taken my body for that of the wolf. Another sighted the animal as it slunk away, and a shot followed. Then, at a gallop, the troop rode forward--some towards me, others following the wolf as it disappeared amongst the snow-clad cypresses.

As they drew nearer I tried to move but was powerless, although I could see and hear all that went on around me. Two or three of the soldiers jumped from their horses and knelt beside me. One of them raised my head and placed his hand over my heart.

"Good news, comrades!" he cried. "His heart still beats!"

Then some brandy was poured down my throat; it put vigor into me, and I was able to open my eyes fully and look around. Lights and shadows were moving among the trees, and I heard men call to one another. They drew together, uttering frightened exclamations; and the lights flashed as the others came pouring out of the cemetery pell-mell, like men possessed. When the further ones came close to us, those who were around me asked them eagerly, "Well, have you found him?"

The reply rang out hurriedly, "No! no! Come away quick-quick! This is no place to stay, and on this of all nights!"

"What was it?" was the question, asked in all manner of keys. The answer came variously and all indefinitely as though the men were moved by some common impulse to speak yet were restrained by some common fear from giving their thoughts.

"It—it—indeed!" gibbered one, whose wits had plainly given out for the moment.

"A wolf—and yet not a wolf!" another put in shudderingly.

"No use trying for him without the sacred bullet," a third remarked in a more ordinary manner.

"Serve us right for coming out on this night! Truly we have earned our thousand marks!" were the ejaculations of a fourth.

"There was blood on the broken marble," another said after a pause, "the lightning never brought that there. And for him—is he safe? Look at his throat! See comrades, the wolf has been lying on him and keeping his blood warm."

The officer looked at my throat and replied, "He is all right, the skin is not pierced. What does it all mean? We should never have found him but for the yelping of the wolf."

"What became of it?" asked the man who was holding up my head and who seemed the least panic-stricken of the party, for his hands were steady and without tremor. On his sleeve was the chevron of a petty officer.

"It went home," answered the man, whose long face was pallid and who actually shook with terror as he glanced around him fearfully. "There are graves enough there in which it may lie. Come, comrades—come quickly! Let us leave this cursed spot."

The officer raised me to a sitting posture, as he uttered a word of command; then several men placed me upon a horse. He sprang to the saddle behind me, took me in his arms, gave the word to advance; and, turning our faces away from the cypresses, we rode away in swift military order.

As yet my tongue refused its office, and I was perforce silent. I must have fallen asleep; for the next thing I remembered was finding myself standing up, supported by a soldier on each side of me. It was almost broad daylight, and to the north a red streak of sunlight was reflected like a path of blood over the waste of snow. The officer was telling the men to say nothing of what they had seen, except that they found an English stranger, guarded by a large dog.

"Dog! That was no dog," cut in the man who had exhibited such fear. "I think I know a wolf when I see one."

The young officer answered calmly, "I said a dog."

"Dog!" reiterated the other ironically. It was evident that his courage was rising with the sun; and, pointing to me, he said, "Look at his throat. Is that the work of a dog, master?"

Instinctively I raised my hand to my throat, and as I touched it I cried out in pain. The men crowded round to look, some stooping down from their saddles; and again there came the calm voice of the young officer, "A dog, as I said. If aught else were said we should only be laughed at."

I was then mounted behind a trooper, and we rode on into the suburbs of Munich. Here we came across a stray carriage into which I was lifted, and it was driven off to the Quatre Saisons—the young officer accompanying me, whilst a trooper followed with his horse, and the others rode off to their barracks.

When we arrived, Herr Delbruck rushed so quickly down the steps to meet me, that it was apparent he had been watching within. Taking me by both hands he solicitously led me in. The officer saluted me and was turning to withdraw, when I recognised his purpose and insisted that he should come to my rooms. Over a glass of wine I warmly thanked him and his brave comrades for saving me. He replied simply that he was more than glad, and that Herr Delbruck had at the first taken steps to make all the searching party pleased; at which ambiguous utterance the *maitre d'hotel* smiled, while the officer plead duty and withdrew.

"But Herr Delbruck," I enquired, "how and why was it that the soldiers searched for me?"

He shrugged his shoulders, as if in depreciation of his own deed, as he replied, "I was so fortunate as to obtain leave from the commander of the regiment in which I serve, to ask for volunteers."

"But how did you know I was lost?" I asked.

"The driver came hither with the remains of his carriage, which had been upset when the horses ran away."

"But surely you would not send a search party of soldiers merely on this account?"

"Oh, no!" he answered, "but even before the coachman arrived, I had this telegram from the Boyar whose guest you are," and he took from his pocket a telegram which he handed to me, and I read:

> *Bistritz. Be careful of my guest--his safety is most precious to me. Should aught happen to him, or if he be missed, spare nothing to find him and ensure his safety. He is English and therefore adventurous. There are often dangers from snow and wolves and night. Lose not a moment if you suspect harm to him. I answer your zeal with my fortune. –DRACULA*

As I held the telegram in my hand, the room seemed to whirl around me, and if the attentive *maitre d'hotel* had not caught me, I think I should have fallen. There was something so strange in all this, something so weird and impossible to imagine, that there grew on me a sense of my being in some way the sport of opposite forces--the mere vague idea of which seemed in a way to paralyze me. I was certainly under some form of mysterious protection. From a distant country had come, in the very nick of time, a message that took me out of the danger of the snow sleep and the jaws of the wolf.

GLOSSARY

Balearic slings: Native inhabitants of Spain's Balearic Islands (including Mallorca, Menorca, Ibiza, and Formentera) are thought to have first used the sling as a weapon.

Bistrtz: City in North-Central Transylvania.

Gratz: Or Graz; the capital of Styria, and, today, the second-largest city in Austria, after Vienna.

The dead travel fast: Stoker based this line on the German ballad *Lenore*, published in 1774 by Gottfried August Bürger. A woman, Lenore, goes on a long and fatal night-ride with the spirit of her dead lover—back to his coffin. The dead man's refrain is, "*die Todten reisen schnell.*" or, "*the dead ride fast.*"

Walpurgis Night: Or Walpurgisnacht; April 30, the eve of the Christian feast of St. Walpurga, an 8th century Francian abbess who was later credited with fighting witches. A night when ghosts, demons, etc. come out. A far more serious Halloween.

AFTERWORD

Stoker tells us the year that Countess Dolingen died, and suggests that, in accordance with an old belief, she became a vampire as a side-effect of suicide. (We never learn how Dracula becomes undead, although there are hints of Satanic rites in his past.) We know almost nothing else about the Countess as a character; but her hometown—Gratz, in Styria—is evidence that Stoker read Le Fanu's Carmilla. ***Stoker's notes also indicate that he had originally considered Styria as the setting for his vampire count's home before he learned about Vlad the Impaler and Transylvania.***

And so, our survey of pre-Dracula literary vampires ends on the very outskirts of the Count's domain…

James Grant Goldin has written numerous non-fiction television programs about fantasy and popular culture, including *Comic Book Super-Heroes Unmasked; The Return of the King: A Filmmaker's Journey; Zombie Apocalypse;* and *Hollywood's Ultimate Super Vixens.*

ALSO AVAILABLE:

VAMPIRES:

FIRST BLOOD VOLUME I

THE FIRST VAMPIRE LORDS:

RUTHVEN, VARNEY...

AND MORE!

www.ingramcontent.com/pod-product-compliance
Lightning Source LLC
Chambersburg PA
CBHW020231110726
47898CB00004B/1230

* 9 7 8 1 7 3 3 5 6 9 0 2 6 *